MY DARLING DIARY

Volume Two
The Girl in and out of Love
Oxford 1944-1950

Also by Ingrid Jacoby:

My Darling Diary – A wartime journal
(Vienna 1937-39, Falmouth 1939-44)

My Darling Diary

Volume Two
The Girl in and out of Love

~ Oxford 1944-1950 ~

Ingrid Jacoby

UNITED WRITERS
Cornwall

UNITED WRITERS PUBLICATIONS LTD
Ailsa, Castle Gate, Penzance, Cornwall.

British Library Cataloguing in Publication Data:
A catalogue record for this book is
available from the British Library.

ISBN-10: 1 85200 123 2
ISBN-13: 9781852001230

Printed in Great Britain by
United Writers Publications Ltd
Cornwall.

In Memory of my Mother.

All the characters and incidents in this book are entirely authentic, and any resemblances to fictitious persons or events are purely coincidental.

My thanks are due to nobody. There are no encouragements to acknowledge. No advice was asked for or given. Sympathetic support or guidance from any persons were entirely absent. All the deficiencies are absolutely my own.

Oxford 1944

As you see, my new life has started. Everything happened very
quickly. I was still in London on 30th September, having no idea
where I was going to live, when a letter from Uncle Bruno in
Oxford arrived saying he'd found digs for me. So here I am, at
66 St John's Road, sitting in my bed-sitting room, medium sized,
quite comfortable, a bit dark. It's 11.15pm and I'm doing something
for which I've been dying – writing my diary!

But to go back to the beginning: I left Falmouth on the 28th as
you know. Connie came to the station and Miss Kitty accompanied
me as far as Truro. My father, Jane and Doris, joined me on the
train at Plymouth, where they'd been on business, and we all
travelled to London. When we arrived we went by taxi to Elgin
Avenue, to Jane and Jack's flat, where my father also lives. Jane's
brother Harry was there. The following day I went shopping the
whole day with Jane – she bought me a coat, a dress, a skirt, a
mack and shoes. It was like having ten birthdays. We had dinner
at Odenino's in the evening – my father, Jane, Jack and I. The
siren went twice but nothing happened. On Saturday Lieselotte
came for tea. It was wonderful to see her again. It was also the
day we heard about the Oxford digs. So, early on Sunday
morning, I caught a train to Oxford with my father. We were met
by Uncle Bruno and taken to my new abode. My new 'guardians'
are a Dr and Mrs Beschorner. He's a Czech, Jewish psychiatrist,

7

linguist, teacher, sportsman, musician and artist (believe it or not), and his much younger, pretty wife is English and called Joan. They have a three-year-old child called Peter. Two girls are the other boarders besides me. We had lunch with the family, I unpacked, played with Peter, and then went out to tea with my father and Bruno. In the evening my father returned to London and I saw him off at the station. On the way home I met a Jewish lady and we walked back together. I knew she was Jewish because she told me so.

Today I started Secretarial College at St Giles, had lunch in a restaurant with a girl from my class called Angela Gale, and tea at Aunt Else's with Aunt Erna, both of whom I had only met once before. In the evening I went to the station to fetch my bike. Tomorrow I'm going to collect my cabin trunk. Once these two beloved objects are with me again – my bike and my trunk – I shall begin to feel more at home – I hope . . .

7th October 1944

On Tuesday morning Erna and I cycled to the country to pick blackberries, and took our lunch. It was somewhere near Woodstock. In the afternoon I had to be at College, where I had my first shorthand dictation. Afterwards I went to the police station to register my new address, and to the food office to inform them of my changed abode for my ration books. The two other girls living at Beschorners are called Pat and Prue. Pat works in an office and Prue goes to the High School. I've been having lunch in the Town Hall restaurant with Pat and Dr Beschorner. Once, when he brought me a cup of tea, a fellow at the next table asked me, "Is he your boyfriend?"

"Oh no," I said, "he's just the man I live with." Afterwards I realised my mistake – and Dr Beschorner wasn't very pleased! He didn't think it funny, which is odd because he fools around with us sometimes, and last night I had fisticuffs with him – in fun, of course – and he gave me a puff of his pipe. So wouldn't you think he could have seen the joke in what I said? He often talks psychology with us in the evenings but doesn't always seem to apply it.

Thursday morning I spent unpacking my cabin trunk. It arrived intact, my white initials still on it, bright and clear, 'I belong to I.J.', the trunk announces to the world, 'and wherever I am is her home.'

In the excitement of preparations for leaving Falmouth I forgot to tell you that poor Miss Davis was bitten by 'a brown mongrel dog in Killigrew Street' and was quite ill afterwards, and in bed for two days. Later it transpired it was really Timothy – her own beloved dog – who had bitten her, and he had to be destroyed, which was a relief to everyone except her. He once went for me when I tried to stroke him, but only managed to tear my dress.

I haven't seen much of Oxford yet. It has been described and praised by so many great men that it doesn't matter much what I think of it, but when I get to know it a bit better, or when I can write like Howard Spring, I might give you an idea of my own impressions of it.

10th October 1944

I am so lonely! I'm used to my crowd of friends and to St Josephs, which was always full of people. Everything is strange to me here, and although I've no complaints about my new 'home', I want to be back in Falmouth, desperately. I tell myself I'm a coward. I tell myself I've only been here for just over a week and in time I shall get used to places and people and make friends. But that appears far off and impossible now – so impossible that just to think of it seems as unreasonable as a mother comforting her sick child with promises of out of reach treats. Never in my life have I felt so much like the refugee I am; never before have I realised so clearly that I belong nowhere. Above all, I hate that secretarial college because I expected it to be quite different. In fact it's not as nice as Miss Hoare's College in Truro, where the girls were much 'better class'. I wouldn't tell my father that though because he's paying a lot of money for me, and he meant well. His business enables him to be generous now. Even so, inside me I hate him more than ever because he gave me illusions which are now battered to bits, resulting in bitter disappointment. He told me that everything in Oxford would be superior to anything in Falmouth, but Oxford is neither the place I imagined or wanted it to be. I feel there is no future for me here, which is a pity as I'm still very young. The once exciting future has become the dull present. I'm in a black dungeon, with four walls to dash

9

my head against. I long for St Josephs and my friends and Miss Davis' narrow-mindedness and Miss Kitty's sarcasm. Poor diary! If only you could have a change of scene. I never get bored with you but you must be very bored with me, forever complaining.

I wrote to the local library today to ask if they had a vacancy. It's very cold and I'm going to bed now. Perhaps I'll wake up somewhere better.

11th October 1944

GERMAN NEWS BY HAW HAW

The GTC (German Tank Corps) reported last night that they had received information through the SHAEF (Socialist Head Affairs and Enquiry Formation) saying that enemy forces were retreating on all fronts and that the Germans would soon hold their own again. This statement was verified by the BUP (Berlin Under Politician) who said that it would not now take long to crush the pestilent and warmongering RAF (Ruddy Alien Forces) and once more regain peace.

The Germans evidently think the war is going well for them! Ha, ha.

I can't make Dr Beschorner out at all. Life is certainly more interesting with him around. He is brilliant. We're all in awe of him, including his wife Joan. Sometimes I think he despises me because of my seriousness and because I don't fool around with him like Pat and Prue, and at other times I think he despises their flippancy. But he's very changeable and he probably does both.

In the past, when I've felt very low, I often wished to die, but now I feel that it would be so lonely to die. It would be no release from my present mood. I think I'll just knock around the world for a bit and not long for a settled home or a steady career any more.

13th October 1944 – Friday!

Not an unlucky but a very lucky day for me! Guess what! I have a job at the Oxford City Library! When I wrote, I had very little hope, but a reply came by return, I had an interview with the librarian (whom I had called the 'manager' in my letter!) and was engaged on the spot. Isn't that wonderful? I am to start there on Monday, as a Junior Library Assistant, at 30/- a week, take examinations and work my way up and finally become a librarian with the letters FLA after my name. Another relief – I'm giving up that awful secretarial college, except for one evening a week. Erna called there today on my behalf and explained the situation. Afterwards we had lunch together. Tomorrow I have to telephone my father in London and tell him the news. Joan Beschorner has asked me to go to the pictures with her in the evening.

15th October 1944

Pat is very keen on woodwork, and this morning I helped her with some sawing in the cellar. Me! Sawing! Imagine it. In the afternoon we all went for a walk in the University Parks – Dr and Mrs Beschorner, Prue, Pat, little Peter and I. In the evening Pat, Prue and I went to a service in Magdalen College Chapel, which is very beautiful. We went there by bus and walked back. It was a nice evening.

I've fallen out with Dr B. on various occasions. I don't take things as the others do – lying down – and occasionally put up an argument. For instance, every evening at 10pm he gets up from his armchair, switches off the radio and orders everyone to bed, including his wife. Only once have I heard her object. She was knitting. "Oh darling, can't I just finish this row?" she asked. "No. Off to bed," he commanded. I objected once when I was in the middle of writing a letter, and he didn't like it at all. I thought to myself, "He's only a refugee, like me. Why should I do what he says?" The Nazis threw him out of his country as they did me and my family and my friends. As far as the British are concerned he's no better than me. I despise him for his typical Continental character. "How I should hate to be Continental," I said to myself. Now you're staring. You can't believe you heard me right, can you? I come from Vienna, you say, and yet I don't consider myself Continental? Quite right. I'm British – British in spirit and behaviour. I speak their language perfectly and I love the British people. I no longer understand the Continental mentality and no longer identify with foreigners. I'm not their kind any more. But in spite of Dr B. I quite like living here, although there'll never be another heavenly St Josephs.

11

Apart from Pat and Prue I've not made any friends yet. I'd like to meet an undergraduate but I suppose that is expecting too much. I often wish you could come out of your papery disguise and come around with me, but then I thank God that you *are* only paper and so much more my understanding friend and comforter than any human being could ever be.

So tomorrow I start my first job. How will it be? I've learnt that however much you change houses, towns and countries, your worries come with you, you can't really get away from anything. Will earning my own living make a real difference to my life?

21st October 1944

My first week as a Junior Library Assistant is over. I work from 9.15am till 7.00pm every day except Thursday, which is half day. In my lunch hour I stand in a long queue at the Town Hall next door to the library, and then eat my (not very nice) dinner unceremoniously and amid much clatter. However, I'm learning a lot about books, and how few I've read! The books are classified by the Dewey System, which I'm beginning to get the hang of. Best of all, I've made friends with the other new junior assistant – a nice girl called Margaret Sanders, known as Sandy, also aged 17. Today we went to town together in our lunch hour. We all, even the senior assistants, have to wear green, short-sleeved overalls for work, of a coarse material and with a belt – not flattering at all. I feel very fat in it.

But I have something more interesting to tell you: there's a secret love affair going on in this house – between Dr Beschorner, the 33 year-old foreign, Jewish psychiatrist, and Prue Dixon, the 15 year-old schoolgirl living here. She told me about it herself. I don't believe half of it but I have noticed what a lot of attention he pays her. She flatters him, and he adores that. What a character! Prue obviously knows how to attract men, but I don't, even though I'm two years older and have seen more of the world. I don't think I give men a chance of loving me and I wouldn't know how to respond to it. And I'm too serious. It must be fun to be carrying on an illicit love affair, and I envy Prue. Of course, she's not a Jewish refugee or a foreigner – that doesn't stand me in good stead even with my own kind! She's a pretty, fair-haired girl, with not a care in the world, and a safe and loving home somewhere in Wiltshire. The reason she's living here is because there's no Girls' High School in her area. She goes home in the holidays.

27th October 1944

I received my first wages today! Now I'm a working girl. My work so far consists of tidying and dusting the bookshelves first thing in the morning, replacing books on the shelves correctly, writing out library tickets and 'buffering' in the basement. This last task is one Sandy and I hate most. It means sand-papering the three edges of the pages until they're white and clean. There's an endless supply of books needing this done and we spend a good part of every day doing it. But it is also an excellent opportunity to read books stored in the basement, and I'm getting quite good at reading and buffering at the same time, though it is strictly forbidden, presumably because it slows down the job. So, at the slightest sound of footsteps, I quickly hide the book I'm reading. It is very lonely all alone in the huge basement, and I'd much rather be in the lending department upstairs, or in the Junior Library, even if it is only to put books away on shelves.

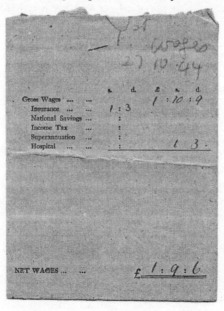

I've had lots of letters from Falmouth. They make me quite homesick. There was one from the Hodgetts today, beautifully written on beautiful notepaper. Mr H. has seen Mrs Belcher, he writes, who told him I was a good correspondent, 'so don't forget to include us in your list'. There are several refugees still living in the tower part of their house, but the Hodgetts have had no rent from them. He asks me, 'Do you think you will return eventually to Austria? I mean after the Huns have been finally settled. I am afraid my scheme for dealing with the Germans is rather too drastic to be adopted by the United Nations – that is the total extermination of the whole race.' That's more or less how I feel.

I've also had a letter from Robin. I think Monica Wills is his girlfriend now.

2nd November 1944

I've been with Pat to the GFS and the YMCA looking for rooms for her, as she's not very happy at Beschorners. I think secretly that she's in love with Dr B. and he treats her very unkindly. We had no luck with the rooms. Mrs Beschorner and I go to the pictures quite often, and on Sundays Prue, Pat and I go to services at different College Chapels. Last Sunday it was New College. I often visit my elderly Aunt Else in her bed-sitting room but find it rather boring. The highlight of the week was last Saturday, when a girl called Joyce who lives next door took me, and two of her friends, to Balliol College for a gramophone recital and afterwards to the posh Randolph Hotel for coffee. I didn't get back till 11pm There's talk of Joyce coming to live here and sharing my room – but how shall I undress then? This quite worries me.

While I was at work on Saturday afternoon, Julia and Sally Kennedy were here for tea; they're school friends of Prue's. When I tell you that they are the daughters of Margaret Kennedy, the author of *The Constant Nymph*, you'll understand why I was so sorry to have missed them.

The first papers of my Correspondence Course have arrived from the Library Association. It is the only way I can study for my qualifications, since I don't live in London, where the only Library College is. I also still go to the Secretarial College once a week, which is not improving with acquaintance.

Next Sunday I'm going to London for the day to visit my father and Putz. I can hardly wait.

9th November 1944

Of course, the train was late again, but I had a wonderful day in London. I left on the 7.30am train and was met at Paddington by Putz. We went to Belgrave Hospital where she works and lives – her bedroom is a small dark cubicle – had lunch at Lyons, then went to Elgin Avenue to see my father. Later he and Jane left for Liverpool on business. In the evening, Jack and Putz saw me off at the station and I caught the train back to Oxford. I fell into conversation with some Yanks on the train.

When I was at a café with Prue one day last week I paid for her because she had no change (she said). I never got the money back. I don't think that's very nice of her, do you?

Canon Roxby has put me in touch with the Rev. Lund of St Aldates Church. I met him today and he expressed the hope that I would attend his church regularly.

Mrs Beschorner is taking me to the theatre next week. I have never been to a real theatre except once or twice in Vienna. There are two theatres here – the New and the Playhouse. Joyce is also taking me to another gramophone recital – at Wadham College this time. Joyce has a friend called Edna to whose birthday party I went last Saturday. It wasn't bad, considering I knew nobody else there.

Prue's brother Giles was here for the weekend. He took us out for a meal. He's the personification of an Englishman, with a nice sense of humour and a quiet, reserved manner. Very upper class.

The war looks good – it *must* end soon now. Putz is happier at her hospital. I hope she's coming down for a weekend soon and I'll do my utmost to find her a young man. I long for her happiness. My father's business is excellent. It seems the whole of England wants knitwear by Playfair – his firm in London. Things are looking up, though I hardly dare write that down, but it would be foolishly superstitious to think it's all going to stop just because I dared mention it. Even I have found a career and am settled in digs. It looks as if my past private battles, like the war itself, are at last to be rewarded with victory. Except that the tragedy of my beloved missing mother makes every happiness impossible.

23rd November 1944

Most people, like most things, change as time goes on. Myself included: from the giddy-brained, empty-headed, light-hearted, gay, loved, spoilt child I've changed into a reserved, silent person. I no longer like garish colours or noisy parties. I'm nowhere more in heaven than quietly in my room alone after a day's work. I used to hate solitude but no longer. Perhaps the war changed us all. Five years of a long, dragging war. Perhaps that is why peace even on a small scale, such as the peace of my quiet room, is such a comfort.

The Assistant Librarian is called Miss Campbell and is a real dragon. I avoid her as much as possible, but we – Sandy and I – always have to ask her what she wants us to do next. She usually replies, "B-b-buffering". She stammers. She doesn't like the junior assistants to talk to borrowers, and if one of them asks us something and Miss Campbell is about she comes straight up and barges in and says: "Can I help you?" to the borrower. I hate that. Borrowers usually only want to know things like if there are any new Ruby M. Ayres books in, or where the travel section is. Another thing we're not allowed to do is counter work – ie, stamp people's books with the date stamp, or find their tickets when they return a book. I'd *love* to do these things, but it seems you have to have worked here for at least a year before this is allowed!

I'm going to London again for the day on Sunday – with Mrs Beschorner. She's a Londoner and is going to visit her family while I visit mine. She thinks I ought to borrow her curlers the night before so that my hair looks nice for London. I've never used curlers in my life as my hair is naturally curly but I don't want to hurt her by refusing them.

2nd December 1944

I've had a letter from the Urbachs! I knew they were in England but we'd lost touch and now they've traced us again! We're going to meet soon. When I first saw their letter it was like seeing a ghost from the past.

Pat left yesterday. She has found herself a bed-sitting room. I shall miss her. I don't think Joyce is coming to live here after all. I'm going to move into Prue's room upstairs; it's a large enough room to share, and the beds are at opposite ends. Next Wednesday

Mrs Beschorner is taking me to the theatre again – the Playhouse – to see *Candida*. She loves the theatre, and she's also very artistic – she can really paint and draw, not like me. There are several paintings of hers on the walls, including a lovely portrait of her son Peter.

Last Thursday, our half day, I was invited to Sandy's house in Witney for lunch and tea. I went there by bus. We played Mah Jong, went to town with her friend Jane and took the dog for a walk. Witney's landmark is an ancient buttercross and Sandy and Jane proudly pointed it out to me, almost as if they had put it there themselves. Sandy's parents are nice, homely people and were very kind to me. Mrs Sanders said we mustn't let Miss Campbell get us down. Sandy replied that this is easier said than done, and I agreed.

When some of us were having our mid-morning horrible watery NALGO cocoa in the basement the other day, where the books in need of repair or otherwise not in current use are stored, I noticed that some were not in alphabetical order, as they should be.

"What's Doris Leslie doing next to Warwick Deeping?" I said.

"Well, you see, Miss Jacoby," replied Betty Argyle, a very nice senior library assistant, "it would take a bit long to go into now, but it's what's generally known as the attraction of the sexes."

We burst out laughing, and laughed for the rest of the all too brief break. It helped me to face Miss Campbell, who actually smiled at me for once. I haven't said anything about Mr Skuce, the Librarian, yet; that's because we hardly ever see him. He sits in his office all day, probably reading, and is as aloof and unapproachable as an army general. Very occasionally he strides into the lending library on his long thin legs, usually during a quiet spell when the assistants are chatting and not doing much. As soon as he's spied everyone busies herself guiltily. Nobody likes Mr Skuce or Miss Campbell.

11th December 1944

A girl in her twenties called Kay Ellison, who's games mistress at the High School, lives here now and has my old room. She keeps to herself and is hardly involved with the Beschorners, and gives the impression of having a fascinating private life. This was

17

confirmed a few days ago when she announced a Maharaja was coming to have tea with her. We – Joan Beschorner, Prue and I – waited by the window in great excitement, expecting him to arrive on an elephant with a retinue in tow. In fact he arrived on a bicycle like any undergraduate. He was very handsome. Kay, like Prue, is only here during term time. On Sunday I attended the Carol Service at the High School with Dr B. Prue was singing in the choir.

Last Saturday was Prue's birthday and she had a party. Kay, Pat, Joyce and her boyfriend Brian and a few others came and we (they) danced, and played games. It wasn't bad. I still can't dance. Aunt Else said she knew a young Viennese who would take me to dancing lessons, but this never materialised.

In her last long letter Miss Davis gave me all the latest news from St Josephs. My room is still empty. It was offered to Keith but he hummed and muttered in his usual way and seemed loath to leave his abode, so he's staying put, and the room is free for the next child occupant (it was the best room in the house). "We miss you very much," writes Miss Davis, "and I often think of you at different times during the day, especially when supper is on the way." They have a new friend in the shape of a USN who's a ship's cook. Miss McCreight still comes to lunch on Sundays, never failing to give full vent to her vocabulary. The wireless is lovely now, with a new accumulator. She says she can't imagine me wearing corsets (which I do now) and she ends: "Well, it is nearly 11.30 and my eyes are blinking. It is pouring with rain, the wind is howling, cats are fighting outside and Keith is snoring inside. Bye bye, write again soon, won't you?" I longed to be back after reading this letter.

20th December 1944

Lieselotte and my father were here for the weekend. He stayed at the Mitre Hotel, Lieselotte stayed with me. We all had dinner at the Mitre on Saturday, and Bruno and Erna too. Bruno is my father's cousin and an art historian. On Sunday we were all at Aunt Else's. She's another cousin of my father's. Next weekend – Christmas – I am going to London and also to Cobham, where Uncle Felix – yet another cousin – lives with his new wife. The Urbachs live in Banstead, which is not far from Cobham, and I hope to visit them too. What will it be like to see them again, after all this time?

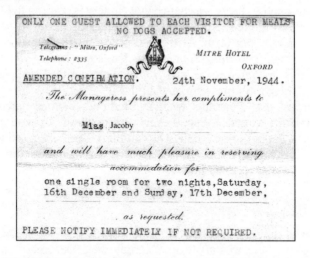

ONLY ONE GUEST ALLOWED TO EACH VISITOR FOR MEALS
NO DOGS ACCEPTED.

Telegrams : " Mitre, Oxford "
Telephone : 2335

MITRE HOTEL
OXFORD

AMENDED CONFIRMATION. 24th November, 1944.

The Manageress presents her compliments to

Miss Jacoby

and will have much pleasure in reserving
accommodation for

one single room for two nights, Saturday,
16th December and Sunday, 17th December,

as requested.

PLEASE NOTIFY IMMEDIATELY IF NOT REQUIRED.

Prue left for home today. I'm getting Saturday afternoon off from the library so that I can catch an earlier train to London. It'll be nice not to have to work for three days, or should I say not to have to do any buffering for three days. I'm getting to be quite a well-read girl thanks to buffering – to date I've read about six books on the job, among them Somerset Maugham's *The Constant Wife*, the *Letters of Jane Carlyle* and some stories by Sacha Guitry. Usually I'm not interrupted. The other day, when I surfaced after about an hour in the basement, Betty Argyle told me what had taken place: the Library recently advertised for a senior assistant in the Children's Library, and one of the applicants who turned up today was a negro. Betty took him to Mr Skuce's office to be interviewed. She knocked on his door, opened it and showed the man in.

"This gentleman has come about the job, Mr Skuce," she explained.

"Well, he can go away again," said Mr Skuce. "We don't have niggers working here." Betty said she didn't know who felt the worse, she or the poor negro.

I had a very nice letter from Audrey. She writes: 'You seem to have an eye for the boys since you left, tut, tut! [I must have mentioned some boys who were at the birthday party.] Is this the

19

little girl who wouldn't look at a boy in Falmouth? Still, I expect the boys in Oxford are heaps nicer than those in Falmouth . . .' I wouldn't know. There's a chance that Audrey is coming to Oxford to do Physiotherapy at one of the hospitals. She doesn't want to stay on in the 6th form. At the end of the letter she says: 'Well Nanks, there isn't much more news. I'm sorry I can't write such an interesting letter as you can.' Oh, and she asks if I still play the piano. There isn't one here, and I miss it.

I heard that Denzil is back in Falmouth – your namesake, remember. I wonder if I shall ever see him again? Do you think I can ever get out of my shell? Do you think I'm born to be an old maid because I'm a refugee? I will leave you with these questions and let you go to sleep now.

30th December 1944

I have so much to tell you I don't know where to start. That is, I do know where to start – on Saturday 23rd December, when I went to London after having lunch with Sandy, and made my own way to Elgin Avenue from Paddington, and had dinner in the evening at the Hungarian Czarda with my father, Jack and Jane – the difficulty is stopping my thoughts from racing on in a disorderly fashion. On to the 24th then, Christmas Eve. We had our presents in the morning, and after tea Putz and I went to Cobham for two days. Although Cobham is only about half an hour from Waterloo Station it was not an easy journey as on account of the war, none of the little stations have their names up and it was pitch dark. Having unsuccessfully tried to count the stops, we ended up having to rely on other passengers telling us when we reached our destination. From the station we walked 15 minutes through pitch dark country lanes till we reached the house – Ann's Cottage, Brook Farm Road. It was worth it! A beautiful, warm, Christmassy room awaited us, with a huge Christmas tree by the window, and a roaring fire round which various relations and friends of Uncle Felix and Anni's were sitting. One of the first things Uncle Felix said to me was: "How's the novel?" I had sent him my novel *Ambitious Failure* to read, with 'Started 24th September, finished 3rd October 1943' written below the title. He had returned it with helpful comments as I knew he would, the most memorable of which was, 'There is no need to finish a novel in a week. Some authors take a week to decide where to put a comma.' I said, "It's still unpublished." In addition to the relations and friends, a parachutist turned up later – not by parachute, as far as I know – and stayed for supper. Later we received more Christmas presents. I had a really useful leather purse from Anni. Putz and I talked in bed until one o'clock.

The next day, Christmas Day, we stayed in bed until 10.30. It was a beautiful day, brilliant blue above and dazzling white on the ground. We – Putz, Felix and Anni, Trude Dawson, Mrs Weber and I had a lovely walk in the Surrey countryside with the temperature below zero, our feet crunching on the hoar frost. When we returned home – after I'd thawed out in front of the fire – I took a photograph of the Christmas tree.

Boxing Day was the day of my reunion with the Urbachs. On my way to Banstead on the train I tried to remember everything I could about them, but I found that even Eva's face was not clear in my mind, and I was afraid I might not recognise them.

How wrong I was. The train moved into Epsom station. I looked out of the window and saw Mr Urbach and Eva at once. They were standing on the platform. As soon as we met we fell into each other's arms. It was a glorious and sentimental reunion, which was repeated at their house where Mrs Urbach was waiting. The tears rolled down her cheeks as she pressed me to her. She could not let me go. The tears stood in my eyes too. We all sat down. I looked at them and they looked at me. We couldn't talk fast enough to satisfy each other's curiosity. Mrs Urbach was laughing and crying. Mr Urbach kept embracing me. And Eva? How about Eva? After all those years of course we have drifted apart and were a little strange with each other. I had expected that, of course. But Eva had no memories. She remembers nothing. "Don't you remember that day we had a fight?" I asked her. No, she had forgotten. I wanted her to be a child again, a child in Vienna, my school-friend, romping and playing with me. I wanted to catch hold of her grown-up hair and uncurl it and put it back into pigtails. I wanted to take her grown-up clothes off and dress her in her little girl's pleated skirt that I used to like. I wanted to squeeze her brain and crush out all her Englishness, her ideas poisoned by England. Poisoned? But England is my country – English is my language! But at that moment they were the murderers of my Viennese past. I longed for us all to be back in

21

Vienna again and that Hitler and the war had never happened. The Urbachs hate Austria because of what occurred in 1938 and never want to go back.

Even the Viennese lunch Mrs Urbach had prepared did not taste as I remembered food tasted in Vienna. And their little house was so different from their spacious flat in the Heinestrasse. It seemed to me they were only visiting here.

Outside it was still white and icy. We were cold going to the bus stop and then waiting for the train. As the doors of the carriage closed and we waved goodbye, our words no longer audible, I was already beginning to erase the new Eva from my mind and replace her with the little pig-tailed girl my mother knew. It had been a strange day, but I had little to think of it again because soon after I arrived back in Cobham my father and I travelled to London, where I spent one more night before returning to Oxford early on Wednesday morning and straight to the library till 7pm. Unfortunately, I missed seeing Aunt Liesel Frank in Cobham – she was due the day I left. I have not seen her since she left Falmouth. Yesterday was the coldest day since 1890, and yesterday was also the day I had an orange for the first time for ages, though not as long ago as 1890. Tomorrow is the last day of the year. May 1945 have more happy days than 1944 . . .

Happy New Year, dearest diary.

1st January 1945

I spent New Year's Eve at home, drinking, smoking and playing cards with the Beschorners. Today I didn't go to the library in the morning as I was sick and had a tummy ache, but had recovered enough to go for the evening session, 5-7pm. More buffering.

My pocket diary for 1945 is a present from Pam. 'Wishing you the best of luck, Ingrid, with love from Pam' she wrote on the front page. How she would disapprove if she knew that I used to pinch a diary from Woolworth's every year!

5th January 1945

I heard on Wednesday that Ruth's mother is dead. It may only be a rumour.

This evening I had supper with Aunt Else. I told her about Ruth's mother. She said I mustn't lose hope about my own mother.

Yesterday I went skating with Sandy on frozen Port Meadow, on borrowed skates. The last time I skated was in Vienna. This wasn't nearly so good as the ice was not smooth and of course there was no music to skate to. Afterwards Sandy came to tea and we played cards.

I had a very nice letter from Miss Davis. They had their usual jolly, noisy Christmas festivities – but without Denzil! He never turned up. It has been very cold in Falmouth too, and they've actually had snow! An American officer has been staying at St Joseph's; he had 'my' room and loved the bed. Miss Davis said that Pam has been to see her and she prefers her to Audrey which quite surprised me. I also had a long, long letter from Miss Kitty. There were no turkeys available this Christmas, she writes, so they had fowl. The letter was full of other news, about people and places I know, and made me feel very nostalgic. Even a glimpse of the various priests who visited St Joseph's would be welcome! Father Parkin very expertly did the carving, wrote Miss Kitty. Although both letters – Miss Davis's and Miss Kitty's – run into many pages and duplicate some of the news, they are very different from each other, with Miss Kitty making a joke of everything as she always did, and Miss Davis more serious and kindly.

I've also had a long letter from 'Uncle' Jack, their brother. He enjoys philosophical discussions and criticising books. He asked me why I became a Protestant and not a Roman Catholic (he's a devout one, like all the Davis's), as the latter is an international religion. I'd better not answer that.

7th January 1945

I was in my room this morning when Mrs Beschorner came to tell me there was someone to see me downstairs. I went down and saw a short, fat young woman standing in the hall.

"Don't you recognise me?" she said. I didn't.

"I'm Susie Riesz. Annemarie Breuer's cousin," she told me. "We met in Vienna once or twice. Remember?" I didn't, but I said I did. I asked after the Breuers, whom I, of course, remember very well. Then Susie told me that she saw me and Mrs Beschorner at the Austrian club on Saturday night where we had gone to hear Strauss waltzes played on records. She wasn't quite sure if it was me but after making enquiries it was confirmed, and so here she was, having done a bit of detective work to discover my address. She lives in Oxford with her parents and brother and has invited me to her house on Thursday, which is also her half day as she works at W.H. Smith's.

In my lunch hour last Saturday I went to visit the Chinese author Chiang Yee, who lives in Southmoor Road. He's a charming gentleman who writes and beautifully illustrates travel books. We talked a little, and then he gave me his signature in Chinese and English.

Kay is coming back tomorrow and Prue on Wednesday. On Tuesday evening Mrs B. and I are going to the flicks. We like seeing foreign films at the Walton Street cinema which is only a few minutes' walk away. Sometimes we buy chips (and even fish!) on the way, just as Connie and I used to. Not fish, we couldn't afford that.

12th January 1945

I had a lovely day with the Riesz family yesterday. It seemed I was back in Vienna, even though I knew quite well it was only Thorncliffe Road, North Oxford. Having as usual had lunch with Sandy, and another girl from the library called Babs House, I went straight to the Rieszs' who welcomed me like a long lost friend or even relative. Mrs Riesz is very warm and motherly, Susie is like her, but Peter is the clever one. He is ginger-haired, 19 years old and an undergraduate reading Chemistry. We talked and talked, had tea, went to the pictures and then had supper, after which I spent the evening with them, more talking, smoking and listening to the wireless. Peter loves classical music and played some Beethoven records. Mr Riesz, home from work, joined us for supper. I had no recollection of ever having met him before. I felt very envious of Susie and Peter living a normal home life with their parents. How lucky they are. We talked of my mother, and Mrs Riesz said the war would soon be over now and we would be together again.

We had our first real snow of the winter today and I fell off my bike three times because the roads were so slippery.

As I have access to a typewriter at the library I stayed on after work to type a story I've written.

17th January 1945

THE RUSSIANS HAVE TAKEN WARSAW! Wonderful news. How much longer now till the end of the war? That is the question everyone is asking.

Tomorrow I'm having the morning off from the library and am going to London for the day as my father wants me to see a specialist about my overactive thyroid gland. I didn't object as it's a good opportunity to have a day off work, and to see Putz. I asked Putz in one of my letters recently if she thought father had slept with Jane, and she replied, typically: "I don't know and I don't care."

The only person at the library who can stand up to Miss Campbell is Zena Davies, the Children's Librarian. She's about 30 years old, wears a pink overall instead of the horrid green one the rest of us wear, and is charming. Every evening a tall, handsome Italian fetches her and takes her home. He's a married man, so rumour has it, which makes it even more exciting. Sandy and I have nicknamed Zena 'Anna Karenina'. Miss Berthold, a senior library assistant, has given me an old copy of *Rebecca*. It is in its red leather library binding, with gold lettering on the spine, but is too tatty to be kept on the shelves. It's not too tatty for me, however, and I took it home as if it were the most precious book in the world.

28th January 1945

Mrs Beschorner was in London this weekend and Prue and I cooked all the meals and looked after Peter. This afternoon, Sunday, I had tea at the Rev. Lund's in the Rectory at St Aldate's Church and afterwards attended a youth meeting in the Church Hall. I didn't know anyone there but walked home with two nurses who also didn't know anyone else.

A girl called Daphne Hall, who works in the same office where Mrs Beschorner works part-time, slept here last Friday. She is enviably blonde and pretty and very upper class. The following

b

day I had lunch with her. Last Sunday Prue and I had a walk in Christ Church meadow and afterwards we went to a service at St Aldate's Church.

3rd February 1945

It has been exceptionally warm for the time of year. Last Wednesday I ate an ICE CREAM! Mrs Beschorner bought it for me. She really is very nice to me. On Tuesday she advised me to skip my shorthand class in the evening as I had a bad cold, and I gladly took the advice. Instead we listened to Hitler's speech on the wireless. I wonder if he really believes that Germany will win the war?

Sandy's mother took Sandy and me out to lunch at Hunt's on Thursday. Afterwards I went to Aunt Else's. It had been a terrible morning in the library and I was very glad it was half day. Miss Berthold had sent me to the Reference Library to ask Miss Campbell to give me the magazine from the windowsill.

"Miss Berthold says could you give me the magazine from the windowsill, please," I said to Miss Campbell, who was sitting behind the counter like a snarling tiger behind bars.

"Well, g. . g. . get it, then," she snapped.

"Where is it?" I asked. She has this effect on me. I could have bitten my tongue as soon as I said it. She looked up from her book and if looks could kill I would have dropped down dead.

"On the w. . w. . windowsill, of course, s. . s. . stupid," she hissed. I felt wretched the rest of the morning.

8th February 1945

I've been to the Rieszs' again today. After tea Mrs Riesz said to Peter, "Are you going to play some of your records to Ingrid?"

"Do you want to hear records?" he asked me.

"Yes, very much," I said.

"Do you like music, too?" I asked Mrs Riesz.

"My mother only knows two kinds of music," said Peter, before she could reply, "the loud and the soft." We all laughed, and Mrs Riesz took it very good-naturedly. She's used to Peter's teasing and mocking ways, I expect. Susie came to listen to the records, too. I found it quite embarrassing to sit in absolute silence for an hour with them, and felt that one should really be alone to listen to beautiful music. Peter played us a Mozart piano concerto.

"What did you think about when you listened to that? Did charming images pass through your mind?" Peter asked me when it was finished. I was about to say that the music had certainly inspired happy thoughts, when I realised in time that the question was a trap and that one is not supposed to think of anything when listening to music.

"I thought about the music," I said. It wasn't entirely a lie.

Yesterday Mrs Beschorner, Prue and I went to the New Theatre to see the Pantomime *Mother Goose*. There was a bus strike on so we had to walk there and back.

I forgot to tell you that the London specialist said my slight goitre was nothing to worry about and is quite common among young girls. It will go away in time. My father also took me to his office where I did a bit of typing for him – boring letters to wholesalers about non-delivery of garments and such like. The best part of the day was having lunch at the 'Vienna', where Putz joined us. She doesn't like nursing any more and would very much like to do something else, but can't because it's war work.

11th February 1945

We have to leave 66 St John's Road! The Beschorner household is breaking up. Dr B. seems to have gone mad and refuses to speak to anyone, and the house is being sold. I don't know if it has to do with the love affair between Dr B. and Prue – and probably Pat as well, which may be why she moved, and stepped out of our lives – or if there is some other reason. When Joan Beschorner gave me the bad news this morning she took my hand and said she loved me and made me promise to remain her friend. I was very surprised and even more so when I saw she was crying.

Now I have to find somewhere else to live . . .

14th February 1945

. . . which isn't easy. A Miss Prager came to see me at the library today about a room she has to let, but it doesn't sound suitable.

27

Yesterday Budapest was liberated by the Russians. The Germans are losing territory everywhere now. It is not only my own life which is in a state of upheaval.

Last night Joan Beschorner and I saw *Othello* in the New Theatre. It was wonderful. After the performance we walked home. On the way we talked about everything under the sun or, more correctly, under the moon. For instance, I'd often wondered why the book by Somerset Maugham about Gauguin is called *The Moon and Sixpence*. "Oh, but don't you see," said Joan, "that was all he wanted. The unattainable, and just enough to live on." I understood at once, and wondered why I didn't before. Then we talked about the war, and wars in general, and Joan said she was a pacifist and would never fight or kill, and was bringing Peter up the same way.

"But if you're attacked . . ." I said.

"If everyone followed my example then nobody would attack you," she replied. It made good sense. I'm a pacifist too. Then somehow we arrived at the topic of her childhood and family in London. She has a favourite brother called Bill whom she would like me to marry! I asked her where she met her husband. At a meeting in London, she replied, and it was love at first sight. She was only 19 when she married him.

"And if I had slept with him he wouldn't have married me," she said. "Remember that, Ingrid." Then suddenly she was telling me about her wedding night, how her husband had made love to her directly after the ceremony, how she had cried, "No! no!" and the more she shrank from him the harder he pushed. I should like to have seen the expression on her face as she spoke but it was too dark. Just before we reached home, she stopped and put her hand on my shoulder and said, "One day you'll know all about these things, Ingrid, but let me tell you one last thing: don't expect too much of it, don't let yourself believe it's all bliss because it isn't. Personally, I was very disappointed."

I went straight to my room when we got back. I wanted to be alone. I drew the curtains and locked the door. Dr Beschorner making love to Joan, and Othello murdering Desdemona in a fit of jealousy, fought for supremacy in my imagination. Both obsessed me. One merged into the other. Then I thought for a long time about poor, nice Joan and the cruel husband she's so afraid of, and of how my own wedding night would be if ever I have

one. I got into bed, and already the room was full of dreams . . .
It has become a beautiful room with heavy velvet curtains down
to the floor and a deep carpet, and I am sitting in my new silk
dressing gown, my hands folded on my lap. It is my wedding
night. I sit waiting. Presently the door opens. My heart beats very
fast. He approaches. He takes my face into his hands. "You are
beautiful," he says. I'm afraid, even though I know that he is kind
and safe and not at all like Dr B. Only minutes away from
understanding the mystery now, and I'm afraid. "Tired, darling?"
he asks. I shake my head. I can't speak. At this moment I am
aware of only three things: him, myself and my fear. He senses
my fear. "My darling," he says, not smiling. His voice is so quiet,
so calm and soothing. "My darling. You are afraid? Of *me?*" . . .
And then, slowly, the mystery begins to unfold.

The room I inhabit has, of course, no velvet curtains or fitted
carpet, and I'm alone in my bed. I remember Othello and Dr
Beschorner – and then I remember the Valentine I received and
have not an inkling who it is from. But it whispers that, perhaps,
one day, my dream will come true, the dream of my wedding
night; as imagined by a virgin.

17th February 1945

On Thursday, my half day, I went to London again. Jane – my
father's business partner, landlady and I don't know what else –
fetched me from Paddington and took me shopping for a costume,
which we didn't get. Afterwards we met my father and Jack for
tea and then Jane and I went to the Old Vic to see *Peer Gynt*. I
wanted to see it because Lawrence Olivier was in it but he only
had a very small part as the button maker and – imagine it – just
as he appeared on the stage, about half an hour before the end – I
had to leave to catch my last train back to Oxford. What a
disappointment. But it was worth getting a glimpse of him. The
last time I saw him in the flesh was at Helford, when he invited
Pam and me to join him and Vivien Leigh in a rowing boat. I shall
remember that occasion to the end of my days.

I've made friends with an unusual Irish girl at my shorthand
class, called Maureen Daly. She's 24 – the same age as Joan – and
wears very thick glasses. On Friday she came to see me at the
Library. We arranged to go to the New Theatre together next

week, which is Celebrity Week at the theatre, to hear Richard Tauber, my one time idol from Vienna. I adore hearing him sing in his beautiful sobbing voice.

Yesterday I treated Prue for lunch. We're good friends now. We don't talk about Dr B.

22nd February 1945

What I'm about to tell you is so unbelievable that I don't expect anyone to believe me. In fact it seems so impossible that it might be a dream: *Richard Tauber has invited me to his dressing room on Friday evening!* This is how it happened: Maureen Daly and I went to his concert last night as arranged. I was in seventh heaven and loved every moment. After the performance I of course went to the stage door to get his autograph. Maureen didn't come with me as she had to catch her last bus home. There was a long queue outside the stage door of people all wanting Tauber's autograph. At last it came to my turn. I was ushered in. A moment later I was face to face with my idol. I handed him pen and paper and he signed his name, barely looking up.

"I'm from Vienna too," I told him. And now he did look at me, and smiled. He looked at me for a long time.

"Are you? Come and see me some time and we'll talk about Vienna," he said. He was charming, and seemed so pleased to have come across someone from Vienna. Friday night after his last concert was arranged for my visit. Can you imagine my excitement? Will Friday evening ever come?

This afternoon Sandy accompanied me in my search for a room. If I hadn't been so happy about my invitation to Richard Tauber's dressing room tomorrow I would have felt truly wretched: all the rooms we went to see were either already taken, too expensive, too shabby or too far away. Where am I going to live? After our fruitless journeys we had tea at Fuller's, went for a walk and then to the New Theatre to hear Rawicz and Landauer. Another wonderful occasion. They played duets on two pianos back to back. There were lots of encores. After the performance Sandy caught her bus home to Witney and I went to visit Aunt Else. Bruno was there. He told us he'd just been to see Egon Wellesz the composer, who's a friend of his, and Mrs von Hoffmansthal was there too. We talked about my plight to find accommodation and both Else and Bruno are going to make enquiries for me among their acquaintances.

Next Saturday Prue's brother Giles is coming to visit her in Oxford and I'm going to the station with her to meet him. But before then the humble keeper of this diary is invited to visit the great celebrity, Richard Tauber.

24th February 1945

If what I told you in my last entry was unbelievable, what I am about to tell you now will almost certainly be considered a figment of my imagination. But truth is stranger than fiction they say, and I have proved this for myself now.

On the appointed evening I turned up at the stage door of the New Theatre. I was beside myself with excitement. I planned what I would say to him. I would talk of Vienna and his fame and his voice and my admiration for his talent. The door was opened to me and once more I was shown into the dressing room of the great man. The door was closed – and I was pulled into my hero's arms. Before I properly knew what was happening he whispered, "How old are you?"

"Nearly 18," I replied, and tried to free myself, but he held me tightly, and then he kissed me and placed his huge hand down my blouse and onto my breast. Still I struggled and still he wouldn't let me go.

"Kiss me, kiss me, please kiss me," he whispered over and over again. Suddenly I was calm, quite calm. It might have been the most natural thing in the world to lie in Richard Tauber's arms. Perhaps the shock and surprise had left me numb. "I'm so pleased to meet a pretty girl from Austria," he was saying (lie!), and for a moment he released me. I looked at him and saw the face I had so often seen on photographs and in the newspapers, the face of a middle-aged man, rather ugly, grinning, lecherous, a monocle in his right eye. Nothing that I wanted was happening, nothing was as I had imagined it, nothing that I had come for was here. He only wanted to make love to me. The next minute he was kissing me again and he put his hands all over me and kept urging me to do something. I didn't know what he meant. I heard him say: "Come on – let me – please!" and I heard myself reply: "No! No!" Suddenly I felt very frightened and wanted to escape. I was afraid of being raped. There was a knock on the door.

"Mr Tauber, your train is leaving in half an hour," came an urgent voice from outside.

"All right, all right. I'm coming," he replied impatiently. He embraced me again and made me kiss him goodbye. He put his tongue in my mouth until I thought I would choke. "Come and see me in London some time," he said, and gave me his address. I said I would and left quickly. I felt ashamed walking past the staff waiting outside and almost ran out of the theatre. Something vile and terrifying had been revealed to me that till now had been hidden behind a beautiful voice, and from now on I would suspect hideous and ugly things lurking underneath all beautiful surfaces. I walked home in a trance, and I cried as I walked.

"Are you all right, Miss?" a kindly policeman called out to me.

"Yes, thank you," I replied. But I should like to have said to him: "I've just been nearly seduced by a childhood idol and I'll never believe in anything or anyone again. If that means I'm all right, then all right is what I am."

26th February 1945

I've found a room! Or rather Erna did. She came to the rescue again. Yesterday afternoon she took me to see it. It is in the house of Mrs Labowsky, an elderly refugee from Hamburg who, so Erna told me, had translated Dante in her youth. The room is beautifully furnished in a modern style, with a lovely mahogany desk from Hamburg in the corner. The rent is 35 shillings including breakfast and Sunday lunch. I'm moving in on Thursday next.

Sunday morning Giles spent with us in the room Prue and I share and to which Dr Beschorner has lately confined us in the evenings, as he's still mad and refusing to talk. Prue thinks he has been to the doctor and has been told he has not long to live! Giles said it's a good job we're clearing out. He took us to tea at the Ritz in the afternoon (after my visit to Mrs Labowsky's) and then we saw him off at the station, where we met a friend of his, who seemed very taken with Prue.

Of course I've told everyone about my adventure with Richard Tauber. Joan said I was lucky to have got off so lightly; Sandy said I should never have gone in the first place – she wouldn't have done; Prue thought at first I was making it all up and then asked me if that was the first time I'd ever been kissed. When I said yes she said don't let it put you off, it can be lovely.

The letter I received from my uncle Erwin in Zurich, in answer to mine, is not encouraging. I have never met him and don't like to bother him too much but am desperate to find out the whereabouts of my mother.

This evening I spent packing and on Wednesday my cabin trunk is being fetched. Kay came to our room for a chat. She's moving out too next week, and Prue has found accommodation in Lucerne Road, not far from where I shall live.

1st March 1945, Thursday

Here I am in my new abode at 47 Lonsdale Road. My pocket diary informs me that, on this day, in 1941, German troops entered Bulgaria. I too am once again in unknown territory. Once again I have to cope with strangeness and the unfamiliar, my beloved cabin trunk and bicycle the only comforting objects around me. Once again I have to cope with a strange present until it becomes as familiar as the past. The Beschorner household has broken up. It was indeed a peculiar six months I had there, what with mad Dr Beschorner, and Joan loving me, and making friends with Prue whom at first I mistrusted, and Pat leaving in mysterious circumstances. Once more I have a new home, a new life, new people to get used to. 'Time, you old gypsy man, will you not stay, put up your caravan just for one day?'

I've made friends in Oxford but not with boys, not counting Richard Tauber. What with studying for my library exam, going to secretarial college one evening a week and now having to do some of my own cooking – and I can't cook in spite of being renowned for my love of food – it doesn't look as if I'll ever have time to find a boyfriend. However, there are a few things to look forward to: Putz (and my father) are coming to Oxford for my birthday, at Easter I hope to go to Ruth's in Portsmouth at last, and in the summer perhaps to Falmouth – ?

May whoever God is lead me safely to where I eventually have to land, wherever it may be, over not too rocky a path.

3rd March 1945

I thought of moving to London when I couldn't find accommodation here, and finding a nicer library to work in, but my father talked me out of changing jobs so soon, so that I didn't follow up the invitation for an interview with Edwards & Co in Sydenham.

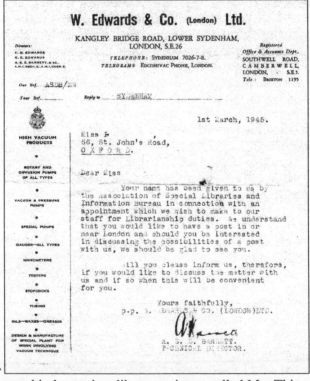

A very kind part-time library assistant called Mrs Thiem, who works at our library, has given me two delicate white china tea cups and saucers and a teapot as a 'house-warming present', with a note saying: 'To a nice girl, when she entertains another nice girl, Sandy, for tea.'

9th March 1945

– My 18th birthday. I had lots of presents and cards, and Prue is coming for supper. Yesterday, my half day, I called at 66 St John's Road as Joan wanted to see me. We fetched Peter from the nursery together. The house was in a very untidy state. Joan remains loyal to her husband and has not explained his strange behaviour, but revealed that he would be leaving soon to take up a teaching post in Harrow and she hopes to go with him.

Last Sunday Prue and her friend Joyce and I went to a service at New College; afterwards I went to a Youth Club meeting at St Aldate's Church: there was a Brainstrust at which Leslie Banks and C.S. Lewis were guests of honour. I got their autographs afterwards, of course. (Quite safe – there were lots of other people around this time!) I had to walk home, about 3 miles, as no bus came.

Tomorrow Putz and my father are coming for the weekend. My father is staying at the Randolph Hotel, Putz with me. I shall be wearing my new costume which is beige with a small check design, and I hope they like it.

'Dear Nanks, I have the most wonderful news for you,' writes Audrey in a letter I received from her yesterday. The news is that she's coming to be a student nurse at the Headington Orthopaedic Hospital in Oxford! That is, if she gets past the interview with the Matron. I'm delighted, and so is she. Then she goes on: 'Nanks, I think your mind is deteriorating somewhat. All that awful rot about Richard Tauber. I'd love to know where the truth ended and your imagination began. My dear Nanks, if he did things like that he would go to prison . . . You've been reading too many novels like *My Son, My Son*. Do write soon and tell me how much of that "affair" was true. Thanks for your photo, it's wonderful – but my my, haven't you grown up, maybe it's all those college boys!!!!!'

I forgot to mention that my father's reaction to my letter telling him about Richard Tauber was a *telephone call!* He sounded quite angry and said I must never do such a thing again, and didn't I know that Tauber is known to be a womaniser? It seems when my father lived in Paris before the war he once stayed in the same hotel as he and they had the same barber. One morning the barber, when he came to shave my father, said to him, "It's disgusting. I've just been to shave Mr Tauber, and he was in bed with a woman on either side of him." That's what my father told me. I can't understand how any woman could like such an ugly man. But, to tell you the truth, now that it's safely over, I'm quite proud of the experience.

15th March 1945

We lunched together at the Randolph Hotel in style, my father, sister and I, Bruno, Erna and Else, we visited the Rieszs', I gave all the relations tea in my room and we went for a few walks. That's how my birthday weekend was spent. Now that I'm 18 I'm no longer entitled to a blue ration book and shall be graduating to an adult one. What an honour.

My father returned to London on Sunday night, Putz stayed till Monday morning and came to the library with me before catching her train back. She has been to St James' Palace again to try and trace our mother but achieved nothing.

On Monday we were given our holidays for the summer. Mine is from 13th-26th July. Sandy and I went to the flicks in the evening.

This afternoon Susie Riesz came to tea – I'm getting quite good at making tea now – and afterwards we went to the flicks. On Saturday Prue and Sandy are coming to supper. As I have no table in my room we either sit at the desk to eat, or else on my bed, with our plates on our laps.

When I returned from work the other day I could hear that Mrs Labowsky had visitors. Her sitting room is next to my bedsitter (downstairs). On my way to the kitchen, they came out and we met in the hall. Imagine my surprise at seeing – none other than the handsome Italian, Zena Davies' lover! Mrs Labowsky introduced us – his name is Lorenzo, and his wife was with him. He gave no sign of ever having seen me before and he very likely hasn't: he has eyes only for Zena, and the rest of us green-overalled assistants are just library fixtures! I didn't let on, of course. If I did, what havoc it might have caused!

24th March 1945

It has been a most eventful week. I'll start with Sunday the 18th. Prue came and we cycled to Blenheim Palace in Woodstock and had tea there (not at the Palace). On Wednesday the whole Belcher family came to see me at the library! It was the day of Audrey's interview at the Headington hospital, and I was expecting them. We had lunch together, and tea at Fuller's, as I finished at the library at 5pm that day. It felt very strange being with Audrey in such different surroundings. I find it difficult to understand that I was once in love with her – and she with me, that is obvious to me now. Is it usual for two girls to be mutually in love? In any case love, like wine, does not travel well and also I have already outgrown it. The world of less than a year ago in which our love flourished seems unbelievably distant. She is coming to live in Oxford to start her nursing career in September, exactly a year after I arrived here.

Another amazing thing happened on Thursday: I met Ilse Rosendorf in town! She was at school with me, though not for long as she left Falmouth after about a year. She's a year older than I and I never knew her well. The thing I best remember about her is that she wanted to join the Girl Guides but objected to the promises she had to make. "He's not my king, England is not my country, and I don't believe in God," she declared, to the astonishment of all present. In the end she relented, however, as it was the only way to become a Guide. We were very surprised to see each other. Later Sandy and I called at her office where she works as a secretary and I invited her for tea on Sunday. Afterwards Sandy and I went to the magnificent Ashmolean Museum and then had tea at the Super Cinema. To finish off this eventful day, I went to the flicks in the evening with Julia Davies and two of her friends. Julia is the daughter of the authoress Margaret Kennedy, and Joan had arranged this outing for us. Unfortunately the film was not *The Constant Nymph*! I asked Julia how her mother came to write this book and she replied, "By watching a family on the beach who took her fancy." I found that a disappointing answer.

Yesterday all the library staff received a bonus, and I got paid double wages! A new assistant has joined us called Miss Jacques. Although she is not a Junior she's a particular thorn in Miss Campbell's eye, probably because she's very shy and unassuming and has no idea how to stand up for herself. I feel terribly sorry for her, and was glad to accept when she asked me to join her for lunch at the town hall today.

It has been the warmest day in March for 50 years! Which reminds me that spring is on its way, holidays are approaching – and Prue has invited me to spend Easter at her home in Wiltshire! This letter from Joan explains how I came to meet Julia Davies.

66 St John's Road
Saturday

My dear Ingrid,

You must excuse the delay in answering your letter – and I know you will understand how busy we are here with packing etc. It's a sad business.

I was so glad you enjoyed your birthday and presents. You certainly were remembered by many friends!

As regards your explanation re the 'meals' business, I knew there had been some misunderstanding and felt sure it would soon be cleared up. I'm sorry you expected me to think you a something liar. You should know me better than that, Ingrid.

The last paragraph of your letter cheered me no end and my husband, too, has been imploring me not to worry about things, but it sometimes goes all round in my head hell-mell and gives me a headache, but never mind, I'm endeavouring to adopt a philosophical attitude towards things. I'm told that life has a little habit of working itself out and as you say, it may 'all turn out all right'!

Now, I have some good news for you. I met the two Davies sisters (Sally and Julia), and told them that you would very much like to meet them and have a chat. As they are modern, broad-minded girls, who do not depend on introductions, why not invite them for tea one afternoon. Give them one or two days to choose from as I know they are always doing different things. You will find their address in the telephone book under Professor Cairns (I believe in Charlbury Road, but don't depend upon it). Perhaps you could give them a ring, and don't forget their name is Davies, as Kennedy is their mother's maiden name.

Life will be pretty hectic during the next few days, so I doubt very much if we will be able to meet in Oxford, but we shall meet again – perhaps in London – never fear. I feel sure I shall see your dear face once more.

I want to wish you all possible luck for your future librarianship and feel sure you will do well in the work you love, no matter how hard the path to your ultimate goal is. In fact the harder the path the sweeter the destination!

Don't forget what I once said about your own personal life. I feel certain you will one day be very happy and my instincts are often right.

Whatever your faults are, that certain something you have (a precious gift which not many people possess) will shine out and lead you along the right track.

All love for now, my Ingrid.

God bless you and thank you for the sunshine you have given me.

Yours,

JB

30th March 1945

Ilse Rosendorf was the same domineering and bossy girl I remember from school, and I felt very inadequate in her company. After tea we cycled to the Refugee Club to look at the 'Missing Relatives List'. In vain, of course. Both her parents are missing. Instead of returning to her place afterwards she spent the evening with me in my room. She told me that she is more or less engaged to a Russian called Ossia, that they are both Communists and intend to live in Russia after the war. Still on that country, on Thursday the 29th the Russians crossed the Austrian frontier! The Germans surely can't hold out much longer now. And still on politics, on Monday Lloyd George died. He was 82 years old. On Tuesday I had my last shorthand class for the term and tomorrow my Easter holiday starts and I'm travelling to Cannings, the village where Prue Dixon lives, and staying until Tuesday. I'm very excited about this visit.

I lost my half day on Thursday, it being Good Friday the following day, that is today, which I spent lazing, packing – and starting my new novel at last! It's called *Why Couldn't Beethoven Draw?* Don't you think that's a good title?

The Urbachs wanted me to visit them for Easter, too. Eva is going to Goldsmiths College to train as a teacher. Lots of girls from my form went to teacher training colleges. Pam wants to be a teacher too. But I'm the only one who wants to be a writer. Pam hopes to go to Exeter University.

Never in my life have I enjoyed a short holiday as much as this one.

It was dark and foggy when I arrived on the tiny railway station of Prue's village in deepest Wiltshire. Mr Dixon was supposed to meet me in his car, but the station was deserted except for one railway official. I told him of my plight.

"Oh, I'll ring Mr Dixon and he'll be here in a jiffy," he said. He was right. Mr Dixon explained that this is the usual arrangement, and we drove away into the night. But what delights awaited me at the end of the journey! The family – mother, father, Prue of course, Giles and a cousin called Rosemary, sitting in front of an open fire with cups of tea at their elbows were as though cut out of a magazine to represent a typical English family, or even characters from one of my fantasies. How warmly they welcomed me! I immediately felt happy there. After a lovely evening talking and listening to the wireless and having a cosy supper by the fire, I was shown into my room. The bed was piled high with blankets and a huge eiderdown as Prue had thoughtfully told her mother I like a heavy covering. On the bedside table was a copy of Jerome K. Jerome's *Three Men in a Boat*.

Mrs Dixon kissed me goodnight and spoke loving words to me, the poor little orphan refugee girl. I cried after she left. I cried because somebody had been especially kind to me, had tried to make me forget my loneliness, had offered me this unaccustomed affection, above all had for a few minutes tried to replace her who is irreplaceable, my mother.

The next day was Easter Sunday. I was brought breakfast in bed! Later we all went to church in the village and afterwards Mr Dixon took me for a drive over the downs. In the afternoon we all went for a walk with the dog and in the evening we played darts and the gramophone. On Monday everyone was beautifully lazy – I played the piano a bit – a grand – and Prue and I walked the dog. On Tuesday Prue and I cycled to Devizes to visit her granny, and had lunch with her. We passed a place called Andover and I said to Prue, "I bet that place dates back to the days of highwaymen."

"Why?" asked Prue.

"Andover your money or else – " I said. Prue always laughs at my jokes however bad they are, and she didn't fail me. On our way back we saw some German prisoners working in a field. It gave me quite a jolt. We visited a church before arriving back at Cannings. In the early evening Mr Dixon and Prue took me to the station and I returned to Oxford.

When I was with the Dixons, at the dinner table, round the fire, or out on a walk, I felt I was an author among my imaginary characters: such tranquillity could not be real; such happy people could not exist. I was certainly not one of them. There was no point at which our lives converged. I was on a different plane. I kept thinking: 'I never want to go back to my old life. I don't like it there, I want to stay here, I want their world to become mine, perhaps they'll teach me, I'll forget the past . . .'

But I'm back again. The old life was waiting for its slave with outstretched arms. Mr Dixon's last words on the station had been: "You are coming down again, aren't you? As soon as you can. Promise?" On the train back I thought about something else he had said. We were all having a serious discussion after lunch and I must have expressed some unusual opinion.

"You are a radical, aren't you?" he said, and smiled at me. I wasn't sure what a radical was but I knew he meant it flatteringly. (I know now; I've looked it up). I will never be able to repay them for this wonderful weekend.

12th April 1945

There's a chance that Ruth might come to Oxford to see me! I've been looking for a room for her, and she phoned me but I was out. I am longing to see her again.

Last Thursday I had tea at the Rieszs' and afterwards Susie and I went to the pictures. Mr Riesz wants me to ask my father if he can offer him a job.

Miss Jacques and I often have lunch together and try to cheer each other up after a horrible morning at the library with Miss Campbell breathing down our necks or telling us off. Maureen Daly, my Irish friend from the shorthand class, and I have been to the pictures together. She's a very strange girl, but I like her.

Yesterday, on the 11th of April, Shirley Temple got engaged. She's only 16. The end of her childhood is definitely the end of mine, too. When I was little I used to long to be like her. I'd still rather be her than me any day.

This is how I spent my half day today: Sandy, her friend Jane and I had lunch at Hunt's, then we went to the flicks, then had tea at Fullers' and in the evening we went to the New Theatre to see Vivien Leigh. Afterwards we went to the stage door as the others wanted her autograph. When our turn came I reminded Vivien Leigh of our meeting at Helford, and she remembered, and I introduced her to Sandy and Jane, who were very impressed. Vivien Leigh is the most beautiful woman I have ever seen. Perhaps it would be better to be her rather than Shirley Temple.

Ilse Rosendorf has been to see me at the library.

Friday, 13th April 1945

VIENNA IS FREE.

How strange that the liberation of a city in Europe by armed forces, this bit of military, political history, should have such an impact on me. Oh, the memories that city holds! Not all the Nazi murderers, not all the Russian tanks and guns in the world can destroy them.

I'm going back to Vienna. I'm going back as soon as possible. I'd go tomorrow if I could. I want to rake up the past and live through it again and save my mother. Perhaps one's birthplace is after all the only corner in the world that offers lasting happiness?

Ten thousand cheers for the Russians. "Rot, weiss, rot, bis in den Tod," said Schuschnigg before the Nazi tyrants led him away at gunpoint, the same tyrants who destroyed me and my home. Vienna is free again but I – I am lost. The Nazis took away my mother, my childhood, my security, my country, my home, my belongings. No liberators can save me. When something terrible happens to you you may get round it but you don't get over it. The Jews, downtrodden, downcast, are all dead in one way or another. But I must be grateful that that city which holds my earliest memories, that richest treasure island on the earth for me, is free once again.

Today is also the day that President Roosevelt died.

15th April 1945

After church today I went to the youth club in the Church Hall for a musical evening and had a chat with the Reverend Markby, but no one else spoke to me.

Aunt Else, being a good needlewoman, has been altering some of my frocks and skirts. Lucky for me, as I'm no good at needlework. Once, when Miss Jacques invited me for a drink in our lunch hour, we got talking about what useless, untalented and impractical members of society we both are, and it made me realise that that was the bond between us, and is also what makes us a target for Miss Campbell's wrath. Useless people have no confidence and are taken advantage of by others. There is not a person who can't live without me, not a piece of work that can't be done without my assistance. Why go on struggling? As Miss Jacques says, to watch God and the Devil, hand in hand, triumphing over one?

Loneliness is killing me. I know I've experienced these moods before and usually something has happened to dispel them, but everything looks too black now for any light to penetrate.

19th April 1945

Mrs Sanders, Sandy and I had lunch at Hunts today, our half-day. In the afternoon I went to the circus with Susie. She pointed Anton Walbrook's mother out to me in the audience! I didn't know he had one, (in Oxford, anyway). Afterwards I went home to supper with Susie, which we had in the garden.

I had an intellectual discussion with Peter; a couple called Anita and Gerhard were there too. I didn't get home till 11.30pm.

Yesterday Ilse Rosendorf and I went rowing on the River Thames, known in this part as the Isis. She called for me and we cycled to Folly Bridge and took a rowing boat from there. She took entire charge of everything, shepherding me into a boat, doing all the rowing herself and expertly manoeuvring the boat back to its mooring again. Needless to say, I didn't particularly enjoy the occasion. I don't get on with German Jews, and if I can't say that here, where can I?

Every time I hear Denzil is back in Falmouth I want to go back to Falmouth, too. By the time I get down in the summer he won't be there any more. One day perhaps we'll meet again, and then we'll stare at each other like two strangers.

26th April 1945

No more black-out or dim-out since the 23rd! Now the war must really be almost over. Pat called at the library on Tuesday. I was very surprised to see her. We had lunch together and talked about the Beschorners and the strange time we had at their house. Prue returned on Wednesday after the Easter holidays and I spent a lovely evening at the house in Lucerne Road where she now lives. Two other girls were there and we all played ping-pong in the garden which goes down to the river. Afterwards Prue and I chatted in her room and I told her how happy I had been at her home and that my father had also written a thank-you letter to her parents.

Last night Maureen Daly and I went to the Playhouse to see *Pygmalion* by Bernard Shaw, which I enjoyed very much. Tomorrow I'm skipping my shorthand class; instead I'm going to Witney with Sandy in her father's car and staying the night as we're going to a concert in the evening. Mr Sanders will take us to the library on Saturday morning by car.

1st May 1945

HITLER IS DEAD! Diary, diary, can you believe it? Tell me I'm not dreaming. Mrs Labowsky is terribly excited as conflicting reports keep coming over on the wireless to which she is glued, except when she is on the telephone. V-Day must be any day now. Mussolini is also dead.

I spent Sunday with Maureen and we went for a walk in the snow! Lorenzo has been here again, and again he gave no sign of having recognised me. One day when I'm feeling mischievous I'll ask him how Zena Davies is! On Thursday Julia and Sally Davies (no relation!) – the daughters of Margaret Kennedy – are coming to tea. I can't concentrate on writing any more today as the death of Hitler makes everything unimportant, and Mrs Labowsky keeps knocking on my door and telling me the latest exciting news.

6th May 1945

I was walking home from the pictures last night where I'd been with Maureen, when I met an RAF chap who insisted on accompanying me, kissed me passionately in the dark street and wanted to make a date with me. I got rid of him in the end. I described the experience to Maureen today, on our walk to Iffley, where we visited the church. She thought I ought to have made a date with him!

Miss Jacques and I had lunch at a Chinese restaurant on Friday – my first Chinese meal. I hope I didn't eat any snake or Pekinese dog.

Berlin has fallen, and so has Austria. I can't believe that I'm living through such historic times and momentous events. Indeed, I've been more directly affected by Hitler than most people I know. Sometimes I think I'm too ordinary to be a refugee, to have had this enormous thing happen to me. I'm miscast.

V-Day – End of European War – *May 8th-9th 1945*

Five years and eight months ago, on September 3rd 1939, war was declared. I was a child then, tasting the first bitterness of the cup of life. Today, the war is over, and I have grown up.

I don't think people have quite taken it in yet, this historic and yet so personal event, to be remembered forever. We're at peace again, it's all over in Europe. I feel bewildered, dazed.

As soon as Armistice was announced yesterday the whole country decided to go on holiday for two days. Swept up by all the excitement I decided then and there to go to London! I just went to the station and caught the first train to Paddington and took a taxi to Elgin Avenue and Jane, Jack and my father gaped with astonishment when they saw me but made me feel very welcome. We all went to Hyde Park and had lunch at the Cumberland Hotel where we listened to Churchill's speech, and then we went to Piccadilly and people were dancing and cheering everywhere. In the evening my father took me to visit Liesel Frank, who disliked it so much at Falmouth and certainly seems much more at home in the environment of a large city. She was very pleased to see me again. We listened to the King's speech on her wireless. The next day darling Putz came and we went to Trafalgar Square and joined in the celebrations. People were quite mad with excitement and at times the celebrating almost became dangerous. Afterwards Putz, my father and I went to the News Reel Cinema and then I caught the train back to Oxford. There were crowds dancing at Carfax, and singing and drinking and kissing each other. All the horrors of the war seemed to be forgotten. Everyone was celebrating victory.

Now that the war is over I must surely get news of my mother. I have waited so long. I *must* hear something soon.

12th May 1945

Life plays nasty tricks on me. When I got back from London Mrs Labowsky said to me, "A young man called for you." My first thought, before I started bombarding her with questions, was that it had been the RAF chap who accompanied me home the other night. But it wasn't – it was Peter! The rest of the evening I wondered why Peter had called – something he has never done before. So on the very next day, after work, I called at the Rieszs' house in Thorncliffe Road. Peter was out and his mother told me he came to ask me to go punting with him and a group of his friends. What a missed opportunity! But that wasn't all. No. 2 was when I discovered that Maureen, with whom I would have celebrated V-night had I not gone to London, had joined a gang of undergraduates during the festivities and later gone to the rooms of one of them where they drank champagne at midnight. This, too, I missed. Will life always pass me by?

The good news is that I'm really going to see Ruth at last – she didn't come to Oxford in the end but I'm going to Portsmouth for Whitsun! She asked me to come early on Saturday so I can go out with her, Mervyn (the son of her foster family) and a Yankee officer, but as I can't get off before 5.30pm I shall miss that, too.

Tomorrow Prue and I are going to a Thanksgiving Service at New College Chapel. In the evening Churchill is making another speech which I shall no doubt hear at Aunt Else's where I'm going for supper and having some more clothes altered.

20th May 1945, Whit Sunday. – For Ruth.

Six years is a long time when one has waited for something, and then at last it comes. One concentrates on little irrelevant things to lend reality to what is happening, and so, when I stepped from the train at Portsmouth station last night and at once saw you rushing towards me, I fastened my eyes on an advertisement and wondered how many times I had seen it before. That was real. But kissing you the next minute wasn't. Being with you again, living in the past in new surroundings after the whole world had been turned upside down before our eyes within seven years, that wasn't real.

Living through the past is no joke. It meant pain and tears – but we enjoyed it. We slept in the same bed and we talked till 4 in the morning. It all came back, faster and faster. And presently I knew, by the way you laughed and passed your tongue across your lips as you used to after speaking, that everything *was* real, that even Hitler, and living in England, and six years of war and separation lacked the power to come between real friends. Of course there were changes that I found hard to accept – your grown up clothes, your hairstyle, your experiences with men, but I wouldn't allow them to interfere. We were still two little girls with short hair and white ankle socks . . . I'm trying to exclude sentiment from my reminiscences, but it's getting the better of me, as you can see.

This reunion marks the highlight of our friendship, Ruth. I am writing this for you, but I won't say any more about myself because the weakest parts of me must remain hidden even from you, with whom I grew up, with whom I witnessed the most evil crimes ever perpetrated by man. So, good night dear little Ruth of 12 years old, in your little red Dirndl, which is how I will always see you, it was a heavenly weekend and we shall see each other again soon. This is only one chapter in our young lives, albeit the greatest. From now on I know that we are forever welded together with hoops of steel!

23rd May 1945

Churchill resigned today!

I'll tell you a bit about Portsmouth, now that the impact of my reunion with Ruth has abated.

After she fetched me from the station we went straight to her house, or rather the house of her foster family with whom she has lived since leaving Vienna. It is a rather poor house, and the family live above their jeweller's shop where Ruth works all day. They are orthodox Jews and I'm sorry to say, reminded me of the Gill family. But they were very friendly and kind and obviously look on Ruth as their daughter. On Sunday I had breakfast in bed and got up late. In the afternoon Mervyn, David (the two sons of the family, aged 20 and 17) Ruth and I went to the flicks and in the evening to a funfair, to which Mr Constad, the father, came too. The next day David, the younger son, tried to teach me to roller skate, not very successfully, took me to watch some canoeing and to see the 'Victory', Nelson's ship. Ruth has to do quite a lot of housework and cooking, which I never had to do, and consequently is much more domesticated than I am. In the evening I returned to Oxford.

25th May 1945

I'm going to London for the weekend for Putz's birthday. She'll be 21. She's going to take me to the National Gallery, and Jane, who's an excellent cook, is making one of her super lunches and a birthday cake for her.

On Thursday evening Maureen and I went to the New Theatre to see *The Pirates of Penzance*. I love Gilbert and Sullivan. Maureen was very late and I waited for her in the foyer for nearly twenty minutes. When we finally went in we had to sit on the steps as there were no seats left. During the interval I scolded her. I said, "No excuses are acceptable. If you have an appointment you must be on time."

"What if I had broken a leg?" said Maureen.

"Then you must come on the other one," I said. We laughed so much about that that all was peace between us again.

I've had the most wonderful letter from Ruth – the first after our reunion. I shall keep it forever. I know she has had an affair with a man and that was the one thing she would not talk about, and she again apologises for this in her letter. I'm reading her diary now and she's reading mine.

Himmler's death was announced today. Soon the earth will be rid of all the Nazi vermin. He committed suicide.

Ruth's Letter

Saturday

My own darling Ingrid,

Thank you very much for your very sweet letter and also the one to Mrs Constad. You silly, silly child, how can you say I have

49

no idea what you felt like seeing me again. Do you think that it meant nothing to me to see you – someone who is a very big part of my life in Vienna! You can hardly imagine how deeply I felt at seeing you again and being able to speak to you about those precious memories that have been just bottled up inside me all these years and I've never been able to share with anyone! I'm quite convinced – now more than ever, that our friendship will last for ever and that I, for certain, will never have another friend who will ever mean as much to me, as you do, especially since we are so much alike.

After reading your diary, especially, why Ingrid – it's just me – feeling exactly the same. There is only one difference, that you feel things deeper than I do where I can take things much lighter in several ways (for instance years ago in Vienna, I should never have been hurt like that over any girl like you were over me). There are so many things I'd like to talk to you about – in connection with your and my diary. That part you wrote for me, Ingrid darling – I keep reading it and I can't hold the tears back – there are many other parts in your diary where I've had to cry – it seems such fate that you and I should have had so many disappointments and it does seem that God enjoys to make us suffer more and more and I really can't blame you for becoming converted – I hardly think there's a god, but I like the Jewish religion very much – there is something very fascinating about it to me – probably owing to the fact I've been brought up that way.

Now to answer your letter. Monday evening, after leaving you, I went to a funfair not far from the station (only a small one. I never knew it was there) and won a few pennies on a machine. Then I went home and stayed there. I didn't go to the dance with Eileen either, I haven't seen her – I went to see *A Place of One's Own* with a girl I used to work with, last night. No, I didn't mind you going out with David on our last day, firstly because as long as you were enjoying it and weren't bored, I was happy, and secondly, it wasn't our last day – as we're going to meet again soon. I'm wondering if you're in London today – did you go up? And what did you do? What is the phone number of your father's flat – where you stay? I might phone you up one day when you're there. About your watch, Ingrid, Mr Constad will do it as soon as he can. I told him you didn't want him to do it for nothing, but I don't think he'll take any money from you.

50

I said goodbye to Mervyn for you, he wishes to be remembered to you – so does David and Mrs and Mr C. They all liked you very much and Mrs C. has been telling everyone what a nice girl you are. David enjoyed your company very much and he kept on laughing about all the funny things you said. So my dear, don't worry and forget your damned inferiority complex, you ought to know that people are always ready to like you, why shouldn't they, you aren't any worse than anyone so why have that silly feeling? (Funny me talking like that. I used to have the same complex but made myself get over it.) I'm very careful to read your diary and not losing any pages and will send it as soon as I finish – which will take ages – but I'm enjoying it very much. (I've got as far as your L.B., how far are you with mine?) Don't send mine but keep it. I do hope you won't mind my copying your idea, but I'm going to write about each member of my family like you did, only more. Do you object? You know Ingrid, I was rather worried about you coming down here and staying here. I didn't think you'd like it here at all and god knows what I imagined, because after all, this is such a different place and the people are so different to what you have known since the last time we met. What a relief it was to me to see you get on so well with everyone and seem to like it here. Ingrid, please send me all details about becoming naturalised. Don't forget! Also Ernst's address!

The way you wrote in your diary that your mother used to write to you to dress yourself warm, well my mother wrote exactly the same way and it used to make me cry too. Gosh, Ingrid, what you and I have been through we could write books and books. Do you think one of us has been luckier? I mean I envied you for having your sister with you all the time and your father, do you think I'm lucky to be among such nice people? I'm very ungrateful in very many ways. Another strange thing is that you always wanted to get married, while I've always wanted to have a good time and be admired by lots of men. So we are very different in some ways but deep down we're just alike.

By the way, Mrs Constad just made another one of those cream cakes and wants to know if you'd like a piece – no I'm kidding but it's time she did just make one.

Well my darling, that's enough for now. There's lots more I could write about if I had the time but we'll talk about all that when I see you. I'm very sorry Ingrid, I do hope you never get too cross with me, for not being able to tell you about my love 'affair', but you'll read a lot about it in my diary, of course not in detail – you'll have to guess the rest. But I found it impossible to explain to you all those things, which are impossible to explain unless you experience them yourself – but I hope you won't experience them before you are married. With me it was different, I've known so many men and they all attracted me in different ways and as I know a lot about this sort of thing I didn't think there was any harm to experience it myself, as I've heard so much about it and was very curious about it. Well, it didn't do me any harm physically, but it did spoil my morals and it has taken me a long time to get back to a decent way of thinking. So please, Ingrid, don't be like me. I do hope and pray you'll never go through what I did – and it all starts with kissing too much!

Please listen to what I've said. I do feel responsible for you in a way, as it was I who told you the facts of life!

Write soon my dear and, once again, it was wonderful seeing you again and you did turn out to be just what I wanted you to be.

For an everlasting friendship.

Your ever loving Ruthy –

Kisses, kisses, kisses

p.s. I still don't know when Johnny is coming. I hope never.

30th May 1945

Actually my diary is at Ruth's again but as it's made up of loose pages I can carry on writing. Maureen and I went to Brett's dance tonight. I thought it was high time for me to learn to dance, and a few times there might get me over my awkwardness. It was really quite nice: there was a soldier there, an RE with dark hair and heavenly blue eyes, with whom I wished very much to dance. However, at the first round, when the gents were asked to choose their partners, a little ginger-haired fellow approached me, and I saw the nice RE dancing with a tall, pretty girl. We had to keep our partners till the second round. When its turn came my hero suddenly appeared before me and asked me to be his partner! I was thrilled, but very shy with him. Now and again, as we danced, our eyes met and we gave each other a faint but reassuring smile, he with his lovely blue eyes, I with my round goggling cow ones that so many people have found attractive (women, mostly), which is beyond my comprehension. We talked little. I wondered if our attraction was mutual. Breaking into my thoughts he suddenly said:

"Have you got a coat here?"

"A coat?" I said, surprised. "No. Why?"

"It's pouring."

"Oh dear. I've only a little jacket here."

"I haven't even got that," he said.

When the dance was over he was gone as quietly and softly as he had come. There came other partners, and then the Paul Jones – and I was opposite him again! I was not too pleased though, because I felt so shy with him. But we didn't dance because neither of us could do the step. And then something disagreeable happened: a tall undergraduate whom I hadn't noticed before persuaded me to dance this dance with him. I said I couldn't do the step. He said he couldn't either. "Oh, we'll pick it up as we go along," he said. And so off we went. It was the dance I had refused the RE. My one prayer now was not that I shouldn't step on my partner's toes but that the soldier wouldn't see me.

This was more or less my first dance, although it was really a dancing lesson, and I hope I shan't feel so inhibited about dancing next time. There's a class at Brett's every Wednesday.

2nd June 1945

On Thursday evening I went to the Playhouse with Maureen to see *This Happy Breed* by Noel Coward. Afterwards we went to the stage door to get Michael Redgrave's autograph. He was very nice to us.

Mrs Labowsky has been on holiday but came back today. Her daughter, Lotte, called on several occasions to see that I was all right. She looks a younger version of her mother, and is equally clever. I wasn't alone in the house as another lady, Miss Lorch, lives here, in a room upstairs. We sometimes meet in the kitchen. Prue brought me some strawberries today!

We are getting our third V-day holiday on Monday – and I'm going to visit the Urbachs in Surrey.

Another awful thing happened at the library: it was my turn to make Mr Skuce's tea. Checking carefully that everything was on the tray – cup and saucer, teaspoon, teapot, milk, sugar, slop basin

– I went off on my mission. I arrived at his door, knocked, opened it and entered. Mr Skuce was in his usual place behind his desk, and opposite him in an armchair sat a plump elderly lady. I placed the tray on his desk. He watched me, but didn't speak. He let me retreat, open the door and almost leave the room before he opened his mouth. "In your country, Miss Jacoby," he said, "do two people drink out of one cup?" I was too shattered to make any reply. "Get another cup!" he barked.

Back in the lending library I told Betty Argyle what had happened. She laughed.

"That was Mrs Pritchard," she said, "the chairman."

"Nobody told me he had a visitor," I said.

"I expect he did it on purpose," she replied. "Never mind, don't worry. I once took the tea to him when she was there, and as I began to pour out he said, 'How do you like your tea, Mrs Pritchard?' and she said, 'Oh, just as it comes, Mr Skuce' – and what came out of the pot was water! I had forgotten to put the tea in!"

"How awful!" I said, but we both laughed. The sting of Mr Skuce's words – "in your country, Miss Jacoby . . ." – is with me still.

6th June 1945

I left for Banstead at 7.30am on Sunday and spent a very pleasant two days with Eva and her parents. We played tennis several times at Eva's Club. How I envy her living with her parents and having her own home – and even a dog.

This evening Maureen and I went to another dancing class at Brett's. I've come to the conclusion that I've no flair for dancing though I desperately wish I had. It seems to come naturally to most girls, but not to me.

I had a distant relation, a young officer in the British army called George Oberländer. We're not a close family and in Vienna I hardly knew any of my father's many cousins etc; my mother didn't have many relatives and those she had were not welcome at our home as my father didn't like them. I never knew George except for the one time I met him, at a Christmas party in London in 1943. I never saw him again and I never shall now because he was killed in action in France, just before the liberation. When somebody you have known dies it makes a deep impression. You really have to believe in death then.

Miss Jacques is a very quiet sort of girl and although we often go out to lunch together I don't know her very well. She's quite a bit older than I am – about 30, I think. She has a habit of picking at her nails which is very irritating. She does not really come into my life at all, however, so why am I talking about her to you? You will see in a minute why. Miss Jacques is the kind of girl one easily feels sorry for, and although I often think I'm a heartless, selfish person and a devil at heart, I'm capable, sometimes quite unnecessarily, of deep pity and sympathy for certain people and animals. I could offer them all I have without turning a hair. Miss Jacques is one of these people. The other day at the library she had one row after another, and the most unkind words were flung at her by her superiors, who take advantage of her meek nature. Her only retaliation are softly spoken apologies. When I saw how upset she was tears came to my eyes. I felt as if all these unkind things had been said to *me*. I wanted to help her in some practical way, comfort her, say to her: "Look here, don't let them get you down, you're just as good as they are, ignore them, show them you don't care, and in a few weeks' time it will be unimportant anyway . . ." But I said and did nothing, because I knew that only the people who had hurt her could undo the hurt. I left the scene – chickened out, if you like – heavy with pity for one of my weaker fellow creatures, and brooding over the cruelty of the stronger ones.

13th June 1945

Today is my mother's birthday. Where are you, my darling mother? Please be alive, please, please come back to me. Whatever I'm doing, that prayer is constantly with me.

When I was at Aunt Else's on Monday for more clothes alterations I told her that my friend Maureen had invited me to a Social on Saturday at Lucy's factory where she works.

"You can't go to that," said Aunt Else, horrified. "That sort of thing is only for working-class girls. Suppose someone sees you there?"

"I can't let her down now," I said. "I've promised." She shook her head in a resigned way, and I wished I wasn't going.

I've been to another Brett dance and my little blue-eyed RE was there – with a girl, with whom he danced the whole evening. I was disappointed, but not too much. I didn't feel so light and gay this time, though. Aunt Else would have thought him too common for me anyway, and to tell you the truth so do I.

When I was on my way to a meeting of young refugees in Oxford I met Peter on his bike. "I'm going to look at some lists," I told him.

"*Look* at some Liszt?" he said. "Not listen to some?"

"I mean lists of missing people," I said, after I realised what he meant. Was it a mistake or a joke? If the latter it was in bad taste. I did not find my mother's or grandmother's names on the lists, of course, no names of anyone I knew, in fact. I am slowly beginning to lose hope.

23rd June 1945

The Social at Maureen's factory was ghastly and I felt completely wrong there. I'm not going to write about it because I want to forget it. It was all wrong, wrong, wrong.

It was amply made up for, however, by the visit of Prue's parents to Oxford last weekend. On Sunday they took Prue and me to tea at the Randolph Hotel and afterwards to a Service at New College Chapel. Then we all drove to my digs in their car as they wanted to see my room, which they liked.

On Thursday all the library staff were given strawberries by one of the borrowers. I'm sure Miss Campbell thought the junior assistants should not have been included!

I've had a letter from Mrs Grice of the Refugee Children's Movement asking me to come to a meeting to discuss how to help children from German concentration camps who are coming to England for rehabilitation. Sunday July 1st is the date fixed for this meeting, and of course I shall go to it. A concentration camp is where Lieselotte and I would have ended up if England had not rescued us. I have written to the King, expressing my gratitude on behalf of all refugee children. On the other hand, I have often wondered if a life of homelessness and mourning one's mother is really preferable to death? I don't suppose the King will reply.

TEL: OXFORD 47302   27 NEW-INN-HALL STREET
CHAIRMAN: REV T.R. MILFORD   OXFORD
SECRETARY: MRS S.H. GRICE

Dear Ingrid,

I know that you will have heard of the sufferings of men, women and children in German concentration camps and wished that you could have given some practical help. An opportunity for doing this will arise in the near future when, with the permission of the British Government, one thousand children from these camps will be brought to this country for rehabilitation. I am sure you would like to play your own part in the effort to collect funds to provide for the care of these children.

It is our intention to hold a meeting of all 'Movement children' who live in and around Oxford to discuss ways and means of helping in this matter. We therefore invite you to come to this office on Sunday, July 1st at 3.15pm for a meeting, and we hope you will also stay on for some refreshments afterwards. Will you please let me know, without fail and as soon as possible, if you will be able to come.

> Yours sincerely,
> (Mrs) S.H. Grice,
> Secretary, Region 6

24th June 1945

I went swimming in the River Cherwell today for the first time. Prue's garden in Lucerne Road runs down to the river and we bathed from there. It was cold but lovely. In the afternoon I visited Maureen in her room and had tea and supper with her. What she told me during our long conversation is so extraordinary that I believe I too have reached the stage where I cease to be able to distinguish between truth and fiction. I will now fill you in on the background history of MAUREEN DALY.

I noticed Maureen at once in the shorthand class because she was unusual. Her individuality attracted me. We made friends. Bit by bit she told me about herself. She's 24, Irish, ran away from home, has a drunkard of a father whom she hates and an aristocratic mother. Her family are very poor. She's extremely short-sighted, always nicely dressed, slim and she writes poetry. She has dreams and ambitions. She has no looks – but she has character. She likes solitude but is never lonely. Gradually we began to see a lot of each other. We roamed about on Sundays and pretended we were penniless bohemians. We invented a sex life. I told her that I longed for a physical relationship. I asked her if she'd ever been to a brothel but she only laughed at me. I think it was she who realised I could not possibly be in earnest. I loved listening to her quiet Irish voice and watching, through her thick glasses, the dreamy look in her eyes, which often seemed to gaze towards an invisible beyond.

Today, suddenly, in a voice odder and dreamier than usual, she said, "You will hate me, Ingrid. You will think less of me and I love you and could not do without your friendship. But there is something I have to tell you."

"Tell me," I said. "I have no morals. You've lived with someone, haven't you? Is that what you're going to tell me?"

"No."

"You've slept with someone once, then."

"Yes." A pause. Then: "I have a child – a son of 5 years."

The sun shining in through the window of Maureen's dreary room seemed to be getting hotter and hotter. I watched a horse pulling a cart through a field at the end of the garden. I said nothing. Then I heard her voice again:

"Now tell me you think no less of me – that I'm still your friend."

"I think no less of you and you are still my friend," I said. I was actually too thunderstruck to say anything else. But she needed encouragement to tell me her story. It was the usual one of a brief love affair with a married man. "And what happened to Derek?" I asked, when she'd finished.

"He was killed in Dunkirk."

"And the child?"

"I was on London Bridge with him once, when he was quite tiny. I wanted to drown myself and him. But a priest came along. He took the child and I've never seen it since."

"Where did he take it?"

"To a Home. I don't know where. I hated it."

58

I had taken in all I could. How was it that all this time, this girl, unbeknown to me, had an illegitimate child, how didn't I guess? I had never thought of her as anything but a virgin, like me. Was it all a delusion? Or the theme of a poem she had written? How can I tell where facts begin and fantasies end? Presently we talked of other things, I told her about Roy and Denzil and Alan and other bits of my past, which of course could not match hers – true or invented. She is my friend still. Perhaps the most unusual one I ever had. I like her. And she loves me. But a cloud of mystery hangs over everything.

As I walked home I thought: Maureen has a child. She is a mother. She knows all about sex. And all the time I thought she was as ignorant as I am.

4th July 1945

Tomorrow is ELECTION DAY, and today I attended a public meeting in St Giles and heard F. Pakenham speak on Socialism. I met Kay Ellison there, and also Betty Argyle.

It felt strange, being among so many other young refugees at the meeting on Sunday. I studied each one, mostly dark-haired and long-nosed, and wondered what Hitler had done to their lives. How quickly we forget after all, I thought, and build up new lives. We were all strangers to each other. We had a common background but probably nothing in common. Some of the young men were quite good-looking, and one in particular intrigued me: he came without a word to anyone, without a smile. He sat down on the floor, clasping his knees. He took no part in the discussion. He ate nothing during the interval when refreshments were served, but stood staring out of the window. He was thin with a pale hollow face, intelligent eyes and a nose to match his long face, and he had dark blond curly hair. He wore a shirt and jumper. Our eyes met briefly when he entered the room. They met again hurriedly later on, and looked away again at once. As soon as the meeting ended he left as quietly as he had come, having never uttered a word to anyone. I had longed for him to speak to me. What had the Nazis done to him? Did he, too, lose a mother? Poor boy. I am going to help with fundraising for the children from the concentration camps. I went home on the bus with a fellow called Donitz or some such name, who had lived on the

Graben in Vienna. We discussed the fundraising.

Tomorrow, besides being Election Day, is also the wedding day of Babs House, one of the senior library assistants. Sandy and I are going to the church and afterwards to the flicks. Babs is marrying her American G.I. But best of all, tomorrow Miss Campbell goes on holiday. Hurrah!

My own holiday starts on the 12th and I'm going first to Portsmouth and then to Falmouth. If it weren't for that and I were writing my autobiography now I should run out of material. I consider my present life an utter waste of time. I might as well be in my grave. When my mother was 18 she was beautiful and popular; she was living in her parents' house, spoiled and loved, in gay, waltzing Vienna, now gone forever; and she was courted by many men. And here am I, aged 18, alone in a bed-sitting room and sometimes so lonely that I think I'll go mad; doing nothing much except going to work, coming home in the evenings, getting myself a scrappy meal, going to bed, and repeating the whole business on the following day. I have a social life of sorts, but suspect it is of the wrong kind. I should study for my library exams but feel too weary and fed up. I want to travel. I want to be a writer. I want to marry and have children. Lieselotte is unhappy too. Her life, too, is being wasted. I want my mother. I want to hug her and hear her voice again. Please, God, give me back my mother! The only positive things in my present life are that I'm writing a novel and that I earn 30/- a week, enough to pay for my bed and breakfast, and I mustn't forget Sunday lunch. But where is it all getting me? Not to the kind of people I want to meet, not to the glittering society I want to be a part of. I want to listen to all the great music that has ever been composed, and I want to laugh from morning till night and get to like champagne and be sophisticated. I want everything I can never have. Because the seeds of greatness are not in me. So now you know. Up to now you thought me frugal, simple, modest? You know better now. You thought I only want 6d? Wrong again. I want the moon.

When I lived in Falmouth I thought once I had passed my School Certificate and had a career and the war was over I should be happy and that it would not be long until my mother was found. But it has not happened like that. I would give anything to be back at St Joseph's again. At least it was a kind of home, and

I wasn't lonely. I can cope with grief and disappointments and longing but not with loneliness.

11th July 1945

This evening I had supper at Mary West's house. Mary is an assistant at the library. When she invited me she said, "I told my parents what a nice girl you are." I hope they agreed after they met me. They were certainly very kind to me, gave me a lovely supper and took me for a drive in the countryside beyond Headington, where the Wests live.

My packing is done and I'm off on my holiday tomorrow. No more buffering for two weeks. I can't wait to see Ruth and Falmouth again. I had a lovely letter from Miss Davis saying how pleased everyone is that I'm coming and what a lot we shall have to talk about over nice cosy suppers in the kitchen. She really has missed me, she says, and Lieselotte too (she calls her Lottie). Keith still sometimes weeps, and speaks untruthfully, which makes her very unhappy; he has been confirmed and has made his First Communion, and she has tried so hard to make him see how wrong it is. He's 14 now and should think a little more seriously, she writes. She often confided in me about the younger children, and I'm glad she still does.

17th July 1945

'The Dance that was not.'

It was Tuesday and Ruth and I were going to a dance. We stood in front of the mirror in her attic bedroom, getting ready. "You must always put on your make-up before you dress," said Ruth, standing in her slip and applying thick red lipstick. She was ready before I was, I suppose because she has perfected the art of preparing herself for a dance. I was still doing my hair when I saw the brilliant spectacle that was Ruth reflected in the mirror. What chance had I of a dance, I thought, with her next to me? She was a peony, and I a dandelion. My heart sank when she said at last, "Shall we go?" It was like going to the doctor's – a nightmare. I was shaking all the way to the bus stop. A voice inside me cried out: "I want to go home, I want to go to bed! I'm scared, I'm not used to this kind of thing, I hate it, let me go, let me go!" But a

61

more reasonable voice said: "You silly fool, you have no home, no country, you are a refugee, your mother is missing somewhere in Poland and you make this fuss over a dance, and act as if you were going to be slaughtered." But the other voice came in again: "I'm only an inexperienced, shy girl. I know nothing about enticing men and I feel so small and ashamed beside Ruth, who is all spruced up, and no longer a virgin and has left me far behind, still stuck in the childhood we once shared . . ." "Go on brooding in your own world then, and go to the devil," said the other now impatient voice. To the devil is where I would have chosen to go rather than the dance, given the choice.

But I had no choice, and here we were. We got off the bus and now we were only a two minute walk away from the dance hall, Ruth informed me happily. My heart was pounding so loud I thought she must surely hear it.

I'm short-sighted (and refuse to wear my glasses unless absolutely necessary) and so I couldn't read the notice on the door until we were fairly close. Before I had properly deciphered it I heard Ruth exclaim, "Oh no!" and then suddenly my heart felt light and the bad taste of fear vanished from my tongue and I was free as a bird: THERE WAS NO DANCE THAT NIGHT . . .

We walked back to the bus stop, poor, unsuspecting Ruth very disappointed but I with a jaunty step and a deep feeling of gratitude to whatever gods may be. I glanced at my best blue frock, the frock meant to attract men, which I'm certain it wouldn't have done but it had been my only hope, the frock I needn't have worn at all to the dance that was not.

Oh Ruth, let's forget it all, let's be children again!

But I'd better go back to the beginning, the beginning of my holiday, I mean. So much has been happening and I haven't had a moment to write. First of all, Ruth and I missed each other somehow at Portsmouth station and I had to take a taxi to her house. They all received me very warmly, the Constads and Ruth. The next day I had breakfast in bed and in the afternoon Ruth and I went shopping and swimming. A lot of her friends were on the beach – all Jewish. On Saturday Mervyn Constad, the older son, came home for the weekend and the three of us went to the flicks. He had an arm around each of us and laughed and flirted with us both and told dirty jokes. The film we saw was *A Tree Grows in Brooklyn*, and I cried from beginning to end, especially every time Peggy Ann Garner appeared. Mervyn handed me his handkerchief. He was very sweet to me and made me feel grown up. Mervyn can give a girl a good time and is quite different from the serious intellectual fellows I've mostly known, but he's very common, which probably explains it all.

On Sunday Ruth and I went to London for two days by an early train. What an adventure! First we went to the Cumberland Hotel where we met my father and Lieselotte. He commented, when a suitable opportunity arose, on what he calls my gadding about. "You seem to be keeping GWR in pocket," he said. It was meant to be a joke – superficially. Then we went to Finchley to have lunch at Ruth's cousin's, Vally, where we were to spend the night. After lunch we visited – guess whom – Louise Herzberg-Frankel, our school friend from Vienna. Even though I never particularly liked Louise it was a very moving reunion. She lives in a beautiful flat with her family – almost as large and beautiful as her house was in Vienna. We had tea with her, but we didn't stay long. Ruth said afterwards that she had been a bit disappointed in Louise. We had dinner at the Cumberland.

On Monday we went shopping in the West End and had our fortunes told by a fortune teller in some grubby side street. It sent us into fits of laughter and for a time we seemed to be two children walking through the streets of Vienna again, arm in arm. Back in Portsmouth in the afternoon, and more visiting of friends, and a glimpse from the bus of Charles Dickens' house.

Tomorrow I'm off to Falmouth, and Mr Constad is taking me to the station by car.

21st July 1945

In fiction one is not surprised at the unlikeliest happenings; they are not true, and you don't have to believe them. In real life one is greatly surprised if something improbable occurs, but it's got to be believed.

On the train to Falmouth from Portsmouth a very strange thing happened: opposite me sat a neatly-dressed, pleasant-looking young Chinese man. I was reading when the train stopped at some station. There was no one left in the compartment except the Chinese man and myself. I felt a little embarrassed but was sure he was too occupied with his books and papers and far too shy to disturb me. Presently he got up and left the compartment – and returned with a cup of tea and a sandwich for me! "Please," he said, and handed both to me. I was thunderstruck and charmed. We began to talk. His English was very poor but he was polite and entertaining. He produced a Chinese newspaper and tried to teach me some Chinese characters. Then I had to write down my name and address. He was going to Falmouth, too. As the train approached our destination we said goodbye and I never expected to see him again. Anyway, I was very excited by now, and when the train slowed down for Penmere Halt I was overwhelmed by a feeling of being HOME. And here was Miss Davis, running towards me as I got out of the train. I stooped to kiss her. She seemed smaller than ever. After saying how lovely it was to see me again she began to chatter straight away, and kept it up all the way to St Joseph's. The priests have a new housekeeper and Keith has had another weeping fit and the religious gardener was dead.

"Have you heard anything about your mother, dear?" she interrupted her narrative to ask.

"No," I replied.

"I'm so sorry. I'm sure you will soon", she said, and then told me some other item of news. I was glad. What has my mother to do with Falmouth?

"It's lovely to be home," I said.

"I'm so glad you think of St Joseph's as home," she said. "Until you're settled. I met Audrey the other day and told her I had a secret."

"What secret?"

"That you were coming. But I think she guessed."

And now we were walking up the long garden path, past the house where the Americans had been billeted, under the arch covered in pink climbing roses by the side of the shed where we ate our meals and played ping-pong in the summer. I may not have been home, but I was back on familiar and much-loved ground.

The following day, Thursday, I visited old friends – the Tamblyns, the Thomsons, Mrs Davis etc., and Robin came and we went to town together. In the afternoon I went to school and had a talk with Miss Frost, and of course the girls from my form. They gave me a wonderful reception. They didn't hide their delight at seeing me. I felt like a heroine. One day, somewhere, this must happen again, I thought, and I *shall* be a heroine . . .

"What's Oxford like?" asked Margaret.

"It has nice buildings," I answered, "and lots of Colleges, and a lovely High Street." And horrid Miss Campbell, I thought. Better not say that.

"What are Oxford boys like?" asked Muriel.

"I wouldn't know."

Mock surprise and laughter. Then Pam said, "Guess who's in Falmouth."

"I am," I said.

"Who else?"

"No idea."

"Anton Walbrook. He's staying at the Ferry Boat Inn. Do you want to see him?"

"You bet." We arranged to go on Saturday. I could tell him I saw his mother in Oxford, I thought.

"Why don't you come, too?" Pam said to her friend, Pauline Mitchell.

"I'd be scared stiff," said Pauline.

"Don't be silly," I said. "Film stars are always awfully nice when you go to see them. Aren't they, Pam?"

"Yes. And so are singers," she replied. Everyone laughed, but I couldn't help blushing a bit at this reference to my meeting with Richard Tauber, about which they all knew. Pauline agreed to come – reluctantly.

In the early evening, just as Miss Davis and I were getting ready to go to the Opera at the Princess Pavilion (to which she treated me) to my utter amazement Chang Cheung, my Chinese man from the train, appeared on the doorstep, for the front door was open, as it usually is in the summer. He had a friend with him, another Chinese man. Chang handed me a large hamper full of food. "For you," he said. This is fiction, I thought, pure fiction. I didn't want to accept it at first. Miss Davis invited them for supper. When we returned from the Opera they were already here, being entertained by Miss Kitty, who afterwards had a good laugh about them because of their funny English and the garish socks they wore. Chang asked me to come to the pictures with him but I pretended I didn't understand him. He asked me again and again but I only smiled and shook my head. Afterwards I felt sorry. They stayed till midnight. The following evening – that was last night – they came again and brought more food – bananas, oranges, dates, chocolates and biscuits – and we talked and laughed together. They are on a ship here in Falmouth and on Monday they are sailing to New York, from where they promised to send me presents.

Yesterday morning I went to town. I wanted to call on the watchmaker and claim my money back for the watch he repaired because the war did not end at Christmas, and that had been our bargain. I expected him to have forgotten. What I didn't expect was – that he was dead. I was very sorry. In the afternoon Connie and I went for a long walk. She's helping at the St Joseph's nursery school and so wasn't free until now. Moyra is in Falmouth and she called to see me today. I've also been to see the Hodgetts, who wanted to know all about Oxford. I've seen so many people that my head is spinning.

22nd July 1945

No time to write – going to church with Sheila, and Miss McCreight is here, and Pam and Jean Pollard are coming and I'm going to the Pavilion with Moyra and Connie – but I *must* tell you quickly what happened at the Ferry Boat Inn yesterday: Pam, Pauline and I went to Helford by bus in the afternoon, as arranged. We entered the now familiar hotel. We asked to see Anton Walbrook. We waited excitedly, pen and paper in hand. Presently he appeared, in the company of a Naval Officer. I approached him, and asked him very nicely and politely if he could give us his autograph. He wasn't smiling. Do you know what he did then? He turned to the guests sitting around on armchairs in the lobby and said to them: "You see what I have to put up with?" Then, to us very gruffly: "Have you got a pen?" I handed him one, he scribbled his name hurriedly and brushed past us and out of the hotel, the Naval Officer close behind. Later we saw them walking arm in arm along the beach.

"That was terrible," said poor Pauline, and I felt very guilty. "What an unpleasant man."

"I'm sorry, Pauline, but that's never happened before. Honestly."

"Not your fault," she said. I felt it was.

Outside, one of the waitresses who had witnessed the incident said to us: "He's a pansy boy. Didn't you know?" We didn't.

My holiday is drawing to a close. What a wonderful time I've had. Miss Davis, or Sheila, bring me breakfast in bed every morning. I'm joyfully received wherever I go. Even Canon Roxby, whom I visited yesterday, seemed pleased to see me, especially when I told him I'd been to St Aldates Church several times. I've been swimming, and played tennis at school and had tea at Pam's and the Eggins' and Margaret Lawrance's and been rowing with her and her boyfriend, John, and I've been to Flushing by ferry with Connie, where we swam and talked and read and talked again, and I've been to a huge Red Cross party and, and, and – are you dizzy yet? I haven't quite finished: last night I spent with the Belchers; I had supper at their house and they took me for a drive in their car, which is one of my greatest pleasures. Audrey and I had a long discussion and it was almost like old times. "It's lovely to see you again, Nanks," she said. No one else calls me Nanks.

"And you," I replied, and could have cried for my lost love. "Anyway, we'll see each other in September, in Oxford," I said. It made the parting less final.

My only consolation at returning to Oxford tomorrow is that Putz is coming: she has left nursing, which she hated, and she's moving to Oxford and will be looking for digs and a job, and staying at the Rieszs' in the meantime.

So tonight is my last evening in the cosy St Joseph's kitchen, and no doubt we shall be sitting round the table after supper and reminiscing about old times over watery cocoa and cheese: about the games of 'Murder' till four in the morning, about Gerty and the turkey legs which still sends Miss Kitty into fits, about the air raids and the many nights spent in the damp, earth-smelling trench, about the time I tried to run away, about little John Cock, the funniest pupil ever to attend St Joseph's school, who wouldn't stop smacking his lips when eating and had his Cornish pasty fed to the dog once, as punishment. And so on. Putz was never as happy here as I was because she could not stand the cold rooms and hard beds and other lack of comforts, such as no electricity. I do hope she will find happiness in Oxford.

26th July 1945

The election results are out and the SOCIALISTS HAVE GOT IN – with a huge majority. Everyone was talking about it on the train. Miss Davis saw me off at the station and I was very sad at leaving Falmouth. I shared the compartment with some soldiers for most of the journey. One of them had never been to Cornwall and was complaining about the hills, which made cycling almost impossible, he said. "It's a case of 'I walk beside you' most of the time," he laughed, and so did everyone else in the compartment.

Soon after I arrived back at Lonsdale Road, Prue and her friend Joyce, who lives in the same house, called. Prue's going home for the summer holidays tomorrow. Joyce's brother Brian, whom I've met once or twice, is joining the Indian army.

Tomorrow Putz arrives.

There's something I'm ashamed to tell you: *I'm extremely keen on Robin Thomas*. Maybe I'm mad, or maybe it's because of my lack of friends of the opposite sex. I like his wit and his strong opinions, although I don't agree with all of them. I enjoy his company. He showed me off to people we met in the street when we were out together, even to Monica Wills. I'm completely at ease with myself in his presence. And yet, when I shut my eyes I see only a little boy in short trousers, the one I've known for so long.

"They'll call me up any day now," he was saying as we walked together on my last day in Falmouth, "but I don't want to fight the Japs."

"I don't blame you. You're only a little boy!" I said.

He laughed. "I wish I was!" he exclaimed.

Perhaps he's just the nearest male on whom to vent my pent-up emotions. Or perhaps I'm being sentimental about a childhood admirer. Anyway, I don't love him. If I did, I should want him to touch me and kiss me and say loving things to me. I seem only to be able to like boys if they don't like me – much.

Conversations with Robin.

"Some of my friends don't know about homosexuality," I said.

"Good God!" he laughed. "Do you know, if I talked about this kind of thing to Monica she'd have a fit."

"You mean she doesn't know about these things?"

"Oh yes. But she wouldn't mention them – to me."

"Well, I don't mind mentioning them to you."

"I'm glad."

"Do you know, Robin, I'd like to come back to Falmouth again. I love it here."

"Oh, Ingrid, I wish you would." (Do you? Do you really? I wonder.)

"I don't suppose I ever will. Come on, let's go to town."

In the Street: It is pouring with rain. Robin is wearing a brown hat. I'm in my mackintosh.

"You'll have to shout now," I said, as we walked through the rain, "because I can't hear a thing through this hood."

"Would you like a cigarette?" he shouted.

"No, thank you. I don't smoke in the street. I'd like one for the train though."

He went into a shop and returned with a packet of cigarettes. He gave it to me.

"What, the whole packet for me?"

"Yes, go on, take it." (When we were children he bought me radishes and buns. That's all over now. We're grown up.)

"Thank you very much." (I'm sure he likes me. I like him, too.) "I don't want to leave Falmouth," I said.

"I wish *I* could!"

Outside the library we parted.

"Don't forget to buy that lettuce for Miss Davis," he said. "Have you money, or shall I give you some?"

"I've got money. Oh Robin, your hat's all wet. Why do you wear one?"

"It's meant to get wet instead of my hair." (Now that's soppy. Why should a boy mind his hair getting wet?)

"Well, goodbye, Robin."

"Goodbye, Ingrid. All the best."

"I'll write to you."

"Good. I like your letters. You ask so many questions that I only have to answer them and hey presto, I've written a six page letter."

"I'll ask you lots of questions, then. I've been thinking, Robin;

69

Aren't time and space queer? I mean, I can touch you now (I did, on his sleeve). Tomorrow I won't be able to."

"I'm intrigued. Explain."

"Nothing to explain. It's just that one can't stop time and space coming between people. I wish one could."

"I never thought about it that way."

"Tomorrow at this time we'll both be in different places. And now I must go. Goodbye, Robin."

"Goodbye, and good luck!" He was gone. I stood for a moment outside the library and felt the packet of cigarettes in my mackintosh pocket. (Later that day, on the train, I remembered that it was Robin's birthday today.)

2nd August 1945

I have a wireless! It came today and sits on my desk. It is rented from Radio Rentals. Mrs Labowsky said I mustn't have it on too loud after 10pm.

Putz is here. She's staying with the Rieszs' until she finds some digs. We see each other on most days – have lunch together, go to the pictures in the evening, or at the Rieszs'. On Bank Holiday, which is next Monday, she, Peter and I are going to play tennis at the Alexander Courts in Summertown.

5th August 1945

Do you think I'm mad? I feel things so deeply that it sometimes frightens me. Tonight I walked home alone from the Rieszs'. It was a beautiful, cool and clear evening. I walked and walked, not towards home at all. I suddenly realised. I lost my way. I walked very slowly, deep in thought. I felt like a mad poet in a film – I could almost hear haunting music in the background. I didn't feel like me at all. Now and then a few passers-by looked at me. I asked some people the way because by now I was completely lost. They were three happy persons, absorbed in each other, caring nothing for the sorrows of a poor, unknown night wanderer. I was back in my room at last. I undressed and washed in a perfunctory way. I was in bed. Now I let myself go. I cried, wanting my mother (as always, when unhappy), wanting a God, wanting love. I lay wrapped in a blanket of self pity. I couldn't sleep. I couldn't cry any more. So I read a little. And now I am writing, and I shall explain to you the cause of this wretched night.

Yesterday I was tearing about on my bike, trying to get addresses where Putz could meet young people because she's lonely and I want her to be happy. When I got back she was out. *She was on the river, punting with Peter Riesz.* He has never taken me punting. I was enraged with jealousy. I never thought this possible, as I want her happiness so much. I was wrong. Being jealous of friends was bad enough, but of my own sister whom I love, and over a boy who means nothing to me, was unbearable. Why, why did I feel like this?

So now you know how low I have sunk. I can't write any more because my eyes are burning from crying and my mind is not at all clear any longer and what's more, somewhere in the Universe my mother is advising me to lie down quietly and go to sleep.

10th August 1945

There's talk of a Japanese surrender! That means the war would be completely over, and if Robin is called up he won't have to fight the Japs.

I have supper at the Rieszs' nearly every evening since Putz has been staying with them, and there certainly seems to be nothing between her and Peter. The other day Peter said: "They've split the atom. It's the most fantastic discovery. The world will never be the same again." I've heard similar statements before from Peter and his friends, uttered to impress his unscientific family, I suspect, and I've learnt to ignore them as he's only showing off.

When the Rieszs' heard that I have kept a diary since I was 10 years old they asked me if they could read it. I said no, but I would read them out bits that I wrote in Vienna when I was a little girl. So on Monday evening, after supper, that's what I did. The effect it had on them was a complete surprise to me. They laughed and cried alternately, and tears rolled down Mrs Riesz's and Susie's cheeks. Peter said it was a gem and I must keep it and publish it one day. Quite a compliment from him. It was the best evening I ever spent at the Rieszs'.

15th August 1945

END OF JAPANESE WAR! PEACE ONCE MORE ALL OVER THE WORLD! This is a very memorable date and, I hope, the start of a better era. Today and tomorrow are public holidays. At the Rieszs' we were all treated to a choc-ice by way of a celebration, and afterwards Putz and I went to the flicks. The King spoke at 9pm. Then the real celebrating started. Putz, Susie and I went down to Carfax; there was a huge bonfire in the centre, crowds of people were dancing around it in a ring, and we joined them with complete abandon. It was intoxicating. I was kissed three times and forgot all my inhibitions. A pity Peter wasn't with us – he's on holiday. Most of my friends are on holiday but I mean to go down to the town again tomorrow night, after the theatre. Putz, Susie and I are going to see *Arsenic and Old Lace*.

16th August 1945 – 2nd V.J. Holiday

I did go to Carfax again – alone. At first nothing much happened. I was just a spectator. Then suddenly everything changed. I became part of the crowd. I was kissed – by everyone there, it seemed. A Yank and I were in the middle of kissing when a bucket of water was poured over us. He wiped me down with his handkerchief. We were separated. Another Yank pulled me into his arms. He was drunk, and he was called Tom or George. We walked around for about half an hour, arm in arm. I got rid of him at last, only to meet him again, and get rid of him again. I heard music somewhere and went towards it, past merry policemen and happy dancing children. A pretty, dark-haired girl was playing the concertina, surrounded by a group of listeners. Now she was playing a waltz. A British army captain stepped out of the group and tried to organise people, but it was hopeless. And then he suddenly stood by my side and said in a lovely voice: "Shall we dance?" And I said "yes", and so it was that I danced in the centre of Oxford with a captain in the British army, and we were the only couple dancing, and it was the middle of the night. "Now anything can happen," I thought. The girl stopped playing and we stopped dancing and he said, "Have a cigarette," and I said, 'Yes, please." He had to strike three matches before the cigarette would catch and I said, "What a shame, to waste so many matches in war time," and then we both laughed because of course it wasn't war time any longer. Now we joined a long line of people holding each other by the waist and hopping down the street, singing. Somehow I got detached from them. I joined other groups and had several more struggles with kissers. I met Tom or George again, who was extremely drunk by now. "Let's dance around the bonfire," he said to me, but I said I was going home. I wished I could have seen my captain with the beautiful voice again. Tom or George put his arm around me and walked a little way home with me. He became rather silly. When he suggested sitting in the park I ran off.

I was walking up Banbury Road thinking what fun I'd had when I heard a quiet English – not American – voice say: "Good night." I turned round and saw a middle-aged, handsome, aristocratic-looking gentleman whom I vaguely knew from the library. "You don't mind if I walk a little way with you, do you?" he asked.

"Of course not," I replied. So we walked together, on this fantastic night of celebrating the end of a world war, and he talked to me about politics and socialism and the railways. Sometimes we walked in silence, and I thought I wouldn't mind kissing someone like that – I've always had a liking for kindly elderly gentlemen.

"Do you often ask strange girls to walk with you?" I asked him.

"No, I don't," he answered, "but I thought we both needed a little company."

He certainly wasn't after sex, and didn't mean to seduce me like that horrible Richard Tauber. Perhaps there's some sadness in his life?

When we were about half way to my digs he said he must go back. "Not that you aren't attractive and very good company," he said, "but sadly I must leave you now." And he did.

I can't get him out of my mind. I'd like to see him again but I fear that, in a less intoxicating atmosphere, he might charm me less and I certainly would have reverted to my childish, inhibited self.

25th August 1945

Ten days into world peace, and it doesn't feel very different. Putz

d

and I have spent the time looking for digs for her. Even Erna and Bruno have not been able to come to the rescue this time, and nor has Aunt Else. We have been to the Playhouse once and met the Beschorners there and once or twice we played tennis at the Alexander Courts.

1st September 1945

Last Thursday, my half day, I went to Witney with Sandy again and spent the night there. We went putting in the afternoon (a silly game) and to a dancing class in the evening with Sandy's friend Jane. On Friday morning Mrs Sanders took us to Oxford by car.

Putz has found a room at last, in Warnborough Road, and moved in on Tuesday. It's a nice large room but a bit shabbily furnished. Next week she starts her new job as Secretary at Wolsey Hall Correspondence College.

Peter is back from his holiday.

I can't get that man who walked home with me on V.J. night out of my mind. If only I could see him again!

8th September 1945

It has been an interesting week. I'll start with Sunday. On that day I finished writing my novel, *Why couldn't Beethoven draw?* As I do not know of any activity that makes me happier than writing, life will seem empty now to say the least. In the afternoon Putz and I went punting on the river Cherwell with Peter, a girl called Veronica and a friend of Peter's called Peter Zadek, a brilliant and handsome undergraduate. He read to us from a novel by Aldous Huxley while the other Peter did the punting. Afterwards we all had supper at the Rieszs'.

On Monday, which was the day Putz started her new job, Maureen and I went to St Giles' Fair till 9.30pm. This is an annual fair lasting two days, and the whole of St Giles is closed to traffic. I find fairs very exciting and thrilling and love the noise and bustle and loud music. I went again with Putz on the following day, but she's less partial to fairs. On Wednesday my father paid us an unexpected visit! I wasn't exactly pleased to see him, but pretended I was, of course.

On Friday evening Putz and I went to a dance at the Town Hall;

it wasn't bad, but we didn't meet anyone interesting.

Today I didn't go to the library; I stayed in bed with a cold. As I lay in bed, with only an occasional interruption from Mrs Labowsky to ask how I was, and the wireless as my sole and obedient companion, my thoughts went something like this:

I want to go away from England. It's funny, but all at once I find myself blaming England for all my unhappiness over the years. Why England? Why not? I long to go back to Austria. My Austria. It contains everything that is missing here. Without my mother life will never be worthwhile but in Austria I'd feel closer to her, wherever she is. I have finished my novel and I don't quite know what to think of it, I've lived in it so much. I'm waiting for other people's opinions. I'm going to take it to Blackwells, the publishers, and I shudder to think how I'm going to face up to the dreadful blow of the disappointment to come. Oh hell, I wish I wish – what? I don't really know what else to tell you about this miserable life or my miserable self. There's nothing like a cold in the head for making you see both – life and yourself – in their ugliest colours, or rather as they really are.

11th September 1945

I met Ilse Rosendorf today. We said goodbye, as she's leaving Oxford and moving to London.

Yesterday I had supper at Mary West's house again. Also invited were two RAF officers called Owen and Jack. We danced to the gramophone. It was a very nice evening and I didn't get home till 11pm.

On Sundays I sometimes don't get up till Mrs Labowsky brings me my tray of lunch at 12.30pm. I eat it at my desk with the wireless on. Last Sunday the first thing I heard when I turned on the wireless was the name 'Laurence Olivier'. "The brilliant Laurence Olivier", I heard, "gave a marvellous performance . . ." It's like hearing about someone I know personally. Which I do. In the afternoon I went to Putz's room. We had tea and talked and talked, after which we came to my room and had supper and continued to talk.

On Thursday we are going to have tea at Fuller's and afterwards we shall go to a concert at the Town Hall, to hear some Beethoven.

On Friday my shorthand class starts again. After this lengthy break I shall be more hopeless than ever, and not be able to read any of the wiggles.

14th September 1945

Sudden happiness! I'd almost forgotten what lovely feelings are stirred up by happiness – self-confidence, magnanimity, a love of all the world. And what is the reason for my happiness? Just wait till I tell you: Two days ago I took my finished novel to Blackwells. I asked to see the person in charge of the publishing department. As I waited, I felt weak in the knees. I wanted to go home. I felt I couldn't face him and talk about what was so close to my heart. Presently a distinguished-looking man appeared. Youngish.

"What do you want published?" he asked me very nicely.

"A novel," I replied.

"Oh, I'm afraid we only deal with non-fiction. We never publish novels. I'm very sorry."

"That's all right. Thank you." I wanted to get away as quickly as possible.

"Is it something you've written?" he asked.

"Yes."

"That's very interesting. Very interesting indeed. Have you got it here?"

"Yes." He led me to his desk.

"Let me see it," he said. My hands trembled as I passed him my beloved work. I gave him an imploring look.

"Please don't read it now," I said. "I'll leave it here if you like." But he was already reading. The humiliation of seeing him read my humble words was unendurable. I turned my head away so as not to have to witness it, and fixed my eyes on the ground, at some books behind me, anything.

"The beginning is awful," I said, to interrupt his reading. "It gets better later." It can't get worse, I thought. "You'll be awfully disappointed." But –

"Not at all," I heard his voice from far away. "On the contrary. It's extremely interesting . . . the force behind it, the style . . . and most unusual . . . quite unique . . ." Did I hear right?

"Pardon?" I said stupidly. He muttered some more praises. Now my eyes were glued to his face as he read. Suddenly my dreams were coming true. Within seconds I had become a budding genius. Basil Blackwell the publisher has praised my work! Fame and happiness are only around the corner now. Mother, you produced a budding genius! Darling Mother, if only I could go home to you now and pour out to you the exuberance that is in my heart, the heart that has known so much sadness. He was speaking again.

"You have talent. A lot of talent. That's certain." He looked up from the manuscript. "Do you know Vienna, then?" he asked. The novel's setting is Vienna.

"Yes. I come from there."

"Oh, really. How long have you been here?"

"Six years."

"Have you ever written or published anything before?"

"Written yes; published no." I answered his questions with childish pride and delight.

"What is your name?"

"Ingrid Jacoby." Some day that name will mean something. People will come from miles away to see its bearer, the writer of famous books. He said I have talent, didn't he?

"I'd be so grateful if it could be published," I said. He was reading again and I don't know if he heard me. After what seemed a long interval he spoke again.

"Look here," he said. "You must get this typed and then bring it along to me again. Here are some addresses of typing agencies in Oxford." He handed me a piece of paper. I dropped it. He gave me the manuscript back and I nearly dropped that, too. Never mind, I was a budding genius being clumsy, not just an insignificant girl any longer. I walked out of Blackwells and the world was my oyster. I felt sorry for everyone who wasn't, like me, one day going to be a famous writer. Not for one moment did I stop to consider how I shall face my disappointment when my book is refused, because, two days on, I can't really believe it will be published. I was, of course, far too easily taken in by those words of encouragement.

22nd September 1945

I've taken my novel to a typing agency. It will take about two weeks. Pruc is back in Oxford after her holidays. She came to see

77

me on Thursday. She asked me why I looked so depressed. I apologised for showing my emotions.

"Why aren't you happy?" she said.

I shrugged my shoulders. "I am sometimes," I said.

Prue is always happy. She stayed for supper.

On Sunday Maureen came to tea and afterwards we went to church because there was nowhere else to go. The following day Mary West came to supper, but I didn't eat much as I had been sick twice at the library that day. I can't entertain my friends in the style in which they entertain me in their parents' homes, eating in dining rooms at polished tables, but they don't seem to mind. I usually give them something cold and we eat it on our laps or at the desk.

Putz has joined my shorthand class, which started last week. Neither of us likes the teachers, Mrs Hall and her sister-in-law, Miss Hall, who has a lame arm. They are both very strict and unfriendly.

I'm writing this with my new fountain pen, which I bought last Saturday. I've also bought some new shoes – white wedges. They are not comfortable, but their appearance makes up for that.

Why have I been thinking of Otto Seifert of all people lately? I'd love to see him again, to know what he's doing, far away in China, a refugee from Hitler. He used to call me "his little bride". I used to sleep with his letters under my pillow. I was only 11. Does he remember his little bride? Or was he really in love with my mother, did he pretend it was her when I sat on his lap? But what does it all matter now?

I've started writing a new story.

24th September 1945

Audrey has arrived, to take up her nursing job. I spent my lunch hour with her and her parents today. I've asked her to come to tea on my half day (next Thursday). It's lovely to see her again, and I think she was pleased to see me, too.

Last night I dreamt vividly of Denzil; I dreamt I saw him in the street and called out his name but he wouldn't stop. I ran after him and when I was quite close I saw that his face was sad and pale. At first he seemed to reject me but then he put his arm around me and we walked in silence through eerie, dusky streets such as only exist in dreams. Presently I said, "Denzil, what is it? Why are you so sad?"

He wouldn't tell me, but he was very sweet and loving. I noticed that he was wearing a very unusual tie. We reached a lovely meadow and sat down on a bench. I felt his body close to mine. He seemed reluctant to speak. Suddenly I felt his hand against my bare skin, under my frock, and with this action he expressed his physical desire for me. For a moment I submitted. Then I jumped up and cried: "Denzil! That's enough! Now pull yourself together. I'm not going that far." He smiled sadly, as if to say "I'm so unhappy I don't mind one way or the other." I knelt down at his side and said: "Dear little Denzil, it's so good to see you again. Don't be sad. Please answer me one question."

"Yes?" he said.

"Are you a virgin?" No answer.

I saw trees all around us, swaying in the breeze. And then I woke up.

Horrid Mr Skuce is back from his holiday. Everyone breathes more freely when he's away. So now we're all choking again.

I had written to my father asking him if he has slacks at his firm, Playfair, in London. Everyone seems to be wearing them. He wrote back: "I would not advise you to wear slacks. They are only for slim girls with excellent figures."

28th September 1945

I've had a letter from Joan Beschorner. She is longing to see me again, she says. Her husband has now left and is teaching in Harrow. Would I come for supper next Monday? She's still at 66 St John's Road. By a strange coincidence I also met Kay Ellison, and we walked a little way together. She thought the Beschorners had left Oxford long ago.

I had lunch with Peggy Jacques at Weekes and we talked shop mostly about how much we hated Skuce and Campbell.

4th October 1945

I have had a sweet letter from my little Chinese man, Chang Cheong. He is sending me some silk stockings from New York! And he wants a photo of me.

79

Last Sunday I went to a farewell party at the Refugee Club; Mrs Grice is leaving. I met a Czech fellow called Otto Schmidt there. He is short and stocky and a ping-pong champion. He asked me for a date, as a result of which we went to the pictures together last night; afterwards he took me home. Next Sunday I'm playing ping-pong with him at a Jewish hostel in Linton Road.

Monday was an eventful day: In the afternoon – I'm always off from 1-5pm on Mondays – I took my typed novel to Blackwells. Luckily Mr Blackwell was not there so I just left it. When I returned to work for the evening session I saw a familiar-looking man in the lending library. He was tall and blond and very good looking – and he turned out to be – can you guess? Yes? No? Then I'll tell you: Mr Collinge from Falmouth, whom Connie and I used to go just to get a glimpse of in Timothy Whites where he worked. What a surprise! I couldn't talk to him much as Miss Campbell sent me buffering, and in any case we – the juniors – are not supposed to converse with borrowers. In the evening I had supper with Joan Beschorner at St John's Road. We had a long

Joan's
self-portrait.

talk and she confided in me that her marriage was very difficult and her husband possessive and tyrannical. I stayed till 10pm. Next Monday I'm going again, and I'm taking her some of my stories to read. She gave me a lovely self-portrait she had drawn.

On Saturday I'm going to a social at the Austrian Club with Putz, Maureen and Susie.

7th October 1945

I've just returned from the hostel where I played ping-pong with Otto and Eric. Eric is also Czech. I liked him immediately. They both took me home. I wished it had only been Eric. If I am going to permit myself to fall in unrequited love again I shall hang myself on the next tree. I want to control my feelings and forbid these frightening emotions to get the better of me.

13th October 1945

Kay was supposed to come to supper on Wednesday but she cancelled it.

Putz and I had lunch with Sandy on Thursday and in the evening we saw *The Gypsy Baron* at the New Theatre. It doesn't sound right in English, but it was quite enjoyable.

I haven't been in love with any man since Roy Lovell. When that was over I promised myself that I was through with unrequited love. It must be mutual or not at all. As you know, since then I fell in love with no one and no one fell in love with me – except a girl! Audrey, by the way, came to see me the other day and I more or less told her how I used to feel about her. I got the impression it was mutual, as I always suspected it was – I don't know how she feels about me now, but as for me, that is all over. Anyway, if you expect me to tell you that I'm in love with somebody again – you're right. It is Eric. I have just seen him on the bus, in his usual jumper, the one he wears for ping-pong, and with the usual sad expression in his eyes. When I saw him, something happened to me. Everything I know to exist somewhere seemed to become attainable: joy, beauty, solid warm security, a looking forward to everything – to the changing seasons, to Christmas, to the company of friends. All this and more, Eric represents. Suddenly I'm a normal young girl again. If it is not possible to love someone one has only seen two or three times and whom one does not know, and yet this is how they make you feel, then what shall I call it? For too long writing has been my only consolation. Once it was to pray, then to draw and play the piano, now and forever more to write, but it is a lonely occupation. When I saw Eric on the bus I knew in a flash that there were other things to life and to live for. And what of my resolve to steer clear of unrequited love? I can only say this in excuse: when Eric replied, "Buried" in answer to my question where his parents were, there was so much pain in his voice that I must accept as my due the pain he may cause me.

Putz has been to a dance with a Polish officer in the airforce. Oh, I'm so happy for her!

15th October 1945

I feel like killing myself. I wish it weren't my life. I wish I could make it someone else's.

I'd been looking forward to Sunday evening all the week because I might see Eric at ping-pong. In the morning I was at Prue's, then at Putz's, then Audrey and I met and went for a walk after which she and Putz had tea with me in my room. Otto had rung me earlier to ask me to go to the pictures with him, before playing ping-pong. I agreed. We caught a bus at 6.30pm. "Eric told me he saw you on the bus the other day. With your sister," Otto said.

The name, Eric, startled me into alertness. "Yes," I said.

Otto smiled.

"Why are you smiling? What else did Eric say?"

"I shan't tell you."

"Yes, you will." Pause.

"He said that you had a nice sister."

"Oh." I thought: I love Putz with all my heart. Why shouldn't everyone else?

"I asked Eric to come to the pictures with us," Otto went on innocently. "But he couldn't."

"Oh." God damn Eric. God damn him for not caring for me.

He wasn't at ping-pong. Otto and I played alone, he usually winning. In between games we drank tea in the kitchen. I watched his chubby little fingers raise his cup and his round sandy-haired head lower itself to meet it, and I felt bored – and disgusted. The sight of Otto sipping tea was not a pretty one. I was unhappy, and I blamed ugly, fat Otto for my unhappiness. No one loves me, no one. In my despair I thought, from somewhere I've *got* to get faith, I must give God a chance. Who else can save me?

Otto took me home. It was very dark and foggy and I stumbled. He took my arm. If you touch me, I thought, if you touch me I shall scream. Let me alone. Presently he let go. I suppose he was decent and sensitive enough to be aware of my unwillingness. But a few minutes later he suddenly and shyly put his arm through mine. I hated but suffered it. He is a decent fellow. And kind. What made me say what I said next? I shall never know. "My sister plays ping-pong, too," I said. "I'll bring her along one day. To please Eric." It was the stupidest, craziest thing I could have said.

"Yes, do," he replied. His hand had crept onto mine.

"What happened to Eric's parents?" I asked.

"They were killed in a concentration camp," he replied. His hand was even tighter on mine now. I must ask him to stop touching me, I thought. I can't bear it. I shall cry in a minute. And I could hear Eric's voice again: "BURIED . . . BURIED . . ." It echoed in my ears.

"Is that why he always seems so sad and quiet?" I said.

"Maybe. I feel sorry for Eric. He's very lonely. He lives in digs. He's queer sometimes. Crazy. But a very nice boy." I said nothing more. A very nice boy. And I'm in love with him, in my usual hopeless, tragic, one-sided, school-girlish way. Only now I'm 18 . . .

Thank God, Otto's instinct didn't let him kiss me, and I escaped. I was back in my room. Once alone, rid of poor Otto, rid of the horrible, unjust world outside, I sat down on my bed. I felt like a frustrated child and, like a child, I wanted to climb on a chair and scream until I got my own way. That would have relieved me for a time. Instead I just sat on the edge of the bed and didn't know how to face God, now that we were alone and after so long. "You let me down," I said to God, whoever he may be. "Why did you?" I would have preferred my mother, instead of this distant vague supernatural being, but my mother is missing believed dead. So I continued to talk to God. "I'm sure you remember how I loved you once," I said. "I want Eric. Can't you make him love me? To show me you exist?" And then my mood changed. "Oh, I'm glad Eric's parents died in a concentration camp. Yes, glad!" I thought, "Why didn't they kill Eric too? I'm glad he's lonely . . . long may he continue to be so . . ." Because

Eric doesn't care for me, and never will. God, if you are there, you hate me now, don't you? So you should, because I'm wicked, selfish and cruel – but not cruel enough to tell Otto I don't want him, I want Eric instead. I could never do that.

If he really likes Lieselotte – she certainly didn't like him much from what she saw of him – then I shall be closer to him . . .

19th October 1945

Life is crazy, completely crazy. Does a little happiness sometimes emerge from this craziness?

On Monday Mr Collinge came to the library again and this time I managed to have a long chat with him. I tried to remember all I knew about him – that he was assistant manager at Timothy Whites, a member of the dramatic society to which Miss Davis belonged, and engaged, though Miss Davis told me this engagement has long been broken off. In Falmouth I was just a little schoolgirl to him, and we barely knew each other. And now here he was, inviting me to go to the theatre with him! I couldn't go on Monday as that is the evening I always have supper at Joan's, so Wednesday was the date fixed. We went to the Playhouse and saw Ibsen's *The Wild Duck*. Discussing the play afterwards triggered off an interesting discussion and exchange of ideas. The next day being Thursday and my half-day as well as his, we cycled into the country. We sat on the grass and left our bikes leaning against a tree. Then we had a long walk by the river. It was very quiet; only a few fishermen were about, and they watched us from time to time, and smiled. Perhaps they thought we were lovers. Once or twice he touched my arm. I didn't mind. I had been frightened before going out with him – I don't know why – but I wasn't any more. He had brought me a box of chocolates and was altogether kind and polite throughout. I felt very safe. After our walk we sat down again for a bit and I was now relaxed enough to notice the beautiful colours of the autumn leaves, and commented on them. When we weren't talking it was very still. Harold seemed quite at ease, stretching his long legs out, lighting his pipe, putting his hands in his pockets. I watched him, fascinated. For the first time in my life I knew that these masculine gestures were meant for me alone, I wasn't watching a film or someone at the next table in a café. When I removed a leaf that had fallen on his trousers, thereby touching his knee, he didn't say anything.

We talked about all sorts of things on our way home: About each other, about work, about music and art. He said he was terribly pleased to have met me; he had never met anyone like me before. I think he's about 28 years old – 10 years older than myself. I enjoyed the afternoon. Next Thursday we're going out together again. It is nice, pleasant and normal and would be more so if I weren't in love with Eric. I shall never have Eric, I know that, not even if Otto dies, and he will have to remain an unfulfilled dream, with his curly hair and head like an Easter egg and the sad, sweet expression in his eyes.

Harold's full name is Harold George Collinge.

20th October 1945

I was so busy telling you about my outings with Harold yesterday that I forgot to tell you I also went to the New Theatre with Sandy and a crowd of her Witney friends – Jane, and three uncouth youths called Pete, Bony and Juddy. We saw George Formby, whom I had previously only seen in films. In the evening I played ping-pong with Otto and others at the hostel (not Eric).

23rd October 1945

Joan and little Peter came to tea on Sunday. Peter is nearly 5 years old and a very sweet boy. I read him the story of *Hatschi Bratschi*, translating it as I went along as it's in German – I loved it as a child but Joan thought the end was terrible. All the children screaming in captivity, before they are rescued, reminded her of children in concentration camps, she said. However, I'm going to translate the book and she's going to do the drawings. I'm having supper with her tomorrow and she has invited Daphne Hall too. The worst thing that ever happened to Daphne, according to Joan, is losing her lipstick on holiday.

I went to the flicks with Otto last night, but what I really want to talk to you about is Sunday night, which I spent at the hostel playing cards and ping-pong with Otto, Putz, a few others – and Eric. He talked to me quite often; he didn't ignore me by any means. Several times I caught his eye. Once or twice we shared a joke. I was completely happy. There wasn't any yesterday or tomorrow. I wanted to touch him without any clothes on, and I knew that it would be lovely and I wouldn't be a bit self-conscious. With other men the very thought of physical contact makes me sick.

On the way home, Otto talked about Eric again. Apparently he loves a Czech girl called Helen who doesn't care for him, and he carries her photograph around. True or false, what difference can it make to me? I know I can never have Eric.

25th October 1945

I've just spent the whole of my half day with Harold. First we had lunch together. Then we went to see the processional march of academics in full regalia, as it was the day of the Encaenia. We had come to see Montgomery and Eisenhower who were marching in the procession, having had honorary degrees conferred on them. They wore the academic fancy dress too, instead of their uniforms. Then we went to the cinema, where Harold knew the organist who performs there during the interval, and he introduced me to him after the film; then a cup of coffee at a café before going to the Sheldonian for a concert by the London Philharmonic Orchestra, conducted by Sir Thomas Beecham. Harold is not the right companion for listening to music with, and detracted from my enjoyment. Finally we had supper at a snack bar in George Street. Sounds exciting, doesn't it? It wasn't.

These last few weeks I seem to have learnt a great deal. I have learnt that a wish fulfilled is not necessarily a desire satisfied, but rather an illusion destroyed by reality. No, I'm not ungrateful, but I know now that a lovely dream was turned into a triviality, and trivialities will not do for me. It is better to do without and wait for something BIG. I must be tremendously satisfied, like a huge starving animal which hasn't eaten for months, not fed with little morsels. Somerset Maugham says if you don't accept the second best sooner or later you will get the first.

All this has led me to believe that it would be best for me to keep Eric as he is – forever; that it would be best if I never got to know him better after all, never touched him with no clothes on, never knew what goes on in his strange mind or fathomed the sad expression in his eyes. Because I'm afraid that my illusions may be destroyed. What, after all, can be as perfect as my imagination? I have no faith in people and I don't understand them. The only thing I really understand are my own thoughts. So it would be best to stay like this, just a silent worshipper.

28th October 1945

Last night Putz and I spent the evening at the Rieszs'. Susie's fiancé Charlie, a Viennese/American G.I., was there too. She has known him a long time and they recently got engaged. I think it must be much easier to get engaged if you are a simple, uncomplicated girl like Susie, even though she's so plain. Peter walked home with us and we laughed and joked all the way.

When I got back Mrs Labowsky bounced out of her sitting room and, before I had even closed the front door, told me that a gentleman from Blackwells had called to see me, and would I call at the shop next week! Mr Blackwell had been here in person! I was elated. It could only mean good news. I was too excited to sleep much that night.

Every time I see Eric I must write about him. Putz and I were at the hostel this evening, Sunday, as usual, playing ping-pong. We'd spent the afternoon in her room practising shorthand as there's an exam coming up, and we were stiff from sitting so long. There were quite a few people playing this evening, among them of course Otto (he had telephoned me in the morning to ask me to be sure to come . . .), Ossy, Gustav – and Eric. (I even had a go at billiards for the first time in my life.) It was decided to play some ping-pong matches, and I have now reached the stage in my account where Eric was playing a single with Ossy, and Otto did the scoring. Ossy being the weaker of the two players, everyone backed him. "Come on, Ossy!" they all shouted. I sat quietly, watching, but in my mind I whispered: "Win, Eric, win, win, win. Win for me and I'll know you love me!" That was reckless of me. He lost the game. God is honest with me, honest but merciless.

Lieselotte says I'm throwing myself away on someone completely indifferent to me, that I'm banging my head against a wall, and of course she is right. If I needed any more proof I had it tonight, when I was alone with Eric for about three minutes before the others arrived, and he asked me casually how I was, as he might ask a complete stranger, an insignificant visitor, and took no further notice of me. How can I go on loving him in such circumstances? Is total real love possible when it is not mutual? What can I do? Nothing, and even if I could there's always Otto whom I couldn't let down.

31st October 1946

My search for my mother meets with nothing but failure. The reply from United Nations Relief is as disappointing as from all the rest of the places I've written to. How can I still go on hoping?

UNITED NATIONS RELIEF AND REHABILITATION ADMINISTRATION

European Regional Office,
31 Portland Place,
London W.1

Letter C.
File Number: DP91/217   Date: 3rd October 1945
To: Miss I. Jacoby,
          47 Lonsdale Road,
          Oxford.

Dear Madam,

We have received your communication of 30th Sept. 1945 concerning the whereabouts of Mrs Emmy Jacoby.

Your letter has been referred to the National Tracing Bureau of United Kingdom at British Red cross Society, Foreign Relations Department, Wimborne House, Arlington Street, London S.W.1.

If this organisation is able to secure any information it will communicate it at once to you direct. If they are unsuccessful in their search, your enquiry will be passed by them to the appropriate tracing bureau who will endeavour through every means at their disposal to trace your relative and will advise you of the result of their efforts.

Whilst every endeavour will be made in order to obtain with the minimum delay an answer to your enquiry, we feel that we should explain that in view of the number of missing persons in Europe and of the difficulties of search and communications, delays are unfortunately probable before the answer which you are expecting can reach you.

Yours very truly,
L.W. Charley, Lt. Col
Chief D.P. Programmes Officer (Germany)
Unc. 1034   D.P. Division

Kay came to supper. I sat on the bed, she on a chair and we had a little table between us which Miss Lorch, the elderly lodger upstairs, lent me. It served as a supper table, and was better than the desk. Kay is fascinating to talk to, and we talked until 11pm. I told her that, in my experience, love is extinguished as soon as it is requited and she laughed and said I was a masochist. I guessed she had had no such experiences, only a lot of happy love affairs. She's blonde and sporty and attractive. I lent her my bicycle to get home as she had missed the last bus.

I've had a letter from 'Mr Blackwell' who isn't Mr Blackwell at all, but Mr Morris, asking me to come to his house on Thursday – tomorrow. Imagine my excitement! I slept with the letter under my pillow. He wrote:

9 St John St.
Oxford
Sunday 28th inst

Dear Miss Jacoby

I'm writing to you in very great haste and ask to be forgiven the use of a pencil. I ask too that I may be forgiven for keeping you so long in suspense. Tout comprendre . . .

You will have had my message to call on me at Blackwells any day next week. I'm writing to tell you now that the odds are AGAINST my being there next week: my doctor will probably insist on my taking another week off. Anyway, if you can arrange to do so, it will be much better if you call on me here at, say, seven o'clock on Tuesday evening, 30th inst.

If that time should be unsuitable, may I suggest Thursday afternoon at three o'clock.

I am, yours sincerely,
M.C. Morris

Today I took my typewriting exam (elementary) and Friday it's the turn of shorthand, which is much harder. I'm afraid I've sadly neglected my studies for the Library exam; occasionally I have a brief lesson with Miss Butt, a senior assistant at the library who agrees with me that doing all the work by correspondence course is very unsatisfactory.

1st November 1945

My new life begins today. Out of the blue. It is almost midnight and very cold, but however late, however cold, I have to write down what has taken place.

I wish I could explain to you what has happened to me spiritually. I wish I could photograph my extraordinary emotions and stick them in here. I wish I could harness the exciting future and pull it nearer to me.

I don't know why I am sitting here, shivering in front of the electric sun, spiritually happy, when I should weep over my disappointment. But something remarkable has happened to me. It happened at No. 9, St John's Street, where Mr Morris lives and where I have been today. At first I was unpleasantly surprised that he only lived in a bedsitter like me, instead of a large house of his own as I had imagined, with a wife and family all waiting to entertain me and praise my book. How differently things turned out! The room into which Mr Morris showed me on my arrival was a veritable Faustian study: Michelangelo pictures on the walls, newspapers and other papers on the table, chairs and floor, and books right up to the ceiling. He offered me a cigarette but I was too unsure of myself to smoke. He asked me to sit down. At first glance there didn't seem to be anywhere to sit. He found a chair for himself near me. For a long time he talked to me quietly, about himself, myself, books, life, anything.

"I know you are dying to hear what I think about your novel," he said at last.

"Yes, I am," I said, and waited. You could hear a pin drop. The atmosphere was electric.

"What right have you to think that your very first novel should be published?" he said at last. "At the age of 18?"

"No right," I said in a dead voice. "I was just hoping."

"What right had you to be so conceited?" I had really known all along that my novel was not publishable, so why were his words such a bitter blow?

"I wasn't conceited," I said lamely.

He smiled at me. He said I was very young. He said I was never to give up writing, had considerable talent, possessed an artist's instincts. A bright future awaited me, but I had a lot to learn, I must put myself in the public's place, above all I must acquire discipline in writing. I wanted to cry, but I wanted to rejoice too. I said I had no patience to wait. I wanted to be happy *now*. Everyone is entitled to happiness, I said. I was bubbling over inside, I wanted to stay in this room with Mr Morris for ever and ever. "Happiness without any obligations?" he said. "No, never." Why not, I longed to ask. "Come along," he said, "I'll take you out to tea. We'll go to Fuller's. Would you like that?"

"Very much," I replied. It didn't feel like me sitting at Fuller's drinking tea and eating chocolate cake with Mr Morris. I was neither a sophisticated young lady out with a much older and brilliant man, nor any longer a silly flapper believing herself to be a future genius. I was nothing, I was in limbo, I was some spiritual being sustained only by Mr Morris's voice, for he continued to talk to me right through tea, during which he drank absently and ate without interest – unlike me. When we had finished and I offered to pay my share he said he would smack me. I was so entirely under his spell and in his power that it would not have surprised me if he had, and I would have accepted it meekly.

Going home on the bus I went over and over our conversation and everything that had taken place. I saw Mr Morris not only as an intellectual influence but as the foundation of my career. I felt born again. I saw an entirely new aspect of life. A life with a visible God, almost.

"Will you come and see me again?" he had asked, on the way to the bus stop.

"Can I?" I tried to keep the excitement out of my voice.

"How about Wednesday?"

"Yes." He smiled and pressed my hand when we said goodbye.

But Wednesday is an eternity away!

6th November 1945

I've been in a state of intoxication all week. I did all the usual things: worked at the library (Campbell is on holiday!) went to the theatre with Harold, had supper with Putz, played ping-pong at the hostel and was taken home by Otto, and saw *The Doctor's Dilemma* by G.B. Shaw at the Playhouse with Putz and Maureen (excellent). But I was untouched by them. It was as if I were standing outside my life, watching myself do these things. My mind was floating in the clouds. When Harold came back to my room with me for a cup of tea after the theatre and stayed until 11.30pm, chatting and playing chess with me, I felt so aloof that I wasn't even bored. He's going to Falmouth on holiday tomorrow.

My father telephoned today. Just a duty call. I don't feel that I belong to him at all.

Only a few more hours to go now until I shall be back in that magical room in St John's Street, among the books and papers and Michelangelos, in the presence of its magical inhabitant, Dr Faustus Morris, the spirit of all my tomorrows.

7th November 1945

I walked along the dimly lit street that leads to Mr Morris's house. I had my novel with me as we were going to discuss it, and also a short story. I was madly excited. I wondered if the second taste of heaven would be as perfect as the first.

There was no heaven. He was out. He had forgotten. There was no message, nothing. Only an emptiness that had once been happiness. But happiness, it seems, is not for me. My young hope was dead.

I went straight to Joan's, to empty my heart out to her. I wanted to know desperately what kind of a man Mr Morris actually is, and Joan might understand. I knew, and Joan would confirm, that life wasn't over, it only felt like it. Only death can end life. There would be other things to live for, the only problem was how to endure life until they occurred again. I had longed to talk to Mr Morris and now perhaps I never would. He had said to me: "You never dip in the same river twice – remember?" Is this what he meant?

Dr Beschorner was at home! I had supper with them and Joan persuaded me to leave my novel for him to read. I did.

10th November 1945

Can heaven be restored?

Today I had to go to Blackwells for the Library, as I sometimes do. He was there. He saw me and called me over to his desk. As soon as I was in his presence I felt this magic aura closing in on me again, shutting everything out.

"What happened to you on Wednesday?" he asked me.

"To me? I came to your house. You weren't there."

"I was there at the appointed time, 7.30." He sounded quietly angry.

"Oh. I came at 7."

"Did you imagine I would be out when I asked you to come?"

"I thought you had forgotten." He looked at me seriously and didn't say anything for a minute. Then he said:

"I am not much of a gentleman in your opinion, am I?"

"Of course you are."

"How could you have thought that? You must have more patience. You should have waited."

"All right. It was my fault." I didn't care, I was wild with pleasure that he hadn't forgotten.

"When can you come again?" He wanted to see me. He wasn't angry any longer.

"Next Wednesday?"

"Next Wednesday. At 7.30. And don't go away again." He smiled at me.

When I had supper at Putz's this evening I couldn't talk about anything or anyone but Mr Morris. After supper we visited Aunt Erna and Aunt Else together. I think Putz was quite pleased to get a break from Mr Morris.

Joan and Peter came to tea on Thursday and we read *Hatschi Bratschi* again, which Peter enjoyed very much. I have almost finished typing it out in translation – all in rhyme. Joan has done the most wonderful illustrations.

13th November 1945

Harold is back from Falmouth. He brought me a parcel from Miss Davis containing some little cakes she had baked for me, and a few other things. How nice of her. Harold said he was pleased to see me again.

Yesterday Putz, Maureen and I went to an ENSA concert at the Town Hall (we skipped shorthand!), and Sunday I spent with Audrey; first we went for a walk, then she came to tea in my room. We talked a bit about love and she told me she's very strait-laced. Things were very different in Falmouth, when I was the one who was strait-laced. Afterwards we went to Putz's room, had more tea, and then on to Audrey's room at her hospital. She likes her job and thinks she has definitely made the right choice of career. In the evening Putz and I played ping-pong at the hostel. The usual crowd was there. I feel it is only fair and honourable to tell you that my brief, passionate love for Eric is over. I'm too impatient to fight for the impossible, and I was a fool to fall for him in the first place, when all the time he loved a girl called Helen. I have Harold and Otto who don't mean much to me but are a comfort.

Two or three weeks ago I thought that not being loved by Eric and not having my novel published would be worse than death. But it isn't – nowhere near it. I didn't understand that an unfulfilled wish can leave a person happier than a fulfilled one. Now I know.

Thank goodness every today is blessed with a tomorrow!

14th November 1945

I have just been to Mr Morris's room. I know now that, whatever has happened in the past, whatever may happen in the future, whatever I may have said and done in the past, or may say and do in the future, these precious hours have been worth living for, have surpassed anything I may have imagined could ever happen to me.

Perhaps you've lost faith in me and don't take me seriously any longer? You think I'm erratic, let my emotions run away with me? Because I have no explanation as to why I feel as I do, I cannot argue with these accusations. But you must believe me when I say that this is the biggest chapter of my life so far. I don't know exactly how it will end but I'm sure it will leave me a better person. So now I will tell you something of what took place tonight, of which I shall never forget a minute or a word that has been spoken. Mr Morris was wearing his mustard coloured jacket and grey flannel trousers which he always seems to wear. Nothing was changed in his room, either. Books and papers filled every available space. The scene was set for a conversation in which nothing would be left unsaid. And so it turned out. It started innocently enough. He asked me if I had any family and I said my sister lived in Oxford. "Is she the Miss Jacoby who does invisible mending?" he enquired. I laughed and said no, her mending was very visible. We talked about music and he said he loved Haydn

94

because he's such a happy composer. We talked about God and I said I often found God in people. We talked about great men and their theories, men like Confucius and Pascal and Voltaire, and we talked about love and sex. When it was time for me to go he asked if I could come again next week. I said I'd love to but was afraid I might be wasting his time. He smiled a little where we stood in the half-lit hall and put his hand on my shoulder and kept it there and I felt none of the repulsion I feel with Otto and Harold. He said: "Wasting my time? Good gracious, I enjoy being with you." And I love being with you, I thought, as I reluctantly left him.

17th November 1945

I had a lovely letter from Joan about my novel which I shall keep forever.

Tuesday

My dear Ingrid,

Suddenly, a clock chimes 12 midnight and I was still reading your book. I haven't finished it yet of course, but I must tell you how beautifully written it is, and how real is the character of 'I' ('I' reminds me of myself a bit, in younger days).

As I sat there by the dying embers utterly enthralled I suddenly, astonishingly, became aware for the first time that the words were written in blue ink. Unaccountably, I felt they should be colourful, vivid, living, moving things instead of your dear untidy scrolls as the work *lives* so much.

Of course, in the technical sense I would say that a lot of your narrative about Hitler and his goings on could have been narrowed down. After all, we more or less know those things, but we *don't know* how a girl like 'I' could feel about them, which is the beauty of that part, especially the part about her ordeal (here you had a most exquisite touch in your description of feelings) with the SA men which on no account must be left out as it is so intensely humanly written. Let me read on now, but I felt before I do, I have to tell Ingrid how I feel about her really beautiful characters both 'I' and Klaus, who were endeared to me immediately.

Yours always,

Joan B.

Two pieces of news: I've passed my typing and shorthand exams – the former 1st class – and I have a new job! As librarian at Wolsey Hall Correspondence College, where Putz works. I had my interview on Thursday and start there on the 26th November. No more Campbell or buffering!

At the Rieszs' last night we had an interesting discussion of a philosophical nature with Peter, who was in great form. Mrs Riesz thinks I did right to leave the library since I wasn't happy there. On Monday I must go to the Labour Exchange to inform them of my change of job.

18th November 1945

My one-time guardian, Mr Robins, has become a big noise in Falmouth. He stood as Independent Candidate in the local elections. I wonder if he or Mrs Robins ever think of the two awful refugee children they took into their home?

Sandy is coming to supper on Wednesday. She's very sorry I'm leaving the library on Friday. I can't wait! She wants to leave too. Harold is taking me to the pictures to celebrate my last day at the library on Friday.

20th November 1945

I've been to heaven again. I've just come back from there. Don't be afraid that I'm going to repeat myself and go over all the emotions that I experienced in that room yet again. I could no doubt find different words for them but I shan't even do that. In the three hours I spent there, from 7.30 till 10.30pm, less than half that time was taken up with conversation of a personal kind, but that is what I'm going to tell you about.

Quite early in the evening he asked me how old I was. I was surprised because I thought he knew.

"Why do you want to know that again?" I said. He sighed and looked away from me and said at last:

"Why? I don't know why – God knows."

"Tell me your age and I'll tell you mine," I said.

He laughed. "That's a fair bargain," he said. "Guess."

"In your thirties?"

"Yes, in my thirties." I didn't enquire which end. He sometimes looks suddenly very sad and I didn't want that to happen.

"I'm eighteen," I said, sticking to our bargain.

"Eighteen," he said thoughtfully. And then – "Tell me – do you mind if I ask you – have you any boyfriends?"

"Yes, but I don't care much for them. They don't interest me."

"One day you will meet somebody," he said. "You will be happy then, Ingrid." I'm Ingrid now; last time it was still Miss Jacoby. He said: "So you've never met the right man. Have you ever made love?"

"No."

"Of course. Yes. Well, you are very young. Tell me, what would make you completely happy?" I knew the answer, but I didn't want to tell him.

"I'll tell you some other time," I said.

"I wish I were twenty-five again," he said.

"You're not old."

"Look at my grey hair."

"Grey hair can make people look distinguished."

"Ah, yes. Tell me, do I look distinguished?"

"You look different from anyone I've ever met."

"Distinguished?"

"Is it a woman's place to pay a man a compliment?"

We both laughed.

"But I want to know what you think I'm like," he said, serious again.

"I wish I knew," I said.

"Do you think it would be wrong for a man of forty to marry a girl of twenty?"

"Not if they love each other."

It seemed natural to talk to him like this. There was no hypocrisy, no embarrassment. At least for me. Perhaps he did feel a bit uneasy because at this stage he got up and went to his bookcase. He took a book on Chinese Philosophy from the shelf and read to me from it. Next it was the turn of Pythagoras. Pythagoras believed in something called the Orphic doctrine, and Mr Morris explained this to me. I'm afraid I didn't listen quite so eagerly any more, though I would have benefited so much from it. A voice inside me was whispering – "He likes you. He needs you. He wants you. He is desperately controlling himself, that's why he's hiding behind Pythagoras and Chinese philosophers again. Go on, tell him how much he means to you, tell him – now!" But I too was controlling myself. I wanted to say to him: "Age does not matter. Believe me. . ." Believe what? I could not express what I felt.

He did not touch me once. But now come the words which will stay with me long after I've forgotten what he told me concerning great men and their thoughts. He had just helped me into my coat and I turned towards the door to go.

"I'd like to say one more thing before you go," he said.

"What is it?" There was a tiny pause.

"It's something of what I'd like to say to you if I were twenty-five."

"What?"

"You have the most wonderful eyes."

And then very quickly, he opened the door for me, told me to let him see what I next wrote, took my hand, said goodbye, and vanished into his room. I don't even know if he heard my reply, accompanied by an embarrassed laugh, "Oh, what a pity you aren't twenty-five then!"

My first novel may not be publishable but it has brought me luck; without it I would not have met Mr Morris and tasted a little bit of paradise.

It is 1.15 in the morning! I'm not tired, but I shall be tomorrow. I'm lying in bed looking at my eyes in a mirror. Are they really wonderful? I don't think they are; I think my hair is nicer. In my imagination I have slept with Mr Morris, I have been his wife and borne him children but I never imagined him saying: "You have the most wonderful eyes." One day, when he is married to a distinguished and intelligent woman, perhaps he will remember the insignificant girl with the lovely eyes. And I, I shall remember him as someone like no one else I've ever known, someone who cast a spell on me. I shall get over him but I shall never forget him, as I got over but have not forgotten my feelings for Otto Seifert (about whom I told Mr Morris!), Roy or Eric.

I don't expect to see him again very soon. With this sad thought I must say good night and try to sleep. Do you think Mr Morris is asleep yet?

24th November 1945

Today I'm on holiday. I've left the Central Library. Not so long ago I was exuberant because I was given a job there – today I'm exuberant because I've left. How could I have foreseen that I would not be credited with an ounce of intelligence, treated with less respect than I ever was at school, and be at the mercy of someone like Miss Campbell? I was not given a leaving present as is usually the custom. I don't know why. I was on good terms with the staff and had friends among them. Maybe the custom of present-giving does not extend to unimportant Juniors who've only been employed for a year. I am my mother all over. That's the sort of thing that would worry her.

She didn't understand the world. The thing she probably understood least of all is why the Nazis came and took her away. Neither she nor I will ever make sense of the evil streak in human nature.

I'm starting my new job at Wolsey Hall Correspondence College on Monday and I'm very nervous. Once bitten twice shy. Will things be the same as in the Library? When my life goes wrong, is it I who am to blame? One can change one's job but not one's nature.

Putz and I are going to a Pouishnoff (can't spell it) piano recital at the Town Hall today, to hear him play Chopin. Afterwards we shall have tea at the Cadena. In the evening we're invited for supper at Aunt Else's.

1st December 1945

One week of my new job is over. It's much better than at the Library. I have my own little office and am in charge of the library, which houses textbooks on every subject for students taking courses here. Putz works in the next room, which is the secretaries'. The atmosphere is much more relaxed than it was at the Library and my boss, Mr Herbert, is a kindly old gentleman mainly interested in betting on horses. Best of all I don't have to work on Saturday afternoons.

This evening I went to Brett's dance again with Maureen. We hadn't been for ages. It wasn't very exciting. Nor was the evening at the Playhouse with Harold last Wednesday. We talked for ages outside my gate when he took me home. I was afraid he might kiss me but luckily he didn't. I think his mind was still too much on John Gabriel Borkman, who sacrificed life and love for his dreams.

Putz and I heard a wonderful performance of the *Messiah* in the Town Hall last Sunday afternoon. In the evening we played ping-pong at the hostel as usual, and then Otto took me home. He was quite flirtatious! Needless to say, I didn't encourage him.

10th December 1945

Prue called and invited me to her birthday party. My father is in Oxford for the weekend. He came on Friday and he is leaving on Monday. When he is here we live in style; he is staying at the Randolph Hotel, the most expensive hotel in Oxford, and we have our meals there, with waiters dancing around us, and go home by taxi, courtesy of my father. Bruno and Erna were invited too last night, and went home in a taxi ordered by my father, instead of their usual mode of transport – bicycles.

Yesterday afternoon the three of us had tea at the Rieszs'. Peter had two of his friends there – George Bell and Bill Emerson – and we young ones all went upstairs to Peter's bedroom while the older generation sat in the sitting room. It was great fun. George asked for my address as he wants to read my novel! Robin has joined the army but he doesn't like it. I didn't think he would.

14th December 1945

I once considered Otto's feelings because I didn't think it fair to ignore someone who was kind and paid me attention in order to run after someone who was quite indifferent to me.

Otto, without a word of warning, has now switched over to Lieselotte and takes her out! She doesn't care for him any more than I do. She says he smells of onions.

I've come to the sad conclusion that no mortal being on this earth deserves the slightest consideration. Humanity is the enemy of humanity.

I still go out regularly with Harold. We have meals at the Ritz, go to the cinema or theatre or play chess in my room. Sometimes Harold's friend, the organist Mr Cuthbert, gives us a lift home in his car. I told Joan that my friendship with Harold is platonic, but she said it may be from my point of view but almost certainly isn't from his.

Putz wants to move. She thinks she has found another room and hopes to move in after Christmas which we are spending in Cobham with Uncle Felix and Anni. I'm very much looking forward to it.

-- December 1945

'Dear Mr Morris,' I should like to write, 'Please forgive me for writing to tell you that I find life without seeing you quite unbearable. I'm not too shy to tell you this because the longing to do so is stronger than any feeling of modesty. The influence you have over me is so enormous, both spiritual and physical, that I don't mind how much you know about me. I am willing to submit to you in any way you wish, in any way you might need me. I don't know what you have done to me to render me so weak and submissive. I feel that every bit of me belongs to you, especially my eyes.

'Why did you talk to me the way you did, why did you invite me to your room? Did you really mean to say all the things you said to me, did you mean them at all? And my novel – were you really interested in it? You seemed to forget about it, and you made me forget it, too. I had staked my life on it, and you made me forget it while I was with you! I often dream of you and, as in reality, I can never reach or understand you but blindly believe in you.

'The last time I was with you, that Tuesday evening, when you talked to me as man to woman, I wanted you to say: "Be my mistress!" Why didn't you?

'When you asked me about other men, didn't you know that at that moment there was only you for me, far yet near, real yet unreal? Oh, the things I should like to have said to you! But all the time I knew you were only playing with me, that you and I lived in different worlds. Did nothing I say betray what you mean to me?

'I want you to know that there is a person in this world, just a silly girl to you but one day a woman, who is completely yours, whom you have completely bewitched, in whose mind you stand out as a human being nearer to God than anyone else.

'Thank you for everything. Thank you for your words, your look into my eyes, the new life you gave me. Thank you for your help and advice, for being interested in me, for exciting me, for taking me out of myself and showing me a far better, greater and wiser being – you.

'With all my love – yes, all of it,

'your slave,

'Ingrid.'

Of course he will never read this letter, because I won't send it.

21st December 1945

Last week was taken up with giving and getting Christmas presents: Erna, Harold, Prue, the Rieszs, Maureen, Joan. From Wolsey Hall everyone received an extra 10/- in their wage packet. On Sunday I went to a Christmas Carol Service at the Town Hall with Putz and Maureen. I've also taken two more exams – Typing Intermediate and Shorthand Speed.

Tomorrow Putz and I are going to Cobham in Surrey by train,

to spend Christmas with Uncle Felix and Anni (who is his second wife). No more work till Thursday 27th December.

WAR ORGANISATION
of the
BRITISH RED CROSS SOCIETY and ORDER OF ST. JOHN OF JERUSALEM

FOREIGN RELATIONS DEPARTMENT
Chairman:
MAJ.-GENERAL SIR JOHN KENNEDY, K.B.E., C.B., C.M.G., D.S.O.

Director:
MISS S. J. WARNER, O.B.E.

TELEPHONE NO.:
REGENT 0211

Allied Prisoners of War Packing Centre
Head of Packing Centre:
MRS. GRAZEBROOK
Gift Parcels Service:
MRS. GRANT.

WIMBORNE HOUSE,
22, ARLINGTON STREET,
LONDON, S.W.1

85, EATON SQUARE, LONDON, S.W.1
(TELEPHONE NO.: SLOANE 8235)

27.12.45.

When replying please   EBP/ONA.
quote reference:—

Miss I.
47. Lonsdale Rd.
Oxford.

Dear Madam,

　　　　　Your enquiry for news of your Mother was passed to this office by the United Nations Relief & Rehabilitation Administration office. We must apologise for the delay in answering this, due to extreme pressure of work in this department.

　　　　　We note from our file that we sent an enquiry to your Mother's address in Vienna in July last. This enquiry was sent to us by your Sister we think ? We hope that perhaps your Mother will by now have returned to her former address, and that you may still receive a reply to this enquiry.

　　　　　With regards to enquiries for people in Polish territory, we regret that we cannot try to trace your Mother, unless we have some indication as to her whereabouts in that country. If you know the name of the camp which she was reported to be in, we will of course do our best to try and trace her for you.

　　　　　We sincerely hope that perhaps by now you have received some reassuring news of your Mother, but if there is anything further we can do to help you, we will be glad to do it. In any case we beg to assure you that we have your Mothers particulars on our files, and that should be receive any news, we will at once inform you.

　　　　　Yours faithfully,

Muriel Monkhouse.
Muriel Monkhouse.
ONA Section.

28th December 1945

I didn't have a moment to write over Christmas. It was hectic as usual. Ann's Cottage in Cobham was full of visitors and there was a huge Christmas tree in the drawing room around which everyone placed their presents. On Sunday Putz and I went to London, had coffee at the Quality Inn and then spent the day at Elgin Avenue. My father gave a party. All his posh English friends and business acquaintants were there. I shan't describe what he looked like doing the *Lambeth Walk* and the hokey-cokey. Quite ridiculous. I didn't join in, and was glad when the dancing was over. Back in Cobham on Christmas Eve – which is much more relaxing than Elgin Avenue – we slept late, and awoke to pouring rain. How much nicer snow would have been! My father came for the day. In the afternoon we went to the flicks in the village with two of the visitors – Elsa Neustadtl and Trude Dawson. In the evening Trude, who's a cousin of Anni's and a glamorous divorced woman, took me to the village pub for a drink. We met a Canadian army officer there who treated us to a glass of sherry. On the way back I asked Trude why she had no children (she's about 40).

"Because I don't think children should be put into this world," she replied. She has a point.

On Christmas Day the Urbachs rang. Unfortunately we are not able to meet this time. My father spent the day in Cobham again. We didn't do much, except go for a walk in the afternoon. The following day, Boxing Day, Putz and I again went to London, this time in order to meet our cousin Herta and her fiancé Gordon at the Cumberland Hotel. My father was there too. We had coffee. I envied Herta her tall good-looking fiancé, who's a naval officer. After a walk, we had lunch and tea at Elgin Avenue and then Putz and I returned to Oxford by train and took a taxi from the station back to our respective digs. Back to work again on the 27th. I now have my little office all to myself as the girl who was teaching me has left, and it is considered that I can cope with the library on my own. When I don't have much to do I go in there and look at the books. I mean to read one book on every subject except mathematics and theology.

Joan came to supper and told me her big news – she's expecting a second baby.

31st December 1945

Last Saturday afternoon I spent at Joan's helping with Peter's Christmas party. There were about a dozen noisy lively children bouncing around. Dr Beschorner was not at home this weekend and Joan was glad of my help. I was quite surprised how much I enjoyed organising the children's games, and all went without a hitch.

Yesterday, Sunday, Otto telephoned in the morning. He has a nerve! Putz and I had tea at the Rieszs' in the afternoon. Susie's fiancé Charlie was there too. Mrs Riesz told me that George Bell was very taken with me!

I have been given an assistant at work. She's going to help me at busy times when books come in from the publishers. How about that, Miss Campbell?

It being New Year's night tonight, Putz and I celebrated with Otto and Harold; we had drinks at the Randolph hotel, danced on Carfax among crowds of people and finished off having supper at a bar until midnight. Harold took me home in a taxi and kissed me goodnight! Or rather he pecked at me like a bird at an apple, and it was about as thrilling. What a way to end the last entry for 1945! No, I won't end it like this, I'll tell you all the things I want next year and then I'll go to sleep with something else to dream about than Harold's kiss. Here they are:

A film revue book

A manicure set

A camera

A three quarter length coat

High heeled shoes

A cigarette case

A petticoat

Pearls

The author's *Who's Who?*

I'll have to start saving coupons. Happy New Year.

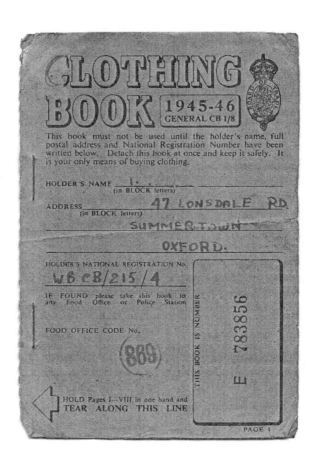

6th January 1946

Connie is in love with Alan Tothill! He doesn't know it, of course. Like me, Connie only falls in love with people who don't love her back.

My first outing of the New Year was, as usual, with Harold. On Thursday he took me to lunch and tea at the Ritz and in the evening to a Spiritualist meeting in St Michael's Street. It was great fun, although I'm sure that is not what we were meant to think. How anyone can believe in this sort of thing is beyond me. It was sad when a mentally very backward girl was placed on a chair in the centre of the room and the Spiritualist laid her hands on her head and said the girl would be made well. The parents believed it, because they wanted to, I suppose.

When I went out with Joan on Saturday afternoon, after having been shopping and to the hairdressers, we talked about the child she's expecting, which she's pleased about, and so is Peter. It feels strange having a pregnant friend. We had tea at the Cadena and afterwards went to the cinema.

Today, Sunday, I had tea and supper at Sandy's in Witney. We went for a walk with her friend Jane, and in the evening played board games with her parents. I'm really sorry for Sandy still working in the library under the evil eye of Miss Campbell. Tomorrow evening I'm going to the Playhouse with Harold.

I've heard nothing from Mr Morris although I sent him a Christmas card. I seem destined to find disappointment even in the sun itself – for he was my sun. I must see him again. One day I *must* hear him talk to me again and feel his leg against mine on the sofa. I am determined to be alone with him one more hour of my life, anywhere, in any circumstances, I want to be drunk one more time with his words. I suppose the only way to achieve it is to send him another story. Then I'll be able to say I write for my living!

8th January 1946

I once thought that, to have a boyfriend, someone to go out with regularly, someone who gives you presents and kisses, is a definite step to happiness, if not happiness itself. Well, I was wrong. Harold is no fun. I've had enough of him – and yet I don't want him to go out with anyone else! Such is my jealous nature! Did you know I was such a dog in the manger? I'm bored and fed up with him, and even his compliments mean nothing to me. He has never for one minute thrilled me, and when he kissed me on New Year's night it was about as exciting as a rainy day. I don't know why this should be. There's nothing wrong with the fellow, he's nice-looking and intelligent (and quite conceited with it), he takes me wherever I want to go, he holds my hand and puts his arm around me and acts protectively, but nothing he does makes me happy, and when I'm with him I just want to go home, to be alone in my bed-sitting room and sit on my bed and cry and ask God (if there is one) why he won't let me love Harold, or anyone. It's terrible not to be loved, but far more terrible not to love.

There's nothing more to be said about Harold. I'm always nice to him and he has nothing to reproach me with, except that I now make as few dates as possible with him.

I continue to wait for someone to whom I can give my whole heart in exchange for his.

19th January 1946

I woke up to SNOW! Lovely! Yesterday I started writing a new story – and stayed up till 1.15am writing it! Lovely! I always feel happy when it's snowing, and when I'm writing.

In spite of what I've been saying about Harold I was out twice with him this week. On Sunday we went by bus to Blenheim Palace in Woodstock and walked in the grounds and had tea at the Bear Hotel afterwards; and on Thursday I skipped shorthand and went out to supper with him at the Town and Gown and then to another Spiritualist meeting in New Hall Street, just for a laugh. Afterwards we had drinks at the Randolph Hotel. I've passed my Intermediate typing exam – 1st class again.

Last night Putz and I entertained Mr and Mrs Riesz and Peter for supper and drinks in my room and it was good fun. They were here till 9.30pm. My room, normally quite spacious, seemed very small with so many people in it. Tomorrow, Sunday, we are going to their house again. This evening Sandy was here for supper and regaled me with library news, mostly of a miserable kind.

I've also seen Joan twice this week, once for supper at her house and once when we went to the flicks together. She says that her days would be very boring if she did not see me regularly to brighten them.

But the biggest thing that happened this week is I had news of the Lambergs! Terrible news. Both Britta and her parents were sent to the concentration camp Theresienstadt, where her parents were gassed but she survived – just. She is now in Pilsen and hopes to come to England. My mother was not at the camp.

25th January 1946

I think I may have succeeded in getting rid of Harold, and feel wonderfully free. I've been a bit cool towards him of late, and last time he wanted to fix our next date I said I would telephone him at the shop to confirm our usual Wednesday arrangement – but I didn't. Wasn't that reckless of me? It was an opportunity not to be missed. I don't think I've ever done anything like it before, but many people have done it to me. Ever since I've known Harold he has been as persistent and pestering as a monkey. I wonder what will happen next?

We've had a LETTER FROM THE ENGLS IN VIENNA! Now that communication with European countries is possible again old acquaintances are giving signs of life, and it is like being woken up from a dream. Mrs Engl was not Jewish and therefore could stay in Vienna. She was a great friend of my mother, and looked after some of our valuables, which otherwise we would have had to hand in. Her daughter Hedi was a schoolfriend of Lieselotte and a 'Mischling' – only half Jewish. Unfortunately the Engls know nothing about my mother and grandmother except that, one day, they were taken away. Always the same story.

Tomorrow I'm going for an interview at Rothesay School, a private school in North Oxford who advertised for a week's help with accounts for two hours in the evening. The extra money would be useful. I typed my story after work and sent it to Mr Morris.

On Thursday Putz and I again skipped shorthand. When we skipped once before Miss Hall said to us the following week: "Where were you last week?"

"My sister wasn't well and I stayed with her," Putz lied coolly.

"The next time your sister isn't well," said Miss Hall icily, "you come on your own."

We'll have to think of a better excuse this time. It won't be the truth – that we wanted to go to a dance. But we changed our minds in the end.

31st January 1946

I got the job at Rothesay School and so, every evening this week, I went there straight after Wolsey Hall and sat with the matronly headmistress in her room doing accounts, sometimes till 8.30pm. I finished today and she paid me £1, with which I was very pleased.

Aunt Else is planning to move to London. Putz and I had

supper with her in her room on Tuesday. I shall miss her nice Viennese suppers. Erna was there too. I sent my novel to George Bell to read, as he apparently said to Peter Riesz that he'd like to read it. Peter told me this when I met him on the way to work the other morning and we cycled along the Banbury Road together.

Harold called while I was out! There's no escaping Harold. Mrs Labowsky said: "Your nice young man came to see you." I wish I could have been more pleased.

On Sunday the 29th I FLIRTED WITH ERIC at the hostel. It happened like this: Maureen and Putz had been to tea in my room, and after Maureen left Putz and I decided to go to the hostel and play ping-pong on the spur of the moment.

The usual crowd was there – Otto, Gus, Eric and a few others. For some reason I felt very 'high'. That is, I said and did whatever entered my head, without inhibitions. I thought: Why can't I always be like this? I felt light as a feather. I was the master of my fate, the captain of my soul – just for that night.

Two people were playing singles, and Eric happened to be sitting next to me, watching the game. He's a very moody chap and for the last few weeks hasn't spoken more than three words to me, so I took little notice of him and was prepared for silence. However, it seemed to be his night, or perhaps he had caught my mood, and he began chatting me up and all at once we were laughing and joking together. I had not seen him like that for a long time. I had never talked to him like that before. I was wearing my fur gloves because it was cold and he said: "Ah, now I can hold your hand."

"Good," I replied, and stroked his face with my fur hand (utterly at ease), "I wear these in bed when it's cold," I said.

"Can't you find anything better to take to bed with you?" he said.

"I haven't tried," I said. Laughter. Next thing – Eric got hold of my key.

"Now I must see you home," he said.

"So that's how you do it!"

"Yes, and now come closer, I'm cold." Someone sitting on the other side of him pushed him and he pretended to fall off his chair – and fell into my lap. "Ah, this is lovely," he said, "now I'm getting warm. Do you mind if I stay?" I laughed and pushed him back onto his chair. Otto was sitting on the other side of me and witnessed the scene.

"You *are* a flirt," he said. But I was too 'drunk' to care.

2nd February 1946

Yesterday was black Friday. First, I met George Bell in the Town Hall at lunchtime *and he did not say one word about my novel.* But much worse was to come. I went to see Mrs Hall after work to tell her that my sister and I would not be coming to shorthand classes any more, since we had completed the basic course. At first she looked at me and didn't say anything. We were both standing up. If looks could kill I would have dropped dead. Her face was stony, her lips thinner than ever.

"I see," she said. "When I tell you that you have failed your shorthand exam, you may like to rethink your decision."

I said nothing.

"And so has your sister," she added.

I still said nothing.

"You have both missed several classes, haven't you?"

"Only one or two," I said.

"Only one or two," she echoed, with a particularly nasty look on her face. "I believe you are Austrians?" she continued, in a tone which implied 'so what can be expected of you?'

"Yes," I said.

The interview was over. I left the room feeling terrible. I didn't believe her about the exam results and mean to write to Pitmans to find out. I immediately went to Putz's digs – I felt too miserable to return to my own and be alone – and told her what had taken place. She said Mrs Hall had behaved disgracefully. A lot of girls are leaving her secretarial college and she doesn't like it, Putz said. She made a cup of tea which always calms her but has no effect on me, and then we went to the Rieszs' and I repeated the incident to them. We stayed for supper. Mrs Riesz said not to return to the college was a wise decision.

Back in Lonsdale Road, Prue telephoned, and we arranged to go to the pictures tonight, which we did, and spent a pleasant evening together. I'd bought some new shoes in the afternoon, feeling rich because of the extra money I earned at Rothesay School, and I wore them to the cinema. To hell with Mrs Hall.

One more incident I have to relate concerns a girl called June

111

Rodway who works at Wolsey Hall. She's very pretty, lively and naughty. She does as little work as she can and has a cheeky manner towards her superiors but manages to get away with most things. She had once said to Putz about me, not knowing I was her sister: "That girl fascinates me." So I've always had a soft spot for her, conceited as I am, but I also admire her for her carefree attitude and devil-may-care courage. Once, when we were all given a rise of half a crown and were disgusted with the smallness of the amount, June went to Mr Herbert and said: "I think this half a crown got into my wage packet by mistake. Do you want it back?" Only Mr Herbert's good nature saved her from anything more than a reprimand. The other two bosses, Mr Knipe and Mr Newell, would not have been so lenient. And so it turned out when June committed her final misdeed. She had given a week's notice, having found a better job, and before leaving decided to have her revenge on a woman in her office superior to her whom she has always hated. When this woman was due to come out of her room at teatime, June lay in wait at the top of the stairs, rope in hand. This rope had a noose at the end of it. As soon as the door opened, June would let the rope down the stairwell and the woman's head would be caught in the noose. And it very nearly was. June was instantly dismissed, without her week's wages, and the bottle party we had arranged for her as a farewell do took place without her! It was a sober affair though, as everyone was still stunned by what June had done, and I for one didn't know whether to be full of admiration or disapproval for her. Wolsey Hall won't be the same without her, that's for sure.

3rd February 1946

Harold has just called again and everything seems to be back to normal. We made a date for Thursday – tea at the Ritz and afterwards the Playhouse. I really think he's far too conceited to have the slightest notion that I might not care for him.

Otto telephoned in the evening, while Putz was here. He seems to think Putz and I are interchangeable. Well, let him.

5th February 1946

Yesterday I MET MR MORRIS. He came running over to me,

calling my name. He said he had been ill. I was so overcome at seeing him I was struck dumb. I am going to his room on Friday. It was as much as I could do to say, "yes" to his invitation. By the time we parted I was shaking all over.

It was too cold to cycle to work yesterday morning. Harold must have been of the same opinion, for I met him in the bus queue (his digs are not far from mine). I wasn't particularly pleased to see him – until a van stopped and gave us both a lift; the driver was an acquaintance of Harold. After work I played ping-pong at the hostel. Unfortunately Eric wasn't there.

Today I went to the flicks with Joan and afterwards had supper at No. 66 with her. As the weather had improved I had my bicycle with me again. Cycling home at night I was stopped by a nice policeman who told me I had no rear lights. I could have been fined for that.

I made a few extra shillings this week by selling some old clothes to a second-hand shop. The elderly lady owner knows me now; as soon as she sees me she says: "What have you got for me today?" And when I show her what I have she always says: "Oh, I've been asked for one of these," and promptly buys it.

6th February 1946

Now that one can write to Vienna again, I wrote to the caretakers of our house in the Wipplingerstrasse, the Gattingers, a little while ago, asking them to tell me what if anything they know about our mother and grandmother. Today a letter from Mrs Gattinger arrived. It was a long letter – in German, of course – full of praise for our family, and saying what terrible times we have all been through, and how much they suffered too, and she was still waiting for her son to return from the war – but she was very sorry, she had no idea of the whereabouts of my mother and grandmother; all she knew was that one day they were taken away. Did she betray them? Reading her friendly letter it seems impossible, but in 1938-9 we knew them to be Nazis.

On very rare occasions one meets a person who is different. This person, to whom one feels mysteriously drawn without even knowing them, whom one wishes to touch for no apparent reason, can be any age, sex or nationality. Such a one is Mrs Labowsky's grown-up daughter, aged about 40, who is here on holiday. As soon as I was introduced to her I knew that she possessed some indefinable quality that few people have. Above all, she was so *kind* to me. You can't imagine what it means to me when people are genuinely kind to me. If I had had half an hour alone with her I would have told her my innermost secrets. On the whole I like people immediately or never.

Only two more days and I shall be sitting with Mr Morris in his room again. Endless fantasies will be replaced by reality. I am madly happy that fate has thrown us together again.

No, I don't love him. I don't love him.

8th February 1946

On this day several things happened ranging from the trifling to the momentous: it was confirmed that I failed my shorthand exam; I had lunch with Putz and her friend Edna Mansell from work; I met Harold on the bus on my way to Mr Morris and told him I was going to visit friends; I met Putz and Otto on my way home from Mr Morris but took hardly any notice of them; and I found my bedroom door lock stuck when I returned to my room, and a locksmith had to be called to let me in. All of these things, however, are of no significance when compared with what took place in Mr Morris's room . . .

For tonight he told me that I had infatuated him from the first; he took me in his arms and kissed me, he held my hand and stroked my hair and asked me if I was afraid of being seduced by him. I laughed and said no. When he put his hand down the front of my dress – my best dress, the maroon one with the white stripes and a V-neck, just wide enough for Mr Morris's hand – I froze. I didn't move. He asked me why I didn't surrender to him. He spoke very quietly. "What do you want me to do?" I whispered. When I felt his teeth cutting my lips I put my hands on his chest and pushed him away. He said trying to conquer me was no joke. I was a hard log to pull. I suddenly realised that I was resisting him. I shivered.

"Are you cold?" he asked.

I shook my head.

"Do you think I want your body?" he said.

I shook my head again. "No," I said. "You don't mean any of this. You're just having fun." I was horrified to hear that my voice was trembling.

He called my name and pulled me into his arms. He said: "Look at me. Look into my eyes. Do you think I'd do all this if I wasn't enormously fond of you? If you didn't wildly attract me?"

"I don't know," I said. And then I suddenly told him how I'd often imagined sleeping with him. He seemed to revel in this. He held my hand tightly and said:

"I'm glad, very glad, because I've pictured myself having sexual relations with you too, over and over again." He looked at me, "So?" he said.

"So nothing," I said.

"But we've both dreamt of it, Ingrid," he said. "And now we have each other . . . I'd make you so happy . . . I promise you."

I shook my head. I was still shivering. "No," I said, "it's out of the question. We don't belong to each other's world."

"But you don't know me!" he cried. "Get to know me. Wait a little, if you like, but let me make you happy – please, please . . ."

"I'll wait," I said, "but please leave me alone tonight."

"Of course." He became very gentle. He admired my hands, my eyes (again!), my hair, my frock. He said he wanted me more than he had ever wanted anyone or anything, but he would never touch me unless I wished it. I smiled at him, because I could not be kind to him in any other way. Over and over I thought to myself – this is true. It is really happening, not just in my unsatisfactory imagination. But I wasn't happy, and he knew it. He said he thought I was frightened. Was I? I didn't admit to it, anyway. I told him about Richard Tauber and he said he hoped I had a better idea of *him* – Morris. During one of my many moments of tension I asked myself desperately why real life is always disappointing, why love-making is only fun in my dreams, why I shrink away from it when I'm face to face with it. I hated myself. I felt a child, but I know he saw me as a grown woman. A frightened one, frightened of being seduced by him, as he kept telling me, but still a woman. But I'm glad I told him I knew he was only playing with me.

And then suddenly I found myself promising to tell him next time whether I would be his mistress . . .

Darling diary, if I haven't told you everything it's because my mind is still in confusion, but I swear to you that I have imagined nothing, that it all happened as I told it to you. Our physical

115

attraction was mutual and yet, when I stood on the brink, I turned back. And so I still have my precious virginity.

But I don't know for how much longer.

10th February 1946

Sunday morning. The doorbell rings. I hear Mrs Labowsky go to open the front door. I hear a familiar voice. I go out into the hall.

"Hello, Nanks!"

"Hello, Audrey!"

I'm pleased to see her, but what a long time ago it was since that name sent me into raptures, and how much has happened since, that stands between us now like a brick wall. During our conversation I told her how much I used to like her when we were at school, which pleased her. She is going home to Falmouth for a holiday next week, and taking lots of messages from me to various people.

In the afternoon Maureen came to tea and in the evening I played ping-pong at the Linton Road hostel. Ossy saw me home. Maureen is going for an interview at Wolsey Hall on Monday; she has applied for a job as a secretary there. I hope she gets it. I often spend my dinner hour in the Wolsey Hall library, dipping into books on various subjects I wish to acquaint myself with.

Prue is coming to supper tomorrow, on Tuesday I'm spending the evening at Joan's and on Wednesday I'm going to the flicks with Sandy. A full week ahead, culminating in another visit to Mr Morris's study on Friday evening.

I cannot stop thinking about last Friday night. I keep asking myself – shall I become his mistress? Or shall I not? I certainly thought I wanted it. I could have had my wish granted, but I ran away from it. How decent he was, and how gentlemanly. I don't know if his intention is to fight until he gets me or to give me up as a bad job. Anyway, he has made me feel very guilty. I have no idea what is going to happen next Friday evening, I only know that I must go to him. I'm afraid, but I must go. But he shall not touch me if I don't want it. I shall be nobody's mistress if it means being afraid.

Friday, 15th February 1946

He has asked me to marry him . . .

It is almost midnight. Far too late to relive my experience on paper. Better go to sleep. Sleep? There's nothing I feel like doing less. I'm wide awake. His voice is still inside my head, his kisses still hot on my lips. How could I sleep?

Mr Morris made love to me solidly from 7.30 till after 9pm. Sometimes I submitted, mostly I didn't. Occasionally I enjoyed feeling his body against my own on the sofa (yes, I'm still a virgin), at other times I wanted to go home, or anywhere away from him.

And all the time, over and over again, I heard his voice telling me how much he wanted me, physically and spiritually, that he could make me happy.

"But it would be such brief enjoyment," I said, "and afterwards we might never want to see each other again."

He laughed, and pulled me into his arms and passionately implored me to trust him, to believe him, to submit, to relax, return his kisses, above all not to be afraid of him. Possessed by the devil, I said:

"But why me? There must be many women who would readily submit to you."

"I want *you!*" he cried. "I want *you!* Don't you understand? Do you think I couldn't have a different woman every night if I wanted to? But I don't. I want *you . . .*"

I suppose I've been disappointed so often by life and people that I felt I must not be deceived, and so I would not let myself believe him. Perhaps he meant what he said, but I was sure in the end we would both be very miserable, and I should reproach myself for having been fooled again. As I lay in his arms, and he whispered that he would be very gentle and that his one wish was to make me happy, and his hand gently stroked my hair as he spoke, the strangest thoughts flashed through my mind. And then, suddenly, I heard him say: "If I asked you to marry me would you accept?" Of course I know he didn't mean it. I was therefore able to reply quite coolly:

"Do you really believe I could make you happy forever? That you could spend the rest of your life with me? I don't think you know what you are saying." A strange reply to a proposal, but it

117

was a strange proposal, as everything has been strange about my relationship with Mr Morris ever since I first met him. He put his hands in his hair in a kind of hopeless gesture, then made love to me more violently than ever to convince me of the sincerity of his emotions.

"Well, I didn't think you would," he murmured.

"I did feel awfully attracted to you, right from the start," I confided.

"Oh, God!" he whispered. "Oh God, thank you for that, Ingrid. Thank you. That makes me very happy. Bless you for that." And then he lay back motionless, his cheek next to mine, and I nearly went to sleep. Until he put his eternal question again. I said:

"No."

"Why not?"

"I don't want to."

Strange, isn't it? A few weeks ago he was the great, unattainable lover I longed for, and physical contact with him seemed one glorious dream. But being a dream, it was of course doomed to perish, if not by non-fulfilment then by fulfilment.

"Will you come again next week?" he asked me, and he looked tired and sad.

"If you really want me to come," I said, "will you write and tell me so?" And so we parted. And I don't know whether to feel happy or wretched, now that I'm alone in my room again going over everything that happened tonight.

18th February 1946

I had to return to my room from work this morning because my period came on unexpectedly and I was unprepared. There was a letter from my father waiting. He has found out that my mother and grandmother were sent to Minsk. I had never heard of Minsk and didn't know where it was, but I felt a glimmer of hope. I telephoned my father in the evening.

"Couldn't we go to Minsk," I said, "and try to find them?"

"Don't be silly," came the reply, "it's almost certain that they never reached there. Have you any idea what such a journey would have been like? Days and days in a cattle truck, herded together in terrible conditions, without food or drink? They certainly didn't survive it." How coldly he said it. My heart sank.

So I must believe that my mother is dead, and I must continue to live forever without her. Long ago in Vienna I saw a Shirley Temple film in which she hears the news that her beloved father has been killed in the Civil War; she refuses to believe it and goes to find him and does. Perhaps I too would find my mother against all the odds? But how can I go to Minsk?

I was glad to spend the afternoon and evening at Joan's today and have my mind taken off my mother's fate. Peter had some friends for tea and I played with the children. When I was alone with Joan after Peter had been put to bed she told me that she always looks forward all day to my visit.

There was an interesting girl called Ellie Horowitz at the hostel on Sunday. She was quite a good ping-pong player, too. Ossy saw me home. Tomorrow Putz and I are having a farewell supper at Aunt Else's; she's going to London for good next week.

I continue to go out with Harold once or twice a week – tea at the Ritz and afterwards the cinema or theatre and perhaps supper. Why? Quite simply because I haven't the guts to say no.

23rd February 1946

I've been working overtime this week – till 7.15pm. Several batches of books have arrived together and they need to go out to the students as soon as possible. Mr Newell, one of the bosses, helped me.

Putz has been to a dance with Edna and her fiancé, Arthur. She told me all about it when we had lunch together at Northgates today. As was to be expected, there was nobody of any interest there. Putz's standards are high, and she can be quite snobbish about people she considers her inferiors. In Vienna she was sometimes nicknamed 'the Baroness' by her friends.

I haven't heard from Mr Morris. I'm glad. It's finished and over and done with. I conquered him but could not conquer myself. He wouldn't remain a divine vision, which I could handle, I couldn't cope with him in the flesh. If ever I do hear from him again I won't go, I won't see him.

I keep picturing my mother on the journey to Minsk but as soon as the picture appears it becomes a blur.

3rd March 1946

For the rest of my life I shall carry with me the memory of having gone to a dance without once being asked to dance! Lieselotte had finally persuaded me to go to the Assembly Room with her last night but we had such a rotten time and there was such a ghastly crowd there that we only stayed about one and a half hours. Do such things happen to other girls? Actually, one weedy fellow did come up to us but we didn't accept him. But why should I care? When a man like Mr Morris has asked me to be his wife, I can't be entirely hopeless, can I? We left early and had a meal at Lyons, which always smells of stale cooking fat, and tried to cheer each other up, and laughed miserably at each other's jokes.

Today we went to a concert at the Town Hall – and who should sit behind us but a girl who was in Lieselotte's form at the Falmouth County High School, Ailsa Clark. What a lot of people from Falmouth end up in Oxford! Ailsa and Lieselotte made an arrangement to meet again.

Mrs Hall was furious when she found out that I wrote to Pitmans querying my exam result. I had also complained about her comment, "You're Austrians, aren't you?" She wrote me a letter saying it would be best if neither I nor my sister attended her college again (which we weren't going to anyway), and adding: "I am equally interested in the welfare of all my students, regardless of their nationality." So she says.

A nurse called Philips, a friend of Putz's from London, is visiting her next weekend.

9th March 1946

I need not tell you what day it is today. I had several presents and cards and went to the Playhouse with Putz and Philips. Yesterday I had my 'birthday outing' with Joan – tea at a café and then the pictures, and next week Sandy is treating me to the theatre. Robin sent a telegram. He always remembers, even now that he's in the army. Two days ago we had a letter from the Schüttes in Vienna. Although non-Jewish they had been good friends of ours up to the time of the Anschluss. I had written to ask for information on events in Vienna after we left. It was the same story – hardship,

120

missing relatives not returned from the war, and Jews disappeared without trace. They were happy to hear from us, they said, and remember so well the two lovely Jacoby girls who played with their daughters when we were neighbours in the Hinzerstrasse.

But no one can, or wants to, supply the missing jigsaw pieces.

12th March 1946

I stayed home from work one afternoon last week with a bad cold – unusual for me. On Sunday Prue called with my birthday present and on Friday we're going to the pictures together. Yesterday Putz went to London for the day for a job interview. I think she's still hankering after London and finds Oxford very provincial – but I hope she doesn't get the job. I went to meet her at the station in the evening – and missed her. She caught a later train. Today we went to a sex lecture after work, which was very disappointing, as we might have guessed it would be. Edna Mansell, who has just moved to digs in the same house as Putz's, told us about it but didn't go herself. Being engaged, I suppose she considers she will soon know all there is to know. Judging from the way she flattens her bosom in a tight vest instead of wearing a brassiere she probably wants to know as little as possible.

After my experience with Mr Morris my life seems very monotonous and dull. Because of that I have nothing more to say to you now except good night.

18th March 1946

Audrey came to tea yesterday and we had a very interesting conversation. I accompanied her to the bus stop when it was time for her to go, and we continued our conversation on the way. Walking home, I allowed myself to think with a little more conviction that her decision to come to Oxford was just a bit influenced by my being here.

George Bell has at last returned my novel. There was not a word with it. I shall never speak to him again.

This morning I went to work on the bus – and sat next to Eric! Out of all the men I know or associate with at the moment, he is still the only one who can excite me, whose voice can make me

f

blush, whose smile intoxicates me. And do you know why? Because he won't submit to me! That holds a queer fascination for me.

When I called at the Rieszs' the other evening only Peter was at home. We had an intellectual discussion until 10pm. He told me, among other less intellectual things, that women don't like the idea of sleeping with him. I'm not surprised! Silly, sexless, immature little boy. Anyway, who'd want to sleep with a *ginger-haired* boy?

I sent a question to the BBC Brainstrust. The programme is coming to the Town Hall on Wednesday evening, with Professor Joad, but I can't go. I shall have to content myself with the Brainstrust book which I bought recently.

22nd March 1946

A girl called Pam Towlson who works at Wolsey Hall came home with me after work yesterday. She's small and fair-haired and very ladylike and really not my type at all, but somehow we've got quite friendly. She sat in the armchair in my room in a genteel fashion while I went to the kitchen to make some tea, colliding with dumpy little Miss Lorch as usual, who's always so self-effacing, and let me have the kettle first, for which I was grateful as I didn't want to keep prim Pam waiting. Over tea I mentioned to Pam that I'd wanted to spend a week's holiday in Stratford-on-Avon this summer but it fell through as my sister had another arrangement and my friend (Connie) doesn't want to go. To my amazement she said: "I'll come with you." What could I say? I agreed with pleasure.

Tomorrow evening I'm going to the New Theatre with Putz and Ailsa Clark, and on Saturday to the hairdressers and the photographers. I'm going to have a liberty cut!

We have a new boss at Wolsey Hall, a Major Ching. He's tall, good-looking, beautifully spoken, about 36 and probably married. Soon after he arrived he got transferred to another part of the building but now he's back on my floor. I wanted very much that he would speak to me – and now he has, because we are working together. He's interested in the running of the library which involves conferring with me quite often during which occasions I sit next to him at his desk. Isn't that romantic? It seems I can't live without having somebody to admire silently and from afar.

23rd March 1946

Harold is getting married!

I knew of course that he had a fiancée in Falmouth called Jean, but he so rarely mentioned her that I thought, as Miss Davis told me long ago, that the engagement was broken off, and I forgot about it. Why else should such an upright fellow take up with another girl (me) to the extent that most people took him to be in love with her? (me). Now I understand his long silence. I had not seen or heard from him for weeks. Then, this morning, I met him at the bus stop. I sensed at once that something was wrong, but of course he couldn't avoid me. He was cornered. There was nothing for it but to come clean.

"I've been to Falmouth for a week," he told me. "I saw Jean and we decided to get married."

For a moment I was speechless and then I stammered: "Oh. Well, congratulations." I felt so relieved to be rid of him that it didn't even hurt my vanity. All the same, I think he has made a great mistake in carrying on with me if he was still engaged to Jean all the time. On the one or two occasions he had mentioned her it wasn't complimentary and he certainly didn't give the impression of loving her. If I were a malicious kind of person this may have had grave results. However, I'm not, so I'd better forget it all and go into the future with another bitter experience in tow, but wiser.

30th March 1946

Putz and I have spent nearly every evening together this week, either at her place or mine, and once at the New Theatre, there being nothing much else on. When we are in her room, Edna usually joins us for some of the time. On Thursday there was a short circuit at 47 Lonsdale Road, and I had no light in my room. I was at Joan's on Wednesday evening and of course told her about Harold. She thought he had behaved disgracefully. He should have written me a letter or come to see me to explain, she said. I agree with her.

123

I'm a sentimentalist, however, and always regret things that are over and finished, never to return. Instead of letting the past quietly recede I rake it up and compare it to the present: I shall never again walk with Harold hand in hand and have to tolerate his boring conversation and chuckle over his boring wisdom. I shall never again sit in the Ritz with him and listen to badly played music we didn't like and eat ice cream we loved. I shall never be at a show or film with him again and feel his arm around me. He will never see me home again or talk to me of his ideas or pay me nice compliments. He will never ring me again and make dates and be polite and give me presents. It isn't him I shall miss, but the cheap pleasures I derived. I think I ought to be annoyed with him, and I wish him every unhappiness in his marriage, a lot of quarrels and at least three miscarriages. If the devil rules my life I shall be a devil back.

5th April 1946

The Aintree horse race took place today. I had a bet on a horse – and lost. Before any race, Mr Herbert always gets the staff to place bets through him and so I did, though I have no interest whatever in gambling. The horse I drew was lame anyway, according to Mr Herbert. I don't think he'll ever make a gambler of me. I worked till 7pm again yesterday and afterwards spent the evening at Joan's.

My father has sent some clothes from his firm – a red jumper and a gathered skirt, which I'm very pleased with, and I suppose I must be grateful for his generosity.

Last Sunday Prue called to say goodbye before going home for the Easter holidays. Then Edna and Arthur came to repair the short circuit – that is, Arthur repaired it and Edna talked to me and Mrs Labowsky. In the afternoon I had tea at Ross's with Audrey and afterwards we had a long walk. In the evening I played ping-pong at the Linton Road hostel.

On Tuesday Pam Towlson and I picked daffodils in a beautiful garden in Banbury Road, at the home of friends of the Towlsons, and on Wednesday Sandy came to tea, after which we had a long walk. But my biggest news is: I HAVE STARTED WRITING A NOVEL. I'm very excited about it. I only hope it won't resemble the style of Denton Welch too much whose book I've just finished and which so impressed me. My novel will be called *Velvet Hours*. It will take my mind off craving for things I cannot obtain and which turn to ashes if I do. I live in a comfortable room, I have a job I like, I have no responsibilities and yet I know all the time that I am wasting my youth, that in fact I'm not living but merely existing. The trouble is I am too egotistic. I look at everything from an egotist's point of view, I am wrapped up in myself, lose touch with the external world and therefore become unhappy because I cannot derive happiness from my own self. It's all wrong and I must try and change.

12th April 1946

Audrey and I spent Sunday afternoon together again. On Monday I worked late, for which Major Ching personally thanked me the next day, and spent what was left of the evening in my room, listening to *Hamlet* on the wireless.

On Tuesday Putz and I were at the Rieszs' and said goodbye to Susie, who's leaving for America next week, to marry her US fiancé. Maureen is also leaving Oxford. I shall miss her. We have never again mentioned her illegitimate child but it is never far from my mind when I'm with her. She wants to work for the British Army in Germany.

A Lieutenant and a Spaniard were at the Rieszs' the last time we were there. I asked the Spaniard whether he had ever done any bullfighting, and everyone roared with laughter. I thought that most Spaniards do some bullfighting, just as most Englishmen play cricket. Not so. Hence the laughter. He did look a bit too weedy to fight a bull. Mr Riesz is going to work for my father in London. It is a return favour, as the Rieszs' so often invite Putz and me to their home. My father went abroad for the first time since the war ended yesterday. He has been longing to travel again for years.

I nearly fell off the bus today. It started moving before I was properly on it. That quite shook me. Fortunately I didn't have to go back to Wolsey Hall on the bus after lunch in town, as we met Mr Belsten, the accountant, and he gave us a lift in his car.

13th April 1946

I've already told you many times that I'm not particularly happy, haven't I? In that case, there's really nothing more to add. My present life is a life of unbearable monotony. Also I'm a jealous and selfish person and happiness does not like such people. Nothing wants me and I want everything. I pray to God and the devil answers my prayers. When I asked Putz the other day if she ever prayed she replied: "I consult with my own God." I wonder who he is.

17th April 1946

The Easter holiday starts on Thursday and Putz and I are going to Cobham, which has become our home during holidays.

Last Sunday morning Pam Towlson and I visited some colleges and took a little boy called Ron with us, who's the child of friends of her parents. The afternoon, however, was a sad occasion: Maureen and I said goodbye in the garden of the house where she has lodged since I've known her. We had tea and gave each other farewell presents: I gave her a nightdress from Vienna (which I've never liked) and she gave me her Kodak Brownie box camera which I've always coveted. She promised to write to me.

Susie left for the USA on Monday.

A woman called Mrs Walker and her children were at Joan's for tea when I was there yesterday. It meant that Joan and I couldn't have one of our serious conversations.

Now I must get on with my packing. We are going on the 7pm coach tomorrow, straight after work.

23rd April 1946

Well, I'm back in Oxford again. The Easter holiday passed quickly and pleasantly. We arrived in Cobham on Thursday at 11pm and everyone was in bed; everyone being the various visitors but not Anni and Felix, who were away until Saturday. On Good Friday we sunbathed in the garden and generally lounged around. I rang Eva Urbach to arrange her visit to Cobham on Sunday. Ruth rang from Portsmouth. On several occasions Trude Dawson took me to the pub for a drink. We usually cycled there, accompanied by Chum the Airedale. Trude is very fond of drinking, unlike me, but she doesn't know about me. I find alcohol quite difficult to swallow, I suppose because I'm so unsophisticated. Eva and I spent a pleasant day together on Easter Sunday, even though we don't have much in common any more. While Ruth is too old for her age, Eva is too childish. I must be somewhere in between.

We arrived back in Oxford at 12.30pm today.

4th May 1946

There's a delicious scent in my room thanks to Joan, who brought me a bunch of my favourite flowers on Sunday – lilac – in gratitude to me for typing a story she has written. I did this on my typewriter at work, after 5pm. She writes poetry too.

Putz has bought Susie's bicycle. She has never owned a bicycle before. After tea at the Rieszs' today we cycled back to Putz's place and spent the evening together. We talked about our mother. I told her of my fear that she might have lost her memory and be wandering around somewhere in Minsk. Putz said this had occurred to her, too. I said: "Don't you think father could have done more to get her out of Austria, when it was still possible?"

"I don't know," Putz replied. "There was grandmother, too . . . as you know, mother wouldn't leave her."

Putz used to love our father, and still defends him from my frequent violent attacks on him. I always envy girls who have a loving relationship with their fathers. The last time I was at the Urbachs, when I was briefly alone with Mrs Urbach, she talked to me about Eva's relationship with her father. "He hangs on her," she said. She was translating from the German meaning 'he adores her'. I didn't correct her. I wished my father would 'hang on me'.

Sandy has at last got a new job and is leaving the library today, six months after me.

8th May 1946

A parcel from abroad arrived today. It was from my father and contained a manicure set in a red leather case. Putz and I are going to London for the weekend to see him.

All this week I've been eating my lunch in the office. Guess what I ate yesterday? A coconut! And guess what I ate today? A BANANA! The war has been over for a year now and we still

127

have rationing and can't get lots of things, or can only get them very rarely, such as bananas.

Last Sunday Prue and I went to a service at St Michael's Church and afterwards for a walk. Maureen was back in Oxford for the weekend. We had tea at Putz's and it was like old times. She still wants to work in Germany with the British Army.

16th May 1946

On Saturday Putz and I left work at twelve o'clock and went to London. Our father fetched us from Paddington Station and we spent the afternoon at Elgin Avenue with Jack and Jane. In the evening Putz and I went to Cobham. We know this journey well now, including the twenty minute walk from Cobham Station to 'Ann's Cottage'. The following day, Sunday, my father came to Cobham. It was a nice day and we were in the garden most of the time. Among the visitors there were a Mr and Mrs Katz and one or two other continental friends and relations of Anni and Felix. They sat on the lawn in deckchairs enjoying the sunshine. Most of them are elderly refugees who live in London bed-sitting rooms, and 'Ann's Cottage' is a haven for them. After tea my father and I took a little walk around the huge and lovely garden, at his suggestion. I think he wanted to find things out about my life in Oxford – whether I had boyfriends and so on – but I didn't tell him anything. As we approached the deckchair brigade again my father stopped. "Look at these people," he said to me in a confidential tone. "Aren't they ugly? What an ugly race we Jews are." I had to agree. Centuries of suffering and being downtrodden must leave their mark, I suppose. In that brief moment my father and I were united in a longing not to belong to this race, to belong to the glamorous Anglo-Saxon one instead, in whose handsome features there is carved their age-old supremacy.

In the evening we returned to London with my father and the Katzs, and then Putz and I caught the train back to Oxford.

I worked overtime again this week. On Thursday I spent the whole afternoon in the principal's office with Mrs Newell, wife of Mr Newell, who's one of the bosses. She comes in from time to time and helps out, usually in the library. She's a very elegant and well-spoken woman and we get on well. I admire and envy her, and she thinks I'm cleverer than I really am. One day she had one of her little boys with her and the three of us were in the library. The little boy picked a huge book off the shelf which bore the title *Revolutions*.

"What's a revolution?" he asked his mother.

She laughed heartily. "You may well ask," she said. And then she added: "Ask Miss Jacoby. She'll explain it to you better than I can."

What a compliment. I felt very flattered, and did my best to explain what a revolution is.

Joan and Peter are coming on Sunday. *Hatschi Bratschi* is nearly finished and only needs to be bound now. Joan's drawings are beautiful, and I'm proud of my translation, all in rhyme, like the original.

22nd May 1946

Ruth is getting married! She has been more or less engaged once before, so this may well fall through again, too. As she has had more boyfriends than I can keep up with – many of them sailors – I'm inclined not to take this new engagement too seriously.

There really isn't anything else much to write about except to tell you I'm still not happy. What does one do when one feels one has finished with life and has no hope left? I suppose one ceases to care, but unfortunately I continue to care. I want a man, I want love, I want to be a writer, I want a house with a loving family all around me. But I am alone, I am miserable, I hate everybody. What shall I do?

24th May 1946

It is Putz's 22nd birthday today. We went to the New Theatre in the evening. We shall have our birthday tea on Sunday. Just the two of us.

Pam Towlson wanted me to go to art school with her on Wednesday evening. I went along with her but didn't join. It was a life drawing class and I'm no good at life drawing.

Putz and I have been to a Brett's dance and it wasn't too bad. It seems to have improved since the days when I used to go with Maureen. Putz is going for a week's holiday to Cobham on Saturday, the 1st of June. She looks on Anni as a substitute mother.

2nd June 1946

Joan and Peter brought me a banana when they came today! After I had seen Putz to the station yesterday I went to work – and stayed till 7.30pm. Mr Newell was there too. Putz's bicycle went ahead of her to Cobham; we took it to the station and put it on the train on Friday evening.

Last Wednesday Titch, the girl who was librarian before me, came to Wolsey Hall with her new baby. It was her moment of glory because all the girls here are living for the day when they can leave to marry and have babies. Titch made the most of it, and stayed nearly the whole morning.

Ruth is coming to visit me on Friday! It being the start of the Whitsun weekend we are going to London and Cobham on Saturday.

5th June 1946

Lovely news from Putz! She has met a man she has fallen in love with! I look forward to hearing all about him when I see her at the weekend.

I had to call on Mrs Guttmann yesterday to get some tickets for a fête. She lives a few doors away and is a good friend of Mrs Labowsky's. Dr Guttmann is apparently a brilliant doctor, and they have a schoolgirl daughter called Eva. I sometimes meet her in the mornings and we cycle together, she to school and I to work. Mrs Guttmann didn't have the tickets but promised to bring them round when she does.

13th June 1946

Today is my mother's birthday. She would be 48 years old. My father is 50. He has had a photograph taken of himself by Dorothy Wilding, the royal photographer, to mark the occasion, and presented us with a copy.

I took Ruth sight-seeing when she was here on Friday. We visited various colleges, saw the Sheldonian Theatre and Bodleian Library and Alice's Shop, and walked in the University parks. We stayed up till 3am celebrating the second anniversary of the Normandy invasion in town, and afterwards talking in bed.

The following day we spent in London – lunch, shopping and the flicks. It was pouring. In the evening we went out to Cobham and again stayed up very late, talking. It seems she's quite serious about getting married. On Whit Sunday my father came out for the day. Putz, Ruth and I went for a walk after he had gone – and had another late night. Ruth left on Monday, and Putz, bike and I returned to Oxford.

15th June 1946

Today I put on nail varnish for the first time. It must be Ruth's influence – she has been telling me to use it for ages. I don't ever remember such loneliness. It's a pity I have to experience every conceivable kind of misery, or so it seems to me. Loneliness is surely one of the worst tortures. When I was a small child my greatest fear was that I would one day wake up in the morning and find everyone dead except me. I would be the only person left alive on earth. I often lay awake at night straining my ears for some sounds of life. It was a long time before it occurred to me that the occasional car I heard in the street below must mean there must be some people still alive.

I have absolutely nothing else to say to you today – except that I am very happy that Lieselotte has found a man.

20th June 1946

I went to a garden fête in Woodstock Road with Putz and Edna today. Various people we knew were there, such as Otto and Ossy. Afterwards I took photos of Putz and Edna on their bikes. The other day I also took a photograph of my room.

I have finished my novel *Velvet Hours* and shall take it to be typed next week.

While Mrs Labowsky was away on holiday recently I had a mysterious telephone call from someone who called himself Harry. He seemed to know all about me, and said he was coming round to see me, as he knew I was alone in the house. Putz said I should tell the police but I felt quite able to cope with Harry myself, should he turn up, which I didn't think he would, and he didn't. Nothing exciting happens to me any more and I have only trifling things to report. What an interesting life I lead! I do too little and I think too much. But thoughts give rise to ideas, and ideas have legs.

25th June 1946

Just a little thing to tell you, to alleviate your boredom.

Lieselotte and I spent this evening at the Rieszs'. (We should have gone last Friday but it was pouring.) At about 10pm we left. I took it for granted that Peter would take Putz home as she lives much further away. He didn't. He walked home with me. I asked him in for a cup of tea – goodness knows why. We drank and smoked and he poured forth the usual philosophical, intellectual stuff, and threw in a few shocking ideas for good measure. Presently the topic of love came up. We don't usually talk about that. The clock in the hall struck eleven and he got up to go. Suddenly he turned to me and said:

"Do you want me to make love to you?"

I was astounded. "Good heavens," I exclaimed, "what on earth gave you that idea?"

"I don't know. I never know what other people's sex impulses are so I have to ask to find out. Do you want to make love?"

"Oh Peter, of course I don't," I said. "Anyway," I added, "You're a bit young, aren't you?" (he's 20, I'm 19). Suddenly we were both very embarrassed. I saw him to the door and he went quickly. I tried to think of something quite ordinary to say, to ease the uncomfortable situation, but nothing came to mind. It was queer because we'd never been personal before. He had told me that he had wanted girls at times, but it went no further. We now said a brief goodnight and I closed the door.

After a few minutes he was back. He knocked on my window. He had forgotten his coat. We laughed. We were still embarrassed. I closed the door a second time behind him and heard him walk away, whistling.

The episode cheered me up a bit for some reason.

I try to play-act in such situations. I pretend I'm very experienced and have long ago lost my virginity, I almost deceive myself sometimes. I adopt an attitude which is really a laughable contrast to the real me. It helps. I don't know why.

29th June 1946

Maureen is in Oxford for the weekend again and we spent today together, in my room, in town, at the flicks and at Putz's.

Yesterday Audrey, Putz, Ailsa and I were going out to tea and afterwards to the theatre, to celebrate the end of Ailsa's exams; she's at university here. In the end Ailsa couldn't come so we celebrated without her, and the 'Falmouth Quartet' was incomplete.

I was blowing bubbles with little Peter Beschorner during the evening I spent at Joan's on Thursday.

"Would you rather have a little brother or a little sister?" I asked him. He knows about the coming baby, of course.

"I'd rather have a little dog," he replied. That made me laugh. Joan laughed too when I told her.

We're having a heat wave. On Sunday Putz and I sunbathed in the garden of her house the whole afternoon and we have acquired quite a tan.

I met Peggy Jacques on Monday, and we had lunch and went shopping together. I asked her if Miss Campbell had changed at all, and she said for the worse if anything. I can't understand why Miss Jacques doesn't leave the library. She's a qualified librarian.

The man Putz has fallen in love with – I almost forgot to tell you – is called Norman and lives in Christchurch. She met him on the train and they write letters to each other. I wonder if something will come of it?

5th July 1946

The heat wave continued all this week, broken only by a thunderstorm on Wednesday night. On Tuesday I had supper at 'Stirway' with Audrey. Afterwards we had a long walk in Headington and then we spent the rest of the evening in her room at the Wingfield hospital. We always have lots to talk about. When I got home Miss Lorch was making cheese in the kitchen. She asked me if I'd like to assist her. I said yes. My assistance consisted of heating the milk to 80° and adding a little sour milk to it. The rest she did and I watched.

When I received my wage packet today I saw that I had a small rise; there was an additional half crown in the envelope. Following the example of June Rodway I took my courage in both hands and, as I was working late again, knocked on Mr Newell's door when most of the staff had gone, and was asked to enter. I thanked him for the half crown but pointed out that I had not had one proper rise since starting work at Wolsey Hall. He gave me to understand that I had done nothing particular to deserve it, and would therefore have to wait until everyone was due to have a rise. There being nothing more to be said I left the room and decided to keep my eyes open for another job.

To my surprise I found myself writing a story in *German*! I wonder why? It just happened. I haven't even spoken German for ages.

My summer holiday starts on 20th July. I'm going to Falmouth for a week – I can hardly wait. This time I'm staying at Connie's.

13th July 1946

Norman should have come to see Putz this weekend but couldn't make it in the end. What a pity. Audrey was here for tea today, and in the evening I listened to *Il Trovatore* on the wireless. Wonderful music. It made me sad and happy – music often does. An indescribable feeling invaded my whole being. I didn't want to let the feeling go, but when the music was over the feeling was over too.

I have taken my novel to be typed. Whether I shall have the courage to send it to a publisher is another matter.

19th July 1946

This week has been a week of 'should haves': on Monday I should have played tennis with Peter Riesz and his friend Derek but in the last minute it was cancelled, and on Tuesday I should have gone swimming with Edna, but it was too cold.

Joan's sister Margaret, about whom she often complains, was staying with her last weekend, plus her children, and as Joan wanted me to meet her I went to 66 St John's Road on Sunday morning. Margaret is short, fat and quite unlike Joan, who's slim (when not pregnant) artistic and a bit airy-fairy; Margaret seemed very down to earth.

On Wednesday evening Putz and I listened to the *Eroica* on my wireless. She prefers my wireless for Beethoven as hers is a bit wobbly, and once a vase of flowers which stood on it crashed to the floor during the finalé of Beethoven's *7th Symphony*.

Surprise, surprise – I had a £14 bonus with my wages today! It will come in very handy as I'm off to Falmouth on the night train this evening. Prue has just been to wish me a happy holiday and Putz will be here in about an hour to come to the station with me. So goodbye – I'm too busy – and too excited – to write any more today.

29th July 1946

I'm back from Falmouth and I loved every minute there. Everyone received me in a way that warmed my heart.

I did not have one minute to write. From the moment Connie fetched me from the station at 9am on Saturday the 20th to the moment when she, Pam and Sheila accompanied me there again on Sunday the 28th my days were one social whirl. I spent them at St Josephs, at school talking to my old friends and mistresses, on the beach, swimming, on the school tennis courts, visiting and having tea with the Tamblyns, Baths, Lawrances, Eggins, Mrs Belcher, Thompsons, Hodgetts . . . have I left someone out? I expect so. Some highlights were:

1) The afternoon I spent with Robin, who took me to the flicks, to tea and for a walk. I don't know what he thinks of me but I think he's quite unchanged, if a little more grown up since joining the army.

2) Meeting Figgy and her baby on the beach. She's married now.

3) Attending the school breaking-up ceremony at which I was *guest of honour*.

4) Being driven about in people's cars.

5) Spending a day sailing with Connie, and Alan and Tommy Tothill in their yacht, the *Uye Tui Tui*. Later I met their parents for the first time and we had tea on Durgan beach. Actually I didn't enjoy the sailing very much. I had never done it before and felt – and was -useless, and knew that Alan and Tommy thought so. It seemed to me that I was so inferior to them they didn't look on me as a girl at all. Love and sex didn't appear to exist for them. Their talk was entirely of masts and booms and fore-and-aft

135

sails and knots and rigging – way above my head. Connie was helmsman.

Old 'Chinnie Row', the grocer, was so pleased to see me again he threw his arms around me and kissed me! I often used to fetch our weekly rations from him.

Pam has a boyfriend called Ben. He doesn't seem good enough for her to me – he's quite unromantic and very common, but she apparently likes him. I went out with them several times – for walks, to chapel, and to see *HMS Pinafore* at the Princess Pavilion. At the Pavilion we met Robin, but I kept him away from Ben, who would have considered him 'posh'.

On one occasion when I was meeting Pam on Gyllingvase Beach and arrived before her I went to get two deckchairs. The man charged me a shilling. "But yesterday they cost sixpence," I objected. "Oh, you live here, do you? I thought you were a visitor," he said. So that's what they do!

Bread rationing started on Sunday. I felt a bit awkward sharing the Davis's ration, but luckily Mrs Davis is friendly with her baker. I talked with her until 1am on the day I arrived, and really got to know her quite well by the end of the week. When I lived in Falmouth I didn't see her often as she hardly ever visited St Joseph's. Not being a Catholic she was a bit of an outsider in the family.

I couldn't bear leaving Falmouth at the end of my week's holiday. I wish I lived there again. I wish I could hide myself away from the world in this enclosed little paradise. When I saw it again after a year's absence I felt I was coming home. I'd told people in Oxford I was going home for my holiday. But I found that this wasn't quite true when someone in Falmouth said to me: "Now that the war is over, will you be going home to Austria soon?" How could I explain that there's nothing and no one left in Austria that could make it 'home' for me, that Austria threw me out and doesn't want me back even though I loved it so much?

On the train to Truro I met Deane Sowell and her brother Bobby and travelled with them. Deane was the cleverest girl in my class but left school after the School Certificate and works in an office, which everyone considered an awful waste of talent. On Bristol station I met another girl from the High School called June Harper. She was not in my form. What a coincidence.

On Sunday night Putz met me at Oxford station in a taxi and

today, Monday, everything is back to normal. Mr and Mrs Newell are going for a fortnight's holiday tomorrow.

3rd August 1946

Today, Putz, Peter Riesz and I had tea at the Cadena and then went to the pictures. I think he enjoys going out with both of us, because he doesn't have to worry about making love – or not making love.

Putz has made friends with a nice girl called Jerry Billinghurst who works in her office, and we usually have lunch together on weekdays. I think she must know nearly every Shakespeare sonnet by heart, because she's forever quoting from them. Putz has always wanted to go to university, and has a flair for making friends with highly educated girls.

When I was in Falmouth I wrote to Howard Spring, reminding him that we had met, and asking if he would read my novel. Today I had his reply, refusing to read it. I'm not really surprised. 'Send it to a publisher,' is his advice.

No work on Monday as it's bank holiday. I'm playing tennis with Putz.

7th August 1946

My friend Joan has had her second baby – a girl. She is to be called Diana.

Today I went to visit Joan in the Nursing home. I have never seen a woman straight after she has given birth. I walked into the

137

room gently and quietly., I didn't know what to say. I looked at Diana and she was a little ugly bundle, not yet human, and who would only be properly so in several years' time. I felt out of place in the room because I had never had a child or known what it is like to be moaning with labour pains. I felt jealous of Joan's experience, and yet I felt sorry for her, and glad that I was still free and young with no responsibilities, and with the whole of my life before me. I looked at the baby again – and now I felt old and weary and beneath its contempt. I wished I could be a mother too, but after it's all over, the pain, and the mess of birth. Joan said:

"Do you know, while I was giving birth and I was only half conscious, I understood the mystery of the Universe. It was all crystal clear. My husband (she never calls him by his name – Hans) just laughed when I told him. But you understand, don't you?" She always overestimates me, which is one reason why I never feel truly myself with her. I didn't want to let her down, especially at such a time.

"Yes, I think so," I replied. And then I asked: "Was it very awful – the pain, and so on?"

"Yes. But then I had this wonderful feeling about the mystery of the Universe being unravelled," said Joan. But she couldn't explain it. I was meant to understand without her explanation.

By the time I left Joan I wanted to know nothing more about childbirth but indulge in my youthful freedom forever and a day. I had briefly been a guest in the world of motherhood, and I wasn't sure that I liked it.

Next week will be one filled with humiliation for me, because I'm going to Stratford-on-Avon for a week's holiday with Pamela Towlson, whom I don't know very well and don't really care for. I think it was a mistake. She's the sort of girl who attracts men easily and I shall be very jealous. Life is completely spoilt for me because of my jealous and envious nature. I can't look forward to anything without this wretched sense of competition and my inferiority complex. And yet I'm filled with this stupid desire to attract attention and out-shine everyone. I can't control it. I wish after all my youth were over!

9th August 1946

How odd that, in my dull and uneventful life, two events happened

138

in one day yesterday – which I must tell you about or burst. I am at 66 St John's Road babysitting, while Dr Beschorner, who's home for the weekend, is visiting Joan. Little Peter is in bed and I'm sitting cosily in the kitchen. The first event is short. I had to go to Blackwell's on business. Almost immediately I saw – Mr Morris. *As soon as I saw him I hated him.* I don't know why. Is it because he did something terrible to my dream? I didn't want him to serve me but it was unavoidable. He said "Hello," and looked into my eyes and I knew that he wanted to talk. But I gave him no chance. I asked him for the books I wanted, was business-like and abrupt and treated him like a stranger. I wanted nothing to do with him. I do not know what caused me to be like this. As I walked away stiffly, thanking him politely, scarcely smiling, feeling his eyes on me, questioning eyes, strange blue-grey eyes that had once stared into mine at close range, I thought – this is the man who was infatuated with me, who made love to me, who asked me to be his wife. Now he is a stranger again, a man in a shop behind a counter. I wasn't sorry it had all happened and yet it is somehow degrading and humiliating in retrospect; and was badly performed. Yes, that was it – badly performed, and it left the same unpleasant aftertaste as a bad play.

Now for the second thing which happened yesterday, which made Thursday the 8th of August the nicest day I've ever had in Oxford: I called at the Rieszs', as I sometimes do on an evening when I've nothing much else to do, and Peter was just going out for a drink with a few of his friends – all male.

"Would you like to come?" he asked me. I hesitated, wondering how much indignity I might have to face from all those brilliant undergraduates, but of course I consented. How glad I am that I did!

We set off on our bikes and it was already quite dark, so there was no need for me to feel self-conscious. I was the only girl, and that was an advantage too. We cycled along the narrow towpath towards the Trout Inn. I had no lights. The path was rough and at times I could hardly see where I was going. I'm surprised I didn't fall into the river. But it was exciting. The boys whistled as they cycled along, and we talked and laughed all the way. They whistled Mozart and Mendelssohn and talked nonsense, such as why isn't it possible to play rugby with the moon. I joined in their mood, I felt I was one of their crowd, I felt they liked me. If they had asked me to swim naked in the river while they watched at the water's edge I think I might have done it. That's how exuberant I felt. At the Trout Inn we sat outside, on the wall, on the table, on the ground, anywhere except on chairs.

"You write novels, don't you?" said Derek.

"I try to," I replied, and for once didn't feel stupid admitting it. In fact I felt so sure of myself that I could have danced with them, then and there, in the garden of the Trout Inn, in and out of the drinkers sitting around the tables by candlelight. I should have liked to have made love with them all, especially Bill Emerson, the lady-killer. But we only flirted mildly. Oh, why can't I always be like this? How sorry I felt for girls who were shy, self-conscious, unsophisticated and had an inferiority complex. Silly, pathetic creatures. They didn't belong here. They deserved their lonely fate.

"Come to the theatre with us on Monday," suggested Peter.

"I can't, I'm going to Stratford," I replied.

"What a pity," said Bill.

"Have a cigarette," said Kenneth.

"Thanks." I took one. He lit it for me. Cigarette smoke filled the air and mingled with our beer. None of them knew it but I loved life that evening. It would be wrong to say I'm always happy in the company of men. That is not true. The atmosphere has to be right. With Tommy and Alan, for instance, in their yacht I was exceedingly miserable because they crushed me with their very looks, which said: what a hopeless girl you are. We only like girls who understand about sailing.

Cycling home along the towpath in Indian file was even more hazardous, pitch dark as it was and intoxicated as we were. Soon they began their silly clever talk again.

"How do you keep a family on thirty shillings a week?" said Bill.

"How?" said everyone.

"Send the wife out to work and the children to an orphanage."

"Very funny," said Kenneth. "How do you eat a banana without peeling it?"

"How?" asked everyone again.

"Give it to a monkey!" shouted Kenneth, who was right in front.

"Ha, ha. How do you make a girl kiss you when she doesn't want to?" asked Peter.

"How?" we all shouted.

"I wish I knew!" said Peter. That got the biggest laugh.

And *I* wish the evening had lasted forever.

I've done my packing and washed my hair and am ready to go to Stratford with Pamela on Monday, whatever it may hold for me. On Saturday Putz came with me to call on Reverend Lunt, to pacify Canon Roxby in Falmouth. Very unexciting.

After Dr Beschorner returned from the Nursing home on Friday we had a little talk. He has never tried to flirt with me as he did with Prue and Pat, which I think was the cause of the dissolution of the household. He always has philosophical discussions with me. He's an atheist. I said I also didn't think there could be a God, but then how did everything start?

"Perhaps outside our understanding things don't have a start. Perhaps things just are," he said. All the way home this sentence went round and round in my head. "Perhaps things just are." One moment I understood it perfectly, the next it made no sense at all.

When Pam and I returned from the pictures on Saturday we met Otto on the bus and chatted throughout the length of the journey. He reeked of onions.

Today I visited Joan and her baby again, and took a present for the baby. She said the answer to the riddle of the Universe which had been so unquestionably clear to her during the birth, was fading. It was fading because the world had already started to lay its dirty finger on Diana. Daphne Hall, the girl Joan used to work with and whom she ridiculed to me for being so dependent on her lipstick, was there too, part of the time. Although I felt drawn to Daphne because she is so upper-class, blonde, blue-eyed and attractive, I dared not reveal this in front of Joan.

20th August 1946

As Pam and I shared a room in Stratford I couldn't write my diary but I'm now back in Oxford and am able to tell you that, on the whole, my apprehensions were unfounded: we got on well, and saw nearly every play Shakespeare ever wrote, as we went to the theatre every evening and sometimes to a matinée as well.

The hotel we stayed at was called Plymouth Arms. The first place we visited on arrival was of course Shakespeare's birthplace, which I loved. Nothing after that came up to this standard but everything was interesting. On Tuesday we took a bus to Ann Hathaway's cottage, where a guide showed us around and Pam sat in the orchard and sketched the cottage while I took a few photos. On fine mornings we sat on deckchairs in the park or went for country walks. On one of these we were walking for some time without talking, which was a new experience for me and I found it rather embarrassing, when Pam suddenly said: "It is a sign of friendship when you can be with somebody without the need to exchange words." This certainly made the situation less embarrassing but I wondered if it was true. Maybe it was also a sign of our friendship when, later on, as we stood waiting endlessly for a bus and I lent against the bus stop post, Pam said: "Don't do that. It looks common." She's very particular about behaviour in public. We always ate our evening meal at a place called the River Hotel, and the manager greeted us in a friendly way as soon as we entered. On our last evening he gave us a special treat — *free* vanilla ice cream!

On Thursday we visited Warwick Castle, had lunch at the Porridge Pot, tea in the Jury Tea Room, went to the pictures and finished the day with supper at a dirty café, which upset Pam very much. I'm afraid I was too hungry (or greedy) to notice the cracked plates and grubby tablecloth until Pam drew my attention to them.

We also spent a day in Coventry. We went there by bus and looked around the town, which wasn't very impressive. The bus tour through Shakespeare villages and a visit to Mary Arden's Cottage, which we did the previous day, was much more interesting and enjoyable; at the cottage there was a funny guide who kept cracking silly jokes, and took a photo of Pam and me.

Early one morning towards the end of our stay I was awoken by a man being violently sick in the room next to ours. The retching, choking and vomiting noises seemed to go on for a long time. Luckily for Pam she slept through them, as I'm sure she would have been very upset by something so disgusting.

On our return journey home to Oxford on Sunday we made the acquaintance of a girl called Doreen on the train. She attached herself to us; and in Leamington the three of us searched for some tearooms before getting our connection to Oxford, but couldn't find any.

Back in Lonsdale Road, I found a parcel from Aunt Else – it

contained home-made Vanilla Kipferl! What a joy. I rang Putz, and she told me that Norman was in Oxford for the weekend. I am so happy for her. Perhaps they'll get married!

On Tuesday 13th August *H.G.Wells died.* I shall never forget his story 'The Country of the Blind' which I read at school. Today I sent my novel to the Authors' Alliance.

I worked overtime both yesterday and today. Just before I was ready to go home late this afternoon Mr Herbert came into my room – and offered me a cigarette! Mr Newell gets back from his holiday tomorrow.

23rd August 1946

Putz is going to London for the weekend today and I'm following on Saturday. Mrs Labowsky is also going away for a few days.

Yesterday Mr Herbert again came into my office, gave me a cigarette and offered to treat me to an evening at the Playhouse! I must tell you that Mr Herbert is quite common and elderly – at least 50 years old – grey-haired and unattractive. However, he is always very nice to everyone and the worst thing he says if he sees any of the girls in his office idling is: "Get on with your knitting!" I thanked him for the cigarette and the offer of the theatre outing, which I declined.

I worked overtime with Mr and Mrs Newell and afterwards Mrs Newell wanted to take me home by car but I was going to visit Putz for the evening.

27th August 1946

I left work at 12 on Saturday (instead of 1) and went to London. I travelled with Miss Senior, a girl who works at Wolsey Hall, as she was also going to London. At Paddington Station I was met by Putz, my father, Jack and Betty – in my father's brand new car, which Jack drove as my father doesn't drive. We had lunch at Elgin Avenue, where Jane was waiting. She's a good cook and a delicious meal was ready for us – continental style to please my father. Later in the afternoon Jack and Dad took Putz and me to Cobham in the new car, and stayed for supper. On Sunday I sunbathed in the garden all day. My father and the Marstons came out again in the afternoon, and in the evening Putz and I returned to Oxford. In the taxi home we had a conversation with a charming air force officer.

Last night I was invited to the Towlsons' for the evening and I showed them my photographs of Stratford. Pam and I discussed a girl called Helen Cox who works at Wolsey Hall and who wears the same dress every single day. She's having a baby and we wondered whether that would be dressed in the same garment every day of its life, too.

Joan's father has died. Her husband came down and I spent the evening with them today and took Peter's birthday present. The baby hasn't got a room of its own as the house is too full of lodgers, and sleeps in the pram in the kitchen! I think that is terrible. Joan was very distressed.

29th August 1946

Oh, why in God's name didn't I marry Mr Morris! Why didn't I abandon all my absurd inhibitions and agree to many him! I didn't marry him because I didn't love him, that's why, and I clung madly to the belief that love exists for me and that one day I shall find it. It was foolish of me. Had I married him I would have seen an entirely new world. Undoubtedly I should have been extremely unhappy with him – but better to be married and unhappy than a spinster and unhappy. He would have been a good lover and the nights at least would not have been lonely. He has a brilliant mind from which my mind could have benefited. Well, it is too late now, it's all over. But I must not wait for love, that much is certain. I can't find it because it is like looking for a needle in a haystack. I feel ugly and distorted with frustration.

Mrs Newell is very nice to me. She often comes to my office at teatime and we have a chat. Today a Nigerian headmistress came to Wolsey Hall – many Nigerians take correspondence courses at Wolsey Hall – and I was introduced to her. "This is Miss Jacoby, our librarian," said Mrs Newell. It sounded very grand.

Tomorrow Putz, her friend Jerry and I are having tea at the Cadena after work and then going to see the ballet at the New Theatre.

7th September 1946

This has been a dull week: overtime, evening at Putz's, evening at Joan's, overtime, evening at Pam's, flicks with Putz, evening at Putz's again, more overtime. Mrs Labowsky has been taken ill, just to liven things up. She asked me to get her a light book from the library, which surprised me as she is such a highbrow, who had translated Dante in her youth, but I obeyed and brought her a Daphne du Maurier. Horrors! She meant a light book in *weight*, as she can't hold heavy books in bed. Afterwards we laughed about it.

I spent most of Tuesday morning seeing the Harrap representative at Wolsey Hall.

8th September 1946

I have waited a week to tell you that I washed the handkerchief of a delightful, tall, fair-haired boy with a beautiful smile and that I liked doing this better than anything I've done in a long time.

It happened like this: I've talked to you of Bill Emerson, the physics undergraduate and friend of Peter Riesz whom I met for the first time about a year ago, the day I met that foolish George. I've seen Bill two or three times since and he made little impression on me. The night we all went to the Trout Inn was the first time I noticed him properly. Then I forgot about him again. Until last Sunday, when he and Peter turned up unexpectedly at Putz's digs where she and I were spending a cosy afternoon talking and listening to music. They wanted us to go out with them. We did not, so they sat down with us and talked. Then Peter suggested we all go to his house for tea. However, there was another girl coming, he said, so we decided to split up. Putz and Bill came to tea at my place, which is only five minutes from the Rieszs' house, and Peter went home to entertain the other girl. We joined them later and listened to gramophone records.

The afternoon was delightful. Bill lounged on my bed and I wished I were alone with him. He seemed to pay me attention but I wouldn't admit it to myself. When he was in the lavatory, Putz said: "He likes you." So I had been right.

I don't mind telling you that, for the whole of this week, Bill has occupied my mind constantly. I hate myself for this. I tell

g

myself that I'm just a frustrated, lonely girl on the brink of spinsterhood who creates visions for herself and falls in love with them, to fill her empty, empty life. Once an idea is stuck in my mind it turns into an obsession and only the bitter, inevitable end will rid me of it. I know perfectly well that Bill loves women and is a flirt, I know perfectly well that he has forgotten me, that I was of no more significance to him than the scenery around him – but I have his handkerchief in my possession which he forgot here, and I washed it, and sooner or later it must take me to him, come what may. And something else too – he asked me to order some books for him, and one of them has arrived. Fate has stepped in, and is about to lead me to – what?

Strangely, the night before that Sunday, during a spell of faith, I made a bargain with God: he would find me a lover and I would never doubt him again. By lover I meant of course someone who loved me back. I'm still waiting, and it is unfortunate that I met Bill again during this period as I feel I have deviated from my path towards this true lover. For a whole week I stopped myself from writing about Bill in the hope of driving him out of my mind. As you see, it has not worked. He said he hoped to see me again, but I know he didn't mean it.

I believe it is easier to have faith in God than in people.

Peter took me home on Sunday night, after an evening of listening to records and having supper at his house.

13th September 1946

Putz was here this evening and we listened to Beethoven's *7th Symphony* on the wireless which made me feel happy, in spite of the sad thing I'm going to tell you in a minute. Last night I had peaches at Joan's, which was another treat. She and the children came for tea on Sunday and I took photographs of them in the front garden.

The annual St Giles Fair was here on Monday and Tuesday. I went with Peter. It was an accident. I had not intended it, neither had he. But now I'm glad I went. We mingled with the crowd, met a few of his friends, spent some time with them, then lost them again.

I cannot tell you how miserable I was. I wanted to be at home, alone or dead. To begin with we didn't find Bill whom we were

146

looking for. I'd love to have seen Bill. And then there was the fact that I wasn't in love. I watched happy girls holding hands with their lovers, enjoyment written on their faces. I could sense the happiness of the crowd but it could not touch me, I couldn't capture the atmosphere, I couldn't be one of the crowd. As always, I was an outsider and spectator. I knew that Peter was miserable too. I knew that he tried his best to be kind and polite. In order to excuse his unaccustomed silence he said that crowds always made him feel sad. I knew that he, too, longed for love and thought as I did that it's no good going to a fair without being in love. A stall-holder called out as we passed: "Come on, buy the lady a lovely rose!" Nothing could have aggravated our misery more. It brought home to us that we had no right to be here together, not in love, not needing each other, not desiring to touch each other. I've always known that love can induce extreme emotions – that not being in love does the same thing was a new discovery. Oh, how I longed to belong to that crowd, to be one of those happy, carefree girls and know how it feels to be in love with the boy who has brought you to the fair! I actually tried to lose Peter once or twice but didn't succeed. We walked aimlessly up and down a bit longer, and then decided to go home. By this time I craved for solitude. As we left St Giles behind us and walked slowly up the Banbury Road, the noise of the fair receding, the silence seemed to welcome us. I know of no more wonderful sensation than to emerge from noisy chaos into orderly peace.

Peter said: "I feel I could have enjoyed the fair much more, had I been with a girl with whom I was in love." I was amazed that I had been so absolutely correct in guessing that he felt as I did. I was also amazed by his frankness. He's an intelligent, interesting and unusual boy but as a child he must have been very spoilt and he never learnt to consider other people's feelings. So it did not occur to me that I ought to be annoyed. I only laughed and said:

"Oh, I don't know. What's love got to do with going to a fair?" I didn't want him to know that I had also longed for love at the fair.

"Everything," said Peter. "The marvellous contrast! The noise, the dirt, the vulgarity, and next to you a vision, a gentle creature, a sacred object of love . . ." I had done with denying my convictions, and made no reply. We continued to talk of love, in an odd sort of way, each thinking the other didn't really

147

understand. I liked his frankness, and preferred it to the dull, tedious politeness of Harold and the sensual, sexual fanaticism of Mr Morris, even though I had played a far more important part with them than I did now.

"I wonder," said Peter, "why I can't fall in love with either you or your sister. I mean, you are both so charming, so extremely nice . . ." There was only one answer I could give him.

"For the same reason, I suppose," I said, "that we could never fall in love with you." We both laughed. He said:

"Forgive me. I've said too much. I'm sorry."

"Not at all," I answered. "Carry on."

He willingly obeyed. "It's a dreadful pity," he went on, "that I can't fall in love with you."

"No, it's not a pity," I said. "It would destroy many things."

"It would destroy nothing. I can never rest until the relationship between myself and a woman is that of love," said Peter.

"Well, you've done your best with me. I advise you to give up now. You're quite childish really, and have some silly notions. Grow up. Anyway, you can't be in love with every girl you know. There isn't room for so much love in the world. And anyway it's probably only a veneer for sex, which is just the instinct to reproduce oneself." You will note the change in my tone. I wanted to hurt him now. My pride, my bitterness, had got the better of me after all. And he said no more.

When two incompatible people are together they can search for love together, they can think and feel identically, but they can find no peace with each other. All the same, as I said in the beginning, I'm glad I went to the fair. The sadness of it made me appreciate that I am not, after all, like the ordinary girls I saw there. I'm glad I know an interesting boy like Peter who dares to declare his deficiency of love. I don't care whether he can love me or not. I don't want to belong to the humdrum crowd. I hope I never see Bill again, for my own good. I never want to chase a phantom again, or search for love hungrily and wait in misery. I learnt a great deal on Tuesday night.

15th September 1946

Putz's friend Philips should have come this weekend but it fell through. She was on duty. It rained all day yesterday and the most

148

interesting thing I can report today, Sunday, is that, according to my pocket diary, it is the 13th Sunday after Trinity and the beginning of Ember Week.

I'm miserable!

17th September 1946

No! Not miserable, nor unhappy any more! Delirious, excited, intoxicated! Why? Because tonight Bill came. Of course it was marred, because I was not alone. For the first time since we've been in England I did not want my sister with me. We were sitting in my room when the doorbell rang. Mrs Labowsky being out, I went to answer it. I opened the door and there stood Bill. I had had an upset stomach all day and didn't know if it was that, or the shock of seeing Bill, that made me feel sicker than ever. I asked him in but I'm afraid I must have been a very uninteresting companion. I don't know, therefore, why, while Lieselotte was outside getting her bike, Bill asked to see me again. I was confused and shrugged my shoulders and said I didn't know when. He suggested going to a dance. No, I said, I don't like dancing. Could he come and see me here, then? All right. I agreed. On Thursday then, at 7pm. The day after tomorrow.

I don't know yet what we shall do. I have an idea he will ask me to sleep with him, so I shall rehearse my refusal between now and Thursday. He stayed until 11pm tonight.

You think that I think I've won now, don't you? You think I feel I've made a conquest. Wrong. I feel more like an excited schoolboy before an important match, and I know it will be a difficult and probably disappointing game. Perhaps you wonder why, now that what I've wished for is coming true, I have no illusions about the future? It's not that I'm ungrateful – on the contrary – but I'm cautious and believe in nothing, least of all in men. But as long as I don't disappoint Bill, I don't mind so much if he disappoints me. This is really a selfish thought and not at all as noble as it sounds.

Oh, hurry up Thursday evening and come quickly and bring me Bill!

19th September 1946

Thursday evening came and Bill came. We had an unimaginably pleasant evening, and talked constantly from 7.20–12pm, with the exception of half an hour when we listened to Tommy Handley in ITMA on the wireless. Bill is an exceptionally nice boy and I'm happy to be able to tell you that he did *not* ask me to sleep with him, and I can't imagine why I thought he would. He's as unsophisticated about such things as I am.

I was so excited all day today I didn't know how I would recover sufficient calm to face the evening. I rushed home from work on my bicycle. Then it suddenly occurred to me that I was a fool, because when I'm happy I always feel that I'm living in a fool's paradise. As I prepared for the evening in my room, I wondered whether Bill would really come. I almost revelled in my masochism. But I knew he would come.

And he did. Punctually. And brought me some pears. We talked about everything under the sun and drank tea and ate biscuits and discovered that we both steal books. Isn't that awful and wonderful? If he does it too it can't be so bad. He's a brilliant undergraduate at Jesus College. I told him that I had recently appropriated The Complete Works of Shakespeare from Wolsey Hall Library costing 7/6d which I couldn't possibly afford (I might if Wolsey Hall paid me more). The time just flew by and suddenly it was midnight and Bill said he must go and asked if he could see me again. As before, I shrugged my shoulders and looked away and said: "I suppose so." I have this obsession about people thinking I don't know I'm being fooled, just in case I really am. In fact I had intended to tell Bill that I know quite well he only wants to see me because at the moment he has no one else, but the opportunity somehow didn't arise. Even if I knew it to be a lie, I would not hesitate to tell Bill that he need not think that I believe myself to be of the slightest significance to him. So when I carelessly shrugged my shoulders it was to convey all these feelings. But then I looked at him and he was frowning in a puzzled way and there was surprise and almost hurt in his face and I was terribly sorry for my attitude. Of course we arranged to see each other again – next Friday; we're going to the theatre. Even as I agreed to this the thought rushed through my mind: you're only serving as an object of momentary amusement to this man. Why should I serve as an object of amusement?

Of course, I'm a pervert, there's no other word for it. Other girls would not think of such things. They would go out and enjoy themselves and not give a damn about the motives of the man or of how much or little importance they are to him.

I'm glad Bill didn't make love to me. Goodnight.

22nd September 1946

Yesterday I went for a walk with Joan and the children, then had tea and supper with them at No. 66 – and had to stay the night because Joan had an attack of nerves. She made me up a bed in the sitting room. Because of the state she was in I couldn't talk to her about Bill. She was very weepy and said she didn't love the baby enough. I bathed Diana and put her to bed in her pram in the kitchen. I didn't like sleeping on the sofa and lay awake a long time, thinking about Bill and my lovely new suede mustard-colour shoes which stood beside my bed, or rather sofa, and about poor Joan. Halfway through the night Joan came in quietly and asked if she could stay with me as she was frightened on her own. Next day, Sunday, I spent most of the morning trying to ring a doctor for Joan, without success. I went home for lunch, prepared as usual for me by Mrs Labowsky and eaten from the tray at my desk, spent the afternoon and evening at Putz's, and rang for a doctor again – with no luck. When I got back to my room there was a message saying that Joan's husband had come, so I didn't need to sleep with her tonight, but promised to do so tomorrow, when her husband will have left again.

On Friday evening Putz and I listened to Beethoven's magnificent *9th Symphony* on my wireless. We sat motionless for an hour and a half, drinking the music in. It was difficult to get back to ordinary life again when it was over.

26th September 1946

Things are bad with Joan. I slept here, at No. 66, on Monday, and again tonight. I'm writing this sitting on the sofa which serves as my bed. After supper Joan handed me a key and said: "Will you do me a favour, Ingrid?"

"Of course. What is it?" I said.

"Take all the knives out of the kitchen drawer and lock them in that cupboard in the hall. It's the only one that locks. And hang on to the key. Would you, please?"

"Yes, of course. But why?"

At first she didn't answer. Then she said, "Because I don't want to hurt Diana."

That shook me. I didn't know what to say or what she wanted me to say. I went to the kitchen drawer quickly and took out all the knives I could find and locked them away, though I didn't really believe she would do anything to Diana. I can't understand what is the matter with Joan and feel helpless, even though she says I'm her lifeline. As far as I can see I'm no use to her at all, except for doing practical things. In the morning I promised to take Peter to the car in which he gets a lift to school, before going to work myself.

I went to the theatre with Putz and her friend Jerry on Tuesday, and on Wednesday evening Putz and I listened to *La Bohème* on my wireless.

Every time I think of my theatre date with Bill Emerson tomorrow night a feeling like terror shoots through me. What if I miss something I should have understood? What if I can't see something he points out because I refuse to wear my glasses in public? What if I want to go to the lavatory in the interval and can't find my way back to my seat? What if, what if . . . the possibilities for disaster are endless. Since childhood, fear, unreasonable fear, often marred what might have been happiness. The day I conquer fear the world will be my oyster. I have never before liked a man with whom I went out. Not even Mr Morris. I mean really liked, really wanted to be with. I haven't told you what Bill looks like, have I? He's very tall and thin and has straight blond hair, green eyes and a delightful smile. His face is oval and pale. He's always moving his eyebrows. I've never known anyone who moves their eyebrows. His whole appearance is delightfully boyish and typically English, and I adore him.

Once a long time ago, when I was waiting at the bus stop in the dark he came by on his bicycle and stopped to talk to me. He had been to see *The Rape of Lucretia* and so had I. I said I didn't like it, and could have bitten my tongue immediately afterwards because it must have made him doubt my intellect. Does he remember, I wonder?

152

27th September 1946

I know now what people mean when they say there's paradise on this earth for everyone somewhere.

The evening did not start too auspiciously. I felt as I knew I would, a little uncomfortable at the theatre with Bill. I wasn't particularly happy but didn't know what was wrong. I didn't like the play and boredom made me fidgety. My thoughts wandered and I remembered my comment to Bill on that beastly British opera, *The Rape of Lucretia*, and felt certain that I wasn't good enough for him, wasn't intelligent, sophisticated or beautiful enough. He will not put up with me as Harold did, who probably didn't understand me. But Bill will see through me in an instant.

We walked home. He came in with me. We drank tea and talked philosophy and books and I was ashamed of my ignorance as I always am with him, although with most other people, I usually feel quite intelligent.

It must have been fairly late, half past ten perhaps. We sat on my bed. I thought at any moment he would get up to go. But suddenly he took me in his arms and kissed me, and I wasn't frightened, and I didn't feel taut or repelled or childish. Quite the contrary. I loved being so close to him, his green eyes, the same colour as the bedspread on my bed, so near to my own, our arms around each other – I never wanted to let him go. I felt his hands in my hair, on my cheeks, somewhere, everywhere, my body, and for the first time in my life, I was enjoying love-making and longed for it to go on 'till all the seas run dry', till the end of eternity. When he spoke it was in whispers, and the words were beautiful compliments. I wanted to protest meekly once or twice, to tell him I knew it was just sport to him, amusing and pleasant but not serious, I didn't want him to think that I believed him to be serious, but my words only came out as vague mumbles. He said he could fall in love with me if I let him go on kissing me but he didn't want to fall in love. He said wasn't it odd that two intelligent people can get such joy out of a simple thing like the meeting of lips in a kiss. I wanted to cling to him and stroke his hair but I didn't want to show my emotions too much. It is difficult to keep one's feminine privacy when one is in the arms of an exciting man.

What I have to do now is to be very diplomatic. I must not give in to him every time because I think he tires of women quickly. Now that we have crossed the Rubicon – so it seems to me – I should feel more relaxed with him, better able to exercise some willpower. That first kiss changes everything. If intellectual love is turned into an entirely physical one I'm sorry about it, but it can't be helped. I'm afraid it will shorten the affair – there is nothing that can be done about that either. It has never happened to me and it had to happen some time. I want to make love with him all the time . . . but intend to stick to my resolution not to give in on every occasion. He said I was the first woman with whom he had ever felt mutual, sexual emotions and I laughed and said hypocritically: "How do you know I do? How do you know?"

"I know," he said. He was right, he was beautiful, I adored him. I thought: don't ever leave me, Bill, stay here, stay here, with me, always . . . I love you, I love you . . .

"You are lovely, you are lovely," said Bill's voice in answer to my thoughts. "I love your hair. It's dark and soft and curly. I love your charm. Dear Ingrid, dear Ingrid . . ." I only answered him in my thoughts for I had betrayed myself enough already, had let myself go far too much, and when he had finally gone I told myself I was a fool and an idiot and I kissed the pale green bedspread which he had touched with his body, and fell asleep.

28th September 1946

You see, I'm writing again to talk to you about Bill because he's never out of my mind. I'm constantly delighted and happy at the thought of him, and the memory of his voice which was like music and his kisses which were delicate as Japanese silk makes me weak in the knees. If I were never to see him again I should surely perish from misery. And if it is not over after next week, when we see each other again, if it goes on and we fall in love, then what? Surely the earth would not be big enough to accommodate so much happiness?

I bought a new frock today. For Bill.

Is God behind this?

30th September 1946

He said he would drop a note in today to let me know about Wednesday or Friday. No note has as yet arrived. I'm not really surprised. Even while we lay on the bed in each other's arms it occurred to me that I might never see him again now that I had succumbed to his kisses, but it was too terrible to contemplate. It seems fantastically unbelievable that he should let me down now. Although I never entered the affair with the remotest illusions, it seems incredible, inconceivable that he should let me down. I shall wait. He will come. He must come.

Same evening:

He came. He stayed only a few minutes because he was on his way to a Liberal Meeting. We're going to a concert on Friday. Bill and music – there can't be a more ideal combination. But afterwards I shall want him to make love to me again. The only trouble is Mrs Labowsky, who has been away, will be very angry if I bring 'a young man' home with me late at night!

If only Bill could fall in love with me!

3rd October 1946

Yesterday I only worked in the morning and went to London afterwards to see my father's doctor and have my thyroid gland checked. I went straight to my father's office from the station. I looked for a coat but there was nothing I liked. The visit to the doctor was equally negative. Afterwards we had tea at Buzzards and dinner at a Czech Restaurant where my cousin Herta joined us. Then I caught the train back to Oxford.

Bill called again last night, brought me some more pears and told me the concert on Friday had been cancelled, so we're going to the Trout Inn instead.

Today I had tea and supper at Joan's. She's having some treatment now, and a girl of about 16 called Sheila sleeps in and helps with the baby, so I hope Joan will soon be her old self again.

5th October 1946

Once again I was aware of a strong desire to escape, a cowardly longing to run away and hide. This is what always happens to me just before I am due to see Bill. All week I long for our meeting and when it gets to the point I am sick with fear of facing something which means so much and in which I have to play such an important part.

Then, when I am with him, when the philosophising and talking is done and we begin making love on my large pale-green covered bed, I feel I can never let him go, if he went away I should die or at least no longer be able to feel whole or sane. The things he says to me when he makes love are like warm sunshine on my skin, like cool sheets, like nectar, like music. All else becomes oblivion.

We had been to the Trout Inn for drinks and afterwards walked along the towpath in the dark. Then he came home with me and we had supper. It was not late, so Mrs Labowsky couldn't object. We talked about this and that. He told me he was a virgin. I believed him. Soon afterwards we were in each other's arms. Now his face was in my hair, now his lips were on my throat, our hands explored each other, we kissed passionately, until we were out of breath, and then we lay in silence and I thought only of him, or of nothing at all, and occasionally we spoke in whispers and he told me all the things he liked about me. Once or twice I wondered vaguely how long all this would go on, and whether it was wise to ignore the future so entirely. I'm sure it won't go on for very long. Such strong emotions are bound to reach a climax soon. Why don't we sleep together? I suppose because we are both inexperienced and a bit afraid. But I have already lost my pride, my sanity, my privacy, my peace of mind through Bill – why shouldn't I give up my virginity too? Such a stupid, useless possession, virginity.

We have decided, however, to be ascetic, and only to make love once a week. Every Friday. The rest of the long week we will think about Friday and about making love on my green bed by the dim light of my desk lamp. Then Friday will come, and Bill will come, and love and happiness.

On Tuesday next we are going to the Playhouse. We will not make love afterwards because it would be against the rules. We don't want to take each other for granted. We shall wait for Friday. And, though I long for him as I have never longed for any man physically, when Friday comes and Bill wants to take me in his arms I shall say: "Suppose I say no, Bill? Suppose I say no? What then?" Perhaps he will smile back and answer, "You won't say no." And he will be right, of course. I won't say no. Life is too short to rob oneself of such pleasures.

Putz and I went shopping this afternoon and I bought a coat. In the evening I went to see Joan and stayed for coffee. Sheila was there. Afterwards Joan walked back with me a little way. She was surprised that I wasn't spending Saturday night with Bill, but Bill won't go anywhere on Saturdays; he says that night is for plebeians.

I'm working overtime again next week as a lot of books have come in from the publishers.

It has turned quite cold and I have started having my electric heater on, though it doesn't give off much heat.

8th October 1946

I've just returned from the theatre with Bill. We met Peter and Derek there and had drinks with them. Derek, you remember, was in the group I went to the Trout Inn with. I wonder what they think about Bill's friendship with me. Are they surprised? I remember now that I flirted a little with Derek at the Trout. So what does he think? Little did he know – little did I know – that the next time we would meet I would be Bill's girlfriend.

It was a glorious night when Bill and I went for a walk after the theatre, with a clear dark sky. We walked across fields and the air was cool but not cold. We walked arm in arm. There was complete silence. We said very little, as if to preserve it. Can you picture the scene? A wide open space, a cool dark autumn night and the two of us walking silently and alone through the universe. Presently we came to a stile. He kissed me. I closed my eyes and stood quite still for I don't know how long – minutes, hours, days, years? "We broke the rule," I said at last. "It's not Friday today." And we both laughed, and didn't care.

I wonder how soon Bill will get tired of me? He is lovely, so lovely.

11th October 1946

I wish I had a gigantic vocabulary, a brilliant command of the English language. As it is I can only repeat myself over and over again. I have no new words left in which to express the beautiful, violent love Bill and I made again on my bed tonight. I shivered with emotion. He asked me if I was cold and I said no. The

157

electric heater was on which gave off a little light and less warmth. If ever I owned any person I owned Bill tonight as he lay in my arms. He belonged to me completely and wholly. We were so close to each other that I felt we no longer possessed a private life of our own. Once I suddenly thought of my mother and my father and wondered whether, if I had lived at home with them, they would have protected me from so much joy, and the pain which must follow. I also thought, fleetingly, of the future, when Bill will be gone and I shall be alone again. Then I heard his voice: "May I, Ingrid?" I thought he meant have intercourse and I didn't answer him at first. But he only wanted to touch my breasts, naked, to feel them in his hand. I was shy, excited, embarrassed, thrilled. Now I feel mean, mean and low, because I wouldn't let him. I only unbuttoned the top of my dress and took his hand and placed it on my covered breast. But he wanted me to remove my slip and brassiere. I wouldn't, and continued to hold his hand, and all that mattered at that moment was that he shouldn't feel my bare, big, breasts. "I wonder," he said, "if we should have married had we met six years later?" I was glad he didn't persist in removing my underwear. Then he said again how he had never enjoyed making love like this before, how much he liked *me, me, me* . . . Did I like him too?

"I like you very much," I said.

"I believe you almost love me," he said, after a pause.

"I wouldn't be too sure if I were you," I said. "Why do you think so?"

"Because you treat me so kindly," he said.

Then we discussed the inevitable: shall we have intercourse? How do two inexperienced people prevent accidents? What exactly did being careful mean? I didn't know any of the answers but knew vaguely that, in order to keep him, I must live up to his idea of me: I felt rather wary having to live up to this. I felt I ought to do something, but I didn't know what. Seduce him? Say something outrageous? But I only pressed him against me harder and drank in the vanilla scent of his kisses and felt his heart beat against mine. I was some substance consisting of nothing except one insane emotion, given wings by this lovely man in my arms. The insane emotion fought and won against reason.

After Bill had gone I thought a long time about him. I knew there would be many other women in his life after me, and possibly a few men in mine. I thought: whatever happens he must always remember me, I must be different, must stand out in his life, must occupy a place into which no one else will ever fit. However many women there will be, tall, beautiful, blondes he will hold in his arms as he did me tonight, they must not obscure the memory of me. And when he compares us he must say to himself. "But Ingrid was more alive . . . I could feel her heart beat against mine . . . Ingrid had a delightful laugh, a sexy body and soft dark curly hair . . . she held my hand in hers, like this . . . This one is not like Ingrid, no, this one will never do . . ."

Gradually I recovered the things that mysteriously vanished during the two hours we were in each other's arms: my privacy, every ambition, every desire except for him. I got myself something to eat and drink, though not long ago hunger and thirst had been totally absent. I did not think it would be like this tonight. I thought the first thrill might have gone. But it was more wonderful for both of us than before. Perhaps it will reach its climax next week and we will really sleep together.

13th October 1946

I was at a concert this afternoon with Lieselotte and her friend Jerry. Just as the pianist sat down to start playing, Bill came in. I was not really surprised as I felt in my bones that he would come. Late as always, and slouching behind Peter and a girl, they took their seats a few rows in front of us. I know the girl and dislike her, and Bill does too, but Peter always drags girls around with him and is never content if he's not in feminine society. But when he's alone with a girl he's gauche and unromantic, as I know only too well.

My first emotion on seeing Bill was a longing to escape, to rush out of the concert hall. I did not, of course, but stayed and listened to the music and watched the back of Bill and imagined him thinking of me and remembering our love making. I was determined that he shouldn't see me for I would not have known how to behave towards him without betraying myself in front of other people.

Sitting on the bus on the way home after the concert I saw Peter and the girl walking home – and Bill was not with them.

I shall be with him again on Tuesday, at the theatre. Then, on

159

Friday, we shall lie in each other's arms on my bed and time will stop, like a machine that has been switched off.

15th October 1946

No, tonight I am not happy, for tonight Bill hurt me twice and I betrayed my mother. We spent the evening at the theatre as arranged, and everything went smoothly. On the way home we went for a walk across the silent fields again and Bill kissed me. As if in anticipation of some impending unpleasantness, the large expanse of meadows meeting the black sky at some distant only-to-be-imagined point had a gloomy effect on me and made me think of the hopelessness of our sensual affair. I wanted to laugh and cry and run away to some place where Bill could not find me. But I had to surrender when I felt his body pressed against mine under the dark sky, I had to surrender and let the future take care of itself when our closeness erupted in passionate kisses. And then the first thing happened that marred the evening for me, and it was my fault. I said to him, in a moment of madness, "No one has ever stroked my hair the way you do since my mother." As soon as I had said it I wished I hadn't. My mother is too sacred to be mentioned to a casual lover. But I had mentioned her. I had mentioned my beloved mother to an infatuated boy whose name I shall probably have forgotten in a few years' time.

Next it was Bill who said something that should not have been said. He had just kissed me violently and his arms were still around me. "Well, Ingrid," he said, "I may not be in love with you but I have certainly never before been physically attracted to any woman so much." I must count my blessings then, I thought bitterly, but said nothing. Honesty is all right if it doesn't hurt you.

The third blow fell when, just as we had almost reached Lonsdale Road, Bill said, "Haven't you any friends? I never see any of them." Nothing is a greater insult to me than to accuse me of having no friends. As a matter of fact I have been rather lonely lately and felt deserted by my numerous friends (for you know I have quite a few).

I said, "Why should you?" He laughed, and then I laughed but I didn't mean it – for me, something very serious had happened.

There's an inevitable barrier between us, something that

frightens me, that makes me feel he ought to be bored with me and exchange me for some clever, light-hearted, beautiful girl. That barrier stimulates all my complexes, makes me play a part I don't know and can't act. And there's a voice that continually whispers into my ear: "Fool . . . Fool . . . fool . . . you are nothing to him and never will be . . ."

I know, too, that he wants to go to dances, but I don't. I should shrink with shame and embarrassment and humiliation if I had to dance with him. I would give all I have to be normal and without inhibitions, and be able to dance as well as Bill can. I can't help thinking that Bill is a sadist, or perhaps only very tactless. He has frequently said things that should have been left unsaid, and they are usually absolutely true and I am defenceless against them. He's often witty with it, and always charming, but I can't stand sufficiently outside myself to admire him for it, I suppose because I'm too selfish, stupid and petty-minded.

The one great thing we derive from each other is a sexual thrill. I do not, therefore, give the whole affair longer than a month. We continue to discuss going to bed together. He is coming again on Saturday evening . . .

18th October 1946

I spent the afternoon and evening at Joan's yesterday. After the children were in bed we sat by the fire in the dark and talked about each other's problems. She understands mine better than I do hers, which I regret. Putz has gone to Cobham for the weekend to stay at Ann's Cottage with Anni and Felix. I am going to a Swiss book exhibition tomorrow afternoon, and in the evening . . . well, you know what's happening in the evening.

19th October 1946

If happiness is not for me, it is my fault alone. Whatever happens is my fault, everything is my fault. I can't stand the strain any longer. Something will have to give.

Tonight, as you know, Bill came. We talked and laughed and ate. Then, much later, we turned the light out so that now only the feeble light from the electric fire enabled us to see dim outlines of each other. We lay close together on my bed, touching, kissing,

161

desiring, thrilling each other.

I don't know what happened to him tonight, I have never seen him like this before and I was frightened, although I must have suspected or even known all along that his true self had not yet been revealed.

He urged me to sleep with him and I remained silent and shook my head and gave vague answers. He cried, "Why not, Ingrid? Why not?" I knew by his voice that something terribly important to him was happening, that he was worked up and not himself and that our future lay in my hands. Suddenly all his passionate tenderness, his gentle voice had vanished. He pressed me against him with all his strength and urged me in a fearful tone to submit to him.

"You'll have other women," I told him, "who will be tall, blonde, beautiful, slim ones with pointed breasts and sophisticated smiles."

"I want to sleep with *you, now*," he replied. "Do you realise that I can strip you and rape you?"

"You won't," I said. "Wait for some tall, slim, blonde . . ."

"And you are short and dark and fat and I want you," he interrupted.

"Not particularly short and fat," I objected, annoyed.

"Yes, short and fat, fat, fat," he laughed, throwing his head back so that now his ear was against my cheek. I wanted to cry and I knew that something was desperately wrong but still I couldn't let him go.

"Of course, you won't want me to marry you afterwards, will you?" he went on.

"It never occurred to me. I thought we were being immoral."

"Yes, but so many women make that condition. But that's all right then, that's settled. You do agree that it would be infinitely pleasant to have intercourse, don't you? We'll be very careful. Look, I brought this book, 'Modern Birth Control for Today'." He pulled it out of his pocket. My heart sank.

"Are you planning to follow the instructions like a cookery recipe?" I asked.

He laughed, and kissed me again, and whispered savagely between kisses, "Why won't you, Ingrid. Why won't you? You like me very much. You make love to me beautifully. I want more than that, more, more. Why not? Why won't you? Oh, woman, torturer of my soul!"

" 'My body', you mean."

"I hope you're miserable, uncomfortable, wretched. Are you, Ingrid? No, I'm cruel, very cruel. I wish I were callous. Callous people are happy . . . Funny, I possess your body wholly at this moment, and yet not at all. Sleep with me, Ingrid, please sleep with me . . ."

Naturally I was miserable. I hugged him as tightly as before but I couldn't bring back his tenderness.

"You are selfish, stubborn and selfish," he whispered into my ear. "Why are you so selfish?" Then hot passion took over again as he kissed me ferociously, "This can't go on," he said. "This can't go on."

"Then why don't you go?" I said, hating myself for it.

"I don't mean that. I mean we have to take the next step now. Ingrid, if I were experienced, would you sleep with me?"

"I don't know. I don't know, Bill." Suddenly he let go of me and abruptly sat up and laughed out loud, until I was frightened and felt sick. "What are you laughing at, Bill?"

"At myself! At myself! Wasting time, trifling with emotions, kissing you, not loving you. Yes, you deserve to be treated unkindly. Oh God, what a life, but what does it matter? 'Nothing is good or bad but thinking makes it so' ."

I felt I ought to escape before it is too late but I was numb, paralysed. To lose Bill now meant to lose everything. At last we got up. We remained in the dark. "You'd better keep that book," he said, "and study it."

"Why?"

"You will need to."

"No, I won't."

"You won't? All right then. Then there's nothing more to be said. And to think I studied it till two o'clock this morning, and made notes."

"Rubbish, Bill."

"Well, anyhow, this is the end, isn't it? If you won't, you won't. Shall I see you again, or not? Monday I go to a Liberal meeting, Tuesday I can't, Wednesday I'm going to a party." He was enjoying himself now.

"I think we'd better not see each other any more, then," I said.

"You think so? Perhaps you're right. I don't know. What about

Thursday though? Can you?"

"No. Leave it this week. Give it a rest. I'll see you next week. Ring me. And Bill . . ." I had not planned this at all. I was completely out of control. "Leave that book. I'll read it."

"And then you'll sleep with me?" he cried.

"I don't know yet. Damn it, give me a chance. You've been contemplating this for weeks and I've only had ten minutes." (Lie!) He smiled. My eyes had got so used to the dark that I could see his smile quite clearly. I went to the desk to write down my telephone number and while I did so he placed his hand on my shoulder and it crossed my mind that this might be the last tender touch of his I shall experience. He didn't kiss me goodbye. Just as he was about to go he sat down again on the edge of the bed and said, "I feel ill. I'd better go home before I'm sick."

"Shall I get you a glass of water?"

"No, thanks. I'm going now. I'll ring you."

"Don't if you don't want to . . ."

"Of course I'll ring you. Goodnight."

"Goodnight, Bill. And if I'm not at home, leave a message."

"Oh God, tuppence wasted!"

This, then is the real Bill, a man to be feared rather than loved. I suppose it is unfair of me to work him up like this and then deprive him of his climax. The point is, why don't I sleep with him? Because we're not in love? No, that can't be the reason. Sexual attraction is sufficient. Because of risks? No, not with birth control. Why then? Fear of losing him? But I shall lose him either way. My dilemma is: shall I lose him with or without my virginity?

I shall think about it tomorrow. I'm too tired now, and too weary and miserable.

24th October 1946

The King and Queen came to Oxford today. All the staff of Wolsey Hall got an extra half hour off for lunch and most of us trooped into town to see the Royal pair. I've had my novel back from the Authors' Alliance with a long letter of criticism and also some praise. They think I've quite a lot of talent.

On Tuesday evening I was at the Rieszs' and Peter took me home. My father has sacked Mr Riesz, which I find so embarrassing that I've hardly been able to face the family, who've been so kind and hospitable to us.

When I asked my father how he could have done this he replied, "He was no good."

"But he was a friend," I said.

"My firm is not a charity organisation," he answered.

Dr Elia, the Rieszs' Spanish lodger, took Putz home.

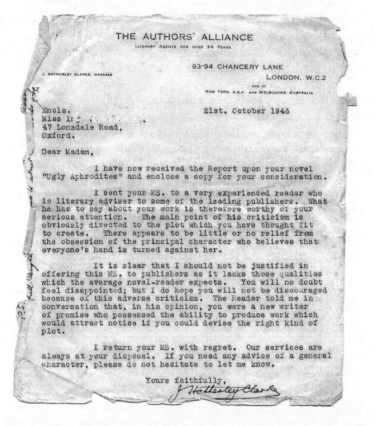

THE AUTHORS' ALLIANCE
LITERARY AGENTS FOR OVER 36 YEARS

93-94 CHANCERY LANE
LONDON. W.C.2

J. HATHERLEY CLARKE, MANAGER

AND AT
NEW YORK, U.S.A. AND MELBOURNE, AUSTRALIA

Encls.
Miss I᠎ ᠎ ᠎
47 Lonsdale Road,
Oxford.

21st. October 1946

Dear Madam,

I have now received the Report upon your novel "Ugly Aphrodites" and enclose a copy for your consideration.

I sent your MS. to a very experienced reader who is literary adviser to some of the leading publishers. What he has to say about your work is therefore worthy of your serious attention. The main point of his criticism is obviously directed to the plot which you have thought fit to create. There appears to be little or no relief from the obsession of the principal character who believes that everyone's hand is turned against her.

It is clear that I should not be justified in offering this MS. to publishers as it lacks those qualities which the average novel-reader expects. You will no doubt feel disappointed; but I do hope you will not be discouraged because of this adverse criticism. The Reader told me in conversation that, in his opinion, you were a new writer of promise who possessed the ability to produce work which would attract notice if you could devise the right kind of plot.

I return your MS. with regret. Our services are always at your disposal. If you need any advice of a general character, please do not hesitate to let me know.

Yours faithfully,
J Hatherley Clarke

On Sunday Joan and the children came to tea and in the evening I fetched Putz from the station after her weekend at Cobham. Before going to bed on Sunday night I made my decision: I shall sleep with Bill. As you know, we were not going to see each other this week. He telephoned on Tuesday: I was out. He telephoned today: I was out again. Mrs Labowsky said, "You must have a

165

very ardent admirer." Little does she know! Today at 10pm, about a minute after I got home from an evening at Joan's to meet her sister Phyllis again, he came in person. I had not taken my coat off yet. He said:

"I'm awfully sorry about Saturday night. I was abominably rude."

"Were you? I've forgotten." What a good liar I am becoming.

"I was feeling ill, you know."

"Poor Bill; come and sit down." I wondered how he really felt about me. He said:

"Have you decided about coming to bed with me?" My heart beat so loudly that he must surely have heard it.

"I'd like to," I said.

"Good. Have you finished the book?"

"No. I'm a slow reader."

"But no getting married afterwards, mind."

"Don't be silly." But he was kinder again. I was wrong when I thought he would never again touch me tenderly. We made love.

"We were going to give it a rest this week," I reminded him.

"Yes. We were," he said. And then he added, "You like me very much, don't you?"

"Just physical attraction," I said, as carelessly as I could.

"Poor Ingrid. What do you see in me? When I look in the mirror . . ."

"I don't care about looks." Another lie.

I did not tell him that I adore the way he moves his eyebrows when he speaks, the way he smiles at his own jokes, the way he strokes my hair, the way he runs his long fingers up and down his legs when he tells a story. Because he will never love me I will never tell him these things.

I wonder what it would be like to have a child by Bill?

1st November 1946

I had another scene with Mr Newell about my salary today. He's very stingy and all the girls complain to him about never having a rise.

On Monday evening Bill and I went to the pictures and afterwards for a walk till 11.30pm. He didn't say anything nice unless you count his repeated declarations of his sexual passion

166

for me. Once I told him that was no particular compliment, as most men want to sleep with most women. I think I behaved remarkably wisely with him, and laughed off his more callous remarks, and generally adopted a don't-care attitude. One day Bill will meet a girl whom he will respect sufficiently to refrain from telling her the naked truth, and with whom the idea of marriage won't be so objectionable. And I – perhaps I, too, will one day meet a man who will feel more than only sexual desire for me. If I do, I wonder what that man is doing now?

7th November 1946

Audrey called last Sunday and stayed for a chat. She asked me if I had a boyfriend and I said yes.

On Tuesday I went to see a Mme Zuccari to arrange German Literature lessons, as I'm considering taking the Higher School Certificate exam in German. She lives in St John's Street, not far from Mr Morris's house. The murderer returning to the scene of his crime! My first lesson has been arranged for Friday the 15th. It being Guy Fawkes Day on Tuesday we had fireworks in the grounds of Wolsey Hall, which was a nice change from sitting in the office.

I don't know myself. I don't understand myself. All my introspection has got me nowhere . . . Last week I had begun to feel quite detached from Bill and was looking ahead to a time when we would no longer know each other. On Monday I burned with desire and passion again while I was in his arms. We said very little, and he was very kind. Not one unkind word left his lips. At times I didn't know what to do; I felt something like an electric current racing through my body, I wanted us to melt into one inseparable being. What shall I do? What *can* I do? My passion is too strong for me. When Bill makes love to me I am just an animal.

He said I had beautiful, beautiful hair. He said, "I hope, Ingrid, that when we have reached our sexual climax we shall still go on being friends." That was one of the best things he ever said. He told me how much he liked me. He hoped it was not only physical liking I had for him. But we couldn't have sex tonight because I had my period.

After supper we listened to Gigli on the wireless. I said *La*

Bohème was one of my favourite Italian operas.

"Since when do the French pronounce the 'h'?" he said in a teasing way. I had mispronounced the word Bohème and deserved his correction, for this, unlike most other things he talks about, is something I should know.

"Bo-ème, then," I said, duly ashamed, and he laughed.

11th November 1946

I wish I could say it was because of my morals that I refused Bill tonight. I wish I could find some good, respectable reason. But I can't. It was fear. Plain, simple lack of courage. Happiness will always be denied me because I am too faint-hearted to fight for it.

You know how badly I wanted Bill. I was determined to sleep with him tonight. I was ready for him. In my own mind everything was arranged. He came. We chatted and had supper, then we lay down. We kissed and embraced in the dark, in the silence, on the green bedspread. I knew that he knew that tonight was the night. He partly undressed me and placed his hands on my bare skin and his face on my breast. He began to take my skirt off. I held his hands and my body shook with fear. I felt like a soldier on a battlefield, awaiting death. Inside my head I was frantically arguing with myself. A thousand voices droned in my ears, all screaming against each other. I heard: "Don't, don't, don't do it! Oh, go on, give yourself to him! Now! No, don't, don't, he'll leave you afterwards! Oh, never mind, let him take you or he'll hate you!" And all the time I wanted him so much. I even told him to lock the door. I knew he was undoing his trousers as he did so. He returned and tried to take my skirt off again. He begged, he implored, he asked why not? I wished I knew. I had no answer. I was utterly miserable. His hands travelled to my thighs in a last desperate attempt but I went rigid. Oh, how I wish I could tell you truthfully that I refused him because we are not in love, because of the risk of pregnancy, because of his frequent outbursts of sarcasm and callousness, because of his inexperience or for moral reasons. But I can't tell you that, because the only reason is that I was too scared. I'm truly a failure in every sense. I failed Bill, and I failed myself. If I can't have his love, at least I could have had his body.

Bill was extremely disappointed. He thought tonight I would

168

consent. So did I. He began to be sarcastic again. It was all my fault. I hated myself deeply. But I did wonder a little afterwards: had Bill been a bit different, more confidence-inspiring and sure of himself, would it have been easier for me? I've heard it said that Englishmen are supposed to be poor lovers – had that something to do with it?

We are going to see each other in a fortnight. If we do not have intercourse then we never shall. If I refuse him then I shall never see him again. I know I am weak, but I'm going to try very hard to keep to my resolution.

I forgot to say that I came home from work this morning as I felt sick, and spent the day in bed. This is no excuse, however.

16th November 1946

Today, my half day, I went Christmas shopping with Putz. Afterwards I was supposed to meet Audrey to go to the pictures with her, but we missed each other. I don't know how. Instead I got a lift home in a car driven by a complete stranger.

Yesterday I had my first German literature lesson with Mme. Zuccari after work. We are going to read Goethe's Faust. Judging by the state of her room she's more interested in literature than personal comfort. I only hope she doesn't expect me to be equally dedicated, or too clever. After the lesson I went to the flicks with Joan and met Peter and George there – without a girl. Joan and I usually go to the Scala Cinema to see foreign films.

Something else happened today: I met Mr Morris. I had popped out to the North Parade shops during morning break to do some shopping, as I often do. On my way back I saw, in the distance, a tall man standing by a telegraph pole in the Banbury Road. He was wearing a mustard coloured jacket and grey flannel trousers. I came nearer. Yes – it was Mr Morris. There is something about his appearance that is unique. He saw me too, and walked towards me. His hair seemed a bit greyer, otherwise he was unchanged. He asked me how I was and I did likewise and then I asked him whether he was waiting for a bus. Yes, he was, he replied.

"But that's a telegraph pole, not a bus stop," I said. "The bus stop is over there." And I pointed towards it.

"How silly of me. Thank you," he replied, and almost ran off,

169

h

because a bus was approaching. I looked after him, a sad, lonely, pathetic figure in the grey morning. I felt sorry for him.

Nobody need feel sorry for me, however, not ever again, for I have to tell you that I have lost a great virtue – honesty. God knows how it happened. Loneliness, frustration, anger at the world, all these, I suppose. Today I stole something in a shop. A little leather pocket diary. I felt strangely justified in this deed. It was an act of retaliation, an escape from my self-inflicted confines. I couldn't convince myself to the contrary. And it was exciting. It seems ironic to be confessing this sin in full view of Miss Frost, my ex-headmistress, who taught scripture and was the personification of good. And here she is, looking at me in – what? Sorrow? Gentle disapproval? Sad understanding? What would she really say if she knew?

IC ASSOCIATION

Candidates - Vote for them

To the Electors of Arwenack Ward

Ladies and Gentlemen,

As your representative on the Town Council, my first consideration would be for the families resident in the Ward. Some need new homes, others need improvement in housing conditions, and I should do everything I could to see that every man, woman and child is comfortably housed.

The principal industry of the Ward is the catering trade. Something might be done to raise the standard of training of the personnel required in this industry. The Town Council could do much to improve the amenities of the town, including the raising of the standard of entertainment, by which both residents and visitors would benefit.

We are fortunate in having on our Town Council a group of men who are sincerely interested in the welfare of the community, and I should be proud to serve with them in furthering your interests.

Having in mind the recent expressions of concern for the physical and moral welfare of children and young persons I should take special interest in this aspect of the responsibilities of the Local Authority.

EDITH M. FROST.

21st November 1946

A few weeks ago Joan said to me, "You know that I want you to be Diana's godmother, don't you?" For a moment I couldn't think of anything to say as this was such a surprise.

"Oh, Joan, are you sure?" I asked her. "It's a terrific honour." I felt really pleased.

"Silly old thing," said Joan. "Who else would I ask if not you? Phyllis is the other godmother." The christening is to be next Sunday at St Philips Church, and Peter will be christened at the same time, since he wasn't done as a baby. On the same day my father, Jack and Jane are coming to Oxford for the day by car. Lucky in a way, as I won't have to see much of my father.

Audrey telephoned yesterday. She waited at the wrong cinema

on Saturday! How wretched I would have been to have missed an outing with her three years ago! We are going to the theatre on Friday and Putz, Ailsa and another girl called Mary (some friend of Ailsa's) are coming too.

I stayed late at work last Monday and Tuesday in order to study as there are some useful books in the library. I'm looking forward to my next lesson with Mme Zuccari on Friday (between work and the theatre). Before I called at Joan's on Monday evening I went to a pub to buy a bottle of something for her, but found the pub closed. I was pleased, as I don't like walking into a pub on my own, and have never done it in my life.

There's an interesting new girl at Wolsey Hall called Miss Lenton. We've been gravitating towards each other for some time, and the friendship was cemented when she gave me a cream bun on Tuesday. She's older than I am and a graduate and very intelligent – unfortunately also rather religious. I've observed that intelligent people often are, and am at a loss to understand it. Like me, she loves the new Third Programme on the wireless which started in September. Mrs Labowsky and Miss Lorch listen to it non-stop. I'm always a bit worried about being labelled a foreigner if I show any intellectual leanings. With Miss Lenton, however, it is different. We're going out to lunch together on Saturday.

I feel uncomfortable about my new decision, queer, uncertain. You see, the next time I see Bill I want to tell him that it is all over between us. I have an idea he has the same intention, and I want to forestall him. He's coming on Monday, in the hope of at last losing his virginity no doubt, after which he will have no further interest in me.

24th November 1946

My father's car, driven by Jack, reached Carfax at the appointed hour this morning, Sunday, and Putz and I were there to meet it. The five of us had lunch at Ross's, then visited Christ Church College and afterwards went for a drive. I left them early to attend the christening, in my capacity as proud godmother. The church was full of Joan's relations, and Dr Beschorner was there too, of course. He came into the church holding Peter by the hand. It appeared Peter didn't want to be baptised. He had never been to a church. The young vicar bent down till his face was level with Peter's and said to him kindly, "You can't go to heaven till you've been baptised, you know. You want to go to heaven, don't you?"

"No," replied Peter, "I want to go home." Joan and I looked at each other and smiled, and Dr B. laughed out loud.

Otherwise it all went smoothly, I didn't drop Diana, and when the vicar said, "I baptise you in the name of the Father, the Son and the Holy Spirit," nobody cried. Afterwards there was a big tea at the Beschorners'. In the evening I went to Putz's to hear how she spent the rest of the day with my father, Jack and Jane.

Tomorrow night, when Bill comes, my future will be decided.

25th November 1946

I wanted real love, and I got sex instead. What made me think that I could be loved so easily?

It has happened. This is the moment I've been waiting for, to tell you that I have slept with a man. Don't look at me like that – yes, of course I was disappointed, of course I'm far from happy, of course I'm wondering if there is anything in life worth having. But let me start at the beginning.

He came punctually at 7pm. We talked, ate and drank. He was charming. I thought I would tell him that we should stop seeing each other after I had failed him again, but he made it harder and harder. He said I was beautiful to him, that since he last saw me an eternity of longing for me had passed, he had desired me, been hungry for me, night and day. He called me his darling. He even said he loved me. The way he stroked me and touched me was more wonderful than it had ever been. He sounded and felt totally sincere. I should have known better. But whatever followed, I shall remember Bill during those moments just before we had intercourse. If it was all a lie then it was a beautiful lie. His urging was gentle and kind and loving. He said, "You make my life worthwhile." I knew that tonight I could not fail him. I got up and went to the lavatory and took my knickers off.

"Don't you wear knickers?" asked Bill, when I had lain down beside him again and his hand felt me.

"Of course. I've taken them off."

"That's cheating," he said. And then everything happened very quickly. It was funny, feeling this thing there. But I felt nothing else, just this fleeting touch. I was so triumphant that I had conquered myself, had at last experienced what had been a mystery since adolescence, that disappointment took some time to set in. It may have been a mystery but there was nothing to solve. It was as ugly as the rest of life with all its promises of vague, unobtainable pleasures. Something was very wrong, and not only for me, Bill was laughing, and it was a horrible laugh. Suddenly there was a different man in my arms. I was afraid.

"What's the matter?" I asked fearfully.

"Well," he said, "that was over quickly."

"What happened?"

"Nothing happened. It's over."

"But you can do it again."

Another laugh, uglier than the last.

"It takes twenty-four hours for a man to ejaculate again," he said.

I hope that no one I like will ever experience anything as horrible as what I experienced during these moments that followed. I hope that no one I like will ever have a lover like Bill. I could not imagine how anyone could change so quickly from being kind and loving to being a cold stranger. I was very glad I had not undressed completely as he had wanted me to. We were still lying close together and I begged him silently with my caresses to be kind, but it was useless. Instead of returning my caresses he said cruelly:

"Now if you had been as beautiful as Simone Simon, Ingrid, we could have done it with the light on. What a pity."

I tore myself away from him and got up. I hated him. I was ashamed that he had touched my body. He listened to my dressing and made little mocking comments but I didn't care any more. I was angry – openly angry with him, for the first time. I told him he hadn't behaved very well. That seemed to amuse him. He told me about some woman he had once loved who had jilted him. His attitude was all at once: up with love, down with sex. He went on to tell me that for the first three weeks of our acquaintance he thought I was a goddess . . . I didn't ask when and why I ceased to be one. He said he was proud that I gave in to him but could not now imagine why he had bothered to have intercourse at all. He didn't think we would again. I said I might insist he unvirgin me completely (for I knew he didn't really do anything to me).

173

Oh God, what's the use of going over it all? It's hopeless. I think I'd rather be lonely than spend any more evenings with Bill. Before he left he said, "I'll see you next week," in a casual sort of way; and then he quoted T.S.Eliot:

"When lovely woman has stooped to folly,
   and paces about the room again alone,
   she smoothes her hair with automatic hand,
   and puts a record on the gramophone."

30th November 1946

More Christmas shopping with Putz this afternoon. Afterwards we visited Mrs Riesz at the Ratcliffe hospital where she had had a minor operation.

There's another new girl at Wolsey Hall; her name is Ann Norton, and she's as beautiful as Miss Lenton is clever. The three of us had an interesting discussion about religion in our tea break on Wednesday. I had lunch with Ann yesterday. After work I had my German literature lesson, half of which was spent discussing with Mme Zuccari the personalities of the learned Faust who says, "I know that I know nothing," and his silly servant Wagner, who in contrast says, "I know a lot, but I want to know everything." Literature is a wonderful antidote against unhappiness. So is talking to Joan. I spent the evening with her as usual on Thursday and told her what had taken place with Bill.

"Oh Ingrid, I'm so glad you're still a virgin," she said, confirming what I believed myself. "Don't give your virginity away. Promise me – wait for the right man." But how long, I wondered, and where is he, and how will I know if ever I do meet him?

2nd December 1946

Tonight for the second time in my life I seriously thought about suicide and there was only the dreadful fear of death to prevent me. The first occasion was when it was clear my mother was dead.

Today I lost Bill. Although I expected it all along I did not know that it would cause me so much suffering. I felt so hopeless when I'd read the letter, so utterly incapable of doing anything that I didn't even think I'd be able to write and tell you about it until at least next week.

It was about 8.30pm. I was just undressing as I wanted to go to bed early and study, it being much warmer there than sitting over the little electric fire. I heard the doorbell. I heard Mrs Labowsky go to the door and open it. I heard Bill's voice. I quickly called out that I couldn't see him as I was undressed. (Ha, ha). I heard him go, and the door close. There was no need for me to read the note Mrs Labowsky handed me. It said exactly what I knew it would say, only more coldly. I didn't open it at first. I am glad he will never know that my first thought on reading that his sexual attraction for me had disappeared and that for us to pretend in a farce would only hurt me more in the long run – was to kill myself. I'm glad he will never know that, when I read that letter, I fell in love with him for the first time. Or perhaps it was just the intense pain, for I always associate love with pain. When I was a little girl I told my mother I was sure that I was destined to have a sad love affair. She laughed kindly and told me not to be silly. Well, now she is dead and I can't prove to her that I was right. I could do no studying that night, of course. I could not stop thinking of Bill, in all his different poses: sitting in my room, his long legs crossed, talking about the wonderful poetry of Baudelaire, his eyebrows moving all the while; that time at the Trout Inn, surrounded by his friends, a glass of cider in his hand, his face lit up with boyish pleasure; sitting next to me at the theatre, muttering cheeky comments on the play; above all lying with me on my green bedspread, his tongue exploring the inside of my mouth. When the other episodes ended – with Mr Morris, Harold, Jimmy, Otto – it was a blow to my pride but I didn't really care. For Bill I grieve with all my heart. I am so unhappy that I can't cry. I long for him and I want him back at all costs. For me it began properly the night we attempted intercourse, however unsatisfactory, and for him it ended. He slept with me and he jilted me. There was nothing else to conquer.

Only my heart. He didn't want that.

11th December 1946

After work on most days I either see Putz or Joan or have my German literature lesson. Last week Mme Zuccari and I had a

175

long talk after the lesson. She asked me if I'd like to work at Exeter College Library for a few weeks in the evenings while the librarian is away. I said I'd love to. She knows the librarian and will arrange it with him.

Last Sunday Joan and the children were supposed to come to tea but Peter was ill so I went to their house instead. Today Daphne Hall came for supper and stayed till 11pm. We talked about Joan some of the time and I'm afraid I was disloyal to her once or twice. We wondered why Joan thought so highly of that unsuitable girl Sheila who helps her with the children. I promised to go to her dance rehearsal with Joan tomorrow to see her in *The Galloping Major*. What a treat in store, said Daphne.

Already over a week since my affair with Bill ended. Everything, the moment it is over, turns immediately into a memory. For a time, the memory keeps coming to the surface, it makes you cry, or it makes you laugh. Gradually it loses its youthful vigour before it ages and gets weaker and weaker. Of course Bill is still a very vivid memory but I know that in time I will manage to forget him – no, not forget him, but not care about him any more. Already I never want to see him again.

16th December 1946

When I was at North Parade, shopping during my teabreak this morning, while standing in a queue I watched two beautiful women chatting to each other outside a shop. Their fair-haired and cheerful children were skipping around them. They were happy housewives leading enviable lives, their untroubled past and probably equally carefree future written into their lovely features. When I returned to the office I had difficulty concentrating on my work because something was stirring in me. I could hardly contain it. Throughout the rest of the long day the labour pains grew worse. At last it was five o'clock. I stayed overtime to finish off some work – collecting books from the library which had to be sent to students – and then I gave birth. On a large piece of scrap paper I wrote:

Listen to the women called Margaret.
Listen to the beautiful women, the women called Margaret.
Listen to the women with beautiful voices,

Chattering about men and places,
Talking vacantly as under hypnosis,
And laughing.

Watch their children called Rosemary.
Watch their beautiful children, their children called Rosemary.
Watch their children with beautiful bodies,
Singing radiantly during their follies,
Exuding ostentation from their bellies,
And dancing.

Listen to me, the mortal.
Watch me, and listen to me, the solitary mortal.
Observe my crude shape with apology,
Stupidly studying etymology,
Ignorant of semasiology,
And weeping.

My first poem had been born.

I showed it to Joyce Lenton the following morning. "Extraordinary," she exclaimed, after an interminable interval. "But I don't understand it." Then she copied it down.

22nd December 1946

Only another two days till the Christmas holiday starts. Putz and I are going to Cobham on Tuesday and not returning till Sunday the 29th. I had supper at the Rieszs' last Tuesday and afterwards listened to the gramophone with Peter and his friend Jack till 11pm. Some of the time I sat with Mrs Riesz in her bedroom, and in the course of our conversation she accused the English of behaving like pigs. "How?" I asked her.

"Because they do in public what we only do in the bedroom," she replied. I was most intrigued as I have never seen English people do anything more than kiss in public. I must keep my eyes open.

Daphne Hall seems to enjoy coming to my room to spend the evening, and has been coming every week. She never invites me to her home. Is she ashamed of me, I wonder, or of her family? Bill never asked me to his home either, although it is quite near here, but I could more or less see the reason for that. But not entirely. In fact, looking back, it is one of the things I resented.

We had coffee at Bruno and Erna's today after lunch. All we ever get there is strong coffee and strong cigarettes, and I don't like either. There were other visitors there, among them Nikolaus Pevsner, the architect, whom Bruno has often told us about, as he's quite famous.

30th December 1946

It was wonderful in Cobham and London. Putz and I left work at 3.45pm on Christmas Eve and went straight to Cobham. On Waterloo station we met our second cousin Lieselotte Webern who was about to catch the same train, so we all travelled together. I discovered that she is a distant relation of the composer von Webern. She's Putz's age – three years older than I. We didn't know her in Vienna and only met her at Anni and Felix's last year. Ann's Cottage was as welcoming and Christmassy as ever, with a huge tree in the sitting room and all the presents arranged around it. We were up till one o'clock, though Anni and Felix retired much earlier. On Christmas Day my Father and Jane's younger sister Betty came, and Lieselotte Webern and her mother left in the evening. On Boxing Day I got up very late again, and visited the Urbachs at Banstead in the afternoon. There were several visitors there. We had tea and Mr Urbach took photographs of us. Eva, with her fair hair, looks like an ordinary English girl and claims to have forgotten everything that happened before she came to England. In the evening I caught the train back to Cobham, which is not very far.

We didn't do much on the 27th except go to the village in the morning. The next day, Saturday, Putz and I went to London, met my father and Herta and went together to the King's Exhibition at the Royal Academy. Afterwards, my father took us out for lunch. Herta's engagement seems to be broken off but she doesn't talk about it. She left us after lunch and my father, Putz and I went to the pictures and saw *Day of Wrath*, which was rubbish. Back to Cobham in the evening, but to London again the next day and at the Marstons' in Elgin Avenue for their Christmas party, at which my father showed his flair for playing the fool. And so back to Oxford in the evening, and back to work today. It wasn't the dull day I'd expected it to be, however, as part of the ceiling came down in the typists' room next to my office, and there was great excitement.

Extract from diary of plays, films and books, 1946.

1st January 1947 – DEATH

It was New Year's Eve. I was sitting in my bed-sitting room doing odd jobs and listening to the wireless. Mrs Labowsky was ill in bed. Around ten o'clock the doorbell rang. I went to answer it, a bit annoyed because I was just listening to something interesting. A strange man confronted me.

"Is this Miss Lorch's house?" he asked.

"Well, she lives here, but I think she's out," I replied, rather bad-tempered, because I'd been interrupted by a visitor who wasn't even for me.

"I'm afraid she's been knocked down," the man said.

"Knocked down?" I repeated stupidly.

"Yes, by a motorbike in the Banbury Road."

"Is she badly hurt?"

"She is dead."

I couldn't believe it. I was shattered. Only a few hours earlier she was talking to me. After the man had gone and I had told Mrs Labowsky the news I returned to my room and thought about death. Every item in my room spoke of it to me. They reminded me that we must all die. I fear death more than I feared my father's punishments as a child, more than I fear loneliness and failure. I fear its strangeness and inevitability. What a way to begin the New Year.

4th January 1947

After shopping Putz and I spent a cosy afternoon and evening in her room today. On Thursday I went to the Pantomime with Joan and Sheila at the New Theatre and had to walk home because I missed the last bus; and on Wednesday I went to the pictures with Ann Norton. We saw *The Citadel* based on the novel by A.J. Cronin.

The other night I dreamt of Bill. I took his face into my hands and kissed it. But I don't care about Bill any more. That's over. Already his features have become indistinct and even in my dream his face dodged me.

If only I could meet someone I could love and who could love me, and if Lieselotte could, too! Her affair with Norman unfortunately came to nothing. God, if you are there, remember us, we want to live, not just to exist!

Miss Lorch's funeral is on Monday.

11th January 1947

There was deep snow on the day of Miss Lorch's funeral.

We've had a letter from Miss Christa in Vienna! She was my father's secretary and she wasn't a Nazi. She knows nothing about my mother and grandmother because Christians were not allowed to mix with Jews, but she expressed her deepest regret at what happened.

When Daphne was here on Wednesday evening we talked, had supper and smoked till quite late. She's coming again next Wednesday, and wants me to read some of my stories to her.

I saw the film *Great Expectations* with Putz and Ann today. We enjoyed it. We met Miss Grimsby and Mrs Harwell there who both work at Wolsey Hall and had come to see the film, they said, as it takes less time than reading the book!

There hasn't been much to do at work this week and I spent some time in the typists' room drinking tea and smoking when Mr Herbert wasn't there. I've also been helping Miss Harwood with the wages.

18th January 1947

My father turned up unexpectedly on Thursday afternoon! He has a chauffeur now, as he doesn't drive himself. His visit was quite a shock. We went for a walk, a drive and out to tea after work. Why did he come? To spy on us? We shall never know. Putz came to Joan's with me on Sunday – and we stayed till 11.30pm!

On Monday morning a young man spoke to me in the bus queue who said he was a friend of Miss Lorch's; they belonged to the same church – the Lutheran. He said Miss Lorch was 70 years old. He knew me from having been to visit her at Lonsdale Road. Poor Miss Lorch. Mrs Labowsky said she was always irritated by fat little Miss Lorch fussing around in the kitchen and getting in her way, but now she misses her. I've been staying late at work, studying.

Today I went shopping with Ann after work. In the afternoon I had tea at Fullers' with Daphne and afterwards we went to the pictures where I met Pam Towlson and her sister Pat. Pam left Wolsey Hall some time ago, which is why I don't see much of her any more. We made an arrangement for next Saturday.

Tomorrow Putz and I are invited to Bruno and Erna's in the afternoon. More black coffee and strong cigarettes.

2nd February 1947

I'm in bed with a cold. Putz came in the afternoon and kept me company. The weather is bitter cold and has been since last Sunday, when we had deep snow, which is still lying on the ground. Putz and I have joined the Film Society. They show mostly foreign films at the Scala Cinema at weekends.

When I was at the pictures with Pam and Pat they brought a tall young man called John along who I think is Pam's boyfriend. He took us all home in his car. At the cinema I met several acquaintances, among them Mrs Thiem from the Public Library, who was so nice to me when I worked there, and gave me the beautiful China teaset. Yesterday I again went to the pictures with Pam – we saw *Frenzy* and I had tea at the Cadena with her. In the evening I had supper at her house and stayed until 11.30pm.

Next weekend Putz's friend Philips is coming from London, and so is Joan's youngest brother, Danny. She has invited me to meet him.

9th February 1947

There really is nothing much to write about. Absolutely nothing. I'm at rock bottom, fed up, discontented and miserable. I should hang myself. I haven't met a man (I like) since Bill. I'm unnecessary to life. In a month's time I shall be 20 – and I'm a failure.

It is Sunday morning. Outside the snow is deeper than I have ever seen it in England. It is very quiet. I am cold, but I love the snow. I'm in bed with heavy blankets covering me and I shall stay here until Mrs Labowsky brings my lunch tray at 12.30. I skipped breakfast and there's no heating in the room because heating is expensive and, unlike my father, I'm very poor. So I stay in bed to save money. Artists always live in unheated rooms, don't they? Geniuses are always poor and cold, aren't they? What a coincidence that I should find myself in the same situation. If only I could find somebody to keep me warm!

18th February 1947

There's a FUEL CRISIS! The icy weather is continuing and the snow has not gone away since January. There have been frequent electricity cuts and I'm constantly cold. In order to feel any warmth from my electric sun I have to sit almost touching it with my feet. Putz's electric fire in her room is not much better. It's too cold to cycle so I walk or go by bus. Today I slipped and fell down twice on the frozen pavements.

What else have I been doing, apart from seeing Putz and Joan? Well, I've worked overtime and been to the pictures with Audrey and entertained Daphne, who has never returned my invitations, and been to a restaurant with Ann and her mother and sister, and had my lunches at work, and of course been regularly to my German Lit. lessons with Mme Zuccari. One morning I met Otto and he gave me a lift to work in his truck. Joan drew my portrait last time I was at her house. She's a marvellous artist. The young man who knew Miss Lorch called on Mrs Labowsky and chatted with me too. He's called Mr Calé. Funny name for a German.

26th February 1947

When I stood waiting in the freezing bus queue this morning a smart car drew up and stopped. The elegantly dressed driver opened the car door, leaned out and said, "If anyone is going into town, I can give two people a lift." A woman in front of me got in. Then a woman from the back of the queue pushed forward, determined to be the other person, but the driver barred her way. He turned to me and said, "Would you like a lift?" I thanked him and accepted, and got in the car in as dignified a way as I could manage. As we drove off I saw the pushy woman stare after us. I could tell from her appearance and her accent that she was a Jewish refugee and I felt ashamed for her, and at the same time triumphant because I could never be like that. It just shows that pushiness doesn't always pay.

Eva Guttmann, the schoolgirl daughter of Dr Guttmann who lives a few doors away in Lonsdale Road, also doesn't cycle in this bitter weather and we sometimes walk to the bus stop together.

Miss Senior, who works at Wolsey Hall, is a member of the Red Cross, which means she can eat at their canteen in St Margaret's Road. Yesterday she took Putz and me along for lunch as guests – and the food was excellent; no wonder, as I discovered later the cook is German. Much better than eating sandwiches at work as I've been doing lately. Putz and I intend to join the Red Cross.

Next Thursday evening I'm going to look after Peter and Diana while Joan is in London, and the following day Putz and I are going to London and Cobham for the weekend, as it is my birthday on Sunday.

5th March 1947

We've had lunch at the Red Cross canteen again and Joyce Lenton came too. The food was as good as before, especially the apple charlotte.

Putz has a new friend who works at Wolsey Hall. She's called Patricia Dorling, is very upper class, intelligent, good-looking and married. I think she has a degree in English. The other day she gave me a banana, which was very nice of her. Ann Norton and I went to the pictures on Monday and saw *Les Enfants du Paradis* with Jean Louis Barrault. It was breathtaking. I can't stop thinking about it. It haunts me. It's hard to come to terms with the real world again after the wonderful dream one of the cinema. Ann feels as I do about this.

11th March 1947

We arrived late in Cobham on Friday evening but Anni had left us a nice supper. The next day Putz and I went to London and had lunch at the Hungarian Czarda with my father and Betty – his favourite restaurant. He made fun of Putz for only choosing ham instead of a Hungarian speciality. Then we went to Jane's flat for tea and afterwards to the Globe Theatre. Sunday was my birthday. I felt sick in the morning. My father came out in the afternoon, this time without Betty. I had a long walk and talk with Lixl, a 19 year old Czech boy and relation of Felix's though not of mine, who's living at Ann's Cottage now. He suffered badly in Czechoslovakia during the war. We all went for a drive in Anni's car later, and then I had my presents from everyone. My father gave me 10/- which seemed a lot – until he told me that he makes £5000 a year now. I was staggered. Back to Oxford in the evening.

Yesterday Putz and I had tea at Pat Dorling's flat. Her husband is called Jim, and he is also very attractive and intelligent. We didn't stay very long as Putz was expecting Ailsa.

Today I went to the hairdresser's in my lunch hour instead of washing my own hair for once, and in the evening Putz and I went to the New Theatre to see *Rigoletto*. I'm sorry to say that I fell asleep during the performance and only woke in time to hear the Duke sing *La donna è mobile* and to see Rigoletto opening the sack and discovering his daughter in it.

A new lodger has come to live in Miss Lorch's old room. She's a gymnastics teacher at the High School.

12th March 1947

Today I saw Bill. I was just getting off the bus with Daphne; we'd been trying to get into the New Theatre but after standing in a terrifically long queue for ages the doors were closed and no more people were allowed in, so we went home. It was dark when we got off the bus, and raining. Suddenly I saw Bill standing there, waiting for a bus. He was wearing his navy blue overcoat and his hands were hanging loosely at his sides. He saw me too. I was overcome by a very strange sensation which I could make nothing of, so I followed my instinct and hurried away in the dark and the rain. The next moment I wanted to run back, to take him into my arms and hug him and kiss his mouth, but of course I did not, and anyway Daphne was with me. It was always like that. I always wanted to touch him and kiss him. Even after that sordid affair was over I longed for his warm, silky lips. Will I always long for them? Will his body haunt me for the rest of my life? He has forgotten me now, I'm just a distant memory, the memory of a dark-haired, kind girl whose body had once been desirable.

I had lunch at the Red Cross canteen with Miss Senior today, and sitting at our table was a pleasant-looking undergraduate named Raymond Fenn from Keble College whom Miss Senior knows. There was delicious apple charlotte again.

15th March 1947

On Thursday I again queued at the New Theatre to see a Carl Rosa opera, this time with Putz and Ailsa, and we again couldn't get in. As the rain became harder a woman in the queue invited me to share her umbrella. When the uniformed doorman (whom Joan and I long ago christened Hitler) came out and told us to go home, a man in front of me shouted angrily, "Why won't you let us in?"

"Because the theatre is not a balloon, that's why," Hitler shouted back, and slammed the doors shut.

However, it was third time lucky today and I saw *Faust* with

Ann and Miss Senior. I met Betty Argyle on the bus; she still works at the Public Library and she was as nice as ever. Earlier in the day Putz and I had lunch at Lyons with Beryl Wood who works at Wolsey Hall – another one of Putz's married friends. There was an unpleasant argument with an Indian who claimed to be keeping a seat for a friend at our table, but he went away in the end. To cheer ourselves up, in the afternoon, Putz and I bought identical summer dresses – hers blue and mine red – with wing sleeves and narrow white horizontal stripes – and that did cheer us up no end, even though they cost nearly £3 each and the weather was still icy and it will be ages before we can wear them. I also bought new shoes.

Instead of having a lesson with Mme Zuccari on Friday, we had a conversation, which was very enjoyable. I can learn as much just talking to her as I can from studying a textbook. At the bus stop I again met the undergraduate I've met twice before waiting for the No. 2 bus, and this time we walked home together.

He invited me to his room but I declined.

On Thursday I felt sick all day and went to Putz's digs in my lunch hour. My period had come on.

19th March 1947

Ruth sent me a letter she had from Susi Roth, our schoolfriend from Vienna, who now lives in America. How long ago it seems that we were at school together in Austria! And now we are scattered all over the globe. For better or worse. It reminded me with a jolt that I'm not really an English girl.

I think I had gastric flu on Monday and stayed home from work feeling sick. In the morning I was in bed but by the afternoon I felt better and visited Mrs Riesz and had a cup of tea and a chat with her. She's a very kind, motherly lady and frequently changes my mood to a serener one.

My father came to Oxford again unexpectedly on Sunday. He was on his way to Cardiff on business, and came in his car, driven by his chauffeur. As Sunday was the day the clocks were put forward one hour it was a short day and by the time he departed there wasn't much time for anything. I spent what was left of the day at Putz's.

Mme Zucarri has arranged for me to attend a German literature discussion group at Pastor Kramm's. I'm going there on Saturday with many misgivings. The job at Exeter College Library has not materialised.

29th March 1947

My cousin Herta was in Oxford on Thursday – for her baptism! It took place at St Aldates Church and I had arranged it for her. I was a witness. I gather it's all hush hush and that she doesn't want anyone in London to know about it. Maybe her fiancé wanted her to become a Christian and her engagement is not broken off after all. Putz and I saw her off at the station with our questions still unanswered.

Some time ago I volunteered to do some work for the Red Cross, as a result of which the Red Cross Commandant, Miss Saunders, got in touch with me and asked me to do some babysitting for a family called Dawson who live in St Giles. I went to see them today and we came to an arrangement.

My half day today, Saturday, was spent in the usual way: lunch and shopping with Putz and Beryl, tea at Fullers' and at the pictures with Daphne.

On Wednesday I had my photograph taken in the lunch hour. For some reason my father wants a photo of each of us.

10th April 1947

Last weekend was Easter. Putz and I went to London for the day on Saturday. I bought a coat at my father's firm and we had lunch in the Cumberland Hotel in Marble Arch with him and Betty. Afterwards we went for a drive – Betty was the driver – and had tea at Elgin Avenue.

Dr Beschorner is home for Easter and I had supper with him and Joan on Sunday; on Wednesday I babysat for them. I've also performed my first Red Cross duty and babysat for the Dawsons' on Tuesday.

Putz had a little supper party at her digs on Easter Monday: Pat Dorling and her friend Joan Lea-Wilson were there. It was very enjoyable. They're coming to me on Friday.

I promised to type a job application for Ann so we're staying behind after five o'clock tomorrow to do it. Afterwards I'll type

187

some of my stories, and another poem. It's not as good.

12th April 1947

Unless it is because I haven't met any men lately, I cannot imagine why I have been thinking such a great deal about Mr Morris recently. I need not remind you what a deep impression that man made on me. There was something about him that I can't put a name to, something uncanny, something indescribable. He had everything, and yet something was lacking. All the necessary material was there but it failed to catch fire. I can't help blaming myself for it. I was so childish, so unsophisticated, inexperienced and silly. I'd like to end the affair properly, but how can that be done?

I've told you before that I steal, haven't I? I am now telling you that I am a thief, I have the mind of a thief. A terrible confession, but what is a diary for if not for confessing? For some perverted reason stealing has a fascination for me that I've found nowhere else.

Having lost my morals and principles, anything goes. Nothing needs justification or has any purpose, reason or aim. This is the sort of thing I do: I obtained permission to borrow 2/- from the cash drawer at work – and failed to return it; 1d fell out of one of the girls' handbags: I picked it up and kept it. I didn't specially want it, but it was exciting. It is a road I have chosen to follow and which no one suspects I am following, since the world still trusts me completely. I'm in a very secure position, you see. You might think I should be ashamed of betraying the world's trust. I have to tell you that I'm not. You might think that the world's trust in me would make me blush and ashamed of myself and endeavour to live up to their estimate of me. I do nothing of the kind.

Today one of the typists left a purse full of money and some ration books with me, while she went to make the tea. I hope that in later life she will choose those whom she thinks she can trust more carefully. I opened the purse when she had gone and felt the money in my hand. I took nothing. But 'if a thief's hands be cut off, he is still a thief'. My case is a peculiar one: I intend to steal, I think like a thief, I'm continually looking out for opportunities and justifying my actions – but I rarely carry out my intentions.

I have given this matter a great deal of thought. I have come to the conclusion that stealing from individuals is wrong, but if I rob the firm which pays me such a miserable salary or a wealthy shop who will never miss what I've taken and therefore suffer no hardship, then I feel no remorse. And if it gives me pleasure – well, where else is pleasure to be derived? No one cares much whether I'm happy or not, and I have nothing to live for, really, so can you blame me if I have thrown my scruples to the wind?

I should like to get a job in Switzerland. It's my dream country.

16th April 1947

How odd! I wanted to see Mr Morris again and instead I saw – Bill! It was last night as I walked to the bus stop with Joan after she'd been here for supper; suddenly there was Bill, only a few yards away from us. He was alone. We looked – no, we stared at each other, but neither of us smiled or spoke. Afterwards I was annoyed with myself for having been so foolish, for not even having said hello: I longed to undo that silly scene but didn't think I would get the chance. Even if I did see him again soon, which I thought unlikely, courage would probably fail me as it did before. I was wrong on both counts. I met him again this morning, on my way to work. We were both on bikes. I overtook him, pedalling very fast. I looked him full in the face and then, with a sudden irresistible urge, I smiled at him and said, "Hello, Bill." I meant to cycle straight on, but he kept level with me.

"Oh Ingrid," he said. "Hello." And he smiled back.

It was performed as if it had been rehearsed and nothing had gone wrong. We cycled together, chatting all the time, almost as if there had been no break in our relationship. He mentioned something about working in the USA and I said I'd heard one had to be as beautiful as a filmstar to get a good job there. Moving his eyebrows at me in his familiar way he said, "Then you would get an excellent job, Ingrid." In fact everything was the same, except that I was no longer Bill's slave. I was a free individual, with nothing to expect, hope for, wait for or fear from him. We had no claim on each other. His words could neither hurt nor flatter me, whatever they might be. In the light of this new freedom I was able to face him as I had probably never faced him before. As for how he feels towards me – that I shall never know.

19th April 1947

Mrs Labowsky has gone to London for a few days and Putz is staying with me till Monday.

I met Sandy today and we both agreed how lucky we are not to be working at the Public Library any more. In fact many of the assistants who worked there when we did have also left, and when I changed my library book the other day I saw several new faces. Betty Argyle introduced me to Elizabeth Jennings who was stamping books at the counter – which I always wanted to do but was never allowed to. Elizabeth also writes poetry besides being a librarian. Better than me, I expect.

Edna and her husband, Arthur, called on Putz today. Edna has turned into a typical housewife, which seems to suit her down to the ground, and I don't blame her. In the evening I went to the German literature discussion group, and again didn't contribute anything. I simply can't get myself to utter a word there, as the others are so knowledgeable, and aggressive with it.

One of the girls who works as a typist in Wolsey Hall knocked on my office door one day last week, and entered shyly, bearing a bunch of primroses which she then handed to me. Wasn't that sweet? I didn't even know her name.

26th April 1947

Yesterday Joyce Lenton and I were cycling together, when a lorry came out of Beaumont Street and almost hit us. We had to swerve to avoid it, and luckily there was nothing behind us. When we had recovered from the shock and were cycling along St Giles, I said to Joyce:

"Do you think we were killed just now and only *think* we are still alive, cycling down St Giles?"

She looked at me and for a moment was silent. Then she said, "It's absolutely extraordinary, but this very same idea occurred to me." That was really uncanny.

This afternoon I went to the Ashmolean Museum with Mme Zuccari. It was founded by Ashmole in the 17th century with a collection inherited from John Tradescant of botanical fame. She is a mine of information, and knew the history of nearly every object in the museum. Afterwards she took me to Exeter College

Library and introduced me to the Librarian, Mr Nicholas. A very intellectual afternoon. Putz is spending the weekend with Beryl and Clem Wood, who live above their chemist's shop in Cowley.

Joan treated me to supper at a café on Tuesday evening. She told me not to thank her as it was to cheer herself up as much as anything. Next week I'm taking little Peter to Miss Harwood's house (she works at Wolsey Hall) to see a puppet show. Puppets are her hobby.

While Mrs Labowsky was away Mrs Guttmann called to see if I was all right. I wonder if Mrs L. thought I might have a man staying here in her absence? She has commented once or twice on my male visitors. Her daughter who's divorced is coming to stay next weekend. Having a divorced daughter, Mrs Labowsky had better not be too critical of me.

A bishop often sits at our table at the Red Cross canteen. It was raining hard the other day, he told us, and he hadn't got an umbrella. He then recited the following:

> *The rain it raineth on the just,*
> *And on the unjust fellow.*
> *But more so on the just because,*
> *The unjust stole the just's umbrella.*

Never having known a Bishop before I was surprised how jovial and down-to-earth he is.

I had a very interesting letter from Britta in Pilsen. If I had survived a concentration camp, as she has, what would I be like now?

2nd May 1947

I discovered at an early age that I must have something to live for, some emotional stimulus, something that transports me away from my hum-drum life, even if into ultimate disaster. And somehow I have always found something, though there were often long intervals in between. Now I have found that something again. After a devastating, soul-destroyingly barren gap of Egyptian darkness, a light has gone on: Pat Dorling has a friend whose husband is a psychiatrist. I told her one day that I've always wanted to be psychoanalysed. "Why not?" she said. And so it happened that, about three weeks ago, she took me along to meet Jim Hayes, who lives in a cottage in Headington with his

German wife, Clare. The following Wednesday I had my first session with him. And those sessions are what I now live for. Do you remember my heightened emotions on entering Mr Morris's room? Jim Hayes' little dark room with a view of his pretty garden, the simple furniture and masses of books and papers has almost exactly the same effect on me. I adore the way Jim treats me, the way he talks to me. I suppose being a psychiatrist he finds it easy to appeal to my emotions. He calls me by my Christian name as if we were old friends, but with something else to it.

He's certainly different from any man I've ever known. He likes me, I think. But then, I'm a good patient. I do exactly what he tells me. After last week's session – I go every Wednesday evening – he touched my hair, and then gently stroked it. Because I'm a nice, good patient . . . Actually it hadn't been a proper session because he had taken me to the pub instead and bought me drinks and cigarettes. He thought that would do me more good as I didn't seem to be in the right mood for talking. He did most of the talking. He told me the greatest poet who ever lived is Gerald Manley Hopkins. He said I was a nice person, a funny, unusual, interesting child. Silly of me to believe him. But he's a clever man, he ought to know.

No, I'm not going to say any more about him now. I'm really ashamed of feeling like this.

7th May 1947

Ruth came to visit me on Wednesday. We had lunch in the Cadena together, and talked and talked. Her engagement to a Norwegian sailor is broken off. I didn't think it would last. She went back to Portsmouth in the evening.

Yesterday I stayed late at work to type a story I'd written called *Needle*; when Pat Dorling came to see me in the evening I mentioned it to her and she asked to read it, so I let her take it home. At the weekend Putz is going to the hospital for a small operation to her hand, to have a ganglion removed, and I'm going to the Woods' and sleeping there on Saturday and Sunday. They have to have Putz and me at different times as there is only one small spare room.

I often meet Peter Riesz or Derek Burgess on my way to work

in the morning, and we cycle together. Derek is very good-looking. I can't say the same for ginger-haired Peter!

9th May 1947 – The 'Joan climax'

I went to Joan's as usual last night, expecting supper, a cosy evening and our customary exchange of confidences – and I found total upheaval. She said her depression had returned and she was going to hospital the following day. I helped her with the children and her packing, and tidied up a bit. Then she took me to her friends in Wellington Square, a couple called Hayes (no relation to Jim) whose little boy Michael is a friend of Peter's. Even in her illness she's concerned about me, and she wants me to spend Thursday evenings at the Hayes', so that, once a week, I would continue to have a home and family to visit.

Today I had tea at Joan's for the last time. Her husband was there as he had come to take her to hospital and the children back with him. The house, No. 66 St John's Road, is finally to be sold. It was very sad saying goodbye to Joan, in the dark passage of her dreary, disorderly house. I promised to visit her at the hospital. It was my babysitting evening at the Dawsons' and so I didn't stay long, which was just as well in the circumstances.

14th May 1947

The weekend at Clem and Beryl Wood's was very leisurely and disorganised: we went for walks with the dog, had lunch when Beryl remembered, got up very late on Sunday, spent the evening in a pub and had supper at midnight. Clem showed me over his chemist's shop.

On Monday I called at No. 66 after work to collect some of Joan's things, and stayed for a two hour discussion about Joan with the tenants still living there. The house was in a very desolate state. Today I went to the hospital to take Joan's things. She came to meet me in the grounds of the hospital, where patients were wandering around like lost sheep. Before I could think what to say to Joan in these strange surroundings she forestalled me. "We don't all believe we're Napoleon here, you know," she said, which left me even more speechless.

"No, why should you?" I said at last. I never thought of her as

j

being mentally ill before, but now for the first time I did. I didn't stay long as I had my session with Jim at seven o'clock, and I didn't want to miss a moment of that. I was glad to leave the hospital.

15th May 1947

Within three months I have rejected two men. It reassures me a little, that's all. One of them was the undergraduate I met at the bus stop some time ago, a serious fellow studying law. I know everything about him except his name. I didn't go to his room when he invited me. Afterwards I couldn't imagine why. Then there's that foreign chap called Calé. I often meet him in the street and he keeps me talking for hours. The other day he shyly asked me to come and see him at Parkers' bookshop, where he works. On another occasion he stopped me in the street and slowly asked me, would I like to go to the Playhouse with him? "Not the Playhouse," I said, stalling. "I prefer the New Theatre," and changed the subject quickly. He was too shy to return to it. I'm not interested, but what made me refuse? Surely it would have been better than nothing? I believe I refused because Bill has frightened me off men, I'm scared of getting involved in another sordid and tormenting affair.

And Jim, my psychiatrist, what of him? Nothing has changed, nothing. If I could marry a man like that I should desire nothing else, not even to become a writer. He sits by me on the couch and he holds my hand tightly in his and never lets it go for the whole of the session. I can feel his long thin fingers, each one separately. Sometimes he strokes my hair gently. Does he treat all his patients like this? At last night's session he suddenly interrupted me and said, "You look charming." He said it very seriously and when I looked into his eyes he looked back into mine. He's terribly kind and quite brilliant and he wants to help me with all his heart. When I keep on about my inferiority complex he insists it is totally unfounded.

"Clare tells me," he said last time, "that you are the life and soul of the lunches at the Red Cross canteen."

"Perhaps there I am," I said, "with congenial people. But nowhere else."

Just talking to him makes me feel so good that I'm quite prepared to believe there's nothing the matter with me. A few

194

days ago Patricia had telephoned me to ask if she could show my story, *Needle*, to Jim as it was so interesting psychologically, and he now congratulated me on it. It was about a girl who would not have any needles in her house for fear of gouging out her eyes in the night in her sleep. Then her baby brother dies and miraculously the phobia disappears. Jim thought it ingenious. I asked him if he thought it could be published. "With a little polishing, yes," he replied.

I tell myself that I'm buying all this help and kindness, buying it for 7/6 a session. It makes no difference. It is a happy purchase. When last night's session was over it was already quite dark and very late as we stood for a moment in the dark room, his hand on my shoulder. Then he drew back the curtain and said:

"Come and look at that tree." I came and looked at it and stood close beside him. "But you don't care for trees, do you?" he said.

"Not particularly," I said. "They're sinister, and they make a mess in the autumn."

"That tree is a living thing like you," said Jim. "Only not quite so lovely." I shall never forget that remark. I smiled in the darkness but said nothing.

Please don't think that this sort of thing is all we do. It is quite impossible to go into the complicated analysis here. Already he knows me inside out and I can tell him things I tell no one else, and he knows exactly how to respond. But I do wish I could tell someone, without destroying the magic, that after the sessions we sit with Jim's arm around me and we smoke quietly and he plays with my ear or strokes my hair. If I were to tell anyone this the magic would be over. Last night, after the session, I did this drawing of Jim at home. It's a good likeness.

17th May 1947

I have spent my first evening at Chris and Ted Hayes' in Wellington Square. Besides Michael they also have a little girl called Valerie. All four of them are sandy haired and short. Chris is no substitute for Joan but a nice, friendly person. She talked a lot about the family who lived in their flat previously, called

Tickell. Gerard Tickell is a well-known writer and both he and his son Crispin have been back to visit the Hayes' on several occasions. I said I'd like to meet him. If ever I have a son I'll call him Crispin. With a name like that success can never be far away.

Mrs Labowsky is away for a week and Sheila, the upstairs lodger, and I feel much freer than when she's here, and don't have to creep into the bathroom after 11pm for fear of waking her.

I had tea with the Dawsons yesterday before commencing my babysitting duty. I watched Mrs D. bath the baby before she and her husband went out. I wrote and read and mended during the long evening.

Today Mme Zuccari called at Wolsey Hall to see me about the Exeter College Library job, which looks like finally materialising. In the afternoon Joyce Lenton and Putz came to tea in the garden, a treat only to be enjoyed in Mrs Labowsky's absence. It was a lovely warm day, and after tea Joyce sat for me

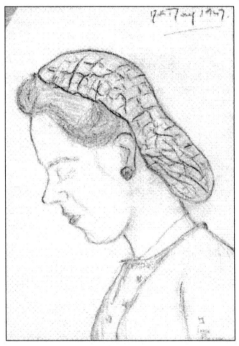

and I drew her. I got a very good likeness. Mr Calé called, but whether to see me or Mrs Labowsky was not clear. Tomorrow evening Putz and I are going to a private concert for which her boss, Dr Parker, gave her two free tickets, and in the afternoon to the Film Society at the Scala Cinema to see a French film.

25th May 1947

It's Whit Sunday today and my father and Betty are in Oxford for the weekend, staying at the Mitre Hotel where we all had lunch yesterday. In the afternoon we went for a drive in the car and took some snaps. Today we visited Bruno and Erna and had lunch in style at the hotel again. They all came to tea in my room. Betty and my father returned to London in the evening.

At last Wednesday's session with Jim I told him about my stealing. His reaction was to look at me, laugh and say, "You're as honest as the day is long. What you are doing is not stealing. You're saying to the world: I hate you for what you have done to me and this is my revenge; listen and take note. See?" I felt quite embarrassed by this benevolent view of my dishonesty, but I didn't contradict him.

After the session Clare joined us and the three of us discoursed until midnight. She told me a joke: a psychiatrist said to his lady patient, "Well, Miss Brown, I'm happy to tell you that there is absolutely nothing wrong with you; the sessions have revealed that you're a perfectly normal young woman."

"Thank you, doctor," she replied, "I always knew it. I only came to you as my relations insisted. After all, there's nothing wrong with liking pancakes, is there?"

"Certainly not. I like them myself," replied the psychiatrist. "Do you eat them often?"

"Oh yes," said Miss Brown. "You see, I have trunkfuls of them."

2nd June 1947

We're having a heat wave. Putz and I spent the weekend sunbathing in her garden. Constance Senior, from Wolsey Hall, joined us on Saturday. Last Friday I visited Joan in hospital again, and I also visited Putz who was home from work with toothache.

A girl called June Pennicot who works at Wolsey Hall has invited me to her 21st birthday party, but as it is on a Wednesday

I told her I couldn't come: I wouldn't miss a session with Jim for anything. I'm having my interview at Exeter College Library after work the day after tomorrow.

7th June 1947

I got the job at Exeter College Library and am starting there, two evenings a week, next month, after my holiday in Cobham with Putz. It looks a very awe-inspiring place and the books are not so much books as items of furniture – huge tomes I can barely lift and much less read.

Yesterday morning Mr Herbert assembled us all in the office and we drew names of horses for the Derby on Saturday. I drew a blank. Just as well, knowing my luck at gambling. I had tea at Joyce's digs, and a drink of cider. In the evening I had supper at Mr and Mrs Hayes'. The Tickells had been to see them again.

At last Wednesday's session Jim gave a demonstration of hypnosis with someone called Robert. I'm certain it wouldn't work with me, and I couldn't really tell how well it worked with Robert, but it was interesting.

Putz is spending the weekend with the Woods. One of the bosses at Wolsey Hall, Mr Lloyd, took me to the pub this morning and bought me a glass of beer, which tasted horrible. Audrey came for tea, and in the evening I babysat at the Dawsons. The heat wave is continuing. What an exciting life I lead.

12th June 1947

This evening I was at the Rieszs' and had supper with them. Dr Elia, the Spaniard, and a Chinaman were there.

The weather still being lovely, I usually spend my lunch hour eating sandwiches and reading in the grounds of Wolsey Hall with some of the other girls.

Daphne called on Wednesday. I'd just got back from the dressmaker's and was about to go to my session, so I couldn't see her for long. At the session Jim decided that a long walk and a visit to the pub would be most beneficial to me, which is what we did, talking all the time, of course. He explained to me the significance of the positive and negative transference of the patient for his psychiatrist, so if I fall in love with him or start hating him I shall know that the sessions are working.

The last time I was at the Hayes' – on Tuesday evening – Chris wanted to know how Joan was getting on at the hospital. I told her all I knew and hope I wasn't disloyal to Joan. I still think she shouldn't have gone to a mental hospital. If she had held out she probably would have got better without this stigma. I may go swimming in the river with Chris if it stays fine.

Joyce Lenton has asked me to go to a service at St Mary's Church with her on Saturday, and meet John the organist whom she loves from afar. I understand only too well how she feels! Afterwards we'll probably have supper at the BR. There's a treat in store!

I've had an invitation to the Laskis' garden fête on Sunday. Unfortunately I can't go as I'll be away. Just my luck.

13th June 1947

It's my mother's birthday. What a shame that she was ever born.

I'm so miserable, I'd like to put my head in a gas oven. I am swimming in a large, drab, completely featureless misery and I am drowning in it. It's the drabness that's killing me. If it were an interesting, exciting sort of unhappiness, full of incidents, I wouldn't mind so much. But mine is dreary, dull, deadly. It is full of empty nothingness. Whatever it was I experienced with Bill has left me hungry and unfulfilled. Are Lieselotte and I unlovable? Don't we have ordinary looks and ordinary brains like other girls? Shall we both die unwanted and unloved? I see the years of our lives ahead as a monotonous road with telegraph poles at regular intervals, and nothing else.

20th June 1947

I worked overtime today as I want to leave work earlier tomorrow morning to go to London. I spent the evening packing, except for a brief visit to Joyce's. Last night I wanted to leave the Hayes' early to go home and wash my hair, but Chris gave me a bottle of shampoo and a towel and said, "You can wash it here." So I did. A woman called Mrs Upward and her children were there for tea.

Putz, Erna and Bruno had coffee in my room on Monday and chatted with Mrs Labowsky afterwards. Joyce had free tickets to the ballet at the New Theatre, and it was twice as enjoyable not having had to pay for our seats.

This week's session with Jim was marvellous. He had his arm round me for the whole evening . . .

Off to Cobham tomorrow for a week's holiday with Putz.

28th June 1947

I've been in Cobham for a week now, and the sun shines day after day, and the heat is at times unbearable. We sunbathe in the garden and swim in the river with Anni and go for drives in her little car, which is called Geoffrey. In the mornings we usually go to the village and have coffee and cakes and Anni never lets us pay. One afternoon we went to Weybridge and one evening I went with Lixl to buy fish and chips for supper. Various visitors have been and gone. My second cousin Liesl Webern arrived today for the weekend, and her mother, Gerta, is coming tomorrow. Liesl has a titled, Aryan father of whom she's very proud, especially as he is related to the composer, Anton von Webern, as I've already mentioned. Her parents are divorced. I spent the day at Urbachs in Banstead today, which always feels a little bit like being in Vienna. When I got back to Cobham my father, Betty and Putz's schoolfriend Betty Crothers were here. My father saw my hideous mottled legs which I burnt by sitting too near my electric sun during the bitter winter weather, and his face contorted into its mask of displeasure and anger.

"What *have* you done to your legs?" he asked me icily.

I explained.

"You must wear stockings," he said. "You can't go around like this."

Anyone would think they were *his* legs. But it's much too hot to wear stockings, ashamed as I am of my legs, which should be a nice golden brown by now.

On Thursday evening Putz and I went to London to have dinner at my father's club; my cousin Herta was there, too. I think my father prefers Herta to me. We also went to Kingston one day, in Jack's car, to visit his sister Doris whom I haven't seen since the holiday in Tenby.

I had promised to ring Joan, and did so on Monday. She's coming out of hospital and going to join her husband and children in Forest Row where Dr Beschorner is running a private school. So she's finally leaving Oxford. I shall miss her. She asked me to promise to visit her.

We had a thunderstorm on Wednesday, but it seemed to be only a temporary break in the weather. Back to Oxford tomorrow. Life here is so different from my life there, with its boring routine of bed-sitting room, work and back again, that the thought of returning fills me with dread.

1st July 1947

Yesterday he came for tea. Then he took me to the Playhouse and for a drink, and saw me home and stayed late. Today he came for tea again and then we walked to Wolvercote for drinks at the Red Lion. I took a photograph of him with a mug of beer in his hand. He came home with me and we made love till midnight, and then we went for a walk. His name is Jimmy Dickens and I shall never see him again and I love him.

That's the bare bones. But of course you want to know more, and of course I want to tell you more. Isn't it funny how, the moment one finds happiness, one completely forgets yesterday's unhappiness – until one comes down to earth again. But I have not yet come down to earth. I'm still in the clouds, at any moment I shall fall, but until then I'm oblivious.

Only a few days ago I wrote of my drab existence and now that is as remote as the stars. It's like waking up one morning and finding that one has forgotten one's own language. But now I must tell you what has happened, though it won't be easy to talk coherently from way up in the clouds: On Sunday night, when Lieselotte and I were returning to Oxford on the train after our week's holiday in Cobham, I found myself sitting next to a dark-haired young boy with a sweet, smiling face. He started talking to me and went on talking to me until we reached Oxford. He told me he was reading German at Brasenose College and I told him I'd started doing a course in German literature but had succumbed to my usual laziness to learn. He laughed and said he was the same and then we played pokerdice and talked some more. Before we parted we arranged to meet.

I foresaw a repetition of the sordid Bill affair; but I risked it. And do you know, a marvellous thing happened. Is it possible that

I am psychologically cured? And who cured me, Jim my psychiatrist or this new man, Jimmy Dickens? I was not afraid with Jimmy, there's no tension, no inhibitions, no conflict. Why not? I don't believe it, I can't believe this has happened to me. I feel now, not as I did after my first meeting with Bill, torn to pieces with wild emotion and chaotic feelings, but a peace, a short sweet peace. And because I am so peaceful now I can face what is to come without being disturbed: Jimmy is only in Oxford for a few days to find out the result of his finals, then he's going home and then he's joining the army for two years. That's why I wrote 'I shall never see him again'. So the episode has a definite beginning and end, no uncertainty about it, with happiness beautifully framed, no time for its elusiveness. No time, too short, too short . . .

. . . We held hands so tightly in the theatre that I thought we could never let go. I loved his hand. We watched a funny play. I was crazy with happiness. It kept me awake all night. The following day, that is today, we walked to the famous Trout Inn after tea, hand in hand, and we sat by the river and we drank something I can't remember the name of and were happy. The garden of the Inn was crowded and occasionally I noticed people watching us, for we were so obviously happy young lovers, and all the world loves a lover. How different it was from the bittersweet days with Bill! I thought it had come at last, real love. So this is it, I thought, so this is it. But I didn't know. Now that he has gone I know. I have fallen in love.

On our way home I counted the hours that were left to us. In my room we made passionate love. He said I was lovely. He said he wished we had met before. At midnight I put my blouse back on again and we smoked one last cigarette together – the same one. I walked a little way along the road with him.

"I thought when I saw you on the train, 'what a beautiful girl!' " he told me, as we walked through the silent streets. He wanted to make another date but there was no time. I knew I would never see him again, and what was the point in prolonging the agony? I thought this was probably just a pleasant episode to him, but for me it would forever be a chunk of my life. A car stopped and offered him a lift. He accepted it.

Suddenly he was gone, out of my arms forever. Suddenly it was all over. From the car he called, "Goodbye, Ingrid! The best of luck, and thank you for everything!" It was the first and last time he said my name. I stood there in the dimly-lit street, a pathetic figure, numb. I refused to believe, now that he was gone, that I should never see him again. It seemed at that moment that there was nothing worse than the inability to accept something that was bound to happen. I walked away and I walked for a long time. I told myself that such happiness could not last more than two days, one could not bear it. I had forgotten to ask him if he'd passed his finals, and he had said nothing about writing to me. I don't even know his address. But I know that he is 21 – and a virgin. And I know that it was just a brief encounter and it is over.

3rd July 1947

And here are the days of tears, and of memories of Jimmy and Jimmy and Jimmy. Just as I expected, only a little worse. And as I sit in my room fingering the stubs of cigarettes in my ashtray which he'd smoked, my misery so large that it swallows me, has he already forgotten the girl whose hand he held so tightly at the Playhouse, whose lips he kissed so sweetly, whose breasts he held in his hands? Who was she? Oh, just a girl, some girl, any girl.

I hate life, it's my enemy. My passionate love belongs to death. At least there it is safe. I want to kill Jimmy, my love, oh my love! I want to kill him so that he will be safe from life.

5th July 1947

I've been to 66 St John's Road, and shall have to go again to collect the rest of the Beschorners' things. Afterwards I spent the evening at the Hayes'. Yesterday Joyce and I walked around Oxford taking photographs – St Mary's Church, the Sheldonian, some of the Colleges. Mr Calé called and again tried to make a date with me. At the last session Jim and I went for a walk and to the pub again. I didn't mention my Brief Encounter. Perhaps I will next time. After all, one has to tell one's psychiatrist everything.

I met Otto today and he gave me a lift in his van. Next Monday Daphne Hall and I are going out to tea at Fullers' and to the pictures. I suppose she'll want to know all about Joan – "Poor Joan," as she calls her, which seems a slight insult.

So life goes on, things are back to normal, and in normal life there is no slot for happiness.

7th July 1947

Is it possible? Is it true? Is my incredible happiness of two days to be extended, stretched out like a rubber band when I thought it couldn't stretch? I have had a letter from my darling Jimmy! He writes:

'My thoughts turn back to Oxford, and in particular to you . . . I wish we might have said good-bye in a more leisurely manner . . . You are a most amicable and lovable girl and I am very sad that so many miles now separate us . . . I print a row of kisses on the paper x x x x x and I only wish I could print them on you . . . There are no girls worth a second look here: I am lonely and unhappy . . . Perhaps you are right that we should be happier in a primitive state – I know where I should go and who I should find if I were not restrained by the routine of my life. Where? Oxford. Who? Ingrid! . . . My best wishes to your room, your bed and your little black doggie (my pyjama case), but all my love to you. Imagine our hands are clasped and our lips pressed together – enough! Please excuse me, I am somewhat distraught . . . Take good care of yourself, they are fortunate indeed who know you . . .'

Oh, how I love him! I shall place my happiness into the hands of providence, or God if there is one, because with me it is not safe. Tonight I shall go to sleep a peaceful soul, because Jimmy likes me.

11th July 1947

I've started my job at Exeter College Library and worked there three evenings this week. I'm all alone in the vast library except for the occasional student who comes in. Mr Nicholas, the librarian, has left me a page of instructions which keep me busy. When not at the Exeter Library I do overtime at Wolsey Hall. Chris was ill in bed on Wednesday, so I visited her in the evening and took her some books to read. Joyce and Daphne came for coffee on Thursday after work and the Library.

Arthur and Edna are here for a visit, and Putz and I had lunch with them on Tuesday. Edna called at Wolsey Hall. On Saturday

Putz and I are going to Watlington by bus with Beryl and her friend Eileen. There probably won't be much to do there except have tea.

And so I do all the things I did before I knew Jimmy, but with this new feeling of belonging to someone that accompanies me everywhere. I am a whole, not a half. D.H. Lawrence says it is a pity that men and women being only one half on their own have to join up to make a whole, instead of being one whole each and making two when joined together. I don't know – is it a pity? Are Jimmy and I a whole? Are we ever going to enjoy love together, will he destroy in me once and for all the devilish instinct which seems to make me seek out torment, which makes me feel unsafe and ridiculous in my happiness, so that I have to hand it to providence for safekeeping? The instinct that Bill scented almost immediately and took full advantage of. But I must stop comparing Jimmy to Bill.

People who know about Jimmy refer to him as 'my boyfriend'. I hate that term. He is not my boyfriend, he is the beautiful love of my life and I think of him from morning till night. To have a boyfriend means you feel mutually about each other, and I mustn't imagine for a moment that Jimmy loves me, or even thinks he does. I read his letter over and over again. Today, as I read it for the 10th time, I suddenly thought: this is only paper and ink – how can it mean so much? Because he touched it? Because it is the only palpable evidence I have that he's not a dream? Perhaps it would be better if he were a dream – or dead: while he lives, others will corrupt him, the world will make him dirty, he will come back to me, if ever he comes back, soiled. But oh, how I long for him! I want to lie beside him, in a small bed in some strange room, both of us naked, hand in hand, without speaking. I want to keep him safe from the world. If only he need not have gone away so quickly, in the middle of my exquisite happiness, and left me so bewildered.

I answered his letter at once and asked if he was free at the Bank Holiday Weekend. You see how shameless I've become. And quite mad.

14th July 1947

I must not be defenceless, I must find some courage from

205

somewhere. And I must be prepared for the worst. I have not had another letter from Jimmy. It is five days since he got mine. Why hasn't he written? It seems such ages to me – doesn't it to him? But today I fetched the photo I'd taken of him: it is beautiful.

When I saw his face again, everything came vividly back to me. I thought my heart would break. I love him so much, so much. I keep looking at the photo and I incessantly torture myself with the thought that he will not write again, he wasn't really serious, I shall never see him again . . . And I look at my left hand which no longer belongs to me but to him because he held it in his for so long and so tightly.

No, this is all no good. I must try and forget. Surely, surely I shall be happy again with some man who will love me back, if Jimmy fails me?

15th July 1947

I went swimming in the river on Port Meadow with Chris and her kids this evening – and when I returned to my room there was a letter from Jimmy! He has been away, that's why he did not reply at once. If I am so happy with his letter, what shall I be like when I'm with him again in person? Perhaps I shall collapse under the heavy weight of happiness. I forgot to tell you that he lives in Tunbridge Wells. He has failed his finals, he is bored, lonely and miserable, and 'walks listlessly about the town like a shadow'. 'I wish I could see you and touch you,' he writes. It is possible he may come to Forest Row over the Bank Holiday weekend, where I shall be visiting the Beschorners. 'I have touched this paper with my lips: make sure you do the same and tell me you have done so,' he says. Touch it with my lips? I nearly swallowed it!

And now let me tell you the second thing that happened today: I was cycling home – and met Bill. I passed him without noticing him, but he caught me up. Almost immediately he asked me to let bygones be bygones and to go out with him again. He told me how he had wanted that for a long time but had not dared to write, how stupid it had been of him to end our relationship so abruptly, how he hated himself for it and regretted it. "Shall we patch it up, Ingrid? Shall we start again, afresh? We could be so happy . . . " he asked, and looked at me, raising his eyebrows. But gone are the days of my fascination with Bill's lively eyebrows: They moved, but didn't move me.

"No, Bill," I said. "I don't think so." But I went for a drink with him at a pub.

"This doesn't mean I want to take up with you again," I told him over our drinks. I longed to hurt him. I longed to repay him for all his sadism, his cynicism, his mocking laughter. I may not have succeeded but at any rate I had learnt to refuse a man. Somerset Maugham says if one refuses everything but the best, sooner or later one gets it.

Bill was talking, or showing off his knowledge about everything under the sun – God, politics, music, poetry, the industrial revolution. I didn't listen. He still wants to impress me, but I don't want to impress him. He asked me if I had met someone else, if that was the reason for my refusal, and I just smiled, I hoped enigmatically, and made no reply.

Then I said, "If we made it up you would only want the same thing again, and I don't."

"You're wrong. I've had sufficient sexual experience now. I want someone I can like."

"And wouldn't any of the other guinea pigs serve that purpose?" I asked wickedly.

"No. They revolt me," he replied.

"That's too bad," I said.

After the drinks he accompanied me home. "Please, Ingrid," he said.

I was heartless for once in my life, and so unlike my kind, gentle mother that I hardly recognised or liked myself. But the bitterness I still felt for Bill had the upper hand. I shrugged my shoulders. "Oh Bill, it's no good," I said.

"Your hair is so lovely," he said, and touched it. I was unmoved.

"You only ever liked bits of me," I said. I wished I could be cruel, subtle, clever. But I couldn't. A few feeble attempts, probably quite ineffective, and that was all. He urged me to think it over and let him know in a week, and on that note we parted.

19th July 1947

I worked at Exeter College Library on Wednesday and Friday evening. Chris has been to supper and left a woman who lives in the same house to feed and put the children to bed, which was a real treat, she said. Putz and I had tea at Bruno and Erna's on Thursday, and Aunt Else was there to say goodbye – she's going to Australia to join her son. Last night I called at the Rieszs' but only Mr Riesz was there – the others are in Switzerland.

Today I treated Joyce and Putz to tea at the Cadena because I'm so happy about Jimmy. Afterwards I went to St Mary's Church with Joyce again to help her admire John the organist, although for the life of me I can't see what she sees in him. Then we went to Springfields to entertain some visiting German schoolteachers and after that we had supper at the G.F.S. (Girls' Friendly Society.)

I turned back some pages of this diary to find out if I ever said I was happy in the company of Bill, or any other man. Reading through my various 'love-affairs' is a sobering business. In every case I used the same passionate, convincing language but I was never as happy as with Jimmy, of that I'm certain. Well, whatever my feelings are now they are wonderful and I call them love.

If only Lieselotte were as happy as I am.

23rd July 1947

Today I finished my job at Exeter College Library and received my cheque from Mr Nicholas. The hot weather goes on and on and Putz and I sunbathe every weekend. I still haven't written that letter to Bill. He has given me up by now, I suppose. Jimmy is my life and my joy. I think of him the whole time. Am I making him into something he is not? Only seeing him again will tell me, and perhaps that will never be. I shall wait and wait for him to come and he won't come, I shall hope and hope that he will tell me he loves me and it will never happen. Then must I go to him, must I tell him I love him? Or what shall I do? Nothing, I suppose, except wait. 'They also serve who only stand and wait.' But I don't want to wait – or serve. Life is like a symphony: an exasperating anticipation for some divine climax.

Oh, to hell with my pessimism, to hell with it. From now on I shall say my glass is half *full*.

26th July 1947

Why, oh why, did Bill have to come into my life again? I wrote that letter to him, telling him that it was finished between us and that I was in love with someone else. It must have infuriated him for he called at the house several times when I was out, and finally left an almost illegible note, *returning my letter*, and saying that he *did* only want to sleep with me, I was quite right; he had thought that his physical attraction for me had disappeared but when he saw me again it returned. I was furious, and decided to ignore the whole business. I will not allow him to force himself into my life again. I tore up the note and threw it away and banished Bill from my thoughts.

About half an hour later we met in the street. That's what I call fate. Or was he lying in wait for me? And now I found myself face to face with Bill at his most charming. He was so charming that I forgot my anger. I told him he had been very stupid and he apologised and said he had not meant to be rude; he said he was sure I would be happy in my love with such a sad bitterness in his voice that I should like to have taken his face into my hands and said something kind. But I was in no mood to be taken in by him again and we soon parted on what I hoped was a note of finality on my part.

One more week and I might be with Jimmy, if he comes to see me in Forest Row.

31st July 1947

I've had another letter from Jimmy and, as he put it 'the worst has happened' – he has to go to Devon for two weeks with his family, as he thought, so we won't see each other at the weekend.

It was such a delightful letter, all about his disappointment and how much he wants to see me and how he can't picture me in his imagination, that my happiness with it almost overshadowed my disappointment. He wants a photo of me. I'm beginning to feel more sure of him and yet I know that I have no right to do so.

Yesterday I accompanied Putz to University College where she has an interview for a job, but she probably won't get it. Tomorrow I'm leaving work early and going to visit Joan at Forest Row for the Bank Holiday weekend, and on the 16th my summer holiday starts – and I'm going to Falmouth for a week. I can't wait!

7th August 1947

Joan was delighted to see me again and so was Peter; Diana is no longer a baby but a little girl, and Dr Beschorner was his usual aloof, cynical self; we don't feel easy in each other's company, but luckily I didn't see a lot of him. Joan and I slept in the same room, and in the morning Dr B. brought us a cup of tea; mine was milky and sweet and I poured it down the lavatory as it would have made me sick to drink it. Joan took me to the village and for a walk in Ashdown Forest and to see some friends called Orange: Mrs Orange is a novelist and she gave me some interesting advice on how to get a novel published. We spent a lot of time in the garden enjoying the hot sunshine. The Beschorners live in a huge old house surrounded by a huge garden. The place is a private school but it being a holiday was almost deserted by staff and children. One morning Joan gave me some potatoes to peel for lunch. I had never peeled a potato in my life and she had to show me how it is done. I was very ashamed. I find I have to be careful what I say to Joan since her illness, as she's very touchy and often misconstrues what I mean. But she was very understanding about Jimmy – as well as my lack of expertise regarding potato peeling.

I was back in Oxford at midnight on Monday. Putz is going on a University summer school course for her holiday for two weeks on Saturday.

My wireless is not working and Mrs Guttmann's son is coming to repair it tomorrow. My room feels very lonely without the wireless's friendly voice. Clare, Jim's wife, always has lunch with us at the Red Cross canteen nowadays. I don't know whether to like or dislike her. She told us about a man who decorated his bedroom with £5 notes instead of wallpaper. Probably a relation of the woman who keeps pancakes in a trunk.

I ache for my love, whose image is becoming hazier and hazier as time goes on. I wrote to him last night and felt I was writing to some creature of my own invention. He is in my head and in my heart. Does he think of me, dream of me, as much as I do of him, and his letter suggests he does? Are men like that? Am I the sort of woman to be the object of someone's passionate love? I think not. Love usually makes a berth round me.

13th August 1947

I've just returned from spending an evening at Clem and Beryl Woods. They are fond of drinking and I had to drink a lot of sherry. Yesterday I went swimming in the river on Port Meadow with Chris and Ted and the children, and we bought chips and ate them on the grass. It was very hot and the cold river was heavenly. I lent Chris my bike. She spent the evening with me in my room. The evening before I had the pleasure of Constance Senior's company in my room for coffee. She's an old-fashioned sort of girl and she always speaks of 'her friend' who seems to be her constant companion, but no one knows whether it's a man or a girl.

Last Sunday I was invited to tea at Ann Norton's in Headington. She lives with her mother and sister and longs for her father, her parents being divorced. After tea we played tennis in the park and took some snaps and walked by the river. Yesterday was also the day the clocks were put back one hour so we had a nice long day.

I've been to the dentist's and have to go again on Friday, the day before I leave for Falmouth. The dentist is called Mr Munz, nicknamed he butcher, as he's very heavy-handed. He's a German. We're getting a BONUS on Friday from Wolsey Hall. I wonder how much it will be? Mr Newell gave me a lift in his car

211

the other day, so I can't very well discuss money matters with him so soon after.

I had an awful dream about Jimmy last night. We were both dead. I woke up thinking: at last we're united. There was no letter from him to cheer me up. I'm waiting breathlessly for his next letter, which perhaps will never come. Today I saw the house he lived in – his digs – when he was in Oxford. I wanted to ring the doorbell and demand to see his room, his bed, the bathroom where he shaved, the table at which he ate. That's how crazy love makes you.

14th August 1947

A letter from him! I could have wept with joy. It was a very long letter. There appears to be less and less hope of our meeting at an early date. He had hoped he might come back to Oxford but they won't let him. He has had an offer of a job in Derby and will take it if he can get exemption from the army. 'You remember when we were on your bed,' he writes, 'and you asked me if I had slept with any girls? I said no. I am naturally rather curious about the whole process. I have never seen a mature woman's genitals. Is there much hair and what is the size? I am hoping these questions won't offend you . . .' We're truly getting to know each other by correspondence. I've never experienced that. I feel very much in harmony with him, and that there is something of him that is me, and that I should never feel ridiculous with him.

If only we could see each other soon!

21st August 1947

Here I am in Falmouth again, staying with Connie. My period came on the day I arrived which meant I missed nearly the whole week of swimming in the sea, and the weather is glorious! Curse the curse, curse it a thousand times! Otherwise everything is lovely. I go out with Pam and her boyfriend Ben nearly every day, I've had a ride on Ben's motorbike, I've been putting and to the flicks and to Flushing and Helford and Maenporth and all the places we used to visit, taking our lunch or tea, when I lived here; I've played tennis on the school courts with Pam, Maggie and Jean and I met Mrs Tohertov and her son Robin – and Denzil, with whom I reminisced at length. At St Joseph's Miss Kitty took me up to the little bedroom which used to be mine, and showed me the ink stain on the floor still there from when I upset a bottle of ink. I remembered how cold I used to be in bed in the winter but now the sun was pouring into the room and it was stifling hot. "Are you still so tidy?" Miss Kitty asked me. "All your things were always arranged so beautifully in those drawers;" and she pointed to the chest of drawers opposite the bed. I laughed and said yes. It seemed as if I had never left Falmouth. Once, on Sunny Cove Beach with Pam and Connie, I suddenly remembered how Pam had nominated me for form captain when we were in IIIB, and the dreadful humiliation when no one seconded it. It made me shudder, and I hoped Pam had forgotten the incident.

There has not been a drop of rain all week.

26th August 1947

I'm back after my lovely week in Falmouth. My love for Jimmy is unaltered. When I think of him a warm current flows through me. It says: peace, joy, happiness. Little Micky – Chris and Ted's son, aged 5 – is coming to have tea with me on Friday, all by himself. Just another young man being entertained in my room! I wonder if Mrs Labowsky will object?

I'm going to the theatre with Ann on Saturday, and Putz is coming to stay for the weekend as Mrs Labowsky is away. We'll probably spend the whole time in the garden, sunbathing, if this weather goes on.

1st September 1947

Whatever resolutions I may make to the contrary, my present life is one of waiting – waiting for Jimmy's letters. I no longer know a boy called Jimmy Dickens for I scarcely remember him, I only love my memory of him. That must be easier to forget and give up. I'm quite sure he doesn't love me as I love him or he would have found a way to see me. So would it not be best to give him up? No – yes – NO!

When I arrived at Paddington Station from Falmouth last Sunday, while waiting for my train to Oxford I telephoned my 'aunt' Anni in Cobham. She seemed pleased to hear me. I told her I couldn't swim for most of the week in Falmouth because of my period and just sat on the beach in my bathing costume feeling hot and looking fat. "You're not fat," said Anni. "You have a nice figure, only your breasts are big but that doesn't matter." I was so pleased to hear this I wanted to thank her profusely but the pips went before I could do so.

I've sent a collection of stories to Patience Ross, the author's agent, as she was recommended to me by Joan's friend, Mrs Orange.

6th September 1947

Mrs Labowsky's divorced daughter, Ruth Miller, arrived today, with a man. Everything about her and the life she leads is fascinating to me and as surely forever beyond my reach as the moon. She's sophistication personified.

I bought some new shoes today. Yesterday I worked overtime. Just before I went home the phone rang. An American pretending to be a student at Wolsey Hall struck up a conversation with me and invited me to a bridge party. I said I didn't play bridge, and hung up.

I'm going to babysit for a new family called Dauries, recommended by the Red Cross, as the Dawsons have left.

Each morning I look for a letter from Jimmy in the post and walk away in the depths of gloom because there isn't one. I try to protect my love, to keep it warm and sheltered and undamaged, but disappointment must leave its scar. I love him so much, why doesn't he love me? How can he neglect me, when I'm ready to give my life to him? I ask myself from time to time: is he really as unique as my fantasy makes him? Of course he is. No, he isn't ... he is ... he isn't ... is ... isn't ...

11th September 1947

I am babysitting at the Dauries' for the first time. They have two little girls called Marion and Joan. There's a piano in the sitting room and it's a joy to be able to play again. But, best of all, for 3 to 4 hours babysitting I earn 1/-. The Dauries live in Marston and it takes about 20 minutes to cycle there.

Putz is going to the Woods for the weekend so I've asked Constance to come over on Saturday, and I'm going to her place on Sunday. St Giles Fair was here on Monday and Tuesday. On the first day I went with Ann and on the second with Chris and Ted. There was a man guessing your age there and he took me to be 16 so I got my money back; there was also a man guessing your weight and he judged Chris to weigh about two stone less than she did, so she too got her money back. She had no idea she weighed that much herself.

Mrs Labowsky returned from her holiday on Tuesday evening.

This morning I met Mr Calé in Banbury Road and we cycled to our respective places of work together – he to Parkers' bookshop, I to Wolsey Hall. Friday night is always Beethoven night at the Proms and Putz and I are particularly looking forward to tonight's concert – the *9th Symphony*.

Will nothing bring me a letter from Jimmy, no tears, no prayers? But I shouldn't be writing such rubbishy sentiment. I should face the situation squarely: What would he think were he to know, my little dark archangel, that I sit night after night weeping for him and playing the tragedy queen?

17th September 1947

What I have been through these last few weeks I cannot go through again on paper. I want to forget it. But the longed-for letter has come at last. He's had an accident on a friend's motorbike and been ill and the Derby job has fallen through – he has to go in the army. Nothing very cheerful, but the letter alone was enough to cheer me up. Years and years ago I used to be unhappy when there wasn't a letter from my mother, and I was reminded of that when Jimmy didn't write.

On Monday I called on Mme Zuccari after work (having stayed late to type a story) and we had a long talk. I gave up the German classes as I didn't want to take the exam, but I still enjoy talking to her. Tomorrow Ann and I are having tea at Lyons after work and afterwards we're going to hear Ronald Strong, the spiritualist, at the Town Hall. Just for a laugh. And at the weekend Putz and I are going to Cobham by coach to meet Felix's brother and his wife, Hans and Leah, who are here on holiday from New York, and whom we haven't seen since we were in Vienna. I

215

remember my mother taking me to the stamp shop owned by Uncle Hans and Uncle Felix, for they are both philatelists. I had never seen so many postage stamps in one place in all my life. After Cobham, having got Monday off from work, I'm going to Watford where Ted Hayes is at College training to be a teacher, as he has invited me and Chris to attend the College Open Day.

1st October 1947

Today I had tea at Clare and Jim's – followed by my last session for the present. I think Jim was quite sorry but I told him he had helped me a great deal and I felt it was no longer necessary for me to have weekly sessions.

My old school friend, Britta Lamberg, from Vienna, who has been to a Concentration Camp, came to visit me in Cobham! She has hardly changed, but her terrible experiences have left their mark. My father and Betty were also in Cobham for the day. And here is my big news: I AM NATURALISED! Since the 20th September I am a British subject! It came about because my father got naturalised and I, being under 21, was automatically included. Putz has to apply separately.

I quite enjoyed the Open Day at Leavesden College; there was an Art Exhibition, a PT display in the grounds and performances in the evening, but I didn't enjoy sleeping in a large dormitory with Chris and the other wives. I couldn't sleep at all. Institutional life is definitely not for me. Chris and I returned to Oxford by coach on Tuesday and I went to work in the afternoon and did overtime till quite late.

Last weekend I stayed with the Woods. As usual, we didn't get up till midday on Sunday and spent most of the time in cafés and pubs.

5th October 1947

Yesterday afternoon I helped Putz move digs. She has left the Blaschkos' house in Park Town and moved in with Mr and Mrs Wren in Plantation Road, where Clare once used to live, and which is much cheaper.

Raymond Fenn, who has lunch with us at the Red Cross canteen, has moved to digs in Lonsdale Road, three doors away from me, and the other day he asked me in. I couldn't go, but chatted with him through the open window for ages! The next day at lunch his look said: "We're friends now, aren't we?" But by today he seemed to have forgotten all about it. He's reading PPE at Keble College and enjoys talking politics and philosophy over his apple charlotte, usually way above my head.

Mr Calé called today and told me there was a vacancy in the foreign department at Parkers' bookshop, and was I interested in the job? I agreed to go for an interview tomorrow. This afternoon there was a little tea party at Constance's to which Joyce, Putz and I were invited.

Next week I am going to 66 St John's Road again, to help Mr Pacis who lives there clear out the cellar, which is still full of the Beschorners' things.

6th October 1947

What a day! A Monday. It started rottenly, there was no letter from Jimmy and everything went wrong. At 5pm I had the dreaded interview at Parkers' – and accepted the job, because the wages are higher. A Mr Brown, head of the foreign department and an ex-refugee from Vienna, interviewed me. I start there on the 20th. After the interview Mr Calé asked me out but, needless to say, I didn't accept the invitation. I decided to stay in in the evening, wash my hair, and look out for Raymond and have a little chat with him. But I did none of these things. I got restless and went to the Rieszs'. Late in the evening Peter took me home – and stayed till one o'clock. We made love *in words!* Very interesting. He's a strange boy, completely devoid of any physical attraction, but apparently longing for sex. A sexual relationship with him would be like incest! I told him all about Bill. I gave him my poems to read – and wish I hadn't now. I'm a rotten poet – no poet at all, in fact. Peter is the last person I expected to be with tonight.

I must to bed. It's nearly two o'clock and I'm not a bit tired. A bad sign.

12th October 1947

I gave my notice in on Thursday. If Mr Newell was surprised or sorry he didn't show it. In the evening Ann and I went to the pictures and then she came for supper. A girl called Joan Lea-Wilson, another of Putz's highly intellectual friends who works at Wolsey Hall, has joined us for lunches at the Red Cross canteen. I babysit every Friday evening at the Dauries' and cycle home 1/- richer. Mrs Dauries told me how much the little girls like me. I'm entertaining someone or other on almost every night this week: Putz, Chris, Joyce, Constance.

Today I was sick but I was all right again in the evening. It was a very dull Sunday and I was reminded of my father complaining of the deadly Sundays in Falmouth, when everything was closed and you couldn't get a meal or see a film and he hung around us and expected us to entertain him. Well, he's lonely no longer. (But I am.)

15th October 1947

A letter from my love! A very long one. He has to join the army and has taken an officer's test; he has been to London; he has a passion for golf and wants to teach me; he thinks Vienna is a lovely place to have been born in; he's been teaching at his old prep. school; he sends his kisses and his love. But not the kind of love *I* mean, of course. When I'd finished reading the letter I thought: I don't know this boy Jimmy Dickens any longer. Time and distance have distorted him. With each letter I know him less. With each letter a stranger is revealed. What's the use of continuing this correspondence? I left this question unanswered, and knew I would continue to write to him.

On Monday I start my new job at Parkers' foreign department, the University bookseller. I liked my job as librarian at Wolsey Hall but I didn't earn enough and I was getting in a rut. And now I'm afraid, as I always am of new things: I long for a new life and when it comes within my grasp I long for the old familiar one back. 'Zwei Seelen wohnen, ach, in meiner Brust!' No, a thousand, not two!

Mr Herbert gave me a good reference.

21st October 1947

This is my second day at Parkers' and I like the job very much. I found a French book on the shelf which neither Mr Calé nor Mr

Brown had been able to find! A good beginning. I went to Wolsey Hall for a chat in my lunch hour, and shall probably visit there again on Thursday afternoon, my half-day.

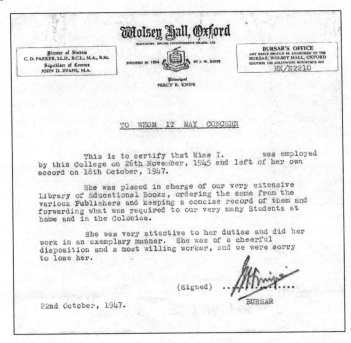

I discovered that Raymond is engaged to a girl in Reading. He's such a nice boy I hope his fiancée is good enough for him. The other thing I want to tell you today is this: I'm going through another of those extraordinary periods of longing for Mr Morris. The thought and memory of him taste like nectar – but unfortunately do not quench my thirst for him. What did he do to me that, after two years, I still cannot forget him? I am haunted by the enigma of the man. The other day I went to Blackwell's, hoping to see him and tell him of my new job, but he wasn't there. So I'm left with his ghost. His shadow has fallen over my life again, but where is the man to whom the shadow belongs? Where is that God of men? One day I'll laugh about my loves and my tears, but now they are the stuff of my narrow, silly life.

31st October 1947

Marion and Joan are asleep, I've read the *Oxford Times* and played the piano and trimmed my hair and there's still about an hour to go till the Dauries are due home, just long enough to partake of my favourite activity – writing this diary.

Yesterday was my half day and I spent it at Wolsey Hall, chatting with the girls and helping in the library as they have not yet found a new librarian. Afterwards Ann and I had tea at Lyons and then were joined by her mother and sister, and we all went to the Town Hall to hear Cyril Smith give a piano recital. He's a brilliant pianist. On Sunday Anni, Felix and my father came to visit us by car for the day. We had lunch at Ross's, coffee at Bruno and Erna's and a ride in the car. In complete contrast, Ted and Chris spent the evening with me on Tuesday, and the following evening I was at their house for supper and we told each other jokes and played cards. I said in 'complete contrast' because I don't think Ted and Chris even know that I have foreign relations who do and talk about such different things. I seem to have two quite separate lives in watertight compartments – three counting Falmouth – and they're like oil and water because they won't mix. Ted used to be in the Air Force and developed an antipathy towards all 'wogs', so I always avoid the subject.

Mr Brown, the middle-aged Austrian manager of Parkers' foreign department, flirts outrageously with me! But my thoughts are not with him, nor with Jimmy – but with Mr Morris! I saw him in the street yesterday; he didn't see me. I let the ideal opportunity slip by and didn't speak to him. I couldn't. I fled. Were he to ask me to marry him again I would say yes. When I think of him sitting in his room among his books and papers and perhaps entertaining some other young girl, my mind runs riot with me.

1st November 1947

Mr Brown calls me 'My darling Ingrid' when we're alone in the shop after five o'clock. He kissed my hand today. It's nice to be called 'my darling' even if only in fun. I promised to live with him for a week and he won't let his wife know! I wasn't serious, of course.

220

On Thursday Lieselotte, Constance and I are going to tea at Raymond's. Today after lunch I went to town with him. I feel very safe with him, partly because he's such a nice person and partly because he's engaged.

I do so long for Mr Morris! God of men! How tired you must be getting of my perpetual repetitious outpourings. But what can I do? I must write down what I feel – or burst. This is, after all, chiefly a diary of my thoughts and feelings.

I wrote to Jimmy – a much less affectionate letter. I don't suppose he'll notice, or care. Only a month ago I wept for him. I was in love with him, and when one is in love one isn't patient or understanding: he did not meet my demands, he didn't come to see me, he didn't say what I wanted him to say. I saw it all coming. Step by step. And was helpless. Now I must take the consequences.

7th November 1947

Several people from Wolsey Hall have been to see me at Parkers'. Today Enid Carter came. We became quite friendly just before I left.

At 2.30pm today I went to an exhibition of French books with Constance, for which we both got time off from work. I hate French books – most of them have no proper covers and their pages are uncut, to stop people reading them in the shop instead of buying them. On my half day yesterday I again visited Wolsey Hall, and afterwards went out to tea twice – first to Rieszs' then to Constance's. No wonder I'm fat. In the evening Putz, Constance and I went to the pictures. Putz and I also went to the Scala Cinema on Sunday evening, where the Film Society we joined show foreign films fortnightly. On Sunday afternoon I had tea at Mary Gammon's. Have I ever done more than mention her? She's the sweet little gentle girl who brought me a bunch of primroses, a year or so younger than I, and who seems to love Putz and me. She often brings us flowers or little gifts. She lives with her family in a house not far from me. I met this family for the first time on Sunday, and Mary must have praised me to high heaven for they couldn't do enough for me, and had laid on a most magnificent tea, everything homemade.

Raymond called at my digs on Monday evening. I had just

washed my hair and felt – and looked – a wreck! Why did he have to choose that moment?

We always play cards at Chris and Ted's now after the children have gone to bed.

8th November 1947

Why particularly today has it suddenly occurred to me that I am alone in the world? Yes, alone, quite alone. Lieselotte is no longer Lieselotte. Something has happened to her. Often she feels like a stranger. Have I been living under an illusion all our lives? If so, that is a terrible thing. I will not even try to go into the subject more deeply now. My father has nothing to do with my life. As for all the friends that I boast of – what are they but props for my vanity and buffers against loneliness? What do they really care for me? Will they remember me at Christmas? Or on my birthday? Life is ugly when one unravels it and clears the path to one's innermost mind. The reflection of a naked, brutal and lonely world is exposed. And the only person in it who ever really loved me died long ago, far away in Minsk, where the imagination doesn't reach. I see her sometimes as if through a veil, my beloved mother, kept eternally young through death.

I'm a jigsaw with vital pieces missing. If God made me in his image he must be a poor specimen. I haven't a single philosophy left. I know nothing and I am clumsy and ignorant and can't hide it from the world. So I expose it for all to see in order that they may take notice of me, lest I become invisible. I belong nowhere and no one cares. I'm as barren as the life around me. I feed on stupid little flirtations and flatteries that lead to nothing. I am no one and I shall never be anyone. No, no! It would be unbearable! It can't be as bad as that, this is just one of those demented unhappy spells that will pass, that can't last . . . But what *is* the point of it all? Life, then death. So much in between, and all so meaningless.

12th November 1947

Enid Carter came to tea today and told me the latest Wolsey Hall gossip. Her father fetched her in the evening. I made him a cup of tea. Enid is from a working class family but is a bright and unusual girl, full of original ideas.

Yesterday evening I was at the Rieszs'. Only Peter was there and we listened to the gramophone and the wireless. Music seems to give Peter confidence when he's with a girl, and he loses some of his awkwardness. He really loves music.

Ruth Miller was here again at the weekend, this time without a man, but none the less glamorous for that. She's always very nice to me. Putz was ill in bed all Sunday so I spent most of the day with her. My mood is in a state of flux – I'm on top of the world or down in the dumps, but mostly the latter.

If only Jimmy and I had met earlier, he might have fallen in love with me and we might have been infinitely happy. But we had no chance and now it is over. One can't expect a man to love a girl he has only known for two days. I was so happy with him. The sadness of this lost happiness breaks my heart. I look at his picture on my desk, the one on which he looks like a pixie, with a mug of beer in his hand, and I could weep for him all over again.

This diary is full of platitudes. How tedious it will be to read in, say, ten years' time.

WB, my boss, made passionate love to me today in the bicycle shed, which is also our cloakroom. It was six o'clock and pitch dark, there being no light in the shed. Despite the unromantic setting, I found it very exciting. He must be a good lover, like most continentals. He is 38, and he wants to come to my room to see me. He frequently informs me that he is very fond of me. I find it thrilling to be touched by him – in fact I can't resist him. Heaven knows why; he's bald and plump and wears glasses and has ugly fat hands – but when I feel them on me I turn to jelly. He said to me, "I am being unfair to you. What can I give you, what can I do for you? I can't even take you to the cinema because we can't be seen together."

"I don't want you to take me to the cinema," I replied, melting at his touch. "It's not what I want at all." But it was a lie.

"You just want my kisses?" he said. I nodded. His kisses – and then what? I thought. I cannot find one redeeming feature about this man's appearance – what is it then that draws me to him, that makes him so physically attractive to me? At first it was all a joke. Now I'm deeply involved against my will. Sometimes I find it difficult to face him, I can't handle the situation, I act like a child often, and then again like a woman of the world. He has noticed this, but he is very kind to me, whatever my guise.

Naturally, for the moment, the memory of Mr Morris has receded.

14th November 1947

Sordidness, like charity, begins at home. Or in a draughty old bicycle shed at work. At five o'clock tonight, I went as usual to the shed to collect my coat and bicycle. It was raining again. I was groping about in the dark when I heard footsteps. WB entered. At first we just stood there, facing each other.

"What brings you here?" I asked him, knowing perfectly well. He always stays at work long after everyone has gone, as he lives in Reading and has to wait for his train. He took me in his arms.

"I had to see you again," he said. "I wanted to say goodnight to you – alone."

We stood there in that unromantic shed. He kissed me passionately, but not on my mouth because he was afraid of lipstick smudges. " – but how I long to kiss you again, properly," he added. And then: "You do like me just a little, don't you? Tell me you like me. Please." I felt so safe and content and relaxed in his arms that I said nothing and only nodded. His body feels like a protective father's and I wanted to stay next to it forever. I was wallowing in the luxury of being the object of such a man's attraction. Presently, we spoke in whispers. And then suddenly we heard footsteps, we quickly moved apart, and Mr Calé entered. Mr Calé is a very odd chap, completely sexless, an eccentric bachelor. He was obviously very surprised at seeing WB.

"Hello, are you going home already?" he asked him.

"No. I – I just came to get something," WB replied, lost for once for an answer, he who is never lost for one with customers, who discourses with dons, who has all the books in the shop at his fingertips. Had Mr Calé been more worldly he might have suspected something, but I don't think he did. Is it worth it, I wonder, to enjoy oneself a little, to give one's body a treat occasionally, if one has to face the foolish embarrassment of a strong, clever man who is like the father one never had? I shall not forget this incident in a hurry. The two of us standing there like guilty children, caught in flagrante, will haunt me for a long time. Our little affair will have to stop.

I have not heard from Jimmy for ages. I don't care.

18th November 1947

I went to an art lecture at the Ashmolean Museum with Mr Calé this evening. It's like going out with a brother or a girlfriend. If he has any masculine desires or characteristics they're well under lock and key. I'm sorry for him, as I am for anyone who's not normal. I didn't tell WB about this evening, but there was really no reason not to.

How beautifully WB can kiss! What an intoxicating lover he must be! The thing between us has grown serious. Our shop is closed on Thursday because of the Royal Wedding but he will be there working, and I promised to go and see him to discuss 'our future'. I think he will ask me to be his mistress. That would be a great compliment to me. After all, though a refugee like myself, he's a clever man, well known and liked by many famous Oxonians – Deakin, Seton-Watson, Lord Pakenham, Isaiah Berlin, and many others – and he is married. It has always been my ambition to have an affair with a married man. What shall I do? This will take more deliberating than the Bill affair. As a matter of fact I'm quite worried about it. What does he see in me? Why does he want me so badly? I think I'm just an ephemeral plaything in men's lives.

I had tea at Ann Norton's again last Sunday, and on Saturday I'm going to the Playhouse with Putz and Joan Lea-Wilson. Isn't it odd that I can be so ordinary and do such ordinary, every day things, when I'm about to be the mistress of a married man?

20th November 1947

If only someone would love me and marry me and take me away from all this sordidness, away from the magic clutches of WB, away from waiting for Jimmy's letters. I want to love and call somewhere in this world home.

I kept our appointment and went to the shop this morning. He was waiting for me. We sat amid piles of books, by a small gas-fire. That was romantic enough. He said we could not go on like this indefinitely, we must either give each other up or live together. He was not content with hurried kisses in the bicycle shed. He again asked me if I liked him and I said yes. He said we might fall in love so hopelessly that we would no longer care about practical details, but until then something would have to be devised. Of course I don't love him and I never shall: I'm attracted to him because he is protective and much older and married and a foreigner and probably a good lover, and because he could be my father. When I'm not disgusted with its sordidness I'm fascinated by the situation, enjoy doing the forbidden, being a conspirator, sneaking behind books to kiss, making secret appointments . . . straight out of the pages of a French novel, one of those horrid ones without a proper cover, and uncut pages. The discussion didn't really get us anywhere. When I got up to go he came up with his trump card: he wants me to spend one night at a hotel with him. French novel style again.

After I left him I visited Wolsey Hall where most people were listening to the Royal Wedding on the wireless, and I joined them. Later I called on Mrs Lines, Maureen's one-time landlady, which I'd been meaning to do for ages. She was pleased to see me.

The evening was a sad occasion because it was my last one at the Rieszs': they're going to the USA, where Susi already lives. I had a last supper with them and then stayed talking to Peter and his friend Jack, and listening to the gramophone, till one o'clock in the morning.

29th November 1947

Putz, Constance and I had tea at Raymond's digs last Sunday, and listened to records on his gramophone. I suppose we help to make him forget the absence of his fiancée. Joyce spent the evening with me on Tuesday, and Chris came on Wednesday. When I was at Chris and Ted's on my half day a friend of theirs, an elderly lady called Mrs Scott, was there, and we played cards for money. I won some and lost some. Mrs Scott's profession is restoring pictures at the Ashmolean Museum, which sounds a very refined job but is in fact done with raw potatoes, she informed me.

I'm beginning to grow very fond of WB, and he is fond of me, too. He smells so nice, and always feels fresh and clean. Today we discussed going abroad together. Of course, one can't travel abroad now, and anyway it would be impossible for us, but we made the trip in our imagination. First we went to France, then to Switzerland and Italy. In Italy we lie in the sun and swim. Paris is where he would really like to take me, he said. We shall go to the Eiffel Tower and the Louvre and all the other famous places I've only heard about. Tomorrow is Sunday.

"What shall we do tomorrow?" I asked him before kissing him goodnight in the bicycle shed-cum-cloakroom. "Shall we walk in the Bois de Boulogne if it's fine?"

"No, darling. We'll stay in bed till lunchtime," he said.

We don't seem able to stay away from each other. We keep sneaking to the rear of the shop where the parcels of books are opened, just to touch each other.

"What will you tell your wife?" I asked him. I genuinely wanted to know.

"Oh, that doesn't come into our fantasy," he replied.

"It does into mine," I said.

No, I don't love him – yet. Nor he me. But he's no longer just sex personified. He's something else too, now. Something much more, as yet nameless. Last Saturday he gave me a present because: "I couldn't wait till Christmas to give you something," he said. It is a beautiful book I've long admired called *Toi et Moi* by Paul Géraldy, a sad love poem with wonderful, simple illustrations. On the fly leaf he wrote 'Pour avoir dans un regard lu des possibilités. To I from W.' It is a quotation from the poem.

I haven't told you much else about Parkers' yet. The three of us, WB, Mr Calé, and I sit at desks in front of our typewriters, I with my back to the shop door so that I get a cold draught every time the door is opened. Mr Calé and I share a desk. Frequently our typewriting is interrupted by customers buying books or wanting information. Right at the back of the foreign department, past the parcels area, there's an office inhabited by old Mr Gronner, a Viennese solicitor and bachelor, who deals with subscriptions, and Mrs Hacker, also from Vienna and middle aged. She's a very nice, motherly woman whom everyone likes. I'm the youngest in the department.

5th December 1947

I didn't go babysitting at the Dauries' this evening because of the bad weather. Yesterday afternoon – Thursday – I was invited for tea at Jim and Clare's, with a free session thrown in. I think the session was meant for Jim's benefit; he told me he's attracted to me! In the evening Raymond and Putz came for supper in my room. Putz and I are being taken out to lunch by her boss, Dr Parker, and his wife and niece on Saturday and then she's going to London for the weekend. Raymond is going home for the vacation next Tuesday and has invited us to his birthday party in January. The Rieszs are leaving for America any day now.

Last Sunday I had lunch and tea at Enid Carter's in Headington. Her parents are very hospitable and there was good, home-made food. I hinted at an affair with a married man to Enid, and she was very intrigued. In the evening Putz and I went to the last Film Society of the term, with Pat Dorling and her husband, and afterwards for coffee at Putz's. Mr and Mrs Wren, her landlord and landlady, joined us, and provided the coffee, or rather the coffee essence.

On Monday after work WB and I went for a long walk. He wants me to go away with him for a weekend when his wife is away. I felt incapable of making any decision. The following day Mr Calé and I had tea at Mme Zuccari's. We're going to another art lecture at the museum.

I shall probably spend most of the weekend with Ted and Chris playing cards – for money, if Mrs Scott is there.

It's all over between Jimmy, my little archangel, and me.

16th December 1947

The Rieszs' departure for the USA was delayed but they are now definitely leaving on Thursday. I had another last supper there this evening and we said a tearful goodbye, though Peter may call at the shop again to see me before they finally depart. I shall miss them very much.

Yesterday I had tea at Lyons with Ann, despite the unpleasant smell that emanates from there, and afterwards we went to the Town Hall for a hypnosis demonstration by Peter Casson. I saw the Dorlings there. At one point the audience was told to link their fingers and put their hands above their heads. At Casson's command we were then told to release our fingers and lower our hands: a sizable part of the audience couldn't, and were marched up to the stage to be freed. Among them was Jim Dorling. I couldn't believe my eyes, and am still sceptical. Perhaps they were all accomplices?

Little Mary Gammon called on Sunday with an invitation to her party. It'll be very boring, but I wouldn't let her down for all the world.

Tomorrow I'm babysitting for Chris and Ted and having tea and supper there first.

21st December 1947

Ted is away for the weekend and I spent the whole day at Chris's today. She told me she's pregnant! They didn't want a third child. She says after this they will have to sleep in separate rooms. It accounts for why she weighed so much more than she thought at St Giles Fair! In the afternoon we took the kids for a walk and in the evening we played cards.

On Friday I had a Christmas drink with the Dauries after my babysitting duty, and yesterday at Putz's I had another one with the Wrens'. I managed to get them both down.

The Rieszs' left on the 18th. I don't suppose I shall ever see them again. It is very sad to go past their empty house. On Wednesday I'm only working in the morning and then Putz and I are going to Cobham for Christmas.

23rd December 1947

It being nearly Christmas no one is doing much work any more. I saw Mr Morris today; He didn't see me. WB says he's in love with me. He is certainly very good to me. I am sorry for his wife.

What do you think? Bill has called! He came last week when I was out and he came again today. For no other reason than to see me, apparently. I was packing. His excuse, he said, was to "maintain a link with Austria," now that Peter and his family have gone. We sat and chatted for some time. How different it was from the old days! Incredible! There we sat stiffly, the two of us, who had once made such passionate love, talking about books and holidays and the Liberals and Christmas. Like strangers. As though we had only just met. The past was wiped out, totally. But it doesn't matter at all now. I don't know what he still wants of me. Beyond a vague suggestion of his that I should come to the

New Year's Dance at the Liberal Club, we made no arrangement. Did he sense that I no longer cared, that he's no longer my master, that he made about as much impression on me as a cat? A stray one.

31st December 1947

We spent Christmas at Elgin Avenue and at Cobham, as usual. We gave and received many presents, though the ones we gave were not of the same high quality as the ones we received. There were the usual relations and friends staying at Ann's Cottage. One evening we all went to the pictures in the village, and occupied nearly a whole row. On the 27th we went to my father's office and I chose a costume. It is pale blue and very smart. Afterwards we had lunch at my father's favourite place, the Cumberland Hotel in Marble Arch, where Herta joined us. Then on to Elgin Avenue for tea at Jack and Jane's flat. There were several visitors there and I helped Jane stuff dates with walnuts.

We got back to Oxford on Sunday evening – my father and Betty spent the day in Cobham and took us to the station – and there was a Christmas card from Jimmy waiting for me. 'Writing soon,' it said. Not soon enough. Too late, too late. Last night at Putz's we had drinks with the Wrens again. Tonight, New Year's Eve, I'm staying the night at Chris and Ted's after seeing 1948 in with them.

Happy New Year!

2nd January 1948

It is all arranged. For Sunday – the day after tomorrow. I'm going to spend the night at a hotel in Woodstock with WB. Do you want to know how I feel about it? I want to die. I feel so awful about it that I want to die. For a week now I've been hoping against hope that something would happen to prevent it, but nothing has. Now you want to know why I'm going. Naturally. I will give you all the reasons I can think of: I am attracted to him; I am thrilled by the exciting adventure; I want to do what people do in French novels; I want to know what sex is really like . . . But I know in my bones that the reality will be very different from all the illusions I have. Oh, I feel so miserable, so wretched . . . I've promised him, I can't change my mind now, nor even postpone the date because Sunday night is the night his wife is away. I feel as unreal as in a dream, in a horrible dream, a nightmare. Is it really me who is going to do this terrible thing? No, it can't be: I'm a little girl, quite carefree, going shopping with my mother on a sunny spring day, knowing nothing about sex.

Bill has started coming again, complete with charm, quotations from Baudelaire and philosophical speculations. Last night we went to a pub and had a drink. I've never yet discovered anything I like drinking, and have whatever the person I'm with is having. Then we did a strange thing: coming out of the pub into the pitch dark we walked aimlessly for a bit and presently crept into a nearby Churchyard. It was about 9.30pm. We groped our way through the cemetery, found a backdoor of the church open and went in. The silence and eerie darkness screamed at us. There was a strong smell of incense. We walked down the nave, holding hands.

I felt relaxed and peaceful, momentarily oblivious of the terrifying event ahead. And then, as though comedy meant spitefully to destroy its enemy, solemnity, Bill suddenly went crash into a chair. It made a terrible noise. In no time a parson came running from somewhere. He turned on the light, and saw us. We explained that we had come to pray, and hurriedly left. We walked arm in arm, and, as if by instinct, to our old hunting ground. Just as of old, only now I had no fear of him. He made love to me. I let him. I didn't think that would ever happen again. I felt so miserable about WB that I didn't care what I said or did. I was suddenly relieved to be in Bill's arms, not WB's. I saw him momentarily as my Deus Ex Machina. I was far away from WB and safe in Bill's arms. We kissed, heavily, like the old, old lovers we were.

Suddenly, in desperation, I told him about WB and the coming weekend and that I didn't want to go. I was almost in tears. Bill was wonderfully sweet and kind. He stroked my hair, and told me not to go. He said he wished he were the man. He told me how he had many times blamed himself for leaving me. He had been a notorious coward. He said I had never ceased to fascinate him. Of all the girls he had met in Paris last summer, none had captivated him as much as I. He has always wanted me back. I wanted to hear him say that over and over again, whether he meant it or not. Dear, charming Bill, who talks streams of philosophy and politics

231

and makes love and flatters you all in one breath.

Of course, he wants to sleep with me again. I'm beginning to wonder who doesn't. I have so much sex appeal, apparently. Or something. I also told Bill about Jimmy. Why? I don't know, for Jimmy lies buried in my memory and in my heart. I should have liked to marry him. But that is another story. I cried with joy when I had his Christmas card. I didn't tell Bill that.

We didn't have our half day off at Parkers' yesterday as we were stocktaking, and we were still doing so today. I was sick in the night yesterday so I went to bed early tonight. Today is also the day Raymond gets back after the vacation. I try to comfort myself with all kinds of things to make me forget Sunday, without much success. I don't suppose I shall write again before the weekend. Perhaps I shall have an attack of some sort and go mad and then I shall never write again. Well, some time ago I wished for lovers. Here they are. Now I must face them.

6th January 1948

Was that really me? Was it I who went with a married man in a taxi to a hotel on Sunday morning and was shown to a double bedroom? No, I cannot believe it. But this is how the dream or whatever it was appeared:

We arrived at the Bear Hotel in Woodstock at lunch time. I had once had tea at this hotel with Harold. How young and innocent I had been then! We had lunch, WB and I. Not that I could eat much. He was sweet and kind to me. He called it 'my day' and fulfilled my every wish, except the wish to go home, which I kept to myself. I wore my red pleated skirt and knee socks, because they're easier to take off than stockings.

After lunch we went to bed. Naked. Yes, it was really I, not one of my characters from a story, nor even myself in one of my daydreams. But I'm racing on. Before that two things happened: we sat at the little table by the window in the hotel bedroom and he took my legs and put them in his lap and we sat like that for some time, talking, I've forgotten what about. I went to bed first and covered myself with the blankets. He stood by the bed. He took my hand. "You look like a little animal that's about to be slaughtered," he laughed. "Have you ever seen an erection?" he said, and showed me this huge thing.

"No." I said.

It surprises me that in all the vividly described sex scenes in books I've read, nowhere is the pain mentioned. The pain was so terrible that I almost screamed. I thought he must be doing something wrong. When it was over I was full of questions.

"It didn't seem to be in the right place," I said.

"Aha, you've been masturbating!" he said, and laughed. "It'll be better next time. Wait till tonight."

"Tonight?"

"Yes, of course, tonight."

"But you can't ejaculate again for twenty-four hours!"

"Who told you that?"

"Bill Emerson."

"Bill Emerson has a lot to learn." And so had I, it seemed. We went for a long walk before dinner. I still couldn't eat. Nothing felt real. He was wrong about it being better next time. The whole night was a struggle and I was sorry for him because he had spent so much money on me. However, he continued to be very kind and comforting, and if sex was a shock and unrecognisable to me from what I'd read, I loved waking in the night and feeling a man next to me.

We returned to Oxford and work separately on Monday morning. When I came into the shop he and Mr Calé were already at their desks, typing.

"Good morning. Did you sleep well?" WB asked me.

"Yes, thank you," I said, and we quickly glanced at each other over Mr Calé's head, with just a hint of a smile.

Back in my own bed that night I slept as if I hadn't slept for weeks. I had got rid of a great weight off my shoulders. I could breathe freely again, and nobody was going to hurt me tonight. Is it possible that some people enjoy being hurt?

10th January 1948

Lots of people come to see me at Parkers', especially girls from Wolsey Hall, but guess who came on Monday? Dr Beschorner! He's on a visit to Oxford and I suppose Joan instructed him to call on me. He didn't stay long.

Constance, Raymond and I had tea at Putz's on Tuesday and afterwards Ray walked home with me. On Wednesday WB came to tea in my room for the first time, and made love to me. He said if anyone was made to enjoy lovemaking it was me, and one day I would, and he only wished it could be with him. I asked him why he had no children and he replied, "All that nappy washing!"

On Thursday afternoon I visited Wolsey Hall and afterwards I had an interview with Mrs Wawerka, a friend of Mr Calé's who runs a typewriting office; I might do some typing for her at home, to earn extra money. In the evening I was at Mary Gammon's party, and so were Putz, Beryl and a few other girls from Wolsey Hall. It was as I thought it would be, very tame and boring. Some of the time we played cards and that livened things up a bit. The best thing was, Mary lent me her brand-new portable typewriter and said I could keep it as long as I like, which is why I am enabled to take on work at home, and why I won't have to stay late at Parkers' typing my stories. She can't do enough for Putz and me and we never know how to repay her. What would she think if she knew where I spent last Sunday night? Or had an inkling that I'm having an affair with a married man? I'm like the moon, for it, too, never shows its other side to the world.

On Thursday the 8th of January *Richard Tauber died*, aged 56. It was quite a shock – almost a personal loss. Shall I go into mourning for him?

15th January 1948

I haven't had that promised letter from Jimmy yet. Perhaps it will never come. All the same, as I sit here in my comfortable bed-sitting room that smells of winter, I feel fairly content for the first time for ages. My restless soul is temporarily still, my relentless instability is temporarily anchored. WB continues to be very good to me. I have started writing a new novel. As from next Thursday afternoon I am going to help with the Red Cross Library at the Radcliffe Hospital. This is voluntary work.

WB was in London for the day yesterday. Mrs Adler, another Viennese lady who works in the office upstairs, came with me to buy a costume in our lunch hour, which I extended on account of his absence.

This afternoon I was at the hairdresser's and at Mrs Wawerka's Typing Office. She's another Lutheran, like Mr Calé and the German lady cook at the Red Cross canteen, even though they are all Jewish. The series of misfortunes in Mrs Wawerka's life, which turned her to religion, are so numerous as almost to be unbelievable: her husband was killed in a mountaineering accident in Austria, her elder daughter died of being given a wrong dose against scarlet fever in Vienna, and her other daughter died in a sailing accident on the river in Oxford, where she and her mother had settled after fleeing from the Nazis. But the Lutheran religion seems to compensate poor Mrs Wawerka for all these disasters, and she won't be pitied.

Mrs Scott was at Chris and Ted's again this evening and we all had tea and supper and played cards. Chris told me that when it is very cold she and Ted sit in the kitchen with their feet in the hot oven, which practice they began during the fuel crisis. Better than scorching your legs over an electric fire as I did!

20th January 1948

My father was here for the afternoon and evening on Sunday. He asked me if I was in love with anyone and said one great love comes to everyone once in a lifetime. Ashamed of my loveless night with WB, I nevertheless hinted at a mysterious relationship. "You should wait till you're in love," he said. It's what Joan had said. He said it quite kindly. I thought: never again without love, never. So perhaps it will be never?

And then he came out with his bombshell: he's getting married to Betty.

"Are you in love with her?" I asked him, because it was all I could think of saying.

"As much as a man of my age can be in love," he said. He's 52, Betty is 30.

"It's certain then, that mother is dead?" I asked in a neutral tone of voice.

"Of course she is dead," he replied. "In any case, I had to put an advertisement in a Viennese newspaper asking for news of her. It was in for three weeks and there was no response."

It was time to go and visit Bruno and Erna which was as well, since the mention of my mother put an end to all conversation. Before he left in the evening, my father gave us 10/-. On another occasion, when he had been to visit us by train – this time he came by car, driven by his chauffeur – just as the train pulled out

235

of the station he handed us a 10/- note, which saved us from the embarrassment of showing our gratitude. This time, because of the shattering news he had brought, I felt the 10/- helped to ease his conscience.

Yesterday Ann came to tea and afterwards we went to the flicks and saw *Monsieur Verdoux* with Charlie Chaplin. It was a bit disappointing. I told Ann about my father's forthcoming marriage, and she said she, too, had felt very bad when her father remarried.

I have an appointment at the Scrivener Press on Thursday as I want to know what kind of things they publish. I shall also help with the hospital library, and hope I don't have to take the trolley of books to the men's ward, as they always make embarrassing remarks to me, and flirt and tease and whistle. I promised Chris to fetch Micky from a birthday party at six o'clock after which I shall spend the evening with them.

30th January 1948

So I've had my night in a hotel with a married man. But what now? Where has it got me? Nowhere. No further to anywhere I want to be. I'm fed up and deadly bored again. From habit we kiss at the back of the shop or in the bicycle shed, WB and I. Sometimes he unbuttons his shirt and I kiss his bare chest. He has such ugly, fat hands. I always notice people's hands. And so I don't look at his, or look at them against my will, with a kind of horrid fascination. Why can't someone be in love with me? When you're in love, everything is beautiful. But I'm rubbish and filth – yes, filth, and who can possibly love filth?

What is the strange chemistry that breeds success or failure? Why do I do all the wrong things?

The Film Society has started again; Putz and I went to the first film of the term on Sunday evening. The Dorlings were there. Afterwards we had coffee with the Wrens at Putz's digs. It's very cosy in their tiny, overcrowded front parlour with a fire blazing in the grate.

I'm writing this on babysitting duty at the Dauries'. They gave me a banana today! I didn't go last Friday because the weather was too bad. Marion and Joan are in bed but not asleep yet. I can hear them talking. When it's all quiet I shall play the piano.

1st February 1948

I spent the weekend at Beryl and Clem's. On Saturday evening we stayed at home and listened to the wireless in their ugly upstairs sitting-room. An hour long tribute to Richard Tauber was the programme we were glued to. The story of his life was interspersed with his wonderful songs which transfigured Beryl's room into the Vienna Opera House. It wasn't his complete life story – they left out the bit about me being kissed by him behind the stage door of the New Theatre!

"I shouldn't want people to say only good things about me after my death," said Beryl. "It gives a false picture." I agreed, but thought secretly, I wouldn't mind. I said:

"There were mostly bad things in Tauber's life. The programme is full of lies."

Of course Beryl knows about my brief brush with the famous man. "As you well know," she said, and we laughed.

We got up very late on Sunday as usual and afterwards went to the pub before lunch. I had some beer which tasted horrible and in the afternoon I played chess with Clem.

Three girls from Wolsey Hall visited me at the shop on Saturday afternoon – Ann, Mary Rowland and Enid. WB always wants to know who everyone is. He wants to be in on every bit of my life. He has noticed that I'm not very affectionate towards him of late, and it seems to have upset him.

3rd February 1948

My happiness is still in its early stages.

On Monday evening Raymond and I were invited to Jim and Clare's. They often have lunch at the Red Cross canteen which is how they know Ray. First Ray fetched me from Parkers' and took me to tea at a café. We got on extremely well and he didn't let me pay for a thing, not even the bus fare to Shotover where Jim and Clare live. Afterwards, I went back to Ray's digs for coffee and we talked seriously about all sorts of things, including his fiancée. Then he saw me home. I felt content and at ease, as I always do when I've been with people who I know like me, and whom I like. I was glad, too, that Raymond has now recognised 'me' – as an individual and not just one of the lunch crowd. The perfect

237

ending of the day was still to come, however: there was a letter from Jimmy waiting for me! He wants to see me again. He's in the army now, stationed on Salisbury Plain. He has not forgotten me. 'I still remember what a pleasant girl you are,' he says. There's no explanation for the long interval, but I expect the army kept him busy.

Are we then really destined to meet again? Was my impression of our Brief Encounter right after all? My lovely little Jimmy, come soon and make me forget my past foolishness, help me to turn over a new leaf. When told at school, as I frequently was, to turn over a new leaf, I never used to know how to set about it. What did one do? One can't change oneself. But with Jimmy's help perhaps I will find the answer. I already know that the French novel lifestyle is not for me, weekends at hotels with married men do not really belong in my life, I must be a child again and listen to my mother and do the things she tells me to do. I thought I had sunk so low that no one would ever be able to love me, but with Jimmy's help I'll come out of the morass again.

10th February 1948

I am very sad to have to report the news of Uncle Jack's death. He was one of Miss Davis and Kitty's many brothers and a special friend of mine. I shall keep his last letter forever.

June Rodway, the naughty girl from Wolsey Hall, works in a shop in town not far from Parkers', I was told recently, and so I went to see her today. She has not changed at all, and looks capable of doing the same things again if necessary. Life holds no terrors for her. Enid was here on Monday after work and we both agreed that we admired June.

WB doesn't like music. Can you believe it? When I asked him why he replied, "Because I don't understand it." How can an intelligent person not like music? I sometimes think I hate him. He's an obstacle to my achieving emotional stability. Why should I feel like that? He has never done me any harm – quite the contrary, as I keep saying, he's extremely good to me. Yes, that's it – his goodness. I hate him for his virtues, not his vices. Everything he does irritates me. For weeks now he has been pestering me to go out with him, to let him come to my room again. I make excuses, one after another. I don't like hurting people, especially those who have been kind to me, but I can't help it with him. He asks me to explain, and I don't know what to say. Finally he walks away, with a kind of hurt grin on his face, but frequently comes back again, with the same request, before the day is over. I'm angry with myself for having mishandled the whole affair.

15th February 1948

Chris went home to her family in Leeds today to have her baby, so my evening with her and Ted on Thursday was the last one for a bit. I bought some new shoes to cheer myself up.

Yesterday I started typing a thesis for Mrs Wawerka which will keep me busy all next week as it has to be finished by Tuesday 24th. However, I'm going to Ann's for tea today, and on Thursday Mary Gammon has invited me to her house for tea and afterwards to a performance of the *Gondoliers* at the Town Hall, for which she has tickets and for which she won't let me pay.

Mrs Labowsky is away on a short holiday. I better get on with some typing – reluctantly, for it is rather a boring thesis. I almost forgot – I had a Valentine card but have no idea who it's from!

24th February 1948

I delivered the thesis at Mrs Wawerka's office in my lunch hour today, and earned £1 for it. I feel rich for a change. I had tea at Ted's and also spent Saturday evening at his house, but it's not the same with Chris not there. He's feeling very lonely. He asked if I would come and keep him company again next Saturday and I said I would. I couldn't very well not.

I had supper and spent the evening at Putz's today – the Wrens were out, so we could talk undisturbed.

I find myself responding to WB's touch again. Only a few days ago I thought it was over for ever. Why am I like this? Do you understand me? I don't. I still don't know whether Jimmy is coming to Oxford for my 21st birthday as I've suggested. We shall see each other again *some* time, I'm sure of that. Do I perhaps seek satisfaction from WB because Jimmy is not here to give it to me? And then am disappointed? I do not know the answer to this, but as you know, I must write down what I feel or burst.

WB told me an interesting anecdote the other day: when he was engaged to his wife, in Vienna, he was sitting in a café with her one day; presently they met a friend of his to whom he introduced his fiancée. The next time WB and his friend saw each other the friend said:

"So this is your fiancée! And you always told me you liked tall girls; but she's quite short."

"That's right," said WB.

"And, if I remember correctly, you preferred blondes. Your fiancée has black hair."

"Right again."

"And she is Jewish. Didn't you always set your heart on a non-Jewish wife?"

"I did."

"So your fiancée is not your type at all. Why are you marrying her?"

"Because I love her."

1st March 1948

I had a very pleasant evening on Wednesday: Raymond invited Lieselotte and me and a friend of his called Stewart to tea in his digs and afterwards we all went to see *Much Ado about Nothing* at Keble College. Actually I didn't see it as I didn't want to wear my glasses. I'd give anything not to be short sighted! Ray saw me home at about 11.30pm. Today he called unexpectedly, and stayed for tea. Putz was here: the three of us had a walk by the river. It was a lovely spring day and the air smelled fresh and clean.

This week two big events are taking place: my father's wedding on Friday, and my 21st birthday celebration on Saturday – a dinner at the Golden Cross.

I am going to finish my correspondence with Jimmy. What a weight off my mind! No more waiting for his letters. Well, I decided some time ago that, if I could not see him for my birthday, I was going to finish with him.

He can't come for my birthday; he can't get any leave and he is over 100 miles away. This time there's going to be no backing down. What's the point of carrying on like this? His last letters have been rather disappointing. I must forget him. I must forget this heavenly boy, the only boy with whom I ever felt completely happy.

4th March 1948

On Tuesday I had some passport photographs taken in my lunch hour, and yesterday I bought a pair of *white* shoes – wedges – at a shop in St Ebbes which always stocks shoes you can't get anywhere else, usually American. They are very uncomfortable but I shall wear them to the wedding tomorrow all the same. Ray brought a bottle of sherry yesterday, for my birthday dinner to which he is coming.

7th March 1948

Putz and I got the day off work on Friday and went to London by coach for our father's wedding to Betty at Maida Vale Registry Office, and afterwards at Elgin Avenue. We didn't want to go. My thoughts were with my mother throughout the day. Betty looked very glamorous in a pale sable fur and a hat with roses and a veil. Only a handful of people were at the Registry; Betty's brothers and their wives, Jane and Jack, Felix and Anni and Aunt Liesel. Putz and I were the only ones not wearing a hat. My father put on his look of disapproval as soon as he saw us, and as soon as there was an opportunity he asked, "How can you come to a wedding without a hat?" We said we hadn't got a hat. It had never occurred to us to wear one. I think it quite spoilt his day.

Aunt Liesel seemed pleased to see me again. "How's Falmouth?" she asked me, probably remembering the miserable time she had there. I remembered her saying to me one day, "You can always ask me any questions you have on your mind, and I'll try and answer them." No doubt she was preparing herself to instruct me in the facts of life.

But what I asked her was: "How is a dictionary written? How can anybody remember every single word in the language?" I think she was momentarily taken aback, but not for long.

"Well, you see, anyone compiling a dictionary doesn't do it out of their head," she explained. "They use existing dictionaries." The next question that immediately occurred to me was, how did

1

the first person to compile a dictionary manage? But of course I didn't ask that. I knew she didn't know the answer. And probably still doesn't.

There were a lot of guests at the wedding reception in Elgin Avenue, and the usual delicious food. Putz and I felt like fish out of water, and I expect my father was ashamed of his two plain, hatless, unmarried daughters. We were glad to return to Oxford in the evening.

My birthday dinner on the following day went off well. There were five of us Putz, Pat and Jim Dorling, Ray and I. The guests provided the drink, Putz and I paid for the meal at the Golden Cross. Afterwards we had drinks at the Randolph Hotel, and then back to my digs for more drinks, till midnight. Ray gave me a huge birthday card on which he had written: "You're a big girl now." I also had a birthday card from Jimmy with four kisses XXXX printed on it. WB gave me a box of translucent, brilliantly coloured bath beads which I wasn't particularly pleased with as I don't use such things and I don't much like having baths anyway. Mrs Labowsky says I'm in and out of the bathroom so quickly she's sure I just run the water and then let it out again.

9th March 1948

Today is my 21 birthday. When I arrived at work I found, propped against my typewriter, an envelope covered all over with the figure '21'. I opened it. It was from WB.

'Hello, little one,' it begins. 'Many happy returns, and all my best wishes, really and sincerely . . . for once I don't want you to misunderstand me . . . for once I hope you'll take my words just as I mean them . . . I wish I could give you flowers, sweets, nylons (no coupons), lovely underwear (too intimate), fruit (you get that from the Konkurrenz) [Percy, the errand boy, always brings me oranges], jewellery (so that you can pawn it), books (das so wie so) . . . one thing only remains. KISSES. Do you want them . . ?' It was such a nice letter it nearly made me cry – and feel very guilty.

My father gave me a ring with a pearl. I neither like it nor shall I wear it, and I don't suppose it is very valuable. Putz gave me a useful shopping basket.

In the evening I went to the pictures with Ann and afterwards we had supper at the Town and Gown. She gave me a pair of white gloves. Just what I wanted.

13th March 1948

Raymond visited me at the shop yesterday, and Jim Dorling came in and bought an expensive art book, much to WB's delight. Today, at lunch, we were introduced to Audrey, Ray's fiancée, who's in Oxford for the weekend. A plainer, more ungainly girl I have yet to come across. It's easy, I know, to find fault with other girls, but I think most people would agree that she's not particularly attractive – and not particularly interesting either. And plump. If a girl like that can get a nice fellow like Ray, then there's still hope for me.

Not that Ray is anything but a good friend, but I've been dreading being introduced to his fiancée as I knew sooner or later I would be. I don't like the idea of his 'belonging' to another girl, and the way we all have to take it for granted, the morality and smugness of it. He belongs to us Red Cross diners, that's where he's at his best. He seemed so different in her presence – a bit subdued, almost. Does he really love her, or is it his stupid morality that is tying him to her? Is there some profound side to his nature that I don't know? It must be awful to be *in love* with a man who's engaged to someone else.

After lunch, as I was walking along the street with Audrey, Lieselotte and Ray walking in front, she suddenly said to me, laughingly, "I hope you take care of Ray." I didn't quite know what she meant, and was a bit taken aback. I think now she didn't mean anything. It was just something to say to me.

Laughing too, I replied, "Well, I don't know that he needs taking care of, does he?" And then I added, quite against my will, "What a nice bed-sitting room he has, doesn't he?" I don't know if she knew I'd been to his room several times, and perhaps my mentioning it was not suitable, but my naughty heart whispered to me: tell her! And I listened to it. She said yes, it was a very nice room. How sure she is of him! And how good and moral they are, like two good children. I pity Ray, spending the rest of his life with this dull girl. He would do better to marry Lieselotte. I am jealous of their happiness.

This evening I'm going to the pictures with Mary Woodward,

a married woman with two small children who works in the office at Parkers'. She's Australian and divorced. As the clocks go forward one hour tonight I shall have to get up an hour earlier tomorrow. I promised to visit Ted in the evening, after Putz has been to tea. We'll sit in the garden if it's nice as Mrs Labowsky won't be here.

20th March 1948

I spent the evening at Ted's and afterwards he walked home with me. Chris still hasn't had the baby.

Mary Woodward left Parkers' today but we are going to stay in touch. She has told me all about her husband's unfaithfulness. Ray has gone down for the Easter vacation. On Wednesday I was introduced to Mrs Brown in the shop. Who is Mrs Brown, you ask? She's WB's wife!

She came to see him, and maybe me too, for I'm sure she knows about me and wanted to see for herself what I was like. It was a pleasant, civilised encounter and I thought her very nice. She must be very understanding, too, for I'm not WB's first girlfriend since his marriage and I don't suppose I shall be the last. It seems that on the continent it is quite usual for married men to carry on in this way, and their wives take it for granted. If ever I marry, I shall not be so forgiving and hope never to be in this situation.

I am – since last Friday the 19th – the proud owner of a British passport.

Next Wednesday I'm going to the pictures with Mr Calé – I've christened him 'the Eunuch' – and on Thursday I'm going to Forest Row to spend Easter with the Beschorners.

1st April 1948

The journey from Oxford to Forest Row on Maundy Thursday was very straightforward: I left at 2.30pm and arrived at 5.30pm. Joan and the children fetched me from the station. Returning on Easter Monday was very different: I went to the station *twice* accompanied on each occasion by the whole family, as there was no train the first time. Then I missed my connection at Paddington, and didn't reach Oxford till midnight. The weather

244

during the three days at Forest Row was lovely. I took Peter for little walks, and we all sat in the garden, and went to the village for coffee and cakes, and Joan and I went to East Grinstead, a typically old-world country town, by bus one evening and saw a film, to which she treated me. We also walked in lovely Ashdown Forest. I took several photographs. Diana is quite a little girl now but she was a bit grumpy and cried a lot.

Ray returned to Oxford yesterday. Today, my half day, I called at Wolsey Hall and later I went back to the shop to stay with WB for a little while; he never takes the afternoon off. His zest for work knows no bounds. Not me – I soon left him to have tea at Fullers' with Ann.

On Saturday Putz is going to London for two weeks on a University Course, and on Sunday I'm going to Bruno and Erna's for coffee, and to help Bruno with the translation of an article from German into English.

9th April 1948

I have met Mary Woodward's husband. I made a mistake: they're not divorced – yet.

I had tea at Jim Hayes' on Tuesday after work. The fact that he knows so much about me makes my relationship with him an easy one. How much about his patients and ex-patients does he tell Clare, I wonder?

Yesterday, after my hospital library duty, I visited Mrs Hacker in the Cowley Road hospital. Poor Mrs Hacker is very ill and not likely to return to work, but she doesn't know this and all visitors from Parkers' have had to swear not to tell her. Then I called at Mrs Wren's and had tea with her, Putz being away. She's very motherly, though she has no children of her own.

Ray came to supper and stayed the evening. Audrey will be pleased to know that he's being taken care of. We have long, interesting conversations.

On Saturday Mr Calé wants me to have lunch with him at a new continental restaurant in the High Street. He never pays for me, so I hope it's not too expensive.

11th April 1948

Mr Morris has left Oxford! I was given this news at Blackwells'. He has opened his own bookshop in London. But he is not yet out of my life . . . some day I shall meet him again . . .

I had tea at Ray's this afternoon – just I, Putz being away. What a strange friendship this is. Who says platonic friendship is not possible? But nevertheless, it doesn't feel quite right. We listened to Beethoven's *9th Symphony* on his gramophone, had supper at the B.R. where Stewart joined us and afterwards walked by the river, the three of us. Then I went back to Ray's digs, we had more food and talked till 11.30pm. He took me home. His digs are in Beech Hill Road now, which is not very far from Lonsdale Road.

The relationship between WB and myself is getting very tense. I feel at any moment something will explode, our animosity will reach culminating point.

Bill called again! It was on the 1st April, but Putz came about half an hour later and he went away. I haven't seen him since. Mrs Labowsky thinks he's a funny boy. She says he never looks straight at her. But then she has never been made love to by him! Why is all the world mad? Is there no one sane and pleasant and ordinary, like . . . like . . . no, I must never mention his name again. I have buried it more or less successfully; I have suppressed his memory with dexterity. I must never think of him again. Only his photograph on my desk shall remind me of him.

PS: Will I ever get married, and be the *only* woman in someone's life?

14th April 1948 (nearly 15th – 11.50pm)

RAYMOND FENN.

At last we have crossed the Rubicon. Ray has kissed me. I thought that it could not go on much longer like this, our friendship. We have been alone together so often lately. It was bound to lead to this and now it has happened, and I'm glad. It happened in the following way: after work today I called at Ted's and afterwards Ray took me out to supper at the 'Tackley', which is a very expensive restaurant – the new continental one in High Street. Then we went back to his digs. Little did I guess that this evening was to mark the end of our long platonic friendship. At first it was like all the other evenings spent at his digs: we talked, and listened to more Beethoven – his *Mass in D major*. Gradually, however the music seemed to fade more and more into the background. I found it hard to concentrate on it and Ray seemed to have given up on it altogether. He told me things I had long wanted to hear from him – that he could talk to me as to no one else, how much he enjoyed my company, that he had resented Stewart's intrusion on Sunday and wanted to be alone with me, that he had had sexual relationships. It should have come as a surprise and yet, curiously, it did not. During the last two weeks slowly but surely my liking for him had increased. I felt we understood each other, felt at home with each other. It even occurred to me that I had held on to Jimmy because Ray would approve of him!

As usual, he saw me home. For the first time he put his arm around me. "So – is our friendship *still* platonic?" he asked me, teasingly. I said nothing. Outside my house he kissed me. Like so many others, and yet it was as new and welcome as spring. And I felt as new and fresh as spring, as if I had never been to bed with WB. I begged him afterwards not to reproach himself. He is so moral. (Or is he?) He promised. He said he was doing what he had wanted to for a long time. Now we have broken down the barrier, we are entering a new phase. But it cannot last. Putz returns on Saturday, and Ray is probably finishing at Oxford in June. And of course he is engaged to marry Audrey.

The kiss is our little secret. And the evening one that I don't think either of us will ever forget. Isn't it a pity that there is always some other woman who has beaten me to it? WB's wife, Ray's fiancée. I'm always second best. All their kisses, however passionate, seem to say: 'You're not to take this seriously.' When shall *I* come *first*?

But see how the first are betrayed!

I must revise this scribble tomorrow because I'm not in a normal frame of mind tonight.

16th April 1948

Now I'm deeply involved with Ray and there's no retreating. I'm still bewildered. How did it happen? Through no fault of mine, certainly. For months I have known and liked him, we have done things together but mainly in the company of other people, we have had interesting conversations over lunch and been good friends. That was all. I have always thought of him as an extremely nice boy who was engaged to another girl and therefore not for me. But now I remember the many, many dreams I had about Ray and Audrey, in which I was always jealous of their happiness. Often Lieselotte and I said what a pity it was that all nice men were either engaged or married. And I remember telling her that I could only think of Ray as a very good friend. Now I can't help thinking that I must have had a great many more feelings for him than I acknowledged. They would probably never have surfaced had he not opened my Pandora's Box of a heart with this kiss, and let them out.

I wish I could introduce you to Ray, or at least paint a clear picture of him. But I can't. He is too perfect. I knew that even while there was nothing between us. Audrey must be an exceptional girl and I probably underestimated her, or Ray would not be engaged to her.

So, how did it happen, what made Ray break the rules? Like this, ostensibly: suddenly, one fine day, we find ourselves alone. Audrey is in France, Lieselotte in London. Because we are friends we invite each other to tea. He takes me home, he puts his arm around me, perhaps because he is hungry for Audrey, he kisses me goodnight. It all began with that kiss.

The day after the kiss, at lunch in the Red Cross canteen as usual, Ray tells me, before the others join us, that he has been longing to see me again and he hasn't slept all night. I now realise there is something between us and that the time has come for me to stop my ostrich politics. However much I want to think of his goodnight kiss as being like any other goodnight kiss I've received, this cannot be: Ray's kiss was a forbidden one.

The following evening we spent together again. It was then that I learnt many things; how fond he has long been of me; what a strange effect last night's kiss had had on him; how much self control he had exercised over the last few weeks and months. We were together until 12pm and made love all the time.

I have lost the old Ray now and am not yet used to the new one. Also I have begun to suffer from that disease which I call a blockade of the brain. It brutally stops me from understanding what is happening or expressing properly the things I want to say to him. As if I had received a shock – the shock of suddenly being confronted with a new Ray Fenn who has sprung from nowhere, like an early morning mushroom that was not there the night before, who had not even announced himself.

With his moral leanings and his logical mind he is now justifying and explaining everything. I myself am not capable of this. I shall just let things drift and follow him.

Today, when we walked for ages in the University Parks after lunch, he said that if he failed his finals he'd blame me! He has not been able to concentrate on his work at all. "The last two days have been like a novel," he said, "with a quite definite plot." The blockage in my brain prevented me from replying.

On Monday he is going to London for three days, to meet Audrey back from France. He is going to find out if I have made any difference to their relationship. He is not telling her about me, and I'm not telling Lieselotte about him. It is our secret.

There is one evil thing about me which disturbs me in the presence of his perfection: *I want him to stop caring for Audrey*. It is probably the most evil thing I have ever wished. Even if I have to lose him, I want the relationship between Ray and Audrey to end. Quite by chance I have found my way into Ray's life. It is a great privilege, but there's not room for both Audrey and me in it.

"If I don't see you at lunch tomorrow," said Ray when we parted, "I'll see you when I get back. Are you quite happy about everything?"

"Yes; quite happy," I lied. Actually, I'm extremely miserable. He has come to terms with himself, or thinks he has, but I've no idea where I'm going to be led. I'm starting on a new journey and I'm scared.

I know that people are often engaged many times, that engagements are frequently broken off, but to Ray an engagement is binding. I know it. Another person's future lies in his hands. I respect him for this. To laugh at it would be vandalism. I must think things out while he's away. I must get back to normality; yesterday I only had one meal and two cigarettes all day! But I took the Red Cross Library trolley around the wards at the Ratcliffe as usual on Thursday afternoon, and afterwards I spent some time typing at Mrs Wawerka's office. She needed my help as she was very busy. While I was there Karl Popper came in with

249

some work to be typed. As he's a very important person she dropped everything and attended to him.

17th April 1948

I knew that Ray would be at lunch today even though he had said he might not be. But fate was against us: Joan Lea-Wilson came in and sat with us. I met Ray's eyes and they expressed what mine must have expressed to him. It was agonising not to be alone together for the last time before his three-day departure on Monday. We parted after lunch on the street corner. It was raining hard. "Be a good girl while I'm away," said Ray. As if I belonged to him. But I don't. Back at work, alone in the bicycle shed, I began to cry. It was all so hopeless. I had once made a casual comment to Ray about nice platonic friendships like ours. He had replied that he wasn't exactly cool as a cucumber my presence. But the music from the gramophone had half drowned his voice and somehow prevented these words from penetrating my brain. Or did I reject them? Why else didn't I recognise them as harbingers of what was to come?

I took little Micky out to tea at a café today for a treat, and then I spent the evening at Ted's. He has asked me to type something for him and I promised to finish it by tomorrow. Late in the evening I welcomed Lieselotte back from London. We chatted till 11.30pm. In her presence I hoped to be able to think of Ray as I once knew him. But I failed. There's no going back.

Everything I have written here about Ray is totally inadequate. By writing about him I'm distorting him. I've never found anyone so difficult to tell you about.

23rd April 1948

How I waited for yesterday! Yesterday Ray came back. And Lieselotte is back too, of course.

When we were sitting at lunch, the three of us, as we have done so many times, and I glanced at Ray, it suddenly occurred to me that I have now lost both Rays – the friend and the lover. The idea would not leave me. I thought, as soon as we're alone together, he would say: 'I am sorry, Ingrid, we must never let it happen again. I realise now that I have done something wrong. I belong to

Audrey and I don't want to belong to anyone else.'

After lunch we walked home together. It was my half day and he was coming for tea, an arrangement we had made before he went away. I waited for him to say he couldn't come. But he came. I waited for him to tell me it was all over between us. An hour, two hours passed. We had tea. I listened to his opinion on the atomic bomb and we discussed whether Communism is preferable to war. I share his left-wing beliefs, on the whole. He said he was getting bored with university votes. He talked of Audrey quite a lot, which reminded me of his old 'I'm engaged to a nice girl, don't-waste-your-time-on-me' manner. I felt exasperated, nervous, restless. I was sure it was all over between us, that he was not going to kiss me ever again.

Anyway, it is an interesting episode in my life, I thought. I need drama, don't I? Here it is. One day perhaps I shall be loved and married and settle down and have kids. Perhaps. And then he kissed me. We were sitting on my bed and I was hugging a cushion and he laughed and said, "You're pretending you've got lumbago again," and he moved the cushion and put his arm around me and kissed me. I felt tremendously relieved. We experienced some delicious moments together but still, I suspected that Audrey was never far from his mind, just as she was never far from mine. What next? I asked myself. Where is this leading? And what afterwards? And, oh, how hopeless and pointless! He belongs to somebody else and I have never really belonged to any man. But he was kissing me passionately. The green bedspread that had witnessed so much should have turned red with shame by now. The cushion was on the floor. I had used it, in the days of our platonic friendship, "to protect myself from his nearness," as he had correctly guessed but I had not even realised.

I used to think how exciting it would be to have a hole and corner affair, to make love with other women's husbands, to do the forbidden thing, not to be dully respectable. The sordid fascinated me. No more. I want to come first now, to be conventional and respectable. To hell with French novels.

Ray will never give up Audrey: he didn't say so, but I know it. No one suspects about us, not even Lieselotte – it's the only thing she doesn't know about me. I'm going to his room tomorrow. At first I objected when he suggested it, but he was quite determined and said he no longer feels any compunction. Is this a good or bad sign?

A new girl came to work in our department on Monday. Chris has had her baby – a boy called Peter – and is coming home at the weekend. I'm looking forward to seeing her again. I spent Wednesday evening at Ted's and he and the children too will all be pleased when she's home.

Mrs Wawerka has put me in touch with a Mrs Fraser who lives in a large house in Headington and wants a letter translated into German: to this end she has invited me for tea in her beautiful garden on Sunday.

Ruth is getting married on the 26th May, and of course I'm invited, but I can't go. It is to be a huge affair. I asked her if her husband-to-be is English. She said yes. I said but Zeid doesn't sound an English name. She wrote back to say it's a Jewish name. So he's not a proper Englishman. No need to be too envious, then.

1st May 1948

I finished writing my novel today. That's always a big event. I also finished typing another thesis for Mrs Wawerka, and delivered it on Thursday afternoon. Chris is back and I spent Thursday evening at her house. It was quite like old times, except for the new baby interrupting us from time to time and having to be fed. Beryl Wood is having a baby too! We were quite surprised to hear this news on Tuesday, as we always thought she and Clem didn't want children. They'll have to change their lifestyle considerably when it is born.

Enid visited me at the shop a few days ago, and a bit later Joan Lea-Wilson. I showed Joan round our department. She has a degree in German and French and is quite familiar with the horrid foreign novels with no covers and uncut pages. She liked the beautiful art books but didn't buy anything, much to WB's disgust. Anyone would think he *owned* the shop. Joan said:

"So you exchanged Liddell and Scott, and Kennedy's *Latin Primer*, and *Piers Plowman*, and *The Leviathan* for *Byzantine Art* and foreign fiction." We laughed. I thought: yes, and I got WB thrown in with it.

This time last week I spent the whole evening with Ray. We listened to Elgar's *Dream of Gerontius*, which he likes very much, on his gramophone. I did not write about this before because – I'm not really sure why. Something held me back. I have not been alone with him since, but it would be futile to pretend that I don't want to be. The thing is, I don't really know what I want of him. His kisses lull me into a false sense of security, but when they are over and we are among other people again, acting as though nothing had ever happened between us, I feel the pang of them, and the uncertain situation they have created. Sometimes our eyes meet across the table at lunch time. Then it is confirmed that there's something between us and I feel uncomfortable about it.

When I was at his digs last Saturday I found his small diary while he was out of the room, and I'm afraid I looked into it. I saw what he wrote about our previous evening together. It was far more impersonal than my own writing. I gathered I'm quite a large chapter in his life but I did not read it all as he returned too soon.

These two days, while we were alone, with Lieselotte and Audrey away, will never be recaptured, like the two days with Jimmy. But has it all ended – so soon? I wanted to ask him to tea but that would only mean one thing nowadays, so I didn't. I wait for him to make every move. The whole affair is a brick wall, and what can I do but try to climb it? Or bang my head against it.

God knows when we shall be alone again. If ever.

3rd May 1948

. . . tomorrow. Yes, we shall be alone again tomorrow evening, Ray and I. During my lunch hour today we went for a walk in the University Parks again. We stopped by the pond and watched the ducks and frogs. Ray told me all there is to know about them, what they eat and how they propagate. And he knows all the names of trees and he told me delightful little tales about them. The sad thing is that everything between us now, even this harmless walk, belongs to our secret hole-and-corner relationship. Neither of us would dream of mentioning to anyone that we've been for a walk together.

"We must have another tête-à-tête again soon," he said. "We haven't had one since last Saturday." I was pleased that the day was fixed in his mind, as it was in mine. He said all last week he wanted to be with me again but controlled himself because being with me prevents him from concentrating on anything else. He's taking his finals in June.

"Come for tea tomorrow," I said, with sudden recklessness. He agreed at once.

Do you remember, some time ago I said Ray would do much better to marry Lieselotte instead of Audrey? I meant that. I wanted them to fall in love because she has no boyfriend and he is such a nice person and I want her so much to be happy. Instead of that I have to live through a lie with her of which Ray is the cause. Everything I say to her seems somehow to be bound up with my affair with Ray, and consequently I lie continually. I didn't particularly want Ray for myself, although I always liked him very much, but now I wouldn't give him up – even for her. I know his touch and his kisses now – and I can't give them up.

Not until June, anyway. After that I shall probably never see him again. We shall have to forget each other. I once saw a film about a couple who only had twenty-one days to spend together. It was a most compelling film and though I've forgotten its title the story remains unforgettable. During their short time together they determined to enjoy themselves and almost managed to defy the awful shadow hanging over them. That is what I must do, with Ray. And after June I shall undo the awful lie and tell Putz everything, and I shall accept the existence of Audrey, which I'm now so forcefully suppressing.

9th May 1948

I spent the whole day at Enid's hospitable home today, Sunday. I had lunch, tea, and supper there, and Enid and I had a long walk on Shotover Hill and visited the crematorium. I was sick on Friday night, after my babysitting duty at the Dauries', and so didn't go out to lunch on Saturday.

Constance came to see me in the shop, and so did Jerry, Beryl and Pat Dorling, all at different times. Sometimes Derek comes into Parkers – Peter Riesz's friend – and we talk of this and that.

Ann and I had tea at Lyons on Tuesday and afterwards we went to another hypnosis demonstration by Peter Cassons in the Town Hall. We left quite unconvinced.

WB has read my novel. "I am proud of you," he said, as he

254

handed it back to me. These words were music to my ears. I spent some time in the shop with him after it closed on Thursday afternoon, and of course we made love, and discussed my novel. "I'm really proud of you, darling," he said again. I almost loved him for saying that.

On Monday I called at the Gammons in the evening to return Mary's typewriter. I felt I had kept it long enough.

14th May 1948

This week was going to be one of *no smoking* for me, but it turned out to be only two days. Mr Calé came for supper on Monday, on Tuesday I spent the evening at Putz's in the Wrens' cosy little sitting room, on Wednesday evening Putz and I had coffee at Constance's digs and listened to Beethoven's *9th Symphony*, and on Thursday I visited Wolsey Hall in the afternoon and spent the rest of the day and evening at Chris and Ted's; we took the kids to the park and in the evening Mrs Scott came and we played cards for money – I won 1/-!

Tonight Putz is going to the St Peter's Hall Ball with the Dorlings. She had to borrow a long dress. She's going to Cobham for the weekend, it being Whitsun.

WB is going to Paris tomorrow for a few days, partly on business. He said he wished I was going with him.

15th May 1948

The last time I was alone with Ray was on Saturday. I again postponed writing about it until today. He came to my room in the evening.

"I have come to a decision, Ingrid," he said, after about two hours. I saw his embarrassment at once and knew what he was about to say. What it comes to is this: after a great deal of deliberating he has come to the conclusion that the situation is becoming impossible, his character was on the point of corruption. Were we to continue in this way his carefully built-up and valuable relationship with Audrey would break down; she trusts him completely, and were his relationship with me to continue he would lose his respect for Audrey for trusting him so foolishly when he was not a person to be trusted. He has a miraculous mind, that boy! How beautifully he has worked it all out, how neatly and perfectly, and how typical of him. I anticipated it, however. I knew it would come, sooner or later. I knew it was not a choice between Audrey and myself but a battle between Ray's morality and Ray's desires. And, as everything Ray does is based on his morals and falls, with a few exceptions, within the limits of his moral code, I suppose I always knew which would win.

It was half-amusing and half-agonising to sit beside Ray that evening and watch him restrain himself, hold himself back with grim determination from kissing me. Poor Ray. And poor me. And poor Audrey, too.

We went for a long walk, till well after midnight. He had his arm round me. That was within the moral code, I suppose. No, I am not laughing at Ray, he is one of the best people I know and I have learnt many things from him, above all that a life dominated by one ideal, several good deeds and hard work is probably the best one to pursue.

He told me, among many other things, how much I mean to him and that he doesn't want to lose me; that he had never looked at another girl since his engagement until he met me; and that no other girl has ever expounded such convincing philosophies contrary to his own.

On Sunday I am going to his digs for tea and afterwards we are going to the University Film Society to which Lieselotte and I belong. She will be away. He says he wants to continue seeing me, but it is the overwhelming physical relationship which must stop.

Well, I suppose it will stop, if I co-operate, and I really feel I must. It would be criminal to watch Raymond being led astray and corrupted beyond redemption. He is far too nice.

17th May 1948 – Whitsun Weekend

I've spent most of the weekend with Ray. I like being with him; to be in his company and know he is near me makes me feel safe. There's something almost sacred about it, like being at church. Indeed we frequently whisper.

On Sunday we again walked until after midnight. I told him, very bravely, that I thought it best not to continue seeing each other, even if our relationship is kept platonic. He answered almost at once: "But only during this fortnight, before my finals . . ." It was a good way out, and made it easy for me to continue drifting and dispense with my feeble attempts to come to some decision. At least I tried, I thought with lazy satisfaction, being really quite unwilling to give up Ray, even if it does cause a rift between him and Audrey, in spite of my mission in life being not to hurt people.

He kissed me goodnight. I hadn't expected that. We had behaved so well until this moment. Agonisingly so. I withdrew quickly – against my will – as though I wanted to make it a kiss that can be forgotten very soon. I could have let myself go, could have kissed him for hours. But I was in control of the situation. I remembered Ray's words, and I wanted to help him stick to his resolution.

I had a horrible idea that it was a last kiss. And I had spoiled it. I blamed myself for the whole hopeless situation.

Then an odd thing happened: we had arranged nothing for Whit Monday. I visited Mary Woodward in Headington – and met Ray on my way back! We spent the rest of the morning together. Let us pretend this is a good omen. He told me he might stay in Oxford for another two years. I'm afraid this would spoil my chances with other men, because, you see, while there is Ray, everyone else will have to be like him, to live up to him. He has set my standard for all men, he represents everything that is perfect.

On Whit Monday afternoon Ann and I had a picnic on Boars Hill, watched a wedding and had a long walk and ices and drinks in a snack bar. Then I visited old Mr Gronner, who is ill, in his bed-sitting room. I felt very sorry for him. He is so old and sick and alone, and the room looked so shabby. Will I end up like this? I spent the evening at Chris and Ted's; Mrs Scott was there and we played cards. I didn't win anything.

Next Sunday Parkers is going on their annual outing – to Weymouth. The whole staff.

21st May 1948

I've been taking quite a lot of photographs this week – of Ray and Putz and Mr Calé and Chris and Ted and the children. Constance came to supper on Tuesday, and on Wednesday I went to the Indian Institute in my lunch hour to see Mrs Scott's exhibition.

Raymond Fenn.

WB came back from Paris on Thursday. I stayed in the shop with him for a bit in the afternoon, after doing the Red Cross Library at the hospital. He is so kind: I happened to mention that I was short of money and waiting for payday, and he put his hand in his pocket and gave me £1. I didn't want to take it but he said, "Let me; it gives me pleasure."

In the evening I went to a meeting of the 'Writers' Circle' in the Shakespeare Room at the Golden Cross. It lasted until 9.30pm. I didn't know anyone there and didn't like it. I don't think I shall go again.

Tomorrow Putz and I are going to see a Marx Brothers' film. They always make me laugh.

Mr Calé, University Park.

In spite of all these other things I tell you, I am waking to the fact that my present life is dominated by Ray. "Would Ray do that?" I ask myself every time I want to do something new, or "Would Ray like so and so? What would he say to this or that? Would he approve?" I want him to approve of everything I do and think and of all the people I know.

Everyone likes Ray. Everyone says what a nice boy he is. And then – then it

258

Chris and Ted.

is brought home to me how awful it is that we don't belong to each other. I've heard it said that perfect people are dull. But Ray is no more dull than a perfect summer day. I know now what it is I want: I want to *be* Audrey. I want to crawl into her and be her. His fiancée as myself, Ingrid, would be absurd, inconceivable, impossible. I have the wrong background, personality, intelligence (not enough), the wrong everything. So I want to change places with the real girl who belongs to him, and that of course is as impossible as the whole situation I'm caught up in. But if there were no Audrey, would Ray have wanted to marry *me*? To this I have no answer.

24th May 1948

Today is Putz's 24th birthday. We had supper in my room and spent the evening together.

The outing to Weymouth yesterday was quite good, except for the weather. It was cold and wet. We set off at the unearthly hour of 7.30am, by private coach. Mr Calé sat by me and regaled me with jokes, at which he excels, and had me in stitches. They were mostly German Jewish jokes. We spent the morning on the beach and ate our sandwiches there. I got talking to a girl called June who works in the New Books department and is engaged to an undergraduate reading English whom she met at a drama group. I said I preferred the books in her department to the foreign ones in mine, though these are better than the ones at Exeter College Library, where half were in languages I couldn't read and the other half might just as well have been. Some of us went for a walk on the pier and I took a few photos. WB and I kept well away from each other, partly from a guilty conscience, I suppose, and partly because we're not on very good terms at the moment; but I watched him from afar and saw him flirt with Cynthia from the office, to annoy me. By late afternoon it was raining quite hard and Mr Townsend, the manager of New Books, took a few of us to the beach café where he treated us to tea and told mildly vulgar anecdotes. Mr Calé sat by me again on the way home and told me more funny stories, and presently everyone burst into song. We stopped in Salisbury and visited the Cathedral which is huge and impressive, and has the highest spire in England. We were back in Oxford by 10pm.

I've been to the dentist today and have to go again next Monday.

30th May, 1948

HEDI ENGL, Putz's school friend from Vienna, visited us today. She's married to an Englishman whom she met when the British army were in Vienna. We had tea in my room and took photos of each other in the garden. Putz and I naturally questioned her about Vienna and our mother and grandmother, and naturally she knew nothing except that they were taken away in November 1941, to an unknown destination. But she did bring us some things from our flat – a leather cover for a telephone book, a bronze figure of Field Marshal Schwarzenberg on his horse, a few photos, things like that. Mementos of another, alien life.

I went to see *The Marriage of Figaro* at the New Theatre with Mr Calé on Friday, as Ann couldn't come. I babysat at the Dauries' on Thursday evening this week instead of Friday, and on my afternoon off I made history by going to the pictures alone to see *Pygmalion*. It was well worth it.

Mrs Labowsky is going away for two weeks on Monday, and Ray's exams – his finals – start on Thursday, the 3rd of June. He won't be coming for lunch at the Red Cross canteen for two weeks.

4th June 1948

Maureen is here from Germany for the weekend. I was really

pleased to see her again and we picked up where we left off without any difficulty. She arrived at 7pm and had tea in my room, after which we went for a walk, had supper and gossiped till 11pm. In one of her letters recently she told me that all money sent to Germany, whether registered or not, will be confiscated, and as I often have to send her money which she has authorised me to draw from her account here, she asked me not to forward any more, but give it to her when she comes to Oxford, which I now did. I was always apprehensive about sending it to her anyway, as the only address I had to send it to, was 'c/o H.Q., N.A.A.F.I., B.A.O.R.' Tomorrow we are going to the pictures and to spend the evening at Putz's.

Last Tuesday evening, I again went to the theatre with Mr Calé, to see *La Bohème*, which was marvellous. Thursday afternoon, I spent typing at Mrs Wawerka's office.

It's Derby Day tomorrow, and no doubt Mr Herbert has placed his bets, but my betting days are over.

6th June 1948

I spent the day with Maureen. We had lunch at Ross's and then I accompanied her to the station as she's going back to Germany tomorrow. In the evening Putz and I went to the last Film Society of the term.

I see my life before me, remaining unmarried (I've caught the disease from Lieselotte, the disease of fear and dread of spinsterhood), and perhaps a third rate novelist whom nobody has heard of, and with barely enough money to pay my rent each week. My good looks will have gone, and of course my youth and all my zest for living. Horrible! I shall have a few memories of buried love affairs, most of them gone wrong and all of them rather sordid. The faces of the men I have known will become blurred, the pleasant sensations I experienced with them beyond recapture, even in imagination.

How futile everything is! My philosophy of life is destroying me. All the friends I have at whose houses I have tea or with whom I pass my leisure hours in some other way – can I really talk to them? One thinks one has friends but woe betide if one really needs one. I look round for one who might understand, but barren lies the land before me. None of them can help me, not even to convince me that my philosophy of life is wrong.

I am rash perhaps, in overlooking and forgetting the many good things that have happened to me, such as being the only girl in Ray's life since his engagement, but 'the evil that men do lives after them, the good is oft interred with their bones . . .' That's how life is, unfair to the bitter end.

13th June 1948 (My mother's birthday)

I've been typing all day today, on a typewriter belonging to Mrs Wawerka, as the work is for her, except for a brief interval sitting in the garden with Putz. I babysat for Chris and Ted last night and did some typing there, too. On Friday, on my way to the Dauries', I had a puncture. Disaster! Luckily I met Jack (Peter Riesz's friend) and borrowed his pump; it was useless, however, and I left my bike at a garage and went to the Dauries' by bus, and arrived very late. They were so pleased to see me that they didn't mind.

Last Monday Jim and Pat Darling came to lunch at the canteen – and Ray was back. He brought me one of his papers on philosophy which I had expressed an interest in seeing. What an entertaining paper! I think I could have answered some of the questions.

In my lunch hour I went to the New Bodleian with WB to see an exhibition of Italian manuscripts.

I won again at cards with Chris, Ted and Mrs Scott on Thursday evening. Lucky at cards, unlucky in love. Too true.

15th June 1948

Yesterday I was so utterly desolate, so miserable and unhappy, that I would have welcomed a major disaster such as an earthquake or the destruction of the world. But today, as so often before, life has beckoned again like the enchantress it is. I can think more clearly, the deadly blindness and deafness to everything around me is slowly giving way to light and sound again.

Of course, Ray is right, everything he does is right. As long as I can go on believing that, can go on believing in the world he has created for me and left behind, I won't have lost so much. If this world that contains all his ideas is as solid as I believe it to be, life

I. General Philosophy from Descartes to the Present Time.

1. What is mysticism ? Is it always reprehensible in a phi-
   losopher ?
2. In what sense is it correct to say that we cannot know
   anything about substance ?
3. Is it important to distinguish time from duration ?
4. Could statistics provide any evidence as to whether you
   will be a smoker or a non-smoker in June 1949 ?
5. The phrase "the self" hardly occurs xxxx in ordinary
   speech. Has this any relevance to the philosophical
   problem of the self ?
6. Can I see anything without having a sense-datum ?
7. "There exist no certain marks by which the state of waking
   can ever be distinguished from sleep" (Descartes) How
   do you know that you are awake now ?

II. Moral and Political Philosophy
                        A.
1."There is no point in defining a right action as one which
   fits the situation, since that after all is only to say
   that it is the right one for the situation". Discuss.
2. "How did I move my hand ?" "By setting myself to do it."
   Is this a fair answer ?
3. One way of finding out what we mean by the word "good"
   would be to try not to use it at all for a time. Discuss.
4. How is the phrase "He did it of his own free will" used
   in common speech ? Is this relevant to the question
   whether the will is free ?
                        B.
5. How do philosophical questions about politics differ
   from other questions about politics ?
6."The mines and railways are now our property." "That house
   has just become your property." What light is thrown by
   these statements on the meaning of property ?

———————

(Some of the questions set)

could go on more or less the same and I shall be a better person.

In retrospect it seems to me that I knew all along that Ray was going to announce his imminent marriage over lunch yesterday. He had never as far as I remember mentioned a date for his wedding before, and they weren't going to get married for a year or two. I thought: "What shall I say when he tells us he is getting married soon? How will I cope with the situation?" And in my lazy way I let it drift, and remained undecided as to how I would react. And so I had no words at my disposal when he announced at lunchtime yesterday that he and Audrey had decided to get married in August.

My eyes met his across the table and I knew mine had a wild look in them. My confusion unbalanced me and I suddenly thought he was gloating. His look seemed to say: "Yes, Ingrid, this is directed against you. Our little escapade is over. Let this be a lesson to you that good always wins over evil."

Then I felt hatred. Bitter hatred and I was furious with him. He had been brutal and selfish. I blamed him unreasonably for everything that had happened between us. "So *that* is how moral people act!" I thought bitterly. But then I realised that, if I lost my belief in Ray's goodness, I shall have nothing left to believe in. I began to find excuses for him. I looked at the situation from every angle and finally persuaded myself that he did the right thing. If I haven't got across to you these last few months what it is about Ray that makes me think so highly of him, it is because an inferior intellect like mine can't possibly describe a superior being like Ray without losing a lot in the description.

So now it is all over between Ray and myself. I have been expecting to write this sentence down for a long time and here it is at last. But I would not be without the memory of his kisses, or our long lovely walks until the early hours, or the knowledge that I am the only girl for whom he deviated from the straight and narrow. I am sorry though that I have seen Ray as a coward. I should have liked to see him depart with the same daring with which he first approached me. He has not been alone with me since the end of his finals. What is he afraid of? I know why he has decided to marry so soon – it is a safeguard: he is locking the door on all further dangers and temptations.

I have told Lieselotte everything, to prove that it is really all over. She was completely taken aback. "I had no idea!" she exclaimed. If only I were as successful in love as I am at concealing my secrets!

18th June 1948

Joyce Lenton came to see me at the shop today. Mrs Labowsky being away, Putz is coming to stay with me for the weekend. We'll be able to sit in the garden as long as we like. Mrs Wawerka gave me the address of a Mr & Mrs Moore, who live in a large house in Woodstock Road and look after young foreigners who come to Oxford to learn English. She asked me to go and see them, and I shall do so on Saturday. I also promised to go to Chris and Ted's to meet Ted's mother who's staying with them.

Last Tuesday I had supper at Mary Woodward's and then babysat for her. She's not a happy person, and in my present mood that suits me very well, and we commiserated with each other. On Wednesday evening Ann and I went to the theatre to see *Arms and the Man* by G.B. Shaw. One of the books I read during my year at the Public Library when I should have been buffering in the basement was Shaw's *Black Girl in Search of God*. It had beautiful woodcut illustrations. That book has stayed in my mind, whether because of its contents or because of the circumstances under which it was (secretly) read, I do not know.

Cynthia, the pretty blonde and blue-eyed girl from the office, has knitted a jumper for me! Wasn't that kind of her? I showed it off to some of the girls when I visited Wolsey Hall on Thursday afternoon, as that's the sort of thing that interests them.

It was foolish of me to assume that my desolation had left me; it has returned, for it hadn't really gone far, cloaked in a dramatic veil. It is nothing new. I can't bear the end of things, whatever shape they take.

I didn't love Ray. I don't know how one can be sure that one loves someone, but I don't think I loved Ray. I may have closed my eyes to his fiancée but I always felt her pull and found it very disturbing, our relationship was too marred. Love needs the right atmosphere to flourish, as plants need the right climate.

He brought Audrey to lunch at the canteen yesterday. I didn't think I could ever face her again. I had intended to plead with him never to let me see her again – but there was no time. For half an hour he sat between us, Audrey on one side and I on the other. I am certain that Audrey knows now what took place between Ray and me, and almost certain that it has something to do with the speeding up of their marriage. I don't know if Ray considers that he has acted justly towards me – I hope so, because if I thought that he didn't, it might shake my belief in him and that, as I said before, must not happen. Maybe I shall be a better person for this profound experience, or maybe it will hurl me to the depths of depravity. At any rate, I'm glad he's leaving Oxford after all. He will fade away, out of my life, and in due time I shall forget him, one of the nicest persons I have ever known. What might have

m

happened had he not met Audrey before me, I shall never know.

He will fade away . . . I shall forget him . . . but in the meantime I remember, one by one, the moments I spent with him, the things he said. They come to me when I'm alone and I can feel them persistently hammering at something inside me. I call it my soul, or it could be my heart.

"The reason I don't suggest the bed, Ingrid . . ." (once in his room when we were making love passionately. What *was* the reason?) "Little, bony Ingrid," (during a walk at midnight; the first man who ever considered me thin!) "We haven't solved our problem yet, have we?" (same walk.) " . . . And then the naughty thought came to me: 'I wonder if Ingrid will be free now?' " "Here's a bit of me," (pulling his shirt out of his trousers so that I could feel his skin. And what soft skin it was!) "Your tummy is all dead. What's the matter with it?" (he to me the first time we made love.) And me: "Oh Ray, you're such a nice person," (once when overcome with forbidden emotions.)

And a thousand, thousand things more. As I shall associate Bill forever with sadism, so I shall associate Ray with morality, from which he strayed but to which, true to his character, he returned.

The day I knew that it was all over with Ray – I asked WB to my room! In my unhappiness I decided to go to bed with him again (which of course I never did with Ray), as a deceived person might kill their sorrows with drink. He came, and brought me cherries, and was very loving. But of course I didn't do what I had intended. I couldn't. I shrank from the very touch of him. He quietly stroked my hair and held my hand. Suddenly I burst into tears. Everything was so hateful and ugly and meaningless. Why was he being so kind to me, asking no questions, accepting my distance? He might have been no more than an Egyptian mummy sitting next to me, but after he had gone I was left with a great sense of relaxation. When the world is falling in, that's when I need him, and when I need him, he's always there.

21st June 1948

We have been to tea at Ray's today, Lieselotte and I. How strange it seemed to go back to the beginning, as though nothing had happened in between, as though there was only a beginning and an end, and a gap in the middle; a gap where there used to be a dream, for it must have been a dream, and it vanished when I woke up. As I listened to the gramophone two things occurred to me.

1. I'm expected to *understand* the situation, not to wait for some clumsily worded explanation from him. He expects me to understand. Our unique relationship should have prepared me for it.
2. Even if he is at the other end of the world and I were never to see him again, his ideas will still be here, in my mind where he planted them. In times of stress, they will sustain me. I shall be able to turn to them for help, as one can turn to the British Consul for help in a foreign country during a crisis.

Then fate threw us together again – alone. Lieselotte went home to study (she's taking the Inter. Arts Exam by Wolsey Hall Correspondence Course) and Ray and I went to Daly's Café in Banbury Road for supper. At first I felt a bit uncomfortable. After all, he had been avoiding being alone with me lately. But the thread of our relationship was broken, the barriers were up, and they served to protect me. A few looks, a few words, confirmed my belief that I'm expected to understand . . . We did not broach the subject of his marriage but stuck to moral philosophy, the topic that played such a big part in our relationship.

"Have you heard from Jimmy?" he presently asked me, for the first time. I had told him about Jimmy because I needed to have someone in the background, as he did. I wondered if he liked to think of me happy and settled after he has gone. I told him I hadn't for ages. Suddenly he said, "I shall miss our little walks to visit the frogs in the Park."

At these words I was seized by a dreadful sadness and I turned away, blushing, and only muttered, "Yes . . . me too," and didn't say all the things I longed to say.

There were long silences as we ate our meal, and I didn't enjoy anything I was eating. But later I said to him, "I wish you every happiness in the world, Ray, because you deserve it, and I believe in you."

"That's nice of you," he said. "I'm sure I shall like my work, it's what I've always wanted to do."

He's going to Lincoln to take up a job with the W.E.A. as a lecturer. I was glad he thought I was referring to his work. After supper we went for a walk and we didn't touch each other. Then we parted.

I think I understand everything now. No more giving him rope to rein him back in. That's all over. Forever.

27th June 1948

I had tea at Ann's today and afterwards we went for a walk and picked bunches of tall wild flowers. I carried mine in my hand but Ann held them in her arms and hugged them against her body. She looked like a girl in a painting. Everything she does is graceful and looks attractive and I envy her her beauty. She wore a white dress. I had on my red one with the white horizontal stripes which I thought I looked quite nice in but which was totally inadequate next to Ann dressed all in white.

Mr Calé took a photograph of me on Friday, and on Wednesday we went to the pictures and afterwards he came for a chat in my room. He lives round the corner from me, in a bed-sitting room, with a landlady who looks after him and her little dog, but prefers her dog, by all accounts. His work is his whole life and all we talk about is Parkers' bookshop and Mr Brown and the customers who come to the foreign department and buy or don't buy our books. There's a nice undergraduate who sometimes comes in called Picton, and I had a long talk with him on Wednesday morning.

Joyce Lenton came to tea on Tuesday. She still worships her St Mary's organist from afar. She had just been to visit an old lady from her church, who was ill in bed. "Are you better?" Joyce had asked her. "There's nothing wrong with me," the old lady had replied. "It's this room. It keeps going round and round."

On my half-day I had tea at the Moores' and played ping-pong in the garden with a few of the French boys staying there. They asked me to go to a dance with them!

Mrs Labowsky is back from her holiday. While she was away, her neighbours, Mrs Guttmann and Mrs Kosman, looked in on me once or twice. Mrs Kosman's daughter is an artist who does marvellous drawings of musicians for a living.

The last time I played cards with Chris, Ted and Mrs Scott, I lost! So will my luck in love change now? I don't think so.

On Thursday we said goodbye to Ray. This then is THE END

OF RAYMOND. He came to lunch at the Red Cross canteen for the last time, and here we took our leave of him. He wore his short, grey mackintosh. As he rode away on his bicycle with the low, white mudguards, I thought: people pass like ships in the night. One day you are in their arms and feel their breath on you and exchange your innermost thoughts with them, the next they are gone forever. I don't know where Ray is going from here, except out of my life. Home to London first, I suppose. I don't want to know. Did I ever tell you that he used to be in the air force? That's why he was rather older than the average undergraduate. He must become again what he was before I met him – non-existent. It is best to forget people once they have left you.

But . . . of course I could never forget Ray. I don't suppose there ever lived a human being who has had such a tremendous influence on me, for whom I wished to change myself to such an extent.

Never again shall I sit with him in his large, warm room in his arms or out of them, on the deep settee which seemed to swallow one as soon as one sat down on it; never again shall I watch the pink and yellow houses opposite change their colour in the fading light, or focus my eyes on the little wooden elephant on the mantelpiece next to Audrey's photograph which I never could avoid . . .; never again watch the little Indian boy with the artificial leg playing in the street below Ray's window, or curse the stairs that creaked when we crept down them, late at night. Never, never, never . . . How I hate that word!

'He who knows what good is will do good,' said Socrates. So Socrates would approve of Ray, for he did good by Audrey in the end. I am left out of the formula.

1st July 1948

A Mrs King and her son Peter, who's an undergrad, usually have lunch with us at the canteen now. – I played ping-pong at the Moores' house again today. On Monday I met Jim Dorling at the travel office and guess what he told me – he and Patricia are getting divorced! I was amazed. If I had such a nice husband, I certainly wouldn't want to get rid of him. In the evening, I went to the Gammons' and borrowed their typewriter again, at

Mary's insistence.

Next week Putz is going to London to sit her Intermediate Arts exams in English, history and Latin, and I promised to spend tomorrow evening testing her in these subjects. I wanted her to come to the dressmaker's with me on Tuesday but she couldn't afford the time.

WB is going on holiday for two weeks on Monday. When the cat's away . . . He's an awful slave driver and expects everyone to work as hard as himself, but we won't in his absence.

The Dauries are also going on holiday next week, so no babysitting on Friday evenings for two weeks and so no extra money.

15th July 1948

Jim and Clare came to see me at the shop last Saturday. It was very busy so unfortunately I couldn't talk to them much. On Friday evening, Mr Calé came to my room for a cup of cocoa, and we read some of the time.

Putz is back from London. We ran out of cigarettes on Sunday and had to go to a nearby pub to get some. Joan Lea-Wilson came for supper in the evening. I admired the skirt she was wearing.

"Yes, it's nice, isn't it?" she said, "except that it's green again. My wardrobe has a habit of turning green when I'm not looking." I suppose you could say the same of mine, such as it is, except it turns red, not green.

On Monday, Putz came to town with me in our lunch hour and I bought my first New Look skirt, a dirndl one – red, of course. It's nearly down to my ankles, which is very slimming. We went to see *This Happy Breed* at the pictures in the evening. I had seen it before and could see it again and again. It is one of the best films ever made. I laughed and laughed.

On Wednesday evening I had tea at Mr Calé's digs and he introduced me to his landlady. We sat in a very drab and poky sitting room, and the landlady and her small dog were equally uninspiring. I'm sorry for Mr Calé living in such dreary surroundings, but he's such an odd person that they have probably escaped his notice. He seems content enough. I call him the eunuch, much to WB's amusement. He's certainly entirely sexless, and very frugal in his needs.

When I was at Chris and Ted's this evening, Ted wanted to go to the pub for a drink but Chris didn't, so she stayed with the children and I went to the pub with him. I'd rather have played cards.

I recently read a story by André Maurois which is so much like my 'affair' with Ray that I copied it out: one day perhaps I will send it to him.

22nd July 1948

WB came back from his holiday on Monday. It was quite exciting seeing him again. I stayed for lunch at the shop and we ate our sandwiches together at the back among the parcels of books waiting to be opened. We laughed about a letter from a Swedish publisher enclosing an amended invoice for some books. They wrote: 'We beg you to disturb the invoice which you have previously become.' WB wanted to know everything that went on in the shop during his absence, so I told him all the good things I could remember and left him to discover for himself the stock cards I haven't filed away and the books on approval that various customers have returned.

Some time ago, I told you that we had a new assistant in the foreign department. Her name is Ditta Adler and she is the daughter of Mrs Adler who works upstairs in the office. They are Viennese. Ditta is a silly, plain and decidedly odd girl and I believe was only taken on as a favour to her mother. One of the queer things she does is sing on the top of her voice, frequently when the shop is full of customers. One day Mr Thomas, the director of Parkers', came to our department, as he sometimes does. It so happened that Ditta was singing her heart out among the parcels at the back. Mr Thomas stopped dead in his tracks. "What's that?" he asked, looking from WB to Mr Calé to me.

"That's our nightingale," said Mr Calé with a smile.

Mr Thomas marched straight through to the back and the singing stopped abruptly, like a canary that has had its neck wrung. Later a dejected Ditta emerged. I felt sorry for her. It seemed harmless if eccentric, and I expect the customers were quite entertained. On another occasion, Ditta was tidying some shelves whose books had got out of order. It was a busy Saturday afternoon and among the many customers wandering around in the foreign department were two women speaking French to each other. I saw Ditta watching them. Suddenly she strode up to them and said, very pleasantly, "What's the weather like in France?" The women looked up from the book they were examining. After a moment one of them said:

"I don't know. We're from Belgium."

"Oh," said Ditta, and returned to her shelf. WB looked at me from behind his typewriter and raised his eyes to heaven.

Putz and I had tea at Daly's Café today and afterwards I spent the evening at Chris and Ted's; Chris is ill. Mrs Scott and I prepared supper, washed up and helped with the children.

On Sunday I'm invited to the Frasers in the evening. I hope they haven't got any more translations for me to do.

31st July 1948

We are enjoying a terrific heatwave and I'm sweating. But it's not the heat that has stopped me from writing until today to tell you of this miraculous forthcoming event – it's because I wanted to be quite sure. Now I am. Jimmy, my long-lost Jimmy, is coming to see me next weekend! This time for certain. He's now an officer cadet stationed at Aldershot. He says he still has the tennis racket I gave him and he has never forgotten me. I'm slightly afraid of our meeting, but very hopeful and happy about it.

Another exciting thing has happened: good fortune, like misfortune never seems to come singly. I've met a fascinating Frenchman – a boy of 21, though in appearance and behaviour much older. He's staying with the Adlers and one day he came to the shop and Ditta introduced us. Several of the girls in the 'New Books' department saw him, and the next day Ditta briefly had the limelight on her when they wanted to know all about him.

"He doesn't give a damn for any of you – except Ingrid," said Ditta brutally. He wanted to make a date with me, so on Tuesday evening we went canoeing on the river and afterwards for a cycle ride. It was very pleasant and we got along beautifully, he with his broken English and I with my rusty school French. I had been to a Bertrand Russell Philosophy lecture at L.M.H. with Ditta earlier, but she didn't join us on the river expedition and seems to have no designs on him herself; she's hors de combat, poor thing.

(See how the French influence is already working!) I considered the whole thing a mere bagatelle, however, and didn't particularly want to go out with him again; but, as you know by now, I can never say 'no' and so he came to supper on Tuesday and afterwards I took him to the Moores' and introduced him to some of his compatriots. That was that, I thought. Then on Friday, I met him in the street, as a result of which we went to the Trout Inn for drinks today and walked back, and I didn't get home till 11.30pm. The wonderful thing is that I feel perfectly sure of myself with men nowadays. I no longer seem to try and mimic the ways of filmstars or sophisticated society women. Maybe men like me as I am best. Is it perhaps WB who has given me this confidence? Ours is a queer relationship; very unstable and with sex always looking over our shoulder, but of course he has his wife and I have other male acquaintances and I tell him about them, and it makes me feel safer. But why am I rambling on about WB? I haven't told you my Frenchman's name yet! It's Jean-Claude Gautier and he's very intelligent and very good-looking and has a moustache.

It's still terribly hot. After doing the Red Cross Library at the Radcliffe hospital on my half day, Chris, Ted the children and I went swimming at Dames' Delight. On Monday I was at a concert at L.M.H. with Mr Calé but it was so sweltering that I couldn't really concentrate on the music.

2nd August 1948 – Bank Holiday Monday – no work today

Ann and I took our tea to Boars Hill but were caught in the rain. We called at the Frasers' where we dried out and had a cup of tea.

My father telephoned in the evening. He had invited me to go to France on holiday with him and Betty, but they were to travel by plane and I by boat, as it was too expensive for me to go by plane, too. I told him I had decided not to go.

We have a National Health Service since last month, which means that all medical and dental treatment is free. The dentists don't like it at all and I have been told that my dentist, Mr Pick (good name), refuses to treat any patient who is a minute late for an appointment, and strikes them off his list if they commit the same crime a second time. Those who get to be treated have to put up with his rudeness. Dental treatment may now be free, but I

273

think I won't be the only person too scared to go!

Jimmy Dickens is coming on the 7th. In my last letter, I told him I'd been reading a book on Existentialism, to find out what it is, and he wrote back: 'You'll have to tell me what it's all about.' So, if all else fails, we can always talk about Existentialism. I attach great importance to my intellectual relationships with men – and women too, of course: I learnt that from a divine being called Ray.

6th August 1948

My hands are shaking! I can hardly write. Tomorrow Jimmy is coming. For days now I've felt a sort of sick excitement, accompanied by a reluctance to face what is about to happen. Why, oh God, why of all times did I have to meet Jean-Claude just now? I've been going out with him all this week, and we have done all the things that I decided to keep from now on for the man I love. But Jean-Claude fascinates me, intrigues me. His boyishness alongside his sophistication, his slight, thin, athletic body, his brown hands . . . on Tuesday we had tea at Ross's and then walked to the Trout Inn along the river, and here he kissed me for the first time, on our way home, at about one o'clock in the morning.

On Thursday I was invited to the Adlers' for supper and Ditta, Jean-Claude and I sat in Ditta's room, talking. When she left the room, he kissed me on Ditta's bed. It was doubly exciting. I was elated. In between we talked of the Adlers a bit and Jean-Claude said, "They have relations all over the world. In America, in Palestine, everywhere." It was said slightly disparagingly. I was glad I hadn't any relations all over the world, only a few distant ones in New York. He thinks of me as his English girlfriend, and English girls have all their families in England, as luckily I have. I stayed at the Adlers' till midnight and then he walked home with me, and we were still walking at 1.30 in the morning when a policeman on the opposite side of the road called out to us:

"Are you all right?"

"Sure we are all right," Jean-Claude called back. He was incredulous. "In France," he said to me, "when a policeman sees me with a girl at 1.30 in the morning, he *knows* I'm all right!" I laughed. He has a very nice sense of humour and often makes

274

me laugh.

"So now you have a French boyfriend," said WB when we were having tea in my room on Wednesday evening and I was receiving his kisses and embraces and caresses. "Have you deceived me with him?"

"No," I replied. But my conscience troubles me: ought I to do this? Ought I to trifle with what Ray called 'the finest thing in life'? How long ago it seems that I knew Ray! Centuries! But gods are immortal and are always there so long as one believes in them.

Jimmy is coming, I keep reminding myself, and if he gives me all I want, then all this other recreation will stop. There will be no more need for it. If only I wouldn't get so involved! I have waited and waited for Jimmy. Now, at last, he is coming. God, lend us your heaven for a few hours and please let me be happy with him as I was last year when we first met. Perhaps I am erring in carrying on with too many men at a time; Ray also erred. I, too, will find the correct path one day, as he did.

11th August 1948

It was 5.30pm on Saturday, the 7th of August when Jimmy arrived and a dream should have come true – but didn't. We had tea. We talked. We were strangers. Then he, Putz, Jim Dorling and I went to the Trout Inn for drinks. I was glad of their company. Putz has always liked Jim and now that he's free – wouldn't it be lovely if they got married? He blames Jim Hayes for the break-up of his marriage and hates psychiatrists! – We all went back by taxi and had supper at Daly's Café.

On Sunday Jimmy and I were alone. I had found him a room in a little hotel nearby, where my father was once supposed to stay when he came to visit us, but left after a few hours to return to London, as there was no hot water coming out of the hot water tap in his room. Jimmy was not so fastidious. But how changed he was! Where is my little archangel of last year? Perhaps I distorted him in my mind? I hardly recognised him. Could it be because he is a soldier now?

We had drinks at the Randolph Hotel in the morning and lunch at the Angel and a walk in the afternoon and finally we went to the pictures and I didn't want to hold his hand and then I saw him off at the station. I have to confess, by the end of the day, when the drab, rainy Sunday at last drew to a close, I was quite bored. What his feelings towards me were I don't know, but I think he likes me better than I like him. He asked if he could visit me in Cobham during my holiday there, which starts on Saturday. I said yes, but I don't care one way or the other. He asked me whether I had met any other men in the meantime and I truthfully told him, yes. He took it like the soldier he is. The thing is, I have grown up and he hasn't. That is my explanation for this drastic turn of the tables. Or could it be because of Jean-Claude? I adore Jean-Claude. Last night I spent hours in a field with him, after babysitting at the Dauries', and didn't get home till four in the morning. I've never done anything like this before. It was a perfect night, absolutely wind-still and quite frighteningly silent. I asked myself several times during those hours with him whether this was real happiness, because I wasn't sure what to call it. I knew of course that it was another one of those ephemeral affairs, impossible and hopeless, for he returns to France on Saturday and I'm going to Cobham for two weeks. I ask nothing more of the affair except to enjoy the hours with him while they last. If ever I see him again, will he be as changed as Jimmy was? Time and distance are cruel, and I wish I could abolish them.

I have just spent another evening with Jean-Claude. (I wrote the above earlier in the day). We were in my room. When Mrs Labowsky discovered that we were in the dark she threw him out! At first I was furious and deeply ashamed and sick of sordidness. But he is such a beautiful boy, I soon forgot the incident. We spent the rest of the evening out of doors. Tomorrow I shall see him for the last time; we shall say goodbye . . .

He would like me to live with him in France, and I shall probably go there in the spring. No, not probably, only *perhaps*.

12th August 1948 – THE END OF JEAN CLAUDE GAUTIER?

When I got back to my room after doing the Red Cross Library today Mrs Labowsky buttonholed me.

"About last night," she said. She sounded contrite, I thought. "I suppose your friend thought me a real dragon?"

"I don't know," I said. I wanted to sulk, not talk. I was still angry.

"You can't behave like that with young men," she said.

"We didn't do anything. We were talking." (Well, some of the time, anyway.)

"I feel responsible for you. How long have you been with me now? Three years? If you had a mother she would react the same way I did."

"He's going back to France tomorrow, anyway. He won't be coming here again."

She was really very nice, I thought, when I was alone in my room again. She had mentioned my mother. Before I could control them, tears were pouring from my eyes. I sobbed my heart out. It was quite unexpected. And now I had to wipe them away quickly for I was meeting Jean-Claude in the University Parks.

He was waiting for me at the entrance of the park. We took photographs of each other, and then spent the evening at his place – he didn't want to face Mrs Labowsky again. We said goodbye at around midnight. It was probably the last time I shall ever see him. All good things in life are short. We liked each other so much. And what a lover he was! Magnificent! (No, we didn't sleep together; all but . . .) Perhaps it's a good thing that it is all over now; after all, it had no future. I spent some of the most exquisite hours of my life with him.

Jean Claude.

Now what I chiefly want is sleep. I'm so tired that I can't write another word. Goodnight. I mean, *bonne nuit*.

21st August 1948. Cobham.

Here I am, at Ann's Cottage with Uncle Felix and his wife Anni. When I am away, I become another person. That's the best part of a holiday – having a holiday from oneself. As usual, the house is full of visitors who come and go. Lixl and John, the Czech and Hungarian boys, sons of relatives of Anni's who had a terrible time during the war in those countries, still live here. Also staying here is a girl a bit older than me called Madeleine who lives in Paris and whose father is a friend of Uncle Felix. The four of us have great fun, singing campfire songs while washing up, going for walks and cycle rides and playing tennis. Putz is on holiday in Switzerland with Constance but is coming to Cobham tomorrow.

On Tuesday I went to Portsmouth for two days to visit Ruth and meet her new husband, David. He works in a wireless repair shop and, after fetching me from the station, Ruth took me to the shop. I was very surprised to see what kind of a man she had married. He's not particularly attractive and quite uneducated. He tried to explain things to do with wirelesses to me – and I suppose thought *me* quite uneducated, on account of my blank looks. They live in a very nice flat and have a car. There's a ping-pong table in the house and we played every evening. Ruth told me that her wedding was a huge (Jewish) affair and cost £300 which the Constads at first refused to pay even though they had arranged it. Over supper in the kitchen, David said to me:

"You work in a bookshop, don't you?"

I said I did.

He said, "Mention any book to me and I won't have heard of it."

"Oh Dave," said Ruth affectionately. "You've heard of Charles Dickens, haven't you?"

"Heard of him, yes. Never read him, though," said Dave.

I kept quiet and tried to conceal the superiority I felt at that moment. Ruth then said they were hoping to buy a television soon and be among the first people to own one. They were going to enter a competition to invent a popular and simpler name for 'television'.

"And first prize, of course, is a television," said Ruth.

"I hope you win it," I said.

We tried to think of some names. Ruth suggested, 'Home Flicks', and I 'See Far', but David didn't think much of either.

I had a nasty shock in the evening. A girl called Anneliese was also spending the night in the flat, and there being only one spare bedroom with a double bed in it, I was to share that with Anneliese. But I knew I couldn't. I couldn't sleep in a bed with a strange girl. But how to get out of it? What possible excuse could I give? As the evening wore on, I got more and more worried.

And then I had an idea. As soon as an opportunity arose and Ruth and I were alone, I said to her:

"I've got my period on, Ruth (not true). Could I sleep on the sofa in the drawing room instead of with Anneliese? It wouldn't be very nice . . ." There followed many protests, Anneliese was informed and added to them, but I was quite determined. I would have slept in the bath or the street if necessary. David said I could sleep with Ruth and he would sleep on the sofa, but Ruth wouldn't hear of that. In the end I got my way and in due course a bed was made up for me on the sofa. When, late in the evening, Ruth came to say goodnight she brought me a large packet of sanitary towels. I felt a fraud and an idiot, but I couldn't help it. Ruth sat with me for some time and told me about her wedding night and how they had taken some bottles of champagne to bed with them.

I returned to Cobham on Thursday morning. Summing up the visit to Portsmouth on the train I decided it had been very relaxing because it had not been necessary to make any effort.

Jimmy telephoned on Thursday evening and is coming to visit me here on Sunday, about which I have very mixed feelings. My father and Betty will also be here.

26th August 1948. Cobham.

Jean-Claude has been gone for nearly 3 weeks. Not even WB has made love to me as J-C. did. A few days ago I had a letter from WB (in German). He misses me. He writes: 'Come soon, it's much more fun with you here.' He chats about Calé being jealous of Gronner and Gronner being stubborn and slow, about his attempt to flirt with Ditta as I had suggested to him, and Ditta taking fright and fleeing; about pretty Cynthia and June being the only bright spots on the horizon in my absence; and about a Gide 'Journal' (Pleiade 43/6) being stolen; he asks if I've heard from Jean-Claude and says I must wait until I do and not write first; he hopes I'll have a nice time with Jimmy; he regrets that he – WB – is not physically attractive enough to me so that I would have no need to turn to others, but the mind and soul of a creative and intelligent girl like me are of course more important to him; other girls have nice bodies if that were all he wanted, though mine is especially nice and round and pleasant; 'You're a sweet, dear, little girl and I love you more than you deserve . . . Be good, don't

279

deceive me too much, and try to be more even-tempered at work and I'll love you even more . . . I'm looking forward to Monday morning when you'll be back . . . another whole week without you . . . I send you a chaste little kiss, please place it on your lovely, soft, peachy cheek, just below your eyes, but if you would prefer it on some other part of you, you can move it . . ." He can certainly write a nice letter, and it warmed my heart.

Since I last wrote Putz and I have been treated to morning coffee and cream cakes in the village several times by Anni, I've been for car rides and played a lot of tennis. Madeleine has returned to France, my clever sister heard that she has passed her exam – and Jimmy was here on Sunday. He cares for me, I think. But alas, I do not care for him. It is very sad. He liked all my relations. I told him I did not get on with my father and never have. He said he and his father also did not always see eye to eye. Tomorrow Putz and I are going to the Albert Hall to hear Beethoven's *4th Symphony* and on Saturday we're going to visit the Urbachs. Back to Oxford on Sunday.

28th August 1948

Ray and I used to talk with contempt about the 'sexy French'. It stood for everything he considered immoral and which I so readily accepted and built round me as a wall of defence behind which I might live in safety and childlike happiness. But now I wonder: am I fit to live behind that wall? Is the real me after all not the moral, righteous, naïve person moulded by Ray, but the sensual animal lying in a field with a 'sexy Frenchman' till the early hours, quite unconcerned with morals? Which is the true me? If I don't know, then how shall I know what sort of a man to marry, should this ever arise? Jean-Claude is by no means only an animal, and I was almost as captivated by his intelligence as by his body, but this does not excuse me.

Perhaps I shall never hear from him and then my compunctions will be at an end.

4th September 1948

WB and I went for a walk in the park after work today. He said he was very happy to have me back, even though I so often argue with him and don't do as he wants; he said I was the only intelligent person in the department and I ought to be on his side and help him, if only for the sake of the sweet things we said and did to each other in the past. It was a real heart to heart talk.

I've heard from Jean-Claude – a postcard from the Riviera. He misses me, he says. All my memories of him came flooding back. I went through the streets he and I used to haunt at night searching for traces of him, like a dog smelling for his master. I know quite well what our 'affair' was all about

WB and myself outside Parkers' Bookshop.

and am not making it into something it was not. This lack of illusion is certainly unusual for me. To leave a thing as it is, as it was rather, is not like me. But I'm determined to leave my imagination out of this for once.

St Giles Fair is coming again next Monday and Tuesday, and again I have really nobody to go with, except poor old Mr Calé, and Chris and Ted. Still, I must be grateful for small mercies. At least Mr Calé won't talk wistfully about not being in love, as Peter Riesz once did!

16th September 1948

There's a nip in the air, soon winter will be here, summer is already only a dream one has dreamt and now woken from. Therefore everything that happened during the warm summer hours must also be a dream. How well Jean-Claude fits into this

281

dream! I had another letter from him. 'My dear little Queen,' he writes. He loved my charming letter; would I write again and again . . . He regrets my hair, my eyes, my cheeks, my lips, my throat and all my body . . . He kisses me once, twice and twice again, a little bit more than friendly; he is glad he taught me his corrupt ideas and found me such a good pupil – 'in fact very often you were ahead of your master.' He's in Marseilles at the moment, but returning to Montpellier to his studies next month. Lovely, lovely Jean-Claude.

There's going to be another staff outing on Sunday. This time to Bournemouth.

23rd September 1948

Today, my half day, I fetched little Micky from Cutteslowe School with Chris and afterwards we went to an Art Exhibition at New College. Enid had tea with me last Tuesday; I occasionally visit Wolsey Hall, where Enid is still working. I'm getting a rise tomorrow and shall be earning more than I would be were I still at Wolsey Hall, and I don't regret having changed my job one bit.

The best thing about the Bournemouth outing was that I went out in a rowing boat with Mr Calé and Mr Gronner. I'm going rowing again on Saturday, on the Cherwell, with Mr Calé. We take a punt and use paddles instead of a pole – quite incorrect in Oxford, but he can't punt.

Last Saturday I spent the evening at Mary Woodward's; we listened to the radio, and in between, she complained bitterly about her irresponsible husband. Still, it's better than no husband. I said so to her, but of course she doesn't agree.

When Putz and I had lunch at the Tackley in High Street the other day, for a special treat, I asked the Viennese owner why Sachertorte was always on the menu but never available. "We'll have it next week," she replied. But I know they won't.

The last time I was at Chris and Ted's, we sat around the fire talking after supper, as we often do. Ted was telling us about a Negro he'd met abroad during the war when he was in the air force. "He was as black as this grate," he said, and laughed. "Bit like Jews really, aren't they?" he went on. "Inferior to us." I went hot and cold, and was so terrified he might have become suspicious of me, I joined in the laughter and made some non-committal reply and quickly changed the subject. What point would there have been in ruining our friendship? Just because some accident of fate made me a Jew I don't want to be.

27th September 1948

Now, with Jimmy firmly in my grip, I no longer want him. I once thought that he was different from all the rest and that I loved him. I was wrong. I am deeply bored with him and contemptuously amused by his absurd attempts at lovemaking, as happened when he was at Cobham. How horrid of me! But he is so uninteresting and there's nothing I wish to explore in him and I am deeply disappointed in the man. He said I am the only girl in his life. God help me! He wants to visit me in Oxford again for a weekend as he's stationed quite near. He's an officer now. The tables, you see, are truly turned: it is he who wants me now, not I him.

Likewise with WB. Poor WB! What has he done, in all his goodness, to irritate me so? I'm irritated by his ugliness, his foreign accent, the way he fawns on customers, the way he throws himself into his work as if his life depended on it. Perhaps the fault lies with me. Perhaps I can only love those who don't want me. I am overcome by a sad frustration, an indescribable melancholy, just as Peter Riesz was when he found himself at the fair with a girl he didn't and couldn't love.

My only joy is Jean-Claude far away in the South of France, or rather receiving his letters; they are delightful and a profound pleasure. But of course there's no future in that.

What, oh what, makes me the way I am? Madness? Boredom with life? Why do I want the moon? In Raymond's world I might have found happiness. In mine I never shall. I knew I wouldn't be strong enough to hold on to that world without his support. Oh, the things I want of life! Everything! To travel, to bathe in Mediterranean sunshine, long warm hours with nothing to do except make love and buy clothes, above all to love and be loved! Because the best things in life are denied ordinary people it makes people mean, bigoted and bad.

I feel dreadful today. Is it the weather, the coming winter? I don't want to read, nor listen to music, nor even to write. All my zest for life has gone. But even as I write these words, I ask myself: If I fail to find pleasure in the everyday things of life, what makes me think I would appreciate any other kind? Is all my longing and yearning just a symptom of youth at a difficult stage, or is it something deeper than that? Perhaps I should go to see Jim Hayes again . . .

I loathe going to work every day from 9 to 5. If only I had money and didn't need to!

3rd October 1948

Ruth Miller, Mrs Labowsky's interesting daughter, is here this weekend. Last Wednesday Zena Davies, the children's librarian from the Public Library, came to Parkers'. She's still glamorous. We had a lengthy talk. She asked me to come and see her at the library.

On my half day Mr Calé and I went boating again and took some photographs. It's quite relaxing being with someone who's sexless, who's a man and yet not a man. In the evening I went to Chris and Ted's. Ted is teaching now. On the table was a pile of exercise books for marking. Ted showed us some of the things the children had written, and we laughed till we cried. One little boy wrote: 'Julius Caesar was a famous Roman. He didn't have much hair so he brushed it all to the front to make the most of it.' That was all he knew about Julius Caesar!

I have written a poem in French! It's called *Un jour je veux être heureuse*. I'm very proud of it.

10th October 1948

Mrs Scott held her own art exhibition of restored paintings in the British Council on Tuesday, and I went to see it in my lunch hour. On Wednesday Putz and I listened to a wonderful performance of Beethoven's *9th Symphony* on my wireless in the evening. Thursday, my half day, I spent in the following way: first Mr Calé and I went to the pictures to see *Hamlet* and afterwards we had tea at Lyons and talked about Hamlet. Then I went to the library to see Zena and luckily managed to avoid Miss Campbell. In the evening, as usual, I had supper at Chris and Ted's. When the children were washed and brushed and in their pyjamas, ready for bed, Ted said, "When they look like this, I can forgive them everything. Don't they look angelic?" I had to agree.

Yesterday my old friend Maureen, on a brief visit to Oxford from Germany, called at Parkers' in the morning and came to my room for tea after work, after which we went for a long walk and finished up at Putz's for coffee in the evening. On Sunday Putz and I had a quarrel in my room and she left early. I washed my hair and went to bed.

20th October 1948

They've just played 'my' French song on the BBC! It was a request programme, and my request was for the song *Quand allons-nous nous marier?* which Jean-Claude taught me and we were always singing together. It was very exciting to hear it on the wireless and brought him back to me vividly.

I saw the film *Anna Karenina* yesterday and was lost to the world for the whole evening, and much of the time beyond. On Monday evening, I visited poor Mrs Hacker at the Cowley Road Hospital with Mr Calé. She is very ill but I don't think she realises it and still hopes to return to Parkers' soon.

Jimmy is coming to see me on the 30th. I wish it was Raymond who was coming: I thought I had buried him but I know now that I shall suffer his loss 'So long as men can breathe and eyes can see'. I'm very miserable these days. Yes, I know, I could make a list of all the things I have, and I have all the things one is supposed to have: health, a good job, freedom, independence, a nice room, some friends, a loving boyfriend(!), my sister, a few nice clothes . . . All these things should be sufficient for me, had I chosen Raymond's lifestyle. The question is, can these things bring ultimate happiness, as he maintained, without him? And without being preceded by a variety of false pleasures and mistakes? The more I think about it, the more convinced I am that one must be led to it, through one's foolishness. That is the only path to it. How did Raymond find it? Through erring, with me? Anyway, Raymond was no ordinary mortal, so how can I hope to live up to him?

28th October 1948

Yesterday was Mr Calé's birthday. No one has any idea how old he is. He is very sensitive about his age. He must be getting on for 40. He had asked me long ago to keep that day free. We had lunch at the Tackley and yes, there was no Sachertorte again. After work I went to his digs for tea. The landlady had made a special effort and there was a cake on the table. In the evening, we went to the pictures. The main film had not started and a cartoon was showing as the usherette shone the way to our seats with her torch – when there issued from the screen: "Happy birthday to you, happy birthday to you . . ." Mr Calé was as delighted as a child.

"What did your landlady give you for your birthday?" I asked him during the advertisements.

"She gave me a box of matches," he replied. There was nothing in his voice to suggest he thought this odd. "It was on the breakfast table, nicely wrapped in pretty paper with a ribbon round it," he went on. He seemed pleased with it.

"How generous of her," I murmured, and hoped he hadn't heard me.

Dr Beschorner and Peter came to see me at the shop today. They were in Oxford on a brief visit. They brought me a letter from Joan. It was my half-day but I did nothing much except help with the Red Cross Library at the Radcliffe Hospital, with a Miss Fry who wore the Red Cross uniform whose severity kept the wolf whistles at bay as we wheeled the trolley through the wards. Jimmy is coming at the weekend. Poor me.

7th November 1948

Beryl Wood has had her baby – a girl, called Rosemary. We haven't seen it yet. On Thursday afternoon, I visited Mrs Hacker in hospital again, this time with WB. When she was first ill, WB said the excessive bleeding was probably due to lack of a sex life during the menopause (she's a widow), but it wasn't that. She has cancer.

On Monday I was invited to tea at the Kings' for the first time and afterwards Mrs King took me to a Red Cross meeting at Rhodes House. She wore her Red Cross uniform. After the meeting there were refreshments. Most of the rest of the week I spent with Putz, at her digs or in mine.

Today is one of those cold, wet, endless Sundays that go right through one, that bring to one's mind the rainy Sundays of one's childhood, when boredom drove one to mischief. I am sitting in my room, by turns content and melancholy. My thoughts are undisturbed and uninterrupted. I try not to think of last weekend when Jimmy was here. The sun was out, but otherwise it was a flop. How he bores me! I was positively unhappy in his company. How could I ever have been so horribly mistaken? True, when I met him, one and a half years ago, I was only a little girl, and I didn't really know him – what little there is to know in him; he has nothing at all, nothing. Throughout the weekend I would not let him touch me, except for one short kiss. I did the Rorschach test with him instead, while we were in my room; I don't think he enjoyed it much. I didn't enjoy anything we did together – not the Playhouse, not the Randolph Hotel, not the lunch at Ross's, not the drinks at the Mitre, not even the trip to Woodstock and tea at the Dorchester. Everything was a complete bore, because he is such a boring person to be with. I tried to make it clear that I consider our relationship at an end, in my fainthearted way, but he may not have grasped it. He is very childish and inexperienced. No crime, but it won't do for me. I am not going to tolerate being called 'his girlfriend' any longer. I am going to wait for the right man if there is such a person (or shall I say, another such person) and should he not come or be too long in coming, only be promiscuous with people who really attract me. In this way I shall at least partly attain my high moral standard.

If I go to France in the spring and see Jean-Claude, shall I still be so attracted to him? Will we live together as we once planned, for two whole weeks and as I so often picture in my erotic daydreams? I wonder.

11th November 1948

Putz and I went to the Scala on Tuesday evening and saw *Der Zerbrochene Krug*; a clever comedy by Kleist. When I see a German film I am transported back to – where? My present life seems to melt away like snow in the sun, I'm a little girl again in some far-off place that may or may not still exist, a little girl for whom life was a carefree time, and I had a mother. I wonder what happened to this girl.

I gave Putz the Rorschach test to do. No two people see the same things in these shapes and blots, but whether it is of any

287

significance I can't tell. But it is quite amusing.

I feel it is my duty to write a little bit about WB now, the to you nameless WB, my father, friend and lover all rolled into one, the married man with whom I once spent a terrifying weekend at a hotel . . .

I have been telling you how much he irritates me, have indicated that I don't like him: this is not so. When I wrote that I was passing through a negative transference phase. I know that now, though I didn't know it at the time. I pass from negative to positive transference with him in rapid succession. He often writes me letters, and from these I know how much I mean to him and they help me to see our relationship more clearly. His letters are messy, badly typed and full of mistakes, but what they lack in presentation they fully make up for in content. He is really one of the kindest and best men I have ever known, the sort of man I always wanted for a father. Anni says you can't be a Conservative (which he is) and nice, but he is. He is constantly helping me financially and otherwise – and his patience with me is endless, for I know I can infuriate him. I can talk to him about things which I would never mention to anyone else; for instance, one day when he said I should feel free to ask him whatever I liked and wished to know about the intimacies of marriage, I asked him what happens if one or the other partner has wind in bed: do you hold it back or expel it? "Well, you try not to be too unpleasant about it," he answered. How is that done, I wondered, but dropped the subject.

The injustice I have done him has for a long time preyed on my mind. There is now an intimate friendship between us, such as we probably would never have achieved without the sexual element, but nevertheless I consider that going away with him for that weekend was not a wise and wholesome thing to do, and I was heavily punished for it (emotionally). My physical love for him is more or less stagnant at the moment.

18th November 1948

Tomorrow I'm going to visit the Beschorners for the weekend. They now live in Marlborough where they run a school at which Dr B. is teaching. It's called Mayfield College. I'm a bit nervous of seeing Joan again, in case we have drifted apart.

This afternoon, when I was doing the Red Cross Library at the Radcliffe Hospital, two things happened: an American patient wanted to make a date with me, and in a bed on one of the women's wards I saw a familiar face, which turned out to be Pamela Tonkin, a girl I was at school with in Falmouth! What a coincidence!

Later that day I fetched Putz from Wolsey Hall, had tea at her place and then went to the Scala with her to see *Le Roi s'amuse*.

I've been to visit Mrs Hacker again, with Mr Calé. She looked very thin and gaunt and is obviously very ill.

29th November 1948

I got Saturday off and went to Marlborough from Friday till Monday. I hardly recognised Diana, but Joan has not changed. She was delighted to see me. We all went shopping in town and walking in Savernake Forest and to church on Sunday afternoon. Joan and I talked well into the night in my bedroom; we plan to go to France on holiday together next year. But I'm broke now, because the fare to Marlborough was 14/3d.

I saw the film *Open City* with Mr Calé on Saturday; on Sunday Putz and I had tea at Clem and Beryl's. Jim Dorling was there too, much to Putz's delight. It was strange to see a baby at the Woods' and even stranger to think of them as parents. In the evening Putz and I went to the last Film Society of the term. Joan Lea-Wilson was there, in one of her green dresses.

I wish I had something else to think about than trying to imagine what J-C's body would feel like in bed. Every night almost I dream the same dream: I'm in bed with him, we make love, and, and, and . . . Then I wake, and I'm ashamed, as ashamed as I am of writing about it. I know, you see, that I'm in love with love and sex, not him. Perhaps it has always been like this? The idea is too awful to contemplate. I ask myself, if Jean-Claude were dead, how much would I care? I don't know the answer to this. My next question is, is he worth all this attention from me? Again I have no answer. He was a delightful boy, but I'm probably overdoing things again, with the result that, if I do see him in France next year, it will be a repeat of the sad case of Jimmy Dickens. Well, *qui vivra, verra*. In the meantime we write nice letters to each other. In the last one he called me: 'My dear little apple'. And he explains: 'Dear, don't be worry (sic) about this new pet name; it is a very sweet one for French lovers . . .'

30th November 1948

I have just had a terrible shock. I can't quite believe yet what I've been told. Mary Gammon, sweet, gentle little Mary Gammon who loved Putz and me and gave us flowers and presents and was forever bestowing little kindnesses on people – is DEAD. I knew she had been ill but had no idea it was serious. She had jaundice. She was 19 years old, the only child of her parents. And now she is dead. I didn't see her again and now I shall never be able to show her my appreciation of her generous nature. I still have her typewriter.

I can't write any more today. It would be an insult to Mary to chatter about myself and my debauched and insignificant life.

2nd December 1948

Is it possible that only three days ago I had nothing to think about except Jean-Claude's body, and then Mary Gammon died and before that event had properly sunk in something else terrible has happened.

This afternoon (Thursday) I was sitting in my room after having been at Mrs Wawerka's office when there was a knock on my door and Mrs Labowsky came in. I was totally unprepared for the bombshell she was about to drop.

"I'm afraid I have something unpleasant to say, Ingrid," she announced. "*I need your room.*" For a moment I didn't speak. It was as if somebody had hit me hard over the head with a rolling pin.

"Why?" I asked at last.

"A very old friend of mine from Germany is coming to live in Oxford. Naturally she wants to stay with me. I am very sorry. I know you've been with me for a long time, but it's unavoidable."

My shock had given way to anger. "Why do *I* have to go?" I asked in an icy voice. "Why not Sheila? I've been here much longer." And Sheila has a home, I thought. This is just a room to her.

"For two reasons," Mrs Labowsky replied. "First, my friend

can't manage stairs easily and needs a ground floor room and second, I couldn't have you upstairs – you have too many visitors."

I made no reply. I was seething.

"I'm really sorry, Ingrid," she said again. "You were only eighteen when you came to me, weren't you? You still had a blue ration book."

I continued to say nothing. After she had gone I put my coat on and left the house, banging the front door behind me. I went to the pictures. I didn't see much of the film.

So I have been turned out of my lovely, comfortable digs and have to find a new room. I've been here for four years. It has been my home. But 'home' is a place you get thrown out of, as I know only too well. I'm like a cat about familiar places, and hate to leave them. Every drastic change leads me to a strange and horrible world. Also I really loved old Mrs Labowsky. But I was wrong to do so, it has turned out.

I'm desperately unhappy as I realise my utter loneliness in the world, my hopeless situation, where nothing is what it seems, nothing is stable or reliable. I am devoured by self-pity. And yet, in some mysterious way, I also feel indomitable – as though I or something in me were stronger than all the things that make me miserable. The more adversity I meet with, the more zest I seem to acquire for coping with life. The more there is to be faced and endured, the stronger I feel to face and endure it. At least that's how it is now. I expect sooner or later I shall be beaten. Something will get me in the end.

In addition to my troubles, my sister Putz is killing herself with unhappiness over a man whom she loves who seems to be quite indifferent to her. The man is Jim Dorling, her friend Patricia's ex-husband. She has never been a very happy sort of person and much as I've always longed to, there was never anything I could do about it. I can't even help myself – how can I hope to help her?

5th December 1948

My father called to see us by car today. He stayed for one hour. Putz came, and we had tea in my room. He listened unconcerned when I told him I have to find a new room, much as he listened or only half-listened when I told him many years ago, in

Falmouth, that, because something had not gone right for me, I no longer believed in God. "What you believe or don't believe is of no interest to me," he had replied with a shrug. And now he would have said the same about where I am to live, I suppose, but had to rush off. Well, the last thing I want is his pity. In the evening Putz and I went back to her digs for coffee and afterwards Mr Wren took us for a drink at the Horse and Jockey. Perhaps he thought we needed cheering up. We did, but weren't.

I've been searching for digs all this week, without success. Even Bruno and Erna don't know of anywhere this time. Mrs Zuccari came to see me at the shop, and I told her of my plight. Enid called too, and was informed of my soon-to-be homelessness. She was very sympathetic.

On Saturday afternoon Putz came with me to buy a new jumper.

9th December 1948

This afternoon, my half day, I stayed at the shop with WB. In the evening, after tea at Chris and Ted's, Chris came with me to look for digs. We rang every doorbell in Wellington Square and nearby roads. Finally we found a house where there was a room to let. I took it. I didn't like it and it had no desk and not even a proper wardrobe and I couldn't see anywhere where my cabin trunk might fit, but I took the room anyway. I was fed up with looking for somewhere to live. The landlady is a Mrs Paddon.

13th December 1948

On Saturday I called at Mrs Paddon's to make various arrangements about moving in. When I got back to Lonsdale Road, Mrs Labowsky popped out of her sitting room as soon as she heard me open the front door. I had not spoken to her since she gave me notice and I had no intention of doing so now. I was about to brush past her when she intercepted me. She said, "Have you been able to find a room yet, Ingrid?"

"Yes," I said briefly, and made for my door.

"What a pity," she said, "because I know of somewhere very nice for you."

The upshot is that I don't have to go and live at Mrs Paddon's, which is a great relief, and instead am moving to a flatlet in 23 Lathbury Road, which is being sublet by Miss Wulf, who is none other than the good German cook at the Red Cross canteen! I went to see it today, with Putz, and I'm moving in on 30th December. My bedroom is a cosy little attic room and I'm sharing a bathroom and kitchen with Miss Wulf. The rent is 35/-, which is 5/- more than Lonsdale Road but there are far more amenities. The owner of the house lives downstairs and is a very old lady called Mrs Pinhorn. Her companion also lives in the house. I'm quite looking forward to moving to Lathbury Road, and feel Mrs Labowsky has in some measure atoned for her injustice to me. I'm glad I don't have to hate her any more.

Daphne Hall came to see me this evening, and I've roped her in to come to Mrs Paddon's with me on Wednesday and break the, to her, unpleasant news that I won't be taking her horrible room after all.

22nd December 1948

I'm writing this in the Dauries' sitting room while babysitting. I'm half asleep because last night Putz and I were at a party at Beryl and Clem's – and Jim's, for he is living with them now – and I was DRUNK for the first and I hope the last time of my life as Clem insisted on making me drink rum and gin and I don't know what else. Everyone was drunk and everyone made love to everyone and I had a taxi home at 1.30am and felt rotten and fell into bed without undressing, which I had never done before. Altogether I think the evening was rather disreputable.

It's Christmas Eve on Friday and Putz and I are going to London and Cobham, and I'm going to Portsmouth on Sunday (Boxing Day) to a Christmas party at Ruth and David's.

31st December 1948

Yesterday I moved into my new digs, with the help of Peter King. It took the whole afternoon. He stayed for tea. This evening, New Year's Eve, I spent at Putz's and we had a drink with the Wrens. I have to get off the bus three stops earlier for Lathbury Road than for Lonsdale Road and nearly forgot to do so going home tonight. Stupidly, I hoped nobody who knew me had seen me get off at

Lathbury Road, as I didn't want to explain about having had to leave my old digs.

I haven't told you about Christmas yet. The festivities began on the train to London on Friday evening: Mrs King, Peter and WB travelled on the same train and we had a drinking party in our compartment! We – Putz and I – spent the night at our cousin Herta's flat in Stanmore. Her friend Marianne was there too. We sat up late trying to solve one of those Chinese puzzles that come out of Christmas crackers and Herta did in the end. The next day, Christmas Day, we spent at Elgin Avenue where we had Christmas dinner and gave each other presents – Jack, Jane, my father and Betty and Putz and I. On Sunday I was in Portsmouth, in the company of an entirely different set of people. It was a huge party and went on till 4am. I spent the night there and didn't get up till mid-day the following morning. We had brunch, and I then proceeded to Cobham to finish Christmas there. Putz met me at the station. And here I am, back in Oxford, in my new home, on the last day of 1948.

Happy New Year.

4th January 1949

Parkers' was closed to customers today and yesterday for stocktaking. We finished early today and I went home to my little attic bedroom. Miss Wulf invited me for tea in her room, which is very large and well-furnished and on the floor below mine. She has a few items of her own furniture in it, one of which is an enormous, wonderfully engraved Dutch wardrobe. She is about 60 years old and very spinsterish, but she seems to like me quite well.

Later, back in my room, I made a list of all the things I want. Here it is:

A dressing-gown	Net stockings	A long scarf
Sunglasses	'Jeans'	A new watch strap
Binoculars	A typewriter	A spring costume
A ¾ length coat	A shoulder bag	White shoes

Will I get them this year? That is another matter.

294

7th January 1949

What a year it has been! In the light of past experience, I face the new year with fear and uncertainty.

I hear occasionally from Jean-Claude who has not forgotten me, nor I him. To see him in France in the spring would be a delight, but I'm frightened to look forward to things. (Deliberate deprivation of happy anticipation = discontent . . .)

My work is a bore and I'm not particularly interested in anything I do. I count the hours from 9-1, from 2.30-5. I long for Putz's happiness and it won't come. My attempts to reduce my desires to a minimum have only half succeeded. In the mornings, in bed, before I get up with the utmost reluctance, I say to myself, in all the languages I know (which is three): "Cheer up!" It doesn't help.

I'm trying to find a reason for my dissatisfaction with life, without analysing myself too much, because that is nothing but destruction. Is it my lack of congenial love-life? Too little love-life? Too much? What man is really right for me? Someone like Raymond? Someone like WB? Someone like no one I have ever met? I'm still very young. In March I shall be 22. When I was a child I thought 20 ancient. I had visions of myself at 21 as a mother of three, two boys and one girl. Can you imagine it?

12th January 1949

On Sunday Putz came for tea and we listened to ITMA on the wireless, as we always do. When it was over she went to the lavatory. While she was out of the room, the news came on. "Tommy Handley is dead!" was the headline. I couldn't believe my ears. Putz returned. "Tommy Handley is dead!" I told her. She was equally disbelieving. It seemed the more incredible because less than five minutes earlier we had been listening to him. And it turned out to be the last time we ever will. I shall greatly miss the programme. Joan Lea-Wilson came in the evening, and the three of us mourned together.

Bill Emerson came to the shop today and we had a long conversation. I have a feeling that he still hankers after me. Let him.

Mrs King and Peter came for supper. It's nice to be able to sit at a proper table with visitors. We ate in the kitchen, which is next to my room. Miss Wulf is teaching me to cook a bit, and my speciality now is a cold rice pudding with whipped cream and raspberry juice. Delicious. Next Tuesday Putz and I are invited to the Kings' for dinner.

The Film Society starts again next Sunday.

20th January 1949

Miss Wulf has a sister called Mrs Drei and we had supper with her at her home last week. A Mrs Zimmermann was there also. I feel strangely at ease in the company of these Jewish refugee ladies, and at the same time totally different from them. They were talking about summer holidays and Mrs Zimmermann, who is very brainy and knows it, said that one doesn't really know how good or bad a holiday has been until some time afterwards, when one looks back on it. This struck me as very true.

Today, my half day, Mrs King showed me round her Red Cross Depot Library; afterwards I visited Mrs Hacker at the hospital with Olive, a girl from the office. We had to remember not to mention that someone else is doing Mrs Hacker's job at Parkers', which was hard. Perhaps she still thinks she will recover and return to work? She gave me a pudding someone had brought her which she can't eat. Afterwards I thought I shouldn't have taken it, and although it tasted very nice, I didn't enjoy eating it. In the evening I went to the pictures with Chris and Ted, and then had supper with them. We saw a wonderful film – *The Fallen Idol* – based on a story by Graham Greene. There's a gorgeous little French boy in it whose name I can't remember.

5th February 1949

Mrs Hacker is dead. She died on Thursday, the 27th January. It is terrible to think that someone you've known and spoken to and touched is no more, is nothing and nowhere. When I was small I used to ask my mother, "Will death be abolished by the time I am grown-up?"

I had tea at Mrs Zuccari's last week, and she persuaded me to attend her French conversation class; I agreed, and am starting next Wednesday. I also visited Mrs Labowsky. She kissed me!

The other day I met Stewart, Ray's friend, in the street and we talked for a long time and, not surprisingly, almost at once of Ray. I wondered if Stewart ever suspected anything of our relationship ... if he did he certainly did not show it. He's a quiet, unobtrusive character, typical of Ray's friends.

On Monday evening, Chris and I went to the pictures to see *Mon. Vincent* with Charlie Chaplin – one of his lesser films; and today, Saturday, WB took me to tea at the Tackley after work. No Sachertorte again, and the Viennese proprietress nowhere to be seen, just like the Sachertorte.

8th February 1949

I could fill pages pouring my heart out to you, but I shall reduce it to one little word: miserable.

I'm beset by unfulfilled desires. While there was Raymond I never masturbated. As a little girl I was afraid to masturbate because of God watching; it was the same with Ray: I had to be good for him all the time. Everything is very unsatisfactory. I'm living the wrong life. I'm the sort of person who is expected to be happy because, superficially, I have so much in my favour: youth, looks, health, a bit of intelligence ... But things are never what they seem.

However, as the dying man thinks that he will get well, as poor Mrs Hacker must have thought she would soon be better, so I feel that soon I shall be happy again.

21st February 1949

On Saturday night, quite unexpectedly, and much to my surprise and annoyance – Jimmy called! He wore a brown hat and had a large boil on his neck. I searched in vain for the little archangel whom once I loved so much. But I felt nothing and couldn't pretend I did. I told him it was finished. He looked as if he could not quite take it in, but he left quite soon, which was a great relief. After he had gone, I was overwhelmed by a mass of contradictory feelings – pity, guilt, regret, anger ... Has my heart turned to stone and will I never be able to love anyone again?

On Friday evening I had dinner at the Randolph Hotel with WB – and his wife Hedi! Afterwards we went to hear Jules Romains give a French lecture. It was very exciting being with WB and his wife. During the lecture he once or twice pressed his knee against mine, and smiled at me when I responded. How could I give my attention to Jules Romains while this was going on? I didn't.

Since last I wrote about WB, things have changed again between us – for the better. I love his strength and bigness and the way I can crawl right inside him when he takes me in his arms, and hide there. I love the way he cossets and spoils me.

Putz, Joan and I have been to a Beethoven concert at the Town Hall, I've had two French lessons with Mrs Zuccari, spent evenings with Chris and Ted and am going to the Playhouse with Mr Calé on Wednesday to see *Death of a Rat*.

No more now: there is nothing more to tell, and I can't invent things for you as I occasionally do for friends, when I run out of things to say. That would never do here.

6th March 1949

Three days before my birthday – and snow! Yesterday morning I looked out of the window and everything was white. Snow makes the most vulgar things look elegant, and even the dustbin looked fit to photograph. Snow is not the only surprising thing I have to report.

What has happened? Suddenly, unexpectedly, I find myself adoring WB. Yes, now at last, I really know what he is like, the kind of man he is. Throughout the various stages of our singular relationship and of my curious, constantly changing feelings for him, he has been indomitable: it is I who changed, not he. He is always the same – solid, kind and good. I believe in him as a child believes in his parents. I go to him with everything. He is my father, my brother, my lover, my friend. For months I trifled with him, at other times I thought I hated him, at yet others I ignored him – and he was always there, accepting my moods without the slightest reaction, and always ready to listen. Now I understand his true worth, and I trust him completely.

I never thought about what life would be like if there were

suddenly no WB any more, but I think it would be like the endless first bitter months after I left my mother, when I came to England at the age of 12. I would be quite helpless, as I was then, I would search for likenesses of him in other people, for recollections of him, and each time I would be rebuffed just as I was then. It must sound a little surprising to you, this remarkable confession about my feelings for WB after all I said about him in the past but I was so wrong! All the noblest people are unimpressive and misleading at first. Was it not so with Ray, too?

And now, because I realise how much he means to me, I have given myself to him without the least shame, guilt or regret. And he, as though he had been waiting for me to arrive at this stage after my turmoil of emotions, has received me, smiling and with wide, open, kind, kind arms.

A few days after I had been to the French lecture with WB and his wife, I said to him at the shop, while we were alone one morning in the parcels area, "Could the three of us go to bed together some time? I'd like that." I have read that people do this, especially on the continent. He laughed, and said he would mention it to his wife. The next day I said, "Well, what does your wife say to my suggestion?"

"She says," he replied with a smile, "that you should learn to walk before you can run." Well, I don't suppose I should have gone through with it, anyway.

10th March 1949 (2am – so actually 11th March)

I had my birthday tea at Putz's yesterday and Mrs Wren, kind, motherly soul, had made a nice birthday cake for me. Today Putz and I went to the Playhouse with Peter King and his friend Timothy and afterwards to tea at the Kings, where Mrs King had organised a little birthday party for me. We went home by taxi at 1am

But perhaps the best birthday gift I had was a wonderful, loving letter from WB. He gave me his present when he came to my flat last Wednesday, but the letter meant more than any present.

9/3/49

Hello, my little one, many many happy returns and all the very best, my dear sweet little girlie, round, soft and female, with the red cheeks.

You are so sweet and you are so dear to me, do you believe me? I really and sincerely hope your next year will see you happy, and I hope I'll be able to contribute a little to make it happy. You deserve to be happy, much more than I can make you. Still sooner or later you'll go on, past me, and find the right one. And until then, we shall be happy together. Often and soon! Believe me, I am looking forward with all my being to our next evening and I am doing all I can to bring it about speedily. And the one after that.

300

And, if when and as soon as possible a longer period than just an evening.

My little sweetheart, don't ever cry again; don't you ever think again, that you have reason for being unhappy and alone, and that, but for me, you would be very unhappy indeed. Much as this flatters me, and you know how I appreciate being flattered, it is not true, and I should like to see you convinced that it is not true.

Little one, my dear sweet Inge, look at me with your beautiful eyes, (but without your famous trick, you don't need that with me any longer), just look at me, and smile at me. We'll soon be happier together than

we have ever been so far! Until then, dream
of it, and think of me!

Little one, my Suge, I repeat my
wish, be happy, ~~there~~ and continue to
be my good, good girlie.

Sweet kisses on your eyelids, and
just below.

My Suge dear, do you know how
much you mean to me?

Yours

Willy

16th March 1949

Today CLOTHES RATIONING ENDED. Now all I need is lots of money to buy all the clothes I want. Tomorrow Putz and I are having the day off and going to London. We shall go to my father's office, choose a dress each and have lunch at the Hungarian Czardas in Dean Street. I also hope to go to Foyle's.

This evening my WB was coming – but in the end it could not be arranged. All good people, in their endeavour not to cause suffering, often inadvertently cause it. If he lied to his wife, who is already jealous of me, or hurt her, then he would not be my WB. He must be the perfect diplomat.

When I knew that, after all, he was not coming, I briefly saw myself as the unhappy mistress I have seen in so many films and read about so often; I felt myself to be an object of pity, always coming second, never first, living a sordid and unsatisfactory existence . . . I saw myself as the tragic heroine of a novel who kills herself in the end. But it is not really like that. I know that, in his own way, he loves me, as I love him in mine. When I am in bed with him I forget all my worries. When I am in bed with him I am someone else. As with Ray, I feel that WB is spoiling my chances with other men.

Ray is in Oxford on a short visit. Somebody told me they met him. "He asked after you," she told me at once. "And after your sister, too." Oh God, I don't want to see him! Not ever again! I couldn't face Ray the idol, Ray the paragon, I don't want to be reminded of our illicit togetherness, of the deep sofa in his room, the elephant on the mantelpiece, the little Indian boy in the street below, and Audrey's photograph staring at me. No, no, never again. And now Audrey is his wife and everything might have changed for all I know, but I dare not risk it, I dare not find out . . .

On the 11th April I'm going to PARIS with Joan Beschorner for a fortnight! She knows a French teacher there who has found accommodation for her, and I'm going to stay with a Madame Oudry who's a friend of Mrs Zuccari's. It's cheaper than the hotel where I was going to stay at first – the hotel Condé, which was 300 Fr per day! I won't believe it until I'm really there. Jean-Claude has written to say I should come to Marseilles for one week, but I shan't. I don't want to rake that up, either. I don't want

303

old things any more that are behind me, they're outdated and tatty and only good for the rubbish dump. I must find new things, things that last, people who don't go away and forget me or change out of all recognition.

"I'd got the bed ready," I lied to WB today when he told me he couldn't come, with all the wickedness of my soul. He looked more dejected than ever. When he is deeply touched by something I have said or done he calls me "my darling" from the bottom of his heart as no man has ever called me it before, and I don't suppose anyone ever will again.

26th March 1949

Bill came to see me again in the shop today. He told me he's going to France, too. We talked for ages. He wanted to make a date. I didn't. As I expected, Ray didn't come to the canteen for lunch while he was in Oxford. Perhaps he's as afraid of seeing me again as I am of seeing him. But why should I keep on about something dead and buried? His return was just an echo.

Today WB's wife telephoned him at the shop; his mother-in-law had died. He had to rush home. It was then that this thought of one day losing him for good occurred to me seriously. As often before, I envied him his life that I am shut out of. I am always shut out of people's lives, though I long to share them. I felt very small and unimportant in WB's life after he had that phone call: he has responsibilities, a wife, a house. I am just the game he plays in his leisure hours. I have no real life of my own. I have schemes and dreams that will make everything come right, but they never materialise.

On Monday I'm invited for supper at Mrs Labowsky's. As Putz will be away next weekend I've invited Mrs King for lunch on Sunday. I wonder how she'll like my cold rice pudding with cream and raspberry juice?

8th April 1949

Mr Dauries is ill, so my babysitting duty has been cancelled tonight. Instead I had supper at Chris and Ted's; two of Ted's College friends were there.

Bill telephoned me on Tuesday and finally persuaded me to

make a date with him on Thursday. But I broke the date! I was too weak to say no, and then did a dishonourable thing. A fine character! On Wednesday evening, WB came to my flat . . . He has given me a book on France. It will be very useful when I go to Paris on Monday. I'm so excited I can hardly wait. I promised to have tea at Fullers' with Mr Calé on Saturday and then I must do my packing (which I hate) as I'm going to London the following day and staying the night at Jane's flat in Maida Vale; I leave for Paris from Victoria Station at 9.05am on Monday morning.

Last Wednesday (I mean the 30th March) Putz and I were at a little party at her friend Joan Lee-Wilson's. Also there was a fascinating psychologist called Markus Jacobus, of obscure origin (ancient Rome perhaps, from his Latin-sounding name) and his upper class (English) wife, Diana.

PARIS, 19th April 1949

I was 'brought up' on Paris because my father knows it so well and was always talking about it. I knew all about its food, its cafés, its nightlife, and its beautiful tree-lined avenues. My next layer of knowledge of Paris came from WB, who loves it too. From him I understood that everyone who comes here is in love or having an affair. Personal experience is always different, but they were right in praising the beauty of the city. Most of the time since coming here I've been accompanied by a wonderful sense of freedom and love of life, a desire to stroll and meditate in a state of happy expectation. But sometimes I feel lost and lonely in this big, beautiful city; I sit, for instance, in a restaurant (I have only been in a restaurant alone once). At a nearby table sits a man, also alone. Our eyes meet. Is he going to speak? Will he come over and ask for a cigarette light? It becomes uncomfortable, slightly embarrassing. And yet the game is exciting. Presently a girl enters the restaurant and sits down beside him. Here the game ends. It is a sad one if it ends like that.

I watch people walking in the streets and again I long to share their lives, to force my way into their privacy. If men in public places stare at me too long I become embarrassed. At night they talk to you, but you avoid them in case they are dangerous. It would be nice to be in love here, but I am prepared to wait for love, as I waited for Paris.

Of all the little incidents in my life that for one reason or another I shall never forget, what happened on Thursday the 14th, when I was returning from the Bois de Boulogne with Joan on the Metro, is perhaps the most enchanting. It was terrifically hot outside but in the Metro it was cool and pleasant. Quite by accident, my knees touched the knees of the man sitting opposite me – not surprising, as there's very little space between the seats. I quickly withdrew them – but immediately his knees found mine again. I looked at the man: he was handsome, well-dressed, perhaps 35, certainly educated. Then it began, our little game. With his knees he rubbed and pressed mine, playing with me, teasing me. I stared out of the window, keeping my eyes glued to the outside darkness. Only occasionally did I glance at him, and every time I did so his grey-blue eyes were fixed on my face. I felt them even when I wasn't looking. Once or twice we smiled at each other. Mine was a half-shy smile, his the charming, come-hither one of a sophisticated man. I began to feel beautiful, in my new green corduroy dress (I hate green, but it was the only colour available in my father's stock) and my new beige suede shoes. They were curious thoughts that passed through my mind during these minutes while this total stranger, this attractive Frenchman, was making love to me with his knees. I could not put these thoughts into words, either then or now. Afterwards I chiefly recalled being overwhelmed because his eyes would not leave my face. While the train was moving, in rhythm with his knees, and I could avoid his eyes by looking through the window, it was easier to conceal both my pleasure and my embarrassment, but when it halted I had to search for somewhere to look.

He got out at Auteuil, two stops before ours. As he moved towards the doors, he was still looking at me, and now I looked straight back and we stared at each other as though we were in love. He beckoned to me to come with him, making gestures with his hands and face, and mouthing something in French. I shook my head and smiled unhappily. He blew me a kiss and was gone. The people in the carriage had been watching us and smiled. In a book or a film we would meet again. But in real life – no. I have looked for him every day – in the streets, in cafés, in museums. Who is he, where does he live, what is his name? I shall never know. We were destined only to enjoy ten minutes of our lives together, and they are over.

The night before I came to Paris I stayed in London at my father's flat, as I told you (he and Betty share the flat with Jack and Jane). As he was away, I slept in his room. Looking through his drawers and cupboard I found boxes of cigarettes, tidily laid-out underwear, shoes in a neat row all perfectly polished, old photographs of my sister and me as children but none of my mother. There were documents too, and many business letters, some in his own spidery handwriting. He is the only person I know who is tidier than I am. Looking through these tidy drawers, I thought how I might have loved him had things been otherwise between us, and how nice it would have been if I had. Those articles spoke of him in a singularly loveable way. I saw him in them in a docile mood, they might have belonged to me, they were familiar and suggested all that might have been between us . . . which never was.

Never mind, I have WB, and a few days ago I wrote to him and told him all about Paris and the man on the metro and when I had finished I wrote: 'I love you very much', and signed off. One of the few things to look forward to on returning to Oxford is seeing him again. Next time I write I will tell you all about what I've been doing in Paris.

22nd April 1949 (late!)

I haven't told you that I met Bill on the train to London and we travelled together. He said he had been meaning to catch a train since the morning – it was 5.30pm now – but it got later and later. It must be nice to be so casual and carefree. No doubt he managed to miss the boat train the next morning, for I didn't see him at Victoria Station. He was very cagey about what he was going to do in France.

Madeleine Schapiro, whom I know from Cobham, met me at St Lazare Station at 7pm and took me to Madame Oudry's flat, which is on the 3rd floor of a tall old-fashioned building in rue Oudinot, similar to buildings I remember from Vienna. "What's that?" I asked Madeleine after we were shown to my room and the first thing I noticed was a sort of extra basin-cum-lavatory, next to the washbasin. She giggled but said nothing. "Is it for being sick in?" I asked her. She giggled even more, blushed and said no. I didn't find out what it was until a week later. Needless to say, I didn't make any use of this thing called a bidet.

On Tuesday, Mme Oudry, a kindly, plump, middle-aged widow came with me to fetch Joan from the station. She showed me Les Invalides on the way. We took Joan to her hotel. Later that day Joan and I went to rue Jardin du Luxembourg and had lunch and tea at cafés. During the next ten days, I saw or visited all the places I have known so long from books and hearsay – Notre Dame, the Louvre, Versailles, Les Halles, the Bois de Boulogne, Montmartre and Sacré Coéur (where an

Rodin's Le Penseur – The Thinker

old woman was feeding sparrows which sat on her hands and shoulders and head), Place de la Pigalle,

A result of my Paris visit

the boul Mich (where the Sorbonne is), the Champs Elysées, the Arc de Triomphe, the Quartier Latin and all the famous bookshops Parkers' Foreign department deals with. I had supper twice with Madeleine and her parents at their flat, and on another occasion with her sister Adele who is married and has four children and lives in a palatial flat with high ceilings and solid furniture. I had artichokes for the first time there and was quite unimpressed: there's nothing to eat in them for a hungry girl.

Last Friday Joan and I were invited to the home of her French teacher friend who lives in the countryside, at a place called

Bellevue. We went by train but almost missed it, as we didn't have the correct money when buying our tickets and the French don't like to give you change. The previous day, while having supper at the Lutetia with Joan (where we often eat), we had a quarrel; it was very nasty and I don't think I shall ever feel the same towards her. She even brought up the incident of the flirtatious man on the Metro which of course she had witnessed, and more or less accused me of vulgarity.

Once, when we were on the tube station together and the train was just rushing in, she suddenly turned to me and clutched my arm and said, "You won't let me throw myself under the train, will you? Promise me."

I was aghast, but replied, "Of course not," perfectly naturally, as if she had asked me not to let her lose her umbrella or something equally mundane. It didn't fit in with being on holiday in Paris for the first time, and I wished my companion were anyone but Joan, as long as they were normal. The quarrel didn't help either.

After visiting the 20th Century Art Exhibition in New York Avenue, we had our fortune told by a fat gypsy at a restaurant, and I took a photo of her. She knew we were English because we drank water with our meal, she said. Not from a crystal ball, then. A glass of water is actually quite hard to come by, and you have to ask for it lots of times before they bring it. I didn't understand half of what the gypsy said, which was probably just as well.

In the Louvre I met a customer from Parkers' called Mr Cassirer. We were both very surprised to see each other. It is still unbearably hot, and by the time I get back to Mme Oudry's at the end of the day, my feet are very sore from all the sightseeing, and I've been tempted to soak them in the bidet! One evening Mme Oudry invited me to supper and made a delicious dessert called Crême Fontainebleau. Saturday being my last day here she's giving a little tea party for me and inviting some neighbours, among them a glamorous Negress I've seen once or twice in the house. It has been a wonderful fortnight and I'm sorry to be leaving on Sunday. Joan is staying for another two days. I almost forgot to tell you that I went to the cinema with Madeleine one evening. The film was without sub-titles of course, and I had to keep asking Madeleine to explain the bits I didn't understand. I think she had over-estimated my French.

I've just opened the book on France WB gave me, to look at some of the places I've been to in Paris, and also at those I missed, when out fluttered a little piece of paper on which was written, in his untidy scrawl:

SOUVENIRS DE PARIS SANS MOI.

I have had two letters from him here, and also one from Jean-Claude.

Au revoir, Paris. I hope to see you again one day.

27th April 1949 (7am)

When did I last tell you that I was in love? Not for a long, long time. I had decided, you see, to forget about love until the real thing came along, hoping to recognise it when it did. And now it has happened, and I am desperately in love. How can I hope to convince you, to convince myself for that matter, that it is really true?

It began on Newhaven railway station. I had just arrived from Dieppe by boat – where incidentally I met another Parker customer, a Mr Latham-Konig – and I was with an elderly lady who had taken me under her wing. There were crowds on the station, and when the train came in everyone rushed forward and pushed in, desperate to get a seat. The lady and I separated, as there were no two seats together, and she disappeared into another compartment, which was the last I saw of her. I sat down on the one vacant seat, greatly relieved. The man opposite helped me get my suitcase into the luggage rack on top.

"Was that your mother?" he asked me.

"My mother? Who?" I said.

"The lady you were with."

I laughed. "Oh no," I said. "I met her on the boat. I don't suppose I'll ever see her again."

We began a conversation about France, about politics, about communism, about birds – and we didn't stop talking until we reached Victoria Station. Three coincidences transpired: he had been staying at the same hotel in Paris as Joan; he's a Jew from Vienna; his birthday is in November (he'll be 29) – and Mme Oudry had only last night read my horoscope to me, which said people born under Pisces (me) should marry people born under Scorpio (him). He told me that he was a barrister in London and graduated at Cambridge. He knows a girl in Oxford, he said, called Gerda Fuchs, and I must visit her. He asked me all about myself. He was quite flirtatious, but I was determined to remain aloof, as a well-brought-up girl should. When he mentioned the poules-de-luxe in Paris I didn't respond. I thought of Ray's morals and made them my lifeline. As we approached Victoria Station he said, "Must you catch your train back to Oxford straight away?"

"Yes, I ought to." I noticed he couldn't say his 'R's'. He said 'twain'.

"Don't. Have dinner with me first."

My lifeline was beginning to slacken. "Well . . ." I said.

He smiled. "Good. We'll have a meal at Paddington."

"And then I won't have far to go to catch my train."

"Exactly."

He had a rucksack instead of a suitcase. I was surprised by this, as I associate rucksacks with hikers and campers, not barristers. A minus sign, I told myself. But it didn't make any difference. At Victoria Station we took the tube to Paddington and went to a hotel for dinner. He steered me to a table and handed me the menu. By this time I was quite light-headed, and was beginning to wonder whether I was dreaming everything. I couldn't take in anything that was written in the menu, and I wasn't hungry, anyway. What I did fully take in was that this man was the most beautiful man I had ever seen. He was slight, not much taller than me, with dark hair and Roman features (I hate big, beefy men).

"Are you a virgin?" I heard him suddenly say. The waitress appeared at our table. Thank goodness.

"What will you have?" he asked me.

"I don't know. I'm not hungry. I'll have whatever you do."

He ordered something. The waitress went away. "So. Tell me. Are you a virgin or not?"

"You don't even know my name yet." I said.

He laughed. "It's not so important. But tell me. Tell me your name."

"It's Ingrid. And you are Jonathan." His look changed to one of surprise. "I saw it on your passport. But not your surname. And I'm not a virgin." I said.

"Aren't you? I thought you were. Never mind. You're a lovely girl. You really are. Lovely."

311

I asked, "What is your surname?" It must be my green dress again, I thought.

"Sofer." He was called Hans in Vienna but changed that to its English version. That came out later. The meal arrived. I couldn't face it.

"Where is the sauce Tartare?" Jonathan asked the waitress.

"We haven't got any."

"It says you have on the menu."

The waitress looked at the menu. "Oh, that's Tartar sauce," she replied.

We both laughed. "Incredible," said Jonathan, when she had left, and began to eat. I just picked away at bits of food on my plate and must have given the impression of someone who's not interested in eating. Totally wrong, of course. What other false impressions of me did he get that evening? This thought, and my anxiety about missing my train, and the unbearable excitement of what was happening to me, made my head spin, and just as I decided I couldn't eat another mouthful, Jonathan's voice stopped me dead in my tracks.

"Don't go back to Oxford tonight," he said, very gently. "Don't go. Stay with me. Please."

"I can't," I said.

"Stay with me."

"I'm working tomorrow."

"You can catch an early train in the morning."

"No." My face was burning. I didn't mean 'no' but I had to mean it.

"Ingelein. Bleib bei mir," he pleaded using the Austrian diminutive of my name, and in my mother tongue, my native language, the language my mother spoke. I looked at him. I had never seen such supplication in anyone's eyes.

"Bleib bei mir, Ingelein," he whispered again. He had an angelic voice. I nodded. He reached across and ran his fingers down my face. I had been weak in spirit, now I felt so weak in body that my knees almost gave way when it was time to get up and go. Jonathan paid the bill and put his arm through mine. "I have to go to the office first," he said. "Just for a minute. Then we'll go home."

The office was the Temple of which, being a barrister, he is a member. I wish I had been in the right frame of mind to absorb what he was saying, but I was not. I stood limply as he looked through the post on his desk, and told me something about there being four inns of court which originated in the 13th century, and they were all damaged in the war. I didn't really believe that any of this was happening. I was completely under his spell, and if it was only a dream, so be it. It was quite late by now.

The next thing I remember is sitting in a taxi with him, his rucksack and my suitcase at our feet, and that he took me in his arms and kissed me. And then we had arrived at his house, 12, Springfield Road. No drunkard ever arrived home at night in a more benumbed state than I was in as he opened the front door for me and I followed him upstairs.

His bedroom was beautiful – large, with one wall all window and curtains from ceiling to floor. He asked me if I'd like a bath. I didn't want one, but said yes. He suggested we have it together, which I absolutely refused. This amused him. He unzipped my green corduroy dress. I escaped into the bathroom. A delicious scent pervaded it, but the door didn't lock. Horrors! I pushed a chair in front of it. "Ingelein, you can leave the bath water for me," Jonathan called.

It was well after midnight before we finally went to bed. He turned the radio on, and found Mozart on a foreign station; he lit some candles and produced a bottle of cognac which he placed on the bedside table. He said:

"You're a brave girl, to go to bed with a strange man."

I wasn't brave, I was trembling uncontrollably.

"You're not a strange man," I said. "I feel I've known you for ages."

We drank some cognac, which didn't do much for me, what I could get down of it. The Mozart music was so beautiful that I wanted to cry, the candle-light made everything magic, and Jonathan lying beside me was like a Roman god. I fell in love with him during that night.

"I thought you said you weren't a virgin, darling," said Jonathan, an unimaginable time later.

"I thought I wasn't," I said.

"Then what's the matter?"

"I don't know." I was in love with him and everything would come right in the end. At some time during the night I went to the lavatory and when I returned Jonathan was sitting upright in bed.

313

o

"You *were* a virgin, darling," he said. "Look, there's some blood on the sheet." I saw it, and felt ashamed. We talked for a time, before trying again. He told me he was married to an English girl called Myra with whom he had been very unhappy, and was in the process of getting a divorce. This made him even more desirable.

The door of the adjoining drawing room was ajar and I lay watching the daylight enter, casting shadows on the soft carpet. Jonathan slept. From time to time I watched his closed eyes and ached with love. Once I took a comb out of my handbag which was on the floor by the bed, and ran it through my hair in case he woke and should see me look dishevelled. I had never combed my hair in bed before, and I had never spent a whole night awake as I did that night. Early in the morning he woke.

"Time to get up," he said, "or you'll miss your train." I felt absolutely awful after my sleepless night. I had hoped to lie tenderly in his arms a little longer but he was already getting dressed.

"I'm not going to catch that early train," I announced. I had quite made up my mind. "Can I make a phone call?"

"Are you going to play truant?"

"It won't matter if I don't get there till the afternoon. Can I use your phone?"

"Certainly."

The phone was by the bed and I reached for the receiver. I know that WB arrives at Parkers' soon after eight o'clock. He answered almost at once, and recognised my voice, sleepy as it was. "Look, I've been held up. I had to spend the night in London. I'll be in straight after lunch. Is that all right?" I mumbled down the phone, aware that Jonathan was listening as he dressed.

"Are you all right?" asked WB. "Or have you been up to something I wouldn't approve of?" It was uncanny. I was glad he couldn't see me blush.

"I'm all right," I said quickly. "I'll see you later. I must go now. Goodbye."

Jonathan said, "Was that your boss?"

"Yes."

"You appear to be quite intimate with him." It seemed I was mismanaging everything and, probably because I hadn't slept, I

314

suddenly felt very miserable. I said that was correct. I didn't care what he thought. I had disappointed him so much already that he couldn't think any worse of me.

At breakfast he introduced me to his cousin Walter with whom he shares the house, and Walter's girlfriend Barbara, who were both students. We all had breakfast together. Soon afterwards Jonathan took me to Paddington Station and we said goodbye. I couldn't bear it.

"I'll come and see you in Oxford one weekend," said Jonathan, and now he was gentle and loving again.

"Yes, please do," I said, and thought, 'it's now I who is pleading.' The train came in, he kissed me goodbye and was gone. I spent the journey re-dreaming the dream of my night with Jonathan Sofer. I had fallen desperately in love with him. He is like me only more so, a not very happy intellectual, a victim of the pre-war generation. I was sure we could be happy together, but already my doubts are setting in: will he write, will he come, did he like me?

It was the craziest anecdote of my life, and now I've got it down on paper, even if I never see Jonathan again, the experience will be with me forever, every detail of it. How do people live without keeping a diary?

29th April 1949

WB wanted to know all about Paris; he didn't know that my two weeks there had been all but obscured by what happened at the end of them. I don't know if I'll tell him about that. He said my filing time will be reduced by half which is all it took him while I was away. Pity. I like to sit and dream while I'm filing and not rush to get on with more taxing jobs. I had forgotten what a slave-driver he is.

Yesterday a letter arrived from Jonathan. Picture how I felt: I was delirious. The fact that he wrote so soon could only mean one thing: he had fallen in love with me too, he was writing to tell me so and to ask me to marry him. What he actually wrote was: (in his left handed scrawl):

Dear Ingelein,
    This is the eighth time I've started this bloody letter. It is an

awfully difficult one to write because I am trying to say that, although sexually the thing just didn't work out at all, emotionally I was so happy to have you with me that I have blessed the day that gave us the idea to come close to each other. I shall come to see you at Oxford some time at the end of next month (if you want me to) although I shall not sleep with you . . . I feel very flat and disappointed that our bodies did not live up to the elation of our 'souls' but it is nice to have found even the limited touch we have managed to find.

Tendresses,
Jonathan

There must be something very seriously wrong with me, my vagina, or both. I read and reread the letter. But, as I recall certain things he said, and the way he behaved in the morning, perhaps there was a hint there of what he is like, that I should have seen . . . I still don't know what he is like. I only know that I love him.

Ditta came to the shop today. I forgot to tell you that she was sacked as she was hopeless at her job. Poor Ditta. I feel sorry for her, and admire her for coming back to see us. I agreed to go to the theatre with her to see *Iolanthe*.

Tomorrow I am going to the pictures to see *Fallen Idol* again. It was such a lovely film.

3rd May 1949

The Red Cross canteen is closed this week and Putz and I and the Kings have been having lunch at Connors', where the food is not nearly so good.

On Sunday we went to the first Film Society of the term and met Dr Markus Jacobus there, to whom we were introduced by Joan Lee-Wilson some time ago. He asked us back to his home afterwards where we had coffee with him and his wife Diana, and stayed till 12.15am. I spent this evening at Chris and Ted's. I told them about Joan (Beschorner's) fear of throwing herself under the metro train, and they thought she was quite mad.

A telephone call was put through to the foreign department at Parkers' today. Mr Calé answered and soon put the receiver down in disgust. A customer wanted a book on French polishing! Mr Calé was not amused. "Those silly girls in the office!" he exclaimed.

I wish I could clear myself of my feelings of guilt, doubt and self-accusation, and believe in my love for Jonathan. I know he is the man I have waited for all my life, but does he know it? And have I waited for the wrong man all this time? Have I been dazzled by trivialities and not seen the man beneath them? What's the difference between thinking you are in love, and being in love? "You only think you are," people often say. But: "I think, therefore I am." And is sex more important than love? Jonathan obviously thinks so. I answered his letter almost immediately but because I couldn't say the things I wanted to say I wrote about nothing much and kept a tight rein on my true feelings.

5th May 1949

I've had another letter from Jonathan. It was very neurotic and left me desolate. 'My body is such a tender plant,' he wrote, 'that I must protect it from shock and disappointment, even at the cost of loneliness.'

Knowing Raymond made me so sensible and uncomplicated that I feel ill-equipped to deal with spiritual torments. Also, I did not realise at the time that the fact that, sexually, we accomplished next to nothing owing to my stupid sensitive vagina, would so deeply affect him. But, being what he is, if it hadn't been that no doubt something else would have got in the way.

I must now put away all memories of that glorious man I met on the train between Newhaven and Victoria, in a hot crowded compartment full of happy people returning home from France, for he has gone forever. I shall not answer this letter, or not for a long time. I can only love a good man, and if Jonathan is not good, if he is selfish and ruthless and only interested in satisfying his sexual desires, then I can't love him, and my brief happiness with him will be relegated to all the other trivia that make up my life.

It is odd that I always run headlong into complicated people. My sister says it's something to do with my continental background. But I don't want these complications, they destroy me, I want peace and quiet, and nice, simple, cosy people, safe to be with. My French landlady, Madame Oudry, always said, "Il faut chercher l'amour; si on le cherche, il arrive." She did not say how long one has to 'cherche' it, before one gives up in despair.

317

My one consolation is that Jonathan did not smoke, and I hate non-smokers.

WB was in my flat this afternoon and evening. I confessed everything. I told him I was in Jonathan's bed when I made my phone call explaining I would be late back; I told him I fell in love with Jonathan, but then I had these two extraordinary letters. He listened in amazement and disbelief.

"What did he say in the letters?" he asked me.

"He said his body was such a tender plant that he must protect is from shock and disappointment. And other things like that," I told him. It met with a burst of laughter.

"Nonsense. Rubbish," he said. "That man needs a good hiding. Forget him."

Sound advice. But I am under Jonathan's spell, since that one magic night, and a spell needs more than sound advice to be uncast.

WB is coming again next Wednesday. I feel a bit better about my lack of sexual skills now because many brides don't learn to relax and enjoy sex for the whole of their honeymoon, according to WB.

10th May 1949

Today I called on Gerda Fuchs, the girl Jonathan asked me to look up. Already on the train he had talked to me of her. Later he compared me to her, saying how warm and lovable we both were. I asked him what his relationship with her was and he had replied, "She's a good friend. Curiously enough, I've never slept with her." Almost the last thing he said to me on Paddington Station was, "Don't tell Gerda that you spent the night with me."

When I saw Gerda today I was at first quite bewildered by her beauty, her charm, her warmth. She's entirely different from what I imagined – tall, dark, elegant, with a round face like mine but there the similarity ends. It's going to be difficult to make friends with her, I thought, for she's so much superior to me. But I liked her.

"Have you known Jonathan long?" I asked her, when we were sitting in her room in Wellington Square drinking coffee.

"Oh, we're ancient friends," she replied with a laugh. How ancient, I wondered, but didn't like to ask as I didn't wish to appear too interested in him. I pictured them as awkward adolescent teenagers together, feeling their way into the grown-up world. I envied her. If ever I felt that Jonathan might belong to my life, I certainly feel it no longer, since meeting Gerda. Gerda is German, not Austrian, and Germans are more domineering and aggressive – another reason for feeling inferior to her. Am I going to be trapped in an emotional triangle again? In the past, when I've been bored with life, it was usually because I was being emotionally lazy, surrounding myself with dull, plain people in order to avoid rivalry and passionate encounters. But choosing easy situations is no solution either. I must have excitement, and I welcome Jonathan and Gerda into my life – if they agree to come, that is, and don't exclude me from theirs.

We went for a walk, and I asked her to tea next Wednesday. In the meantime she will see Jonathan when she goes to London for the weekend. Lucky Gerda.

Last Saturday at Putz's, I was introduced to her boyfriend, Geoff Hancock, whom she met at the Communist Club. Did I tell you that she joined the Communist Party some time ago? Geoff is tall and very English and two years younger than Putz. They seem to get on very well together. He had tea with us, and then left to attend to some Communist business.

16th May 1949

Putz and I spent the evening at Clem and Beryl's today. We had supper, admired Rosemary, the baby, and played with the dog. On Saturday I went to the Scala cinema with Mr Calé; we saw *Ammenkönig*. Afterwards I had supper at Putz's and we talked about Geoff. The previous evening I was at the Thomas Mann lecture with WB, his wife and Mr Calé. Afterwards we went to St John's gardens, and then I went babysitting at the Dauries'.

A new girl is working at Parkers' foreign department, to replace Ditta, and about as different from her as is possible. Her name is Sara Mostyn, she's blonde and attractive and from a very upper-class family descended from Henry Fielding. They recently returned to England after living in Rhodesia where they grew tobacco for a living. Sara's mother is a novelist, which may in part account for Sara wanting to work in a bookshop.

319

18th May 1949

I spent a strange and fascinating evening with Gerda. She stayed till 11.30pm. We talked a lot about Jonathan, and I learnt quite a bit about him, but not enough. Once I asked her, "What exactly is the matter with him?" after we had agreed that he had a tormented soul. She replied:

"I can't discuss that with you."

Why not? Why couldn't she? I longed to know. Years ago, when I was still at school in Falmouth, I asked one of the Catholic priests visiting St Joseph's, why he believed in God. "I can't discuss that with you," he had answered, leaving me flat and disappointed, and ashamed that I had asked. Now I felt the same. After Gerda had made her cutting reply she changed the subject and talked of her love-affairs and the various men she knows, and about her pottery in Plantation Road.

Now Jonathan has been made more real by someone who knows him well and I'm afraid of this new stranger who is waking me from my dream. How unfair when, during our night together, I was frightened to touch him for fear of waking him.

I glimpse, but in no way understand, some profound relationship between him and Gerda from which I shall be forever excluded.

23rd May 1949

Tomorrow is Putz's birthday and we went on her birthday outing tonight – a visit to the New Theatre to see *Cosi fan tutte*. The silly plot in no way detracts from the superb music. On Wednesday I'm going with Mr Calé to see *Carmen* – a very different story but the music almost as breathtaking.

Chris and Ted have acquired an allotment on Port Meadow and spend much of their free time there. Last Thursday I went with them, and helped them with a bit of digging. Afterwards we went for a walk and bought some chips and then I went home to supper with them and played in the garden with the children. While doing such innocent things I give no hint to anyone that this same girl spent a night with a man she had met only hours earlier. I even fool myself.

On Sunday morning I did some drawing in the garden. I do still occasionally get the urge to draw, and especially like pastel drawing. But most people are much better than I, and when I see Ted's work I feel I shall never put pencil to paper again. Last Saturday evening I went to Magdalen College School with Chris and Ted for a performance of Handel's *Water Music* on the Cherwell. It was a fine, warm evening and we sat in the beautiful grounds awaiting the start of the concert. When the first chords were heard drifting up the river Ted whispered, "Here comes Handel doing the breaststroke."

Next Thursday Mr Calé has invited me to tea at his digs, his landlady presiding, no doubt, and on Sunday I'm going to Sara Mostyn's for the whole day. She lives in Whealtey, in a house called Bleak House. I'm very much looking forward to meeting her family, especially her novelist mother. She writes under the name of Ann Mary Fielding.

25th May 1949

Yesterday, on her 25th birthday, my sister Lieselotte GOT ENGAGED to Geoff Hancock.

Now, with my prayers at an end, I can ask nothing more of life – at least not for a long time. What has for years been my and her greatest wish has been fulfilled. She has spent years of misery, unhappiness and loneliness during which I longed for her happiness. In much of that time things looked quite hopeless. It still seems incredible, and I'm terribly happy for her. This is the one beautiful, unselfish thing in my life, the way I feel myself to be part of her. If it had happened to me I doubt if I could be happier. My own troubles are now dormant; I am lost in Putz's bliss. It is wonderful to love so unselfishly. I'm truly delighted for her. They are not getting married for about a year. That is until he has taken his Finals. For her birthday he gave her a book on Communism.

How paltry and insignificant my feelings for Jonathan Sofer seem, in the light of my sister's engagement to a nice, reliable man. I feel ashamed, and sick of myself. "Il faut chercher l'amour . . .", but I never was any good at finding things. Oh Jonathan, Jonathan! Why mustn't I love you, why can't I recall your voice, your smile, the touch of your body, without pain, why not with the happiness they gave me?

I had a letter from Jean-Claude. He wants to come to Oxford

for three months and he wants me to find him a job. He still can't forgive me for not visiting him in Marseilles while I was in Paris. But no letter from Jonathan though I wrote and told him I would be in London for the weekend of the 4th and 5th of June.

3rd June 1949

Someone called Ronnie rang me today. I had no idea who he was until he reminded me that we met at Ruth's party in Portsmouth. I had lunch with him at Ross's. He is short, fat, Jewish, not at all intellectual and totally uninteresting. We talked mainly about Ruth and David's emigration to Australia. He returned to Portsmouth in the evening.

Both WB and Mr Calé have been to my flat this week, but separately, of course, and in very different circumstances!

On Monday after work, Putz, Geoff and I went on a coach trip to Stratford to see *A Midsummer Night's Dream*. I think it was organised by the Communist Club. As soon as we arrived they wandered off and left me to myself. They even sat somewhere else in the theatre. Fortunately I met a girl from Wolsey Hall with whom I used to work, otherwise I would have been quite alone. I wasn't very pleased, as you can imagine. In fact I was very hurt. We didn't get back till after midnight.

But it is Tuesday evening, the evening I spent at Gerda's that I want to tell you about and that overshadows everything else. As I walked home late at night on that Tuesday evening I felt so utterly miserable and wretched I wanted to die. I walked like a wound-up doll, lifeless. Crying would have been some relief, but the pain was too deep below the surface to erupt in tears. If there had been a bridge with deep water below . . . What crazy ideas enter one's head when one is beside oneself with misery.

We had tea. I felt slightly uncomfortable and sort of vaguely excited. I longed to ask Gerda if she had seen Jonathan in London, and whether she had heard from him; I still haven't. But she talked and talked about her friends, her love affairs, her pottery. I got bored and even annoyed. I decided she was selfish, I was glad that she was not after all as nice as I had at first thought and that I was free to dislike her.

Suddenly I told her that I had had an affair with Jonathan. There was no warning that I would come out with this. I had not meant to. I had promised him I wouldn't tell her. "Don't tell Gerda that you spent the night with me," he had said. Strangely enough, I felt no pangs of conscience. Just a weight off my mind. We were sitting in the dark by the electric fire and I could not really see the expression on her face but I learnt soon enough how little impression I had made on her. "Did you think that I had slept with him?" I asked her, longing to hurt her, or to betray Jonathan, or God knows what. She answered:

"I don't think I ever thought about it." That was a lie, I felt sure. But the cruel words reminded me once again of the time I told my father, after much heart searching, that I didn't believe in God, and he had shrugged his shoulders and said it made no difference to him what I believed or didn't. I know now that this is called throwing your pearls before swine, but I fall into the trap again and again. She must have seen, or perhaps sensed, the unhappiness written all over my face, for a moment later she said:

"I should like to save you from Jonathan. He can make women very unhappy, his charm can be lethal." I hated her deeply by now. She went on: "I don't want to upset you but please don't take the whole thing too seriously. Jonathan is a wonderful person but he has a weakness for women and sleeping with them means little to him."

"He liked me," I said, in a voice devoid of all life.

"Oh, I'm sure he did!" she cried, aware of her tremendous superiority, and with that maternal manner I had noticed once or twice before in her speech. "Why shouldn't he?"

"There are things you don't know," I floundered on. What things? That he handed me a glass of cognac in bed? That he lit some candles to make love by? That there was blood on the sheet? "All the things you have told me about Jonathan are good things, and yet you have distorted him for me and he now seems a rogue and a liar." I was obviously going mad.

"What has he promised you?" she asked, surprised by my outburst, I suppose.

"What should he have promised me? It's what he did, not what he said." Except that his pleading words, "Bleib bei mir, Ingelein, bleib bei mir," are as indelibly imprinted on my brain as a sailor's tattoo on his arm, I thought. "I don't want to be cheated. I don't want to be just a woman to be spent a night with and then discarded," I said. "It's what rotters do. So he must be a rotter."

323

"You mustn't say that about Jonathan," said Gerda, telling the naughty child off. And then she said, "Don't take this to heart, but you are not really Jonathan's type, you know. He likes the Nordic type, women that bully and mother him, he likes to be a weak little boy. And anyway, he really likes my sister, he would marry her if she would have him, but she won't."

My arguments were at an end. There was nothing more I could say. And I said nothing.

"I don't want you to be unhappy over this," Gerda went on. "I know what it can be like, to love someone . . ."

"Who said anything about love?" I cried, roused out of my stupor. Lying is easy, when it is a matter of life and death.

She said, "Then what are you worrying about?"

"Nothing," I said. "Let's talk of something else."

She had poisoned my memory of Jonathan. She's a witch. She had treated a story I gave her to read with a similar lack of interest, and I should have learnt from that. But she's a witch, and witches can make you do and say things against your better judgement.

I don't understand why I'm constantly hurt by people but it must be because it is deserved or in some way necessary. Now I never want to think of Jonathan again. Nothing lasts forever and my unhappiness will pass too, at some impossible to envisage date. Meanwhile I shall side with Candide, who said that everything is for the best, in the best of all possible worlds.

8th June 1949

I had the day off on Saturday and Putz and I went to London and then to Cobham for the weekend. Geoff was to come too, but didn't in the end. It seems very strange. Even stranger in my opinion was the occasion of their excursion into town to buy the engagement ring: Putz wore an old jacket, flat shoes and no lipstick! How could she go dressed like that to buy an engagement ring with her fiancé? When I asked her she just shrugged and said it didn't matter. Could that be a part of the Communist creed?

In London everything reminded me of Jonathan, for I had not been there since. Paddington Station was worst of all. My heart is broken. But I must not think of him. We went to my father's office, had lunch at the flat in Elgin Avenue, cooked by Jane and delicious as usual, and then took the train from Waterloo to Cobham. Arriving at 'Ann's Cottage' is almost like arriving home. Almost, but not quite.

On Sunday we lounged in the garden, went for a walk with Chum, the Airedale, and for a drive in 'Geoffrey', Anni and Felix's little car. The next day being Whit Monday and a holiday I played tennis with Lixl, the Czech boy living at Ann's Cottage. On the way we passed a village fair. My father and Betty came out in the afternoon and we all sunbathed in the garden, had tea and drove to Oxshot Woods. My father said instead of acquiring a nice tan in the sun, my face looked like a beetroot. It was supposed to be a joke.

In the evening, Putz and I returned to Oxford. Now the waiting begins again. Does being hurt by people make you into a bad person? I hope not. I still try to live up to Ray's standards.

12th June 1949

Maureen Daly is in Oxford for a week, on leave from Germany. She came to the shop yesterday, and was here for tea today. She hasn't changed. I told her about Jonathan, for I did not vow not to speak of him. "For one night I loved him. Yes, yes. I loved him!" I told her fervently, because she understands these things. "How can anyone act in such a way, so outrageously, so brutally?"

"Men can be beasts," said Maureen.

"I've tried to forget him," I said. "I can't. Only *he* can end my misery."

"You will forget him," she said. "Be patient."

In the evening I went to the last Film Society of the term with Putz and Geoff, and this time they didn't go away and sit by themselves. They sat with me.

The fine weather continues, and on my half-day Mrs Pinhorn, my landlady, invited me to have tea with her in the garden. It was served by Edith, her companion. Edith has an illegitimate daughter and had been turned out by her family. But for Mrs Pinhorn, who offered to take her in, she would be homeless. Mrs Pinhorn is about 80 years old but still washes her blankets in the bath! In the evening I was at Chris and Ted's. Ted drew a portrait of me, a pencil drawing. He is going to frame it.

Ted's portrait of me.

13th June 1949

It occurred to me that perhaps I can destroy all my memories of Jonathan more quickly by getting rid of them on paper. I have never told you, for instance, for I find it difficult to write about intimacies, how he buried his head in my left breast and kissed it almost viciously, biting and sucking it so that I cried out with joy and pain. "God, what lovely breasts you have," he had exclaimed, in German. No, no, I can't go on with this, I can't write it down, not even here, I don't want to remember it, or perhaps I don't want to destroy it. But it was happiness, the happiness of total intimacy . . . we were so close, so close the whole world could not separate us. Oh, I hate you, Jonathan, I wish my nipple had choked you, I hope you die alone with no one to love you. I was a nice girl before I met you and now I am bad and I hate the world.

But do you know what, I am once more, at long last, creative. I've been drawing quite a bit, and have written poetry. Jonathan, that glorious, evil monster, has inspired me. Some good comes of everything. Just as Candide says.

The 13th of June is my mother's birthday, but I mustn't think about her either.

20th June 1949

Today Sara treated me to lunch at the 'Continental'. She quite likes working in the foreign department but frequently complains about all the books being in 'outlandish tongues', so that she can't even read their titles.

"Nothing very outlandish about French," WB told her the other day. "Didn't you learn French at school?"

"I didn't go to school," said Sara. I believe it. She was a debutante, or her mother was. I expect they were all privately educated, by tutors at home.

In the evening Mr Calé and I saw *The Tempest* in Worcester College Gardens. (I've just got back). It was magical. Worcester has a lake, which provided the right setting. Unfortunately it got very cold as the evening wore on, and most people sat covered with rugs. We hadn't any.

Yvonne Leroy, a French girl I once met at Cobham and a friend of Madeleine's, called unexpectedly at my flat last Wednesday, while Chris and Ted were with me. I was very surprised to see her. She stayed for coffee. I've been seeing Maureen on most days, of course. On Friday we found Daly's Café in Summertown closed and decided to call at a house a few doors away to ask if the residents might know why. Who should answer the door to us but Mr and Mrs Howard, who used to live next door to the Beschorners. They invited us in and were most hospitable. Mrs

327

Howard was nursing her baby which cried most of the time we were there as it wasn't well. They couldn't tell us anything about the café unfortunately.

It was little Micky's birthday on Sunday and we took him fishing in the park. On the way we ran into a Communist gathering on St Giles. I saw Catherine there. Catherine is Putz's friend who first introduced her to Communism, and so ultimately to Geoff. I didn't see him there. Putz is on holiday for a week.

On Wednesday I'm going to visit Mrs Labowsky in the evening. I expect she will show me my old room and introduce me to its new occupant.

I haven't been going to the Dauries' babysitting for two weeks as one of the children is ill. This means that I am 2/- worse off, and have had to cut down on lunches.

21st June 1949

The whole day I carried with me the letter I had from Jonathan this morning, unopened. I hadn't the courage to open it.

After I had made up my mind not to think of him any more my life became quite unbearable although, as usual, outwardly I gave no sign of anything wrong and no one suspected. I knew that, with all the good intentions in the world, I couldn't forget him, because I didn't really want to. To people to whom I had related the episode the story was a simple one: I met a charming man on the train, he became infatuated with me, he was an oversexed continental, his charm had the desired effect and I succumbed to him. As far as he was concerned, it meant nothing. But even in the depths of my unhappiness, I couldn't believe that the story went quite like this. And in a way I was right.

Apparently the fact that we did not achieve physical sublimation (and that he doesn't think we ever will) seems to be the crux of the matter. He was frightened of a repetition of this failure, and he went to France for Whitsun so as not to have to come to Oxford to see me. He went to France because of me. He ran away from me. He wrote: 'I liked you more than I have liked any other woman for a very long time and I expected our mutual attraction to immediately translate itself into a physical harmony without which all else is incomplete . . .'

Now at last I think I understand. As with Ray when I did not

328

understand anything until the last evening at the café with his remark: "I shall miss our little walks in the Park to see the frogs . . .", so with Jonathan and his longish letter putting everything in perspective. After Ray's remark I had to let go, and now after Jonathan's letter, I must do the same. It's not their fault that I was stupid and misunderstood everything.

Perhaps one day, in years to come, I shall meet Jonathan again, we shall sit together in some London or Paris restaurant where there is dancing, and I shall work out his problems with him that aren't there. But for now it is over. I should like things to have been different, above all less complicated. I should like Jonathan to have been my dream come true. Had we reached what he called physical sublimation, who knows where we might be now? It was not to be. I disappointed him and now he is having his revenge. Because I disappointed him I have lost a man I loved and could have gone on loving and who might have loved me. WB said that from such a man I could only derive unhappiness (I still tell WB everything) because such a man himself is never happy unless he is unhappy. I expect WB is right.

The letter ended: 'Ring me if you feel like it next time you're in London.' Just what one stranger might say to another, without really meaning it, of course.

24th June 1949

'I liked you more than I've liked any other woman for a very long time . . .' It has become like a line in a well-loved poem and I can't get it out of my head. I say it to myself all the time. I carry it around with me everywhere, to reassure myself, and with infinite pride. I wear it in my heart as a soldier wears his medals on his chest.

This sex business at which I have only hinted is now beginning to worry me, since Jonathan made so much of it. I can't understand why I've never been able to do it properly. It started with Bill, but that was his fault; then with WB, when it hurt so much; later with WB, much later, and it was still uncomfortable and certainly not enjoyable. And then with Jonathan, who was so excited, so wild, he couldn't penetrate at all – he who expected heaven from me because he liked me so much. Poor, poor Jonathan. I shall never forgive myself. I feel utterly guilty. For the rest of my life I shall carry the knowledge around with me that I failed him. I didn't mean to. During every moment spent in his company I longed to make him happy, and the very opposite happened . . .

Today, as I was standing in the kitchen near the window, I saw Bill coming to the house. A moment later the doorbell rang. I didn't answer it. How much longer will it go on, Bill pursuing me and I avoiding him?

26th June 1949

Oh no, oh no, oh no! Do you know what has happened now? I've been out with Bill again! Apparently determined to see me, he called at the shop yesterday. Although I was wearing my glasses, he didn't seem to be put off. In the end I agreed to see him last night. It was Saturday. He must have been desperate, for he always refused to go anywhere on Saturday nights because that's when the plebs are out.

Early in the evening he fetched me from Lathbury Road. We walked along the river to the Trout Inn, our favourite old haunt. It was a beautiful evening, hot and quiet. He chattered way all the time, wittily and brilliantly, though I must admit at times I only half listened and thought about other things. He works at Pressed Steel now, as a physicist. He has grown up a lot, I thought, but lost none of his boyish charm. He no longer frightens me, and so things were easier between us.

At about 9 or 9.30, after we had had a few drinks we called at the little church in Wolvercote village. Here he kissed me passionately. I think he must find the combination of irreverence and lovemaking particularly exciting. I thought, as he stared wildly and greedily into my eyes, men always ask for the same thing, with the same pleading look, the same methods of bribing; nobody has anything new to offer me. But, strangely enough, I wasn't miserable. How could I be, when Bill was paying me the most elegant compliments in a soft and alluring voice? We left the church and climbed to the top of the hill. By now it was quite dark. He threw me into a haystack, and I laughed. For four hours he pleaded with me, even for my love, making me promise he meant something to me. But I would not submit to him. The days of our innocent and inexperienced youth were over though not forgotten, and I had learnt my lesson.

"Come away with me, Ingrid," he begged, the words tumbling out of his mouth in between his kisses. "Come to Malaya with me (he has been offered a job there), come to Cambridge when term starts (he's going to do a PhD there), come to London with me for a weekend! Will you? Will you?"

"Where in London?" I said, and thought of Jonathan.

"The Cumberland Hotel," he replied.

"Ask me again when you come back from France," I said. He's going to France for six weeks tomorrow.

"Promise me. Promise me now."

I was really amazed by him. He was so adamant, so sincere. But hadn't I heard it all before? I shivered. It was getting chilly.

"You are cold, darling," said Bill.

I didn't really know whether I was cold or excited.

He said, "Are you happy, darling? Are you happy with me? Do you love me?" No, that was not the Bill I remembered from three years ago.

"Are *you* happy?" I asked him.

"Terribly. I'm terribly happy with you," he said.

Some time later I told him that I wasn't very good at sex. He was very sweet and said it didn't matter and it would be all right when we were together. I had hoped to put him off. What I did not tell him was how wonderful I thought he was now, and how hard I was finding it to keep him at bay. For the first time he seemed to be a real person, not an elusive ever-changing spirit.

We arrived home at 3am. He had wanted me to stay all night with him under the sky in the haystack, and I was glad I had been strong-willed enough to refuse.

"I'll write to you," he promised, when we said goodbye.

"I don't believe it," I said.

"I will. Until the end of August then!" he called, as he went away.

He had told me that, when in Paris, he lives with a French woman he once loved. It must be her doing that he has grown up so much. I told him little about myself. When he said that he found me more attractive than ever I gave no hint of my experiences which might have made me so, but I expect he guessed. When, as we were walking along in the early part of the evening, he asked me if men always stared so much at me in the street, I replied, "Yes. Usually," as carelessly as I could, and felt pleased.

How much longer will Bill come back to me? I should like to remember him as he was last night because that was Bill to perfection, Bill perfect like a Mozart sonata. He said he loved me, but I don't believe it. He continues to dazzle me with his brilliance – he's cleverer than anyone I know – and I'm very flattered that someone like that should want me so much, should force himself again and again back into my life. Will I go to London with him? If I feel tempted, when he returns at the end of August, I shall remind myself that I can't dance and he loves dancing, and is probably as good at it as he is at everything else; that will stop me.

Where, oh where, is the world of Raymond now? Forgotten? Discarded, obsolete? No, no, never. One day I shall return to it, when experience has moulded me into the person I want to be, when I am fit to live in it.

1st July 1949

Yesterday one of my dreams came true: I went to Wimbledon! With Peter King. Mrs King obtained the tickets for us, which was very kind of her. I had the morning off work and we went to London by coach and arrived in Wimbledon in time for the tournament which started at 2pm. We saw the Americans Schroeder and Mulloy beat the Australians Sidwell and Brown, which was what I wanted. Peter took a photograph of them. We didn't have very good seats but just being there was wonderfully exciting. We stayed till 8pm. During the interval I met my Uncle Bruno – also a tennis enthusiast. Peter and I had supper in London before returning to Oxford.

The heat is terrific. It is so hot in my little attic bedroom that I can't sleep in it, and Mrs Pinhorn has lent me another room, downstairs, to sleep in until it gets cooler. On Monday evening Gerda called and we went for a walk. It was too hot to sit indoors. She has invited me to visit her at the pottery next week and then spend the evening with her. We did not discuss Jonathan again.

Sara is staying at a house in Beaumont Street, with friends called Drummond, this week. On Tuesday we ate sandwiches in St Johns' Gardens in our lunch hour and afterwards she took me to the Drummonds' house.

WB goes on holiday for two weeks on Monday.

10th July 1949

We heard today that the Red Cross canteen is to close. Terrible
news! No more lovely and cheap lunches. No more apple
charlottes.

Mr Calé knows a German professor of Theology who needed
some typing done. He asked if I would do it. I agreed. Mr Calé is
also involved with typing for him. On Monday evening a taxi
collected us and we were driven to Wadham College and met by
the German Professor. We were shown into his study, put before
a desk with a typewriter and he began to dictate. I typed steadily
until 11.30pm but was almost asleep well before then. The word
'faith' appeared many times in the dictation, but as he could not
pronounce the 'th' I typed 'face' every time – until I realised my
mistake. It was very embarrassing but Mr Calé and I laughed
about it afterwards. I was well paid for my efforts. We went home
by taxi again.

The hot weather continues. Both Mrs Pinhorn and Miss Wulf
are away and Edith and I are alone in the house. Today Putz and
I sunbathed in the garden all the afternoon in our bathing
costumes. We're quite brown now.

At Chris and Ted's last Thursday we were also in the garden
most of the time, playing games with the children and eating our
supper there, picnic style. Mrs Labowsky is coming to see me
tomorrow evening.

The last letter I had from Jean-Claude was written entirely in
French. At the beginning of the year he had sent me a book of
French cartoons called *Carrizey*. Inside he wrote: 'A une petite
chou avec mes souhaits de bonne année 1949, et un peu plus à
Ingrid.' He asked if I had read the book yet. He finished his
studies in June and is coming to England from August to October.
I wasn't very lucky with finding him a job: one was at a college
library but his Latin wasn't good enough; one was on a farm but
he didn't want that; and the other was at the Warneford Hospital,
for which he applied but received no reply. So he will stay in
London and come to visit me here. He had invited me to go
camping with him and a gang of friends somewhere in the South
of France, but I knew that was not for me. He signed himself
'Always your little French boy.' Isn't that sweet?

If you think I have forgotten Jonathan or am seriously

interested in anybody else, you are greatly mistaken.

11th July 1949

I noticed the wedding ring at once, and was appalled. Not because it reminded me that he was married but because I thought only men with moustaches and suede shoes wore wedding rings. And here was Ray wearing one. But let me start at the beginning.

Last night I dreamt of Ray. I dreamt of him because someone at the canteen told me that they met him and that he was coming to the shop to see me. I blushed furiously. The night before my 'affair' with Ray began I also dreamt of him. I dreamt that he was lifting me off a tree and kissing me. When I woke I felt ashamed of the dream, ashamed of dreaming about a physical relationship with a man with whom there was none. That was a year or more ago. Later, after lunch, after I had been given the news that Ray was in Oxford, I thought: "If he's here for two weeks I bet I'll meet him in the street." I was in town when this thought came to me. I turned a corner – and was face to face with Ray. And the first thing I saw was his wedding ring. He was wearing a short-sleeved white shirt and he looked quite unchanged. We stood where we had met, the sun beating down on us, and we talked. I don't remember what we talked about but it lasted for ages and I was getting hotter and hotter. Despite his familiar "don't-waste-your-time-on-me-I'm-already-spoken-for" manner which I detected again, something told me he remembered every moment of our illicit togetherness with pleasure. But maybe that was only wishful thinking on my part.

It seemed very strange being face to face again with the person who became a model for goodness and decency. I thought of the ancient prophets hearing God's voice and I felt as I imagine they did. I felt so right with him that I wondered if it had not been a mistake after all, all that constraint; perhaps it was wrong to go against one's instinct and listen to morals? Was he feeling that, too? No, no, nothing Ray did or will ever do is wrong, not even marrying Audrey. In years to come, when the time is ripe, perhaps we will meet again, and then he will say: "It is really you I loved, not Audrey. It has always been you." But it is not love that has made Ray so unique to me, although in last night's dream we did love each other. But that was a simple formula for something very complicated.

A postcard has come from Bill. He means business.

23rd July 1949

The heat continues. I've been on the river, punting with Gerda, and also with Mr Calé (we paddle). WB is back from his holiday and, as usual, found much to criticise in the work done – or not done – in his absence. I've had to have time off for visits to the dentist this week, which didn't please WB too much either. *Tant pis.* Today I went swimming at 'Dames Delight' with Chris and the children. It's the only way to keep cool! I'd like to have gone swimming on my half day too, but instead I did my voluntary work at the Radcliffe Hospital, taking library books round the wards.

I met Markus (yes, he spells his name with a K) last Saturday and we stopped and chatted in the street. I also met Joan Lee-Wilson and we cycled together. She said, "I'm looking for a flat, a bathing costume and a boyfriend." I laughed and said: "The first two shouldn't be too difficult. The boyfriend is a bit harder." She is 30 years old. If I am still looking for a boyfriend when I'm that age I shall give up all hope.

Sara invited me to 'Bleak House' for the weekend last week. Her mother was going away and Sara didn't want to be on her own. She lives with her mother and little 3-year-old brother, Trevor. She also has another brother and sister away at school. Her mother is separated from Sara's father. So I cycled out to Wheatley on Sunday morning and helped Sara prepare lunch, which threatened to be rather revolting. In the afternoon, we visited a very muddy farm belonging to friends of hers, and I took photographs of Sara and Trevor in the garden.

At some time in the evening I heard Sara yell in the kitchen and went to investigate. "There are weevils in the flour," she said in disgust, and began to fish them out.

"Oh Sara, you can't use that flour," I said.

"There isn't any other."

"Never mind. Throw it away."

Luckily I managed to persuade her, and shuddered to think what would have happened if I hadn't gone to the kitchen.

On Monday I'm going on the river with Mrs King and Peter and they're going to teach me to punt. I expect I shall fall in the water.

I did not see Ray again during his fortnight in Oxford. He didn't come to the shop. Either he doesn't care any more, or he still does. Both could be reasons, but I'm tired of trying to understand people. I should like to believe the latter, but the former seems the more credible. Whatever his reason was, it was a good one. I must keep Ray as a sort of comforting religion somewhere in the back of my mind. I may do things he would not approve of – I mean to lead the gayest and fullest life possible – but into it all Ray shall fit. He must always fit into everything I do and think.

30th July 1949

Gerda called on Wednesday but I was going babysitting at the Dauries' and couldn't see her for long. On my afternoon off I went to Chris and Ted's allotment with them and then we all cycled to Wolvercote and had drinks at a pub. Ted saw me home.

Yesterday was a very sad day: we had our last lunch at the Red Cross canteen. I wish they weren't closing. I have such happy memories of the place.

In the evening Bill telephoned me. He's back from France, early. Tonight we went out together – punting on the river, for drinks at the Victoria Arms and then for a long country walk. He found a haystack again, and I undressed a bit. It was just out of kindness to him, to see his pleasure and delight, much as one likes to give presents to people and enjoy their gratitude. He wants me to come to Cambridge the weekend after next. I said neither yes nor no, but I know I won't go. I'm not really in harmony with Bill. I don't know why he pursues me so persistently, when he must know that he means nothing to me any more.

Monday the 1st of August is a Bank Holiday, and do you know where I'm going for the weekend? To Reading – to WB and his wife . . ! Pity he's not an Arab for then I'd most certainly be his second wife. I'd rather like to live in a harem.

2nd August 1949

If Ray is my spiritual lifeline, then WB is my fleshly one. Aren't I lucky to know two such marvellous people? I like WB's wife, too; she's nice. She shows no signs of jealousy at all, but why should she? He will belong to her for the rest of their lives, I only borrow him occasionally. I believe I'm satisfied with this arrangement, although sometimes it is a little sad. The closing of their bedroom door, for instance, and myself shut out in a little guest-room alone, and waiting for him all night to come, that was sad. Of course, it was impossible that he should come but I am stupid, stupid. In the evening before we all went to bed, he came to my room and brought me a piece of chocolate. We kissed. I pretended I was his second wife in a harem. "Do you like me a little?" he whispered.

"Yes. Sometimes I even love you a little. Like now," I said. I don't know why I said it. Perhaps because he is the greatest friend I have, and doesn't one love one's friends? I can't really explain the psychology of our strange relationship and my even stranger emotions for him.

It was wonderful to see him in his own home where, like everyone else, he's at his best. His wife is a marvellous cook and we had a real Viennese lunch on Sunday, with Schnitzel and cucumber salad. We were all quite at ease with each other.

"Do you know the joke of the three shopkeepers and their slogans?" WB asked me, while we were eating delicious coffee cream cake.

"No. Tell me."

"Well, the first shopkeeper had an advertisement in his window which said 'We sell everything you need from the cradle to the grave!' The second shopkeeper saw this and thought: 'I can do better than that!' And he placed an advertisement in his shop window which read: 'We sell everything you need from the womb to the tomb.' Then the third shopkeeper came along and he was very impressed. 'But I can do even better,' he said to himself. Can you guess what his slogan was?"

"No. I can't," I replied. What could be earlier than the womb and later than the tomb?

" 'We sell everything you need from erection to resurrection'," proclaimed WB, his face beaming, and was rewarded with hearty laughter from his audience.

On Monday morning, while Hedi was in the kitchen, WB and I were alone in the drawing room. He took me in his arms and kissed me, and later I saw that he had had an ejaculation; there

337

p

was a wet mark on his trousers. Presently Hedi came to join us, wearing an apron. I was just wondering what delicious meal she was preparing for us when she said to WB, "What's that on your trousers?" It was a bad moment. He glanced at where she was pointing.

"Oh, I must have splashed them in the bathroom," he said.

I'm sure she believed him, and no more was said on the matter, but I felt decidedly guilty and it was the only event that marred the weekend.

In the afternoon we went for a walk in Sonning, which is a beauty spot. He walked between us, his arm through Hedi's on one side, mine on the other. I took his hand. I felt so in harmony with them, I couldn't help it. She saw, but it didn't matter. We all seemed to understand each other. Life could be so easy. Why wasn't it always like this? Why do we make it so difficult? How nice people can be.

But returning to Oxford on the train in the evening my sense of peace left me. I felt an ugly sort of pity for myself. All my relationships have to take place secretly, I thought, during a few snatched and hurried hours, when landladies are out, or in the open when the weather is fine. But no – I'm still young, it won't always be like this, some day surely the bedroom door will close behind me and the man who belongs to me alone, with whom I won't have to wait for landladies to be away or for fine weather. Won't that be nice? In the meantime I can pretend to be WB's second wife and hold his hand, as his first wife doesn't seem to object to that.

7th August 1949

Sara left Parkers' today. She doesn't really need to work and only does so when the fancy takes her, for something to do or for pocket money. Her next job will probably be something totally different, and she won't stick to it much longer then she did to Parkers'. I shall miss her.

I did the hospital library again on Thursday afternoon, with Miss Fry. I usually have my lunch at the hospital first.

It has been a dull weekend: Saturday evening I spent at Putz's and Sunday she spent with me. I'm afraid the engagement is going wrong. I doubt if they will marry. I am angry and disappointed. Does happiness never last long? He's a queer chap, her fiancé. I so wanted to see Putz happy and settled. Still, having been engaged once will have given her confidence and things should never be quite so bad again.

They're pretty bad for me at the moment. Today has been one of those days when I don't want to be alive, when I wish I had never been born. A lot of it has to do with WB. We had a row a few days ago – about work, of course – and I hated him. I had given him a story of mine to read, and he didn't even mention it. Usually he likes my writing and is helpful and kind about it. Once he had said, "I'm proud of you," after reading a novel I'd written. I always feel it is I who am in the wrong, I who am stupid and aggressive. He brings out the most amazing streaks in me. "Why do you always lose faith in me so quickly?" he had once asked me, and I had been stunned for a moment. It was so true. I can't hide anything from him. Whatever disguise I may take on, I can never cheat him.

Gerda has moved digs and I'm having supper with her on Tuesday. On Saturday Putz and I are going to Cobham and I'm meeting Jean-Claude in London . . .

17th August 1949

Bill writes: 'I am longing to see you, Ingrid. Can you get over to Cambridge the weekend after next? I've fixed up a room for you in my digs . . . I do hope you'll decide to come. Forget the times before . . . this time everything will be comme il faut – and besides, Cambridge is beautiful.' Before I could answer, I had a telegram from him. It said: 'Very worried. No reply. Do come.' Is he crazy? I wish he would leave me alone.

But never mind Bill – I've seen Jean-Claude again! There are not many people whom I've met again after one year and found so unchanged and as delightful as ever. I'm glad he didn't fade out of my life, glad that I have a little longer with him. He is charming, amusing and good company. We didn't have very long together – I just went to his hotel, and we had tea at Lyons before Putz and I caught our train from Waterloo out to Cobham – but he's coming to Oxford at the weekend. I can't wait.

In Cobham I spent Sunday sunbathing all day in the garden. Father, Betty and Trudl Dawson were here for tea. In the early evening Anni and Felix left for Belgium and Putz and I returned to London in my father's car, had dinner there, went to the News Theatre and returned to Oxford.

Last Wednesday I didn't go to work in the afternoon because I felt completely exhausted – emotionally. I had been on the verge of tears all the morning and I couldn't face WB another minute. Once at home I cried for a long time and went to bed and slept. For a few hours normality had been suspended and I didn't like it, but the next morning I felt cleansed. WB was so pleased to see me back, everything was forgotten.

On Tuesday Ted, Chris and I went pub crawling as it was such a fine evening. Yesterday Gerda had lunch with us at Connors'. Putz doesn't like her much; she thinks she is insincere.

Tomorrow is Beethoven night on the radio; and then it's Saturday and my little Jean-Claude is coming . . .

23rd August 1949

It was a perfect weekend with J-C. He is perfect company. With him there are no difficulties; he wouldn't recognise them if there were any. Life is a joke to him, and he makes me flippant too. I got a glimpse of marriage during that weekend, of a light-hearted, carefree relationship between two people who get on well together. I cooked the lunch while he lounged on my bed in the next room, smoking his pipe and reading. I brushed his clothes and fed him chocolates and he accepted everything with charming indifference. What is it that makes the French so good with women? For instance, while I was washing up he brought me a lighted cigarette and put it in my mouth, just as men do in films. One can be playful with him and make love passionately, and talk politics all in the same breath. Of course, there was no opportunity to sleep with him – he's staying at Chris and Ted's, but the weekend after next I'm going to London again and we shall stay in a hotel together.

We went to the Trout Inn on Saturday night and walked back a long way round through fields and didn't get home till 1.30am. On Sunday we went to Blenheim Palace in Woodstock and had tea at the Dorchester.

I positively long to go to bed with Jean-Claude and do hope that, this time, everything will be, as Bill says: 'Comme il faut'.

I wrote to Bill, incidentally, and declined his invitation. He wrote back immediately expressing deep regret. 'I suppose I'll never persuade you at a distance, dear Ingrid,' he wrote. 'I'll have to come to Oxford and take you. When is the Frenchman leaving?' He said too that he's more attracted than ever to me now that my figure has improved so much. Cheek!

I lent Jean-Claude an airtax shirt because it was so hot, and he wore it all day. Since then I've taken it out of my drawer every day to see if the smell of him is still on it.

26th August 1949

This is the week of weddings. My cousin Herta got married on Wednesday to a Czech doctor, and for their honeymoon they are going to Palestine to visit her parents – my aunt Grete and uncle Kurt. I have had an invitation to Monica's (Connie's sister) wedding in Falmouth, and guess who's getting married on Saturday the 3rd? Joan Lee-Wilson! Not long ago she told me she was looking for a boyfriend! I suppose the flat and the bathing costume don't matter any more now. Putz and I are invited to the wedding, which is in Sussex.

Putz is going on holiday this week. I said I would call on Mrs Wren, her landlady, and at the same time I'll go to Gerda's pottery which is opposite the Wrens' house in Plantation Road. Gerda promised to show me how to make a pot, which I'm sure is fascinating, but I have no desire to do it myself. Erna is in the Radcliffe hospital, where she's recovering from some illness. I shall visit her too.

We had sweetcorn for supper at Chris and Ted's yesterday. The last time I ate that was in Vienna. They ate it with butter. I've only ever eaten it with salt.

By this time tomorrow I shall be with Jean-Claude.

30th August 1949

Did I say Jean-Claude made me flippant? No longer. I'm serious now. I began being serious on the coach to London on Saturday. I left Oxford at 7pm, feeling very excited. But, as we got nearer and nearer to London and Jean-Claude, the old familiar feelings of apprehension and anxiety overcame me in anticipation of this

341

coming thing I had wanted for so long and imagined so often. If someone had given me a sweet and offered to take me to a Punch and Judy show I would have been the happiest girl on the coach, for I wanted nothing better than to be a little girl again. Then I wouldn't have to endure these adult pleasures.

It was dark when the coach reached London. I saw J-C at once, waiting for me, his hands in his pockets. He greeted me warmly, with his laughing face and eyes. "You are tired?" he said. "You mustn't be tonight, you know." I said nothing. I thought: 'I can't see this thing through. I'm not up to it, I'm not ready for these hungry, greedy men. I am really only the child I want to be.'

He took my hand. It sent shivers down my backbone. I closed my eyes and let him lead me through the dark. We went to a bar near the hotel for drinks. And there an extraordinary thing happened: sitting at a table by the window was the Greek boy we had met and played ping-pong with at Mrs Moore's last year! We recognised him at once. "Look, the Greek from Oxford!" cried Jean-Claude. Then the Greek saw us too, and got up. I noticed that he was as fat and greasy-looking as before, with the same penetrating look in his black eyes that seems to undress one. At another table, flirting with the waitress, sat another Greek, a friend it turned out. He came over and we all had drinks and talked and laughed a great deal. It was quite an orgy – thoroughly continental and slightly debauched. I felt happy in a reckless sort of way. The bar was badly lit, it was dark and hot, the customers looked slightly grubby and sensual, the waitresses were foreign and spoke with indefinable accents; and I was happy. I looked at Jean-Claude and I was proud to be with him. Our eyes met.

"Shall we go?" he said. It was still fairly early.

"Yes," I replied. The Greeks looked at each other and grinned. They knew. It was so obvious; I had my little case with me.

We arrived at the Osborne hotel. The first thing we did in the bedroom was to move the two beds together. Then we got into our night things and lay on the beds on our stomachs looking out of the window. I told him – and it took a great deal of courage – that I had never been successful with sex. "You will be successful with me. J'en suis sure," he said, with the confidence of his gender and his nationality. He looked delightful in pyjamas. I remembered a sweet and sleepless night with Jonathan but it might have happened centuries ago. I knew that the moment J-C

342

touched me a delicious sensation of complete submission would sweep over me. I knew he had had many women but it didn't matter. That night I was his. And suddenly I wasn't and didn't want to be a little girl any more. I was fully grown-up and I lay, once again sleepless throughout most of the night, next to my charming French lover, the parts of my body touching his the only bits I was conscious of. This is a situation from which I do not want my mother and father to come and take me away, I thought. It must be because I had finally ceased to be a child.

Unlike Jonathan, who was lazy and impatient (but I loved him), Jean-Claude woke often and made love meticulously. After the first time he whispered passionately, "Oh chérie, chérie, I am so happy, my darling!" I love making men happy. At three o'clock I produced pears and chocolate and cigarettes and we munched and smoked and talked about the French government, I've forgotten why.

"So, am I the victor?" he asked, laughing, as he yawned and stretched in the morning.

"You are the victor," I said, not quite truthfully, for it had still hurt. It was a beautiful morning. The sun shone into the room and it felt warm and a scent of high summer wafted in through the window. We had breakfast with another French fellow and he and J-C told each other dirty jokes which J-C afterwards translated for me. I didn't think they were particularly funny.

We went to Windsor for the day and saw Eton College and the castle which I told J-C is the ancient residence of English sovereigns and that the flag is flown when they are at home. We couldn't see one. Afterwards we sat on a bench in a little park in the hot sunshine and he didn't touch me. I looked at him. His eyes were reaching out in all directions but not in mine. Once you have gone through the forbidden door men change their masks. They put on a different disguise. There is no way back through that door. I was overcome by a sadness which was in complete contrast to his careless and flippant mood. I felt lonely and melancholy, insecure and cheap. For me, going through that door had meant becoming totally involved with a person who now no longer seemed to exist.

We returned to London. Walking along Regent Street we classified cars and I tried to be as flippant as he was. He became quite devilish, and made me look through girls' dresses to see

343

what knickers they wore. As WB says, if a woman likes a man he can get away with anything. We went to Studio One and then back to the hotel where we said goodbye. I was angry because the other French fellow was there again. So had it all meant nothing at all to Jean-Claude, our night together? I remembered his sweet and loving words as we lay together. But what a man does in the night belongs to the night, in the morning you don't talk about it. Now, though certainly not before, he means more to me than I do to him; which is not entirely unsatisfactory as it is more exciting than the other way round. What a masochist I am! I want more and more of him now, but for him it is probably the end.

My sister said I am well on the way to the whorehouse! But she is wrong. With each step I make in the wrong direction Raymond's world beckons brighter. I know quite well which way I should go.

7th September 1949

Last Saturday Putz and I went with the Jacobus family to attend Joan's wedding at Oxstead in Sussex. A car fetched us from the station in style and we were driven to the little village church where Joan's father is the vicar and the marriage was to take place. When we were introduced to Joan's mother she took our hands – Putz's and mine – and said, "I've heard so much about you, and how much you have both gone through. I hope with all my heart that you will both soon find happiness, too." I was deeply moved, and Putz said afterwards that she was, too.

Miss Wulf is on holiday for two weeks. I shall have to cook my own Sunday lunches, as she usually cooks for both of us. I visited Erna in hospital again today, with Putz. Bruno was there too. Erna fled from the Nazis with him although she is not Jewish, and I think they love each other very deeply.

St Giles Fair was here again on Monday and Tuesday. I went with WB in our lunch hour. We talked of the Wurschtlprater in Vienna to which my father took us every year on Whit Sunday. It was the highlight of the year for me and imbued me with an eternal love of fairs.

"You must go and see *The Third Man*," said WB. "It takes place in Vienna and there's a scene in it in the Wurschtlprater." That will probably make me cry, I thought. Fairs always make me feel sentimental.

We made a strange bargain, WB and I: If I kissed his p . . . s until he ejaculated, he would give me £1! A whole £1! Half my rent almost. Twenty evenings of tedious babysitting. How could I refuse?

On Tuesday in the lunch hour, therefore, as soon as the shop was closed and everyone had gone, we went to the rear office where old Mr Gronner sits and where there is a large table for extra-large and costly art books. WB let the blinds down which wasn't odd as the day was sunny, and so nobody could see us through the shop window. He cleared a few books off the table and lay down on it. In doing so, his foot knocked one of the art books onto the floor. It was a very expensive Braque and will probably have to be remaindered now. However, everything else went off as planned and when the shop opened its doors again I felt a bit sick but was immeasurably richer.

The experience didn't do much to cheer me up. Since my night with Jean-Claude, I have felt flat and sad. Can it really be that once a man has slept with a woman, there is nothing more? Even with nice men like J-C? I'm hurt and miserable. He had been so happy with me. Has he forgotten? Or does a Frenchman take this for granted, like a good meal. Yesterday I had a letter from him which did not refer at all to anything that had happened between us. It was all about some money I had sent him in exchange for French francs. It ended: 'This weekend I am unhappily not free. Hoping to see you before I return to France . . .' (I have put it into proper English, but couldn't alter the meaning.)

I want so much from men to whom I have been so close. So much warmth, so many words. This brutal indifference scares me, there is no way I can tackle it. Already I am taken for granted in J-C's life. Other women are admired in my presence and I haven't the privilege of being his wife or even his mistress; like the pathetic Sartre heroine, Marcelle, who is made pregnant by her lover and then immediately deserted. It is as if I were not allowed to love. For me our union was a whole chapter in my life, for him, who knows, probably only a paragraph, a sentence, a word, a punctuation mark . . .

He used to call me 'St Thomas' because, like St Thomas Aquinas, the disbeliever, I often didn't believe things he told me, such as some of his strange and colourful stories of the South of

345

France. But I believed in his sincerity. Maybe each relationship has its preordained end, and we have reached ours. Then there is nothing more. But, oh God, why was it so short, so fleeting? I have always been content with him. Now, although my heart cries out for one more night with him, just one more – no, two, three, a hundred – I must turn a deaf ear to it and face the end of my affair with lovely, laughing Jean-Claude, the sooner the better. Once I even thought I should like a child by him to bind myself to him, or perhaps to make my suffering complete, but of course that would be insane.

I know now that I can never go to bed with WB again because with him I always dither and have all these feelings of guilt as if I were committing incest; I know now there must be no dithering and no doubt. I must want it without wavering, fully and completely as I did with Jean-Claude and Jonathan, when reason stopped and I went unquestioningly to them. WB is a very good friend but he cannot serve me as a lover any longer.

It is a sad and upside-down world. Nothing makes sense. Ray always put me right when I complained to him that nothing made sense, but I have forgotten his formula in the hurly-burly of all that has been happening to me since. I must never let J-C know that our affair meant any more to me than it did to him. He must believe that for me too, it was only a good meal which, after it is digested, is forgotten.

9th September 1949

I spent last night at the Jacobuses. It was a pleasant evening. I stayed quite late and Markus took me home. We talked Psychology most of the time, as we had done at his house. He asked me if I liked children and I said yes, and told him about taking little Micky Hayes to St Giles Fair on Tuesday. He has two children: Anthony is 8 and Mary 6. When we had travelled back on the train after Joan's wedding, Putz and the Jacobuses and I, he had sat next to me and I had been fascinated by his conversation which seemed so worldly and learned to me, but I was surprised when he asked me if I'd like to have dinner with him one day. "That would be nice," I said, and changed the subject. Now, as we approached my house, he said:

"Can I come to see you on Saturday evening?"

"Well . . ." I was trying hard to think of some excuse.

"You left that book at my house," he said. "I'll bring it on Saturday. All right?"

"All right." I wanted to say, bring Diana too, but I didn't. If he wants to play a little game, I'll join him, just for the fun of it. The only problem is, what role am I going to have in it? I remember now that, on the train back from Joan's wedding, he'd said:

"A fascinating young lady like you will soon follow Joan's example," but I took it to be a harmless bit of flattery. Was I wrong?

12th September 1949

The awful thing was that I didn't want to resist, all the guilty feelings in the world did not make me wish to resist. I was thrown into a sweet and sluttish trance from which I woke finally, to find that I was carried far beyond my bounds and was faced with an unmanageable situation.

What is there for me to say? I feel helpless. I shall go away. I shall go away from everyone and everything, work out my life carefully and start again. I am exhausted, everything is suddenly too much for me, too many emotional entanglements have destroyed my peace. I want to get away from myself. I'm so fed up with myself I never want to see myself again.

Markus has been my lover, and he loves me. Perhaps that is true, perhaps not. He says he loves me.

It was Saturday evening. He came punctually and brought the book. We talked psychology again, and he read bits from the book out loud. Sitting opposite each other in the kitchen over supper, we began to gaze at each other. Suddenly he said, "You are beautiful. But of course you know that." He always paid a lot of attention to me, right from the beginning, and though I was flattered, I don't think I encouraged him. But here we were alone together in my kitchen and I could no longer pretend I didn't notice. He asked me about my life, my love life, he wanted to know everything about me. After supper, back in my room, he took me in his arms and kissed me, very gently. And that was when I began being unable to resist.

Afterwards we went for a walk until midnight. "I have this curious feeling," said Markus, holding me very close to him as we walked in the moonlight, "that you are mine, utterly mine. In the way Mary is mine. I love you. I had no idea you could do this to me, evoke these wonderful feelings . . . You have made me so happy . . ."

I see two possibilities ahead: either it will be just another very brief affair and it will end hopelessly, or I shall fall passionately in love with him and that will be equally hopeless. And it will be my fault. So you see why I despise myself so much.

Perhaps my inner goodness will only be released by true love, like the girl trapped in a swan's body in Swan Lake?

The next day, Sunday, we cycled to Boars Hill, had tea at a hotel, then lay for hours somewhere high up, in the grass surrounded by trees. He was my lover here. "Tell me that you love me," he commanded, but I evaded him. I don't know if I love him – yet. It was quite dark when we got up and cycled back to Oxford.

We had dinner at the Taj Mahal, whose manager we both know. He seemed a bit surprised to see us together but looked as if he was accustomed to keeping secrets. There was a candle on each table, the rest of the room was in darkness, and it was very romantic. Markus said, "Now you belong to me. You must give up everyone else – the Frenchman, everyone. There must only be me now, as there is only you with me." As if he guessed what was in my mind he went on: "You and Diana have nothing to do with each other. My love for you doesn't interfere with anything." I thought not so much of Diana but of his children at home, waiting for him, wondering why he's not there, wanting him to play with them. I couldn't rid myself of the image of his children waiting for him at home.

I promised Markus to say nothing of our affair even to Lieselotte, but I know I shall not be able to keep that promise. I have already lied to her about this weekend, and the weight of this lie, together with my guilt, is a burden I find too big to bear.

He had asked me about other boyfriends and I told him that I could never have a casual boyfriend – each one is engraved in my heart and mind forever, and that, while the relationship lasts I am totally dedicated and probably much too deeply involved. He replied, "That is why you will never be soiled." I loved him for that.

After dinner we went for a walk in the moonlight again until

348

one o'clock in the morning. I was coming under his spell. He already owned my body, soon he would own my soul, too.

I am frightened – yes, frightened; of what will happen to us, of his love, of my own great potential love for him, of how it will all end.

16th September 1949

Yesterday we had our staff outing to Bognor Regis. As usual we went by coach, Mr Calé told me jokes on the way, I sat on the beach and talked to June, Mr Townsend took some of us out to tea at the beach café and the weather was grey. On the way home we stopped at a pub for drinks. It was a change from going to work, anyway.

Last Tuesday I spent the evening at Gerda's and was introduced to somebody called Peter there, one of her boyfriends, I supposed. Afterwards I went to the pottery with her. Putz and I usually have lunch at Connors' now, often with the Kings and occasionally with Putz's friend Catherine. I still miss the Red Cross canteen – the food, the people, the nice atmosphere, everything. The other day I met Mrs Scott at the Connors'. She doesn't often come to Chris and Ted's now but I didn't ask her why.

I had a letter from Jean-Claude saying he's returning to France on the 15th, partly for financial, partly for family, reasons. How strange! Quite suddenly and very conveniently I am rid of two lovers: Jean-Claude and WB. Not that there has been anything much between WB and myself lately. We are continually quarrelling and haven't spoken for a week. He knows me too well, that's the trouble. So the path is clear for Markus. Everything has been happening too quickly: the quarrels with WB, the departure of J-C – and now Markus. I feel as if I have been on a very fast roundabout which halted abruptly and left me stupefied and dazed. (Of course I never replied to Bill again.)

Markus was here this evening and we listened to Beethoven's *9th* on the wireless. I cannot tell you how much I long to see him again. There is only Markus now, just as he wants it to be. We shall have a beautiful and sad love affair, but I'm not quite sure how it will leave us.

23rd September 1949

Sara fetched me from the shop yesterday. She said, "I don't know how you can work with that Mr Brown. I couldn't stand him." (WB)

"Oh, I don't know," I said. "He's not so bad." I was glad she said that, and yet I had to defend him. We are having lunch together on Saturday.

Today, after work, I had tea at Putz's and then we went to a stamp auction in Holywell for Uncle Felix (who's a philatelist). He had commissioned us to bid for some stamps he wanted, but we didn't get them as somebody else made a higher bid. Catherine came too. It was interesting.

Markus said, "Tell me that you love me. Quickly, quickly."

I said, "I love you when I'm with you. It's when I'm not with you that I'm uncertain."

"Why?" he demanded. Because I don't quite trust us, I thought.

"I don't know," I said.

Markus. Who is Markus? A strange and enigmatic man, brilliant, infinitely wise. He must not be questioned. He must be accepted, no questions asked. He's of Polish origin but was born in Japan – or was it China? He has joined the procession of people weaving their way in and out of my heart but he is unique because of his pleas for my love, and his love for me.

I was wondering if I'm ruining my life, if I've become morally unhealthy. A week ago I could have given Markus up. Now it is too late. He is in my life. I wish I could laugh about it, but even that I can't do any more.

We make plans to go abroad together. We talk of Paris and of many days and nights with each other.

But I want to settle down, marry, have children. Markus will never do that for me. Being with him is wonderful but it has no future. Besides, I don't understand him. I shall live through our affair in a hazy and youthful trance, staving off love as long as I can. When I was 8 or 9 years old I had an intense affinity with the trumpet player who played in the dance band on Saturday nights at the Hotel Kuchner in Waldegg, where we spent our summer holidays. That the relationship was one-sided didn't trouble me. I didn't want to dance with the grown-ups as the other children did.

I spent Saturday nights standing by my idol and watching him play his trumpet. One day he gave me an apple, and that was happiness: Why am I remembering that now? It was so innocent.

I've had a great and terrible row with WB. He criticised my attitude to work, my failure to complete all the tasks he sets me daily, my occasional late arrivals at the shop after lunch, and what he calls my outbursts of bad temper. I shall leave the job. I need never see him again. I can escape from everything with which I can't cope – I am free. My struggles can be reduced. I don't need WB any longer. I need Markus now. He must give me all he has. In return I shall tame my feelings for him. I shall not let them become wild, nor allow them to be my master.

I shall be their master.

25th September 1949 – Sunday

I have just returned from a cycle ride to Woodstock with Markus – and his little son, Anthony.

I didn't know he was bringing his son. It was a curious situation. I was again reminded of my father once telling me that, when Putz and I were small, there was a woman who loved him. He used to take us for walks on Sunday mornings and she would stand at a pre-arranged place and watch us go by. "Because," my father said, "she loved everything that was mine, everything that I loved." Oh no, that can't be true. I don't believe it. That isn't human nature. If my father believed her he must have been very naïve. Now that I am faced with a similar situation I know that one's lover's children are a thorn in the eye, a painful reminder of an unshared life. I don't want Markus's children to exist, I don't want to hear anything about them. I am jealous of them and I don't like to think of Markus as a father. When I am with him I pretend that there are no children, but he sometimes talks of them. A father has no business to be a lover.

Later: After Markus had taken his son home he returned to me. We went for a walk. Then he came to my flat. Even as we made love I could see Anthony's face and imagined him at home in bed, waiting for his father to get back. I could hear Markus again calling him during our afternoon excursion, his voice echoing across the fields: "ANTHONY!" – pronouncing the name as if it began with a 'U'. How isolated and excluded one is when a father calls to his son. The little boy didn't take much notice of me. Did he sense something unsavoury? As for Markus – he was a stranger to me that afternoon. Now and then our eyes met, once or twice he whispered something to me.

But they were the look and words of a stranger.

But when evening came, and the father once again became the lover . . . I forgot everything . . .

9th October 1949

I spent Monday evening at the Howards, the German, Jewish couple who used to live next door to the Beschorners. They live in Woodstock Road now. She's a very good cook and makes continental delicacies, which is the main reason I like going there.

On Tuesday Putz and I went to the Scala Cinema to see *Kings*

Row with Ronald Reagan. It's one of those films that isn't really good, wasn't my type, but somehow you can't forget. There's one scene especially, when Reagan wakes up after an operation, legless, gropes down the blanket and, finding nothing, screams: "Where's the rest of me?" It haunts me. Putz, as usual, was fairly unimpressed.

I did a pastel drawing of Mr Calé when he was at my flat for supper on Wednesday evening and he liked it, but I didn't. He wasn't easy to draw.

Peter Beschorner is now a boarder at the Dragon School and today

I fetched him and brought him home for tea. Now 9 years old he's still the same nice little boy with brown curly hair and blue eyes like Joan's. Putz joined us later. Did I tell you that her engagement is definitely broken? She has returned the ring. I am devastated, even though I didn't really feel he was right for her. She does not approve of my relationship with Markus, incidentally; this evening they were both here, as Markus called unexpectedly. Yesterday he and I went to the pictures, to the Randolph Hotel for drinks and to the Taj Mahal for dinner again where the manager was very welcoming and his look said: "Don't worry, your secret is safe with me." We had a lift home in a car. It was raining. Very few people know about Markus and me – not even Chris and Ted. If I don't want people to know something I simply don't talk about it. As my friends are mostly in separate compartments they don't overlap.

It is strange, isn't it, that, at the age of 22 I have many of the things I ardently desired as an immature schoolgirl – lovers, even married ones, independence, a semi-bohemian lifestyle – and yet I'm not happy. I was right in desiring these things, I could have had no conception of how right I was, how worth having they are, but obviously happiness does not lie here. But can I have made such a mess of my life, if I've obtained so much of what I once wanted, I wonder?

It occurred to me in bed this morning, Sunday, that all at once I seem to lead a curiously detached existence, as if I were an idle spectator of my antics. I don't want to get involved. I want to maintain an indifference. It is my protective armour. If I didn't always only think about my own problems I might be able to help other people who have similar emotional struggles to which in theory I imagine I know all the answers. Above all, I might be able to help Lieselotte. If only I could!

Keeping a diary makes you self-centred. But through knowing yourself you get to know the world. I think I read that somewhere.

Next Thursday Markus is taking me to the OXFORD UNION Opening Debate. He's a member. The motion is: 'That in the opinion of this House, socialism is undermining the energies and liberties of our people,' to be opposed by Uwe Kitzinger, who often comes into Parkers' Foreign Department.

Ten years ago, when Markus and his wife Diana were on a long and luxurious honeymoon in the French alps, in Italy, in Switzerland, I was a wretched and bewildered refugee child on my way to England. Little did I know then that one day our paths would cross. How fortuitous life is! As if it mattered; as if anything mattered. I am Markus's mistress. So what? As if that were of any importance. Sirius is a star, and the earth rotates around the sun in a universe in which time is measured in light years, and what significance could human events possibly have in this unimaginable vastness? When I was very little I once saw workmen dig a hole in some Viennese Street. I looked down this hole and it was black, totally black, with no end to it. But it must end somewhere, I thought. Later, when I learned the word eternity, it looked like this hole. On the many nights of my childhood that I woke up, frightened after some nightmare perhaps, I thought of the hole and of eternity and the universe, beside which all else dwindled into nothingness.

But daily life is all around you, and who can think of the universe when one is hungry or a lover has deserted one or one's mother has died?

I suppose it is more common than I realised, men who have been married for years and years having love affairs with other women without the slightest intention of getting a divorce, and continuing to love their wives at the same time. When I am with Markus he always seems to be incapable of taking care of himself, and everything is left to me. He is even less practical than I. Perhaps he needs two wives. The other evening I was at his house. Diana was there. I like her very much. If she was the odd one out it was only because she is English and Markus and I are not, but it made her superior. In this triangle the inferior one is me. How much does she know? However much it is, it can make little difference, it can never shake their married lives or the stability of their home with their children.

I see Markus two or three times a week and I always look forward to it. Not that we have accomplished anything much physically, and I'm often difficult with him, but he's not the vigorous lover Jean-Claude was and perhaps he needs other things from me, too. When we are together I like to imagine that he has no other life.

28th October 1949

I introduced Markus to Miss Wulf last Thursday, and on Sunday
he had lunch with us. He stayed for the rest of the day. It was
raining and we didn't go out. Although he made himself very
pleasant to Miss Wulf I don't think she cared for him.

Yesterday, after doing the hospital library, I had tea with Mr
Calé at his digs – it was his birthday. Afterwards we went to the
pictures and then for drinks at the Lamb and Flag. I still don't
know how old he is. He's as ageless as he is sexless.

On Monday I saw *The Glass Menagerie* at the Playhouse with
several members of Parkers' staff, among them Mr Calé, Miss
Turner and Eileen. I felt a great sympathy for the heroine and
wished Putz had been sitting next to me instead of Miss Turner,
so that I could whisper comments to her. On the way home Mr
Calé, who is from Berlin, talked about the Berlin blockade and
how Britain and America foiled the Russian attempt to starve the
Berliners by dropping supplies from the air. It was a far cry from
the plight of the Tennessee Williams characters, on which my
mind was still dwelling.

I haven't seen Markus for days. He was supposed to come on
Wednesday but didn't turn up. Ever since I've known him I've
expected him to do some mad or unaccountable thing. I once told
him that I thought of him as brittle, as if he would crumble if
handled too hard. I said that I sometimes thought if only I would
try a bit harder I would catch him out. I don't quite know at what
I would be catching him out, but the fact is I have always had a
visceral mistrust of him – there is something about his character
which is unsound. Perhaps the affair is over. I don't care.

I never loved him, you know that, of course. Maybe I have
never really loved anybody, except long, long ago when I was still
almost a child. I have often wondered whether I shall ever again
feel as strongly about anyone as I did about Otto Seifert or Roy
Lovell because I could love these two as one can love God,
without having one's love pulled out of shape, and without
rejection. But then I was innocent and infantile and such simple
love could not go on forever.

1st November 1949

Markus has been ill, and of course there was no means of letting me know. Hole and corner affairs have many drawbacks. Yesterday evening, after the longest interval since our affair began, I had first the unhappiest and then the happiest moments I have ever had with him.

He arrived in a peculiar mood – worried, restless, more neurotic than usual; I was angry and felt aggressive towards him. While he carried on absurd monologues I tried to come to terms with myself. I told myself that I can give Markus up at any time I choose. But I know now that it would not be easy at all, that he means a lot . . .

At ten o'clock we suddenly found ourselves on my bed. Nothing that had gone on before had led me to expect this. It was going to be the first time we had not had intercourse in my flat. But I had been wrong.

It was quite different from all the other times. To begin with, the moment he touched me a submissive desire swept over me, completely in contrast with my previous aggressive feelings. It erupted in elation, which was mutual and we were both happy and hopeful for the future within its limited scope.

But Diana suspects something, Markus said. I asked no questions. First, because I was still too happy and relaxed; second because I don't want to know; and third because it is his problem, not mine. I wish I could catch the moments during which I like Markus best and always hold them before me. I wish he wouldn't change so much. When he is unpleasant I make plans to end the affair, but I know now that I'm really making plans to perfect our relationship. I don't want to end it at all – yet.

5th November 1949

We had a bonfire and fireworks in Chris and Ted's garden this evening and the children were very excited.

I meant it when I wrote that I would look for another job and duly applied for a post at the Occupation Centre which is a school for mentally deficient children, as this is something that has long interested me. On Wednesday I had the morning off in order to go for my appointment. I was shown round the school by the

356

headmistress, and she must have noticed my distress at seeing children in their teens learning colours, many behaving oddly, making animal noises and playing with toys suitable for toddlers. I did not get the job (and I didn't want it) but I got a lift back by car and I missed a morning's work.

On Thursday I again fetched little Peter from the Dragon School, and this time I took him out to tea at Fullers' where he ate a lot of chocolate cake. Afterwards we went to Chris and Ted's. In the evening Markus took me to Somerville College for a meeting of the Psychic Society. Psychic phenomena are of great interest to him.

Next Thursday evening, Putz and I are invited for supper at Bruno and Erna's – a rare treat, as Erna doesn't much like cooking and usually only invites people for coffee and cigarettes. But I bet she can cook well, and just can't be bothered.

10th November 1949

The most extraordinary things happen to me!

On Tuesday I was at a small party given by Gerda. I was first to arrive and found her sorting some jumpers in a drawer which she said had not been washed for a year. That done, or half done, I helped her get a few things ready for the party.

Among the guests there was a German mathematician called Victor Gugenheim. He was small, pale, thin and puny with dark blond curly hair. Gerda had told me some time ago that she knew a brilliant mathematician from Magdalen College, 26 years old, and I assumed this was he. I didn't take any notice of him as he was totally uninteresting. I always know in an instant whether I like somebody or not, and have never yet been wrong – so imagine my amazement when I found him staring at me, and presently coming over to where I was sitting and squatting down on the floor at my feet. His eyes did not leave my face the whole evening. At first I thought it was some kind of a joke. I felt extremely uncomfortable, and decided to leave early. When I got up Victor got up also, so I changed my mind. We all talked about this and that and suddenly it was 12.30 and now it was really time to go home.

"Where do you live?" Victor asked me.

I told him.

"I'll take you home," he said.

What could I do? As soon as we were out in the street he took me in his arms and whispered, "I adore you!"

"But you don't know me!" I cried.

"I adore you, I adore you," he repeated.

I was quite bewildered. All the way home he pleaded with me to let him see me again. I talked about other things but he would not be diverted and returned again and again to the same topic. My heart is with Markus but even if it weren't I could never find a place for Victor in it. In the end, however, I gave in, and agreed to see him on Saturday. People who like me make me think better about myself, and then I'm indebted to them and can't be unkind; and then they think I like them. And I am trapped.

Gerda told me that Jonathan was in Oxford on Sunday.

He didn't come to see me. WB is my greatest friend, my heart is with Markus because he needs me and I need him, but for Jonathan I wanted to lay down my life. For a brief, an all too brief spell, because that flower was not allowed to open, he was the wind in my hair, the sunlight on my face, the music in my ears, my heartbeat, my everything. But he didn't want me. Now, with Victor, the situation seems to be reversed. Poor Victor. Poor me.

In half an hour I shall be with Markus and that is what matters now. There has been trouble with Diana but I don't care. For the time being Markus is mine, and he must be mine for as long as I need him.

14th November 1949

Joan Beschorner was in Oxford for the weekend. We hadn't seen each other since Paris. She stayed with Chris and Ted. On Sunday she and Peter and Putz had tea with me. In the evening Putz and I went to the Film Society. The obvious rift between Joan and me interfered with my enjoyment of the film.

As for Saturday – I have never behaved so stupidly in all my life with any man. But then, no man has ever been quite so stupid with me. It's about that silly and quite unattractive Victor. He says he worships me. He behaves like a suffering poet. No girl would behave like this. First he took me out to tea at Kemp's. Here he had himself reasonably under control. I was foolish enough to let him show me his digs in Hernes Road. At first we talked about

E.M. Forster's novel which was lying on his desk called *Where Angels Fear to Tread*. I had read this book a long time ago and had forgotten about it and I was delighted to come across it again. My pleasure was brief, however. As soon as I sat down on the sofa he tried to eat me. Being touched by a man who doesn't attract me is one of the worst things I know. I can't stand it. When I wanted to go home he suggested having supper at the Indian Restaurant. I gave in. At least I was protected from his pawing in a public place. No doubt the manager's look would again say, "Your secret is safe with me," for of course he would notice that I was with someone else.

When I got home I wrote Victor a note saying it would be best if we didn't see each other any more as there was no point in it as far as I was concerned. Before the note reached him he had called on me again. I must have been horrible – I suppose WB would have called it one of my shocking outbursts of bad temper – for I left him miserable and almost in tears. Oh God, I couldn't help it! I was disgusted. I couldn't bear him to touch me. And I won't tolerate it. I'm attractive to men (it seems), I don't have to put up with the twopenny love of weedy and inexperienced schoolboys, however sincere they may be.

Besides, there is only Markus now. I count the days till I see him again. One day it will be the last day; one day he will say, "Diana is angry. I must give you up. I can never see you again." But there's still time.

There's lots wrong with Markus, but he is irresistible. He has a curious power over me. And I shall always remember him as the man who taught me to enjoy sex.

19th November 1949

Putz and I had intended to go to Cobham this weekend but dense fog prevented it. We had lunch with Joan (Holden) and her new husband Hyla today, and also in my lunch hour I met my one time friend Ann Norton; we had a long gossip. Later in the day Gerda and her friend Alastair came to the shop. She bought an Art book, to WB's delight, and we made an arrangement for Tuesday evening.

Mr Calé, it appears, has, like me, for some time known the Howards, and we are both invited there next Wednesday evening, for coffee and cakes. A quite different invitation has come from unexpected quarters:

My father has invited Putz and me to go to Paris with him and Betty over Christmas. What an honour. We are going – provided we can get the extra time off from work. I hate asking for time off and shall have to brace myself to do it, and risk upsetting WB even more.

Chris told me that Joan Beschorner behaved very strangely while she was staying with them. For instance, she became thirsty in the night and announced at breakfast time that she had to drink the water out of her hot water bottle. When asked why she didn't get a glass of water from the kitchen or bathroom, she replied that she didn't wish to disturb the household. She also said some nasty things about me, which annoyed me quite a lot. I wrote and complained to her.

Do you remember when I thought my affair with Markus might be over, and that I didn't care? It's odd, but I think true, that only then did the affair really begin. Now I need him more than he needs me. There was that extraordinary afternoon last Thursday. I had been longing for him all week. On Thursday morning he telephoned to ask me if I'd like to go to the pictures. He is like that – always changing his mind in the last moment, always doing erratic things. I wanted to be alone with him in my flat, but I agreed. So we went to the cinema, and afterwards to a café. The café was empty. There were only the two of us sitting in a corner at a table for two in a large and deserted room. I told him about my meeting with Victor and his pursuit of me. I said, "But you know, of course, don't you, Markus, that there is only you now? I'm not interested in anyone else."

He put his hand on mine and looked into my eyes. Did I tell you that he is slightly bald and reminds me a bit of Charles Boyer and is wildly attractive in a continental sort of way?

"Darling," he said quietly. "Sweetheart. Darling."

I was lost in his words, absorbed by his voluptuous voice.

"It is unkind of you to have made me feel like this, Markus," I said sadly.

"But I am selfish enough to be happy," he replied.

The next day he made love to me more beautifully than ever. There is a lot to learn about sex. I still have much to learn.

Of course, I'm not fooled. I can see through the situation

perfectly. After eleven years of marriage a man needs a mistress. When Markus needed one I happened to be there. But then I needed the love and affection of a man, so all is well – or is it? Diana doesn't like it, for a start. His children probably miss him greatly during all those hours he is with me. But that is his problem. He is taking me to his College, Christ Church, on Friday.

I know all Markus's faults and yet I want to be with him every available moment of our lives. The thought of any other man touching me makes me shudder.

23rd November 1949

I have had a reply to my letter from Joan. She writes: 'It is true that I said some things about you to Chris but you'll make allowances for decorations, won't you?' It didn't do much to reconcile me to her.

That sentence I wrote in my last entry: 'The thought of any other man touching me makes me shudder,' was a bit rash. I should have said 'of most other men'. As you know, I'm still friendly with Gerda. It is her doing, our friendship. When Jonathan faded out of my life I wanted to finish with Gerda, too. I didn't want to be reminded of him. But she didn't oblige, frequently ringing or calling at the shop. The other day she said, "I mustn't forget Jonathan's birthday next week," and I remembered with a stab of pain that he had told me that his birthday was in November, and my pleasure at hearing this because according to the horoscope my French landlady had read to me, people born in March should marry people born in November. I could still weep over Jonathan. I remember particularly my first impression of him: he was wearing a blue suit and a red tie and we talked among other things of communism and bird-watching. I have often tried to finish the story. I give it various endings, each one as unlikely as the other, but always including a plea to give me another chance to prove that I'm not a frightened, frigid virgin any more. Sometimes it ends with my marrying him. But the Jonathan I knew is a phantom and perhaps it is better for him to remain one and that I should abandon my hope of meeting him again. It will be my unfinished symphony. Who knows what the *Unfinished Symphony* would be like if Schubert had finished it?

q

A few nights ago, I was violently sick and had diarrhoea and returned to bed shivering and shaking. In the morning I was all right again and went to work as usual. On Monday evening Chris came for supper, the following evening Mr Calé and I were at Howards' again eating cakes and whipped cream, and on Wednesday Bruno, Erna and Putz came for coffee. Yesterday Markus was here – and brought me a lot of typing, as he had done the previous Saturday. It is for his Psychology Group. Then, last night, I was again sick, had diarrhoea and felt quite feverish. I went to see Dr Brown who diagnosed gastric flu and ordered me to bed. So here I am, feeling very ill. Worst of all, the Paris holiday which was due to start on Friday had to be cancelled. Parkers' didn't much want me to go and probably now think I'm malingering. I feel too unwell to write any more.

5th December 1949

Still in bed. I have a high temperature and can't eat. Miss Wulf is looking after me. At the moment I feel a bit better.

Last Thursday, when Markus was here from 4.30 till 11pm and we talked business and did typing the whole of that time, we had a row. It was in connection with this wretched work. He is absolutely making use of me, and I resented it. With his questionable character he can't afford to behave like that. Last night, while Putz was with me and I was ill in bed, he came again, an hour and a half later than arranged, with more typing for me. Finding me ill, he pretended to be very concerned about me but wasn't particularly nice. I searched in vain for some signs of authenticity in him, I tried to sort out the genuine things he said from an unaccountable number that are false and mean nothing, and was left with very little. In Putz's presence, however, this was perhaps a bit unfair. Just before he left he took my hand and patted me and gave me a look and a smile which brought a lump to my throat. I wanted to say: 'Thank you, darling, for not letting me down.' Stupid of me. No one likes Markus and I always defend and try to protect him. Putz went to the kitchen and Markus quickly whispered to me that I mustn't mind about not going to Paris, one of these days we would go together, he and I.

"If one could only believe a word you said, Markus," I replied, and laughed, ill as I felt.

10th December 1949

Markus wrote me a letter. 'My dearest Ingrid,' it began, 'I am terribly sorry you are ill. The "German hen" clucking around you as if you were an egg she was hatching must be quite an experience. She told me not to come to see you! Just the same I will come tomorrow. I could kick myself for being so difficult on Thursday when you were probably feeling sick like hell! Sorry . . ."

And he did come. So did Putz, Mrs Pinhorn, Chris and Ted, WB, Erna, Mr Calé and even Victor. All with presents – flowers, fruit, drinks, calvesfoot jelly, books, magazines. The doctor has been twice too. Mr Calé read to me from *Klein Erna* which made me laugh so much that I almost forgot I was ill. WB brought me *The Naked and the Dead* by Norman Mailer which is 600 pages long and would normally take me weeks to read, but as I read most of the day in bed, I'm nearly a quarter way through this marvellous book. WB told me that, last time he visited me, Mrs Pinhorn asked him to post a postcard she had written. Of course, he read it. She wrote: 'My young tenant is ill and has a lot of visitors – mostly men.' He was very amused. I wasn't, and hope she doesn't think badly of me because of that.

Putz went to Paris with my father and Betty on Friday. Mrs Wren will visit me while Putz is away. WB says he wouldn't be surprised if my illness wasn't brought on psychologically – to get out of the Paris trip!

17th December 1949

I got up for the first time on Wednesday, after being ill for two weeks. For some of that time I felt really wretched – high temperature, stomach ache, completely blocked nose, splitting headache, boiling hot and freezing cold . . . It felt quite strange being out of bed again. I was weak as a kitten. The doctor paid me a visit again that first morning I was up, and told me to take things easy. My hair had grown quite long and looked a real mess. I scraped it back and tied it up, which I had never done before.

There's a lovely feel to convalescence. It almost makes being ill worth while. I can't put the feeling into words, but I'm sure it's familiar to everyone. You feel reborn, at peace with the world. Everybody is nice to you.

I had tea with Mrs Pinhorn in her drawing room on that day I first left my sickbed. It was served by Doris. Not a word was said about my male visitors so I don't think Mrs Pinhorn really minded. Thank goodness.

During these two weeks I learnt a great deal about Markus. Can I have been wrong about him? Is he really a nice man underneath the doubtful exterior? Of course, he will never be a Raymond, but perhaps he is a good man, in his own way? While I was ill, he came nearly every day (as did WB and Victor and a few others); he had exactly the right bedside manner, he brought me grapes and books and magazines, ignoring Miss Wulf's hostility, he refused to let me get up when I wanted to. I thought that he must really like me. Why else was he so kind and considerate? He even fetched my medicine. And yet . . . and yet . . . I wish I had never met Markus. I am tired of trying to figure him out, tired of not being able to resist him, of feeling restless and frequently unhappy in his company. I think the day my feelings for him really changed was the day on which he returned to me a story I had written for him and replied with a shrug, in answer to my question how he liked it: "Not much." Just that. Nothing more.

But the spell is not yet broken. I don't know whether I am trying to ignore a genuine love for Markus by pretending that he is worthless, or whether he is really worthless. I know I have just praised him for the way he was when I was ill – but how will he be tomorrow, next week, next month? This morning we had coffee together at Ellistons. He gave me my Christmas present: Freud's book on Psychoanalysis, which he knew I wanted. In the afternoon he was again with me, and stayed the evening (WB having been to see me in his lunch hour!). Perhaps I see too much of him? Maybe he doesn't like his home? He certainly doesn't care for Diana's cooking and often complains of it to me.

On Thursday I went shopping for the first time in two weeks, in Summertown. Afterwards I had lunch with Mrs Labowsky. Eva Guttmann was there. Next Saturday is Christmas Eve and I am going to Cobham, as usual. "Are you going home for Christmas?"

people often ask me.

"Yes," I usually reply. Wishful thinking.

22nd December 1949

I went back to work on Monday. WB said, "What *have* you done to your hair? You can't go like that." So I untied it. I've been Christmas shopping with Putz and I resumed my babysitting duty at the Dauries' last night. Today Chris and I went to an Art Exhibition at the British Council. Things are back to normal. Well – not quite . . .

I hate sex. Markus said I'm still much too taut and stiff, I don't relax, I don't seem to enjoy it, I don't really know how to make love. He is right. And I don't want to. All this time I have only been pretending. How can anyone like sex? It's stupid. I never did get the hang of it. All men are mad, crazy. Perhaps there is something wrong with me, but I don't care. We quarrelled again. Not for very long, just a little. Over the typing. He wants everything done at once. And he always sees through me, my motives, my unconscious wishes. Perhaps

TELEPATHY

To the Editor of the "Oxford Times"

SIR,—An experimental investigation of telepathy is being conducted under my supervision, and it is hoped to secure data for the scientific evaluation of the effects of incentive, learning and mental habits on telepathic ability.

There appears to have been some misinterpretation of facts with regard to the investigation. I wish, therefore, to make it clear that the investigation has no official connection with any department of the University; and though persons interested in the subject of telepathy are invited to subscribe towards the cost of the investigation it must be emphasised that the investigation is not conducted for financial gain.

Any suggestion to the contrary would deprive the results of the investigation of scientific validity.—Yours faithfully,

M. JACOBUS.

Christ Church, Oxford.
21 December, 1949.

he isn't a fraud at all, perhaps I am the fraud. Afterwards I hugged him. "Markus, don't be angry, darling, please don't be angry with me. Kiss me." So he kisses me. Passionately.

"There are things you don't understand," he says. "We don't see eye to eye about some things."

"No, but don't be angry."

"I'm not angry." He is nice again. He does like me. Perhaps it's not important to find out what he really is, just accept him as he is . . . It's lovely once he's inside me, it's just the entry that is uncomfortable and always a shock, the anticipation of that huge thing inside this small space, and the insecurity and sordidness and danger always lurking somewhere. (Psychological? Or physical?)

Everything in life, life itself, all the people in the world, are a great big lie. One can twist everything that is said and done to have any meaning one chooses. And I am the biggest lie of all. I walk through the streets or sit in a restaurant, apparently perfectly sure of myself, well-groomed, attractive, knowing men are looking at me, enjoying it. To the world I'm a pretty girl, sexy, gay and probably good at dancing. But look at me closely. I'm totally vulnerable. I never dance, I'm not very fond of parties, I don't go anywhere exciting and sex is a closed book to me. I don't open up, but I probably look as if I never had my legs closed. Occasionally I am a bit proud of being different, of being a pretty girl and yet quite unlike what a pretty girl should be, of being a sphinx, albeit a sphinx without a secret. But only occasionally.

Dear Markus, dear incomprehensible Markus, if only I could run away from you, from sex, from everything.

Life without Markus? It sounds sheer fantasy at the moment.

Cobham, 25th December 1949 – Christmas Day

It's OVER! It's THE END! It's FINISHED! I have had my FINAL ROW with WB and I am never going back to Parkers' again. Never. This is what happened:

It was Saturday afternoon, Christmas Eve. The shop was full of people buying last minute Christmas presents. I was looking forward to Christmas in Cobham; I was going straight to the station after work, and Putz, who was already in London, was meeting me at Paddington. I had just finished serving a customer. It was half an hour before closing time. I went to the back – and almost collided with WB. He was standing just behind the door, as if lying in wait for me. "Where have you been?" he said angrily, "I asked you to take these books back to . . ." His face was quite red.

Suddenly something snapped in me. I became hysterical. It was as if someone had passed an electric current through me. Shaking and beside myself, my teeth clenched, I shouted, "I was just going to do it – but I'm not now!" and I rushed past him and out.

"Ingrid," he called after me, in quite a different voice. "What's the matter?" I didn't reply. I fetched my bag, I didn't say goodbye to anyone, I went to the bicycle shed to get my coat knowing it was for the last time, and left the shop.

"I'm never going back to Parkers' again," I said to Putz, as soon as we met at Paddington Station.

"Why not?" she wanted to know.

I told her what had happened.

"You'll have to give a week's notice," she said.

"I'm never setting foot there again," I said.

She could see I meant it.

I described the incident several times more at Ann's Cottage. Anni was entirely on my side and reminded me that she told me long ago that a Conservative can't be a nice person. Trudl Dawson said that she hated her boss too, and had given her notice in. Old Elsa, another regular visitor to Cobham, said, "You'll soon find another job." Uncle Felix, as usual, kept his own counsel. In the afternoon we all went for a walk with Chum, the Airedale.

"I'll have to write to Mr Thomas, the director, and give in my notice," I said to Anni. "What shall I tell him?"

"Tell him the truth," she advised. "That you can no longer work with this man. He has cost you your job. That's a serious offence."

I was grateful to her for taking my side. Tomorrow I suppose I shall have to tell my father when he and Betty come out for the day. I don't expect the same sympathy from him.

31st December 1949

As I wasn't going back to work I asked Anni if I could stay in Cobham till the New Year, and of course I could. On Tuesday, therefore, Putz returned to Oxford without me. We had spent the day in London at Jane's party, with the usual relations of hers present, and in the evening after Putz had left, Jack took me back to Cobham by car and I continued to be a lady of leisure, with no idea what I was going to live on the following week, or the week after, come to that and, amazingly, not caring. Not quite a lady of leisure, actually, as Anni asked me to help her clean the house. She gave me a brush and pan and I cleaned the stairs, a job I had never done before but which Anni said I performed to perfection.

The rest of my stay here was spent very pleasantly, going shopping with Anni, having morning coffee with her at Grieves in the village, going to the pictures, playing cards. Yesterday Lixl's girlfriend, Hannah, came to lunch. She also came for a drive in the car with us. The film we saw was *The Third Man*, which briefly transported me to the city of my birth. Tonight we shall see the New Year in with champagne and tomorrow – back to Oxford, with no job and possible starvation. Still, I shall have the champagne inside me to sustain me, though what people like about champagne for the life of me I can't see.

2nd January 1950

After lunch yesterday, Lixl walked to Cobham station with me. Putz met me at the station in Oxford and then I went to her place for tea with the Wrens and for some comfort before facing the rigours of poverty. However, on the train journey back to Oxford I felt deliciously carefree. Freedom lay ahead. True, by next week I might be starving, but at least I would have something in common with artists and writers. I was reminded of the last occasion when I planned to do something wild and rash – the time I tried to run away to London from Falmouth. This time I had already committed my rash deed, and now I must face the consequences. As it turned out, there was nothing to face, I won't have to go without food or shelter and I shan't know after all what it feels like to be a starving artist or writer. Pity. But listen:

First thing this morning, Monday – well, second thing really, for I went shopping first, to buy bread and cheese in readiness for the lean days ahead – I called at Mrs Wawerka's office. On the way I met Ann, and told her what had happened.

"Come back to Wolsey Hall," she suggested.

But I wasn't that desperate. "No, thanks," I said.

I was still feeling light-headed and free when I arrived at Mrs Wawerka's, and not very worried that I was without a job. Mrs Wawerka's typing would do for the moment. I told her I had left Parkers', without going into details.

"Have you got some typing for me?" I asked her.

"I'm afraid I haven't at the moment," she replied. "Christmas and New Year are quiet times."

"And no vacancy at your office, I suppose?" I said, beginning to feel anxious and wondering if it might have to be Wolsey Hall after all.

"No," she said, "but wait a moment. I think Rosenthals' still need a secretary. They rang me up the other day and asked if I knew anyone."

"Who is Rosenthals'?"

"The Antiquarian bookseller. I'll give them a ring." She picked up the receiver and dialled. I waited and listened. It sounded all right. She put the receiver down, and smiled, the way people do when they have good news for you.

"They're desperate for someone," she said. "But it's only temporary."

"Never mind," I replied.

"Here is the address," she said, handing me a piece of paper on which she had written it.

"Go and see them straight away. Dr Ettinghausen is expecting you."

I thanked her and departed. I looked at the bit of paper 'A. Rosenthal Ltd., 5 Turl Street' was written on it.

Ten minutes later I was climbing up the narrow staircase at the top of which I came to a door marked 'A. Rosenthal Ltd.' I knocked. "Come in," said a deep voice. I wasn't a bit nervous as I like interviews – they're always more promising and interesting than the work you're being interviewed for, and anyway I didn't much mind whether I got the job or not. I opened the door.

I was quite unprepared for the sight that met my eyes: I saw a large room *with a carpet*, at the far end of which sat an elderly man with a grey beard at a big desk piled high with books. On the floor beside him lay a black mongrel dog, also with a grey beard. I had the feeling of having entered a drawing room not an office. The man left his desk, came towards me and shook my hand.

"You're Miss Jacoby, are you? Take a seat, and tell me what you can do. I'm Ettinghausen, by the by. Albi Rosenthal, my partner, is out at the moment."

I told him what I'd been doing in my previous jobs.

"Can you take down letters from dictation?"

"Yes, but not in shorthand. I can write very quickly, though."

369

"I don't mind how you get them down. What about foreign languages? Could you take letters in French and German?"

"Yes," I said rashly.

"Well, you look intelligent, anyhow. Can you start now?"

My heart sank. I needed a breather. I hadn't even got a pencil on me. "Can I start tomorrow?" I asked.

"All right. Tomorrow then. 9.30. By the by, you know the job is only temporary, don't you? Say six months. Till the rush is over."

"I know. Mrs Wawerka told me."

"Have you got any references, incidentally?"

"Yes, I have one from Wolsey Hall." I hoped desperately he wouldn't ask for one from Parkers'. "Shall I bring it tomorrow?"

"You can if you like. It doesn't really matter."

It was all over. I had done something crazy and dishonourable by leaving Parkers' the way I did, without giving notice. My father had of course greatly disapproved, and yet I seem to have been rewarded for my behaviour, not punished. I went straight away to the Labour Exchange to inform them of my change of job.

In the evening I called at Bruno and Erna's; as I expected they not only know of Rosenthals', Bruno has bought books there from time to time.

"Ettinghausen engaged you straight away? Without any references?" asked Bruno.

"Yes. He said I looked intelligent," I told him with a laugh.

"Intelligent? I suppose he meant Jewish." That took the gilt off the gingerbread. Typical of my uncle Bruno.

Tomorrow evening Markus is coming for supper and on Wednesday I have an appointment at Dr Brown's so that he can give me a clean bill of health after my attack of gastric flu.

Looking at this picture in the *Radio Times* I lived through that unforgettable film *Les Enfants du Paradis* again. Why can't life be more like films?

Jean-Louis Barrault, 'the Olivier of France,' who plays the part of Baptiste, the clown, in a scene from the film with Arletty

370

Jean-Claude has written to say that he is joining the army. He is going to the École d'Artillerie to become an 'officier'. I don't hold out much hope for him, then. The army does awful things to men.

So tomorrow I start my new job at Rosenthals'. I've never found that I've gone wrong when I've acted on impulse, and I seem to have been proved right once again. The week during which I was unemployed I was as happy as a sandboy. Not having to go to work made me feel superior to my fellow creatures. And did I perhaps have some premonition that everything would work out all right?

7th January 1950

I've had a wonderful week at Rosenthals'. My office is next door to the large carpeted one I was interviewed in, and I share it with Mrs Ettinghausen, Dr E's wife, who comes in most afternoons. Sometimes we are joined by Bonny, the elderly black mongrel who is adored by his master: he comes and lies in front of our gas-fire for a change. I often get up from my typing to stroke him and he returns my affection with a few wags of his old tail.

I've now met Mr Rosenthal, the other partner. He's married and has three children. I think he's a musician and he comes from Germany. Dr Ettinghausen is a Sanskrit Scholar. Both the offices as well as a little room at the back are stacked to the ceiling with antiquarian books in many languages. A youngish man named Peter Grainger presides in the little back room and packs books all day to be sent to customers, mostly abroad. Everyone is very nice to me.

On Friday afternoon, just before 3.30pm, Dr Ettinghausen came into my office and said, "Put your things away. Time to go home."

I looked at my watch, then at him. "But it's only half past three," I said.

"Start of the Sabbath," he said. "Nobody works here over Sabbath."

If he was surprised or shocked that this was something entirely new to me he didn't show it. I finished the letter I was typing and went home.

On Tuesday I met Mr Townsend in the evening. He invited me

to a pub for a drink and we had a long talk. I think he sympathised with me, having had to work under WB for so long, but how much of the truth he guesses I couldn't tell. I have agreed to have tea at Victor's on Sunday. Silly me.

Today, Saturday – I don't work on Saturdays of course – I went to town with Markus in the morning, he came to tea in the afternoon and the evening we spent wandering around the town, window-shopping.

13th January 1950

I always make up my mind quite firmly not to quarrel with Markus over this typing business. But we always do. He says things I know he doesn't mean, he has absurd whims, he changes his mind a thousand times, he infuriates me. Today, when the typing was over and he became my lover again, assuming his charming manner, my anger for once did not immediately abate. My thoughts ran something like this: 'This is a stupid and dull affair that has had its day. I wish I could escape, but I can't. He won't let me go. I'm caught in a spider's web. But he's not indispensable, that's nonsense, I don't really need him at all, I wish I were free of him, I'm bored, even now, even with his p . . .s in my hand, hard and huge, driving him crazy, but what am I to do with it? It suddenly seems so silly . . .'

Once he had said to me, jokingly, "You're a wicked girl and I'm going to sever my relations with you." My immediate thought had been: 'If only you would. Then I would be free'. Just because he is unavailable, a married man, however, I can't give him up. What makes married men so desirable? Another thing he had said once was that everyone in this world gets everything back in the end, but does he include himself in this? Anyway, I don't believe that everyone gets their due.

I'm sticking to my New Year resolution and have not smoked since the 1st of January. But I still miss it, especially when I'm with people who smoke, as last Monday evening when I was at the Howards'. Once the eating is over it's a bit boring and I long for a cigarette, although on Monday we listened to an old ITMA programme on the radio, which made me forget all about smoking.

Victor, puny, neurotic, brilliant Victor, still pursues me with an obstinacy such as I have never before encountered. He offers me his love, his life, everything. But, as with Markus's p . . . s, what should I do with it? At least, with Victor, I'm not emotionally involved, and never could be. Poor Victor. I had a long, mad letter from him begging me not to reject him after so few meetings. 'You may have all you want, yet should not miss what I can give . . . And I will not leave you politely and in silence but come to see you tomorrow . . .' I ought to feel very sorry for him because I know all about unrequited love: for years I was too childish, plain and unsophisticated to hope for anything in return for my passionate feelings, and derived my satisfaction only in my fantasies. But beware of pity. I would only get more deeply involved.

14th January 1950

Oh God, oh God. Or shall I say: Oh Markus, oh Markus! When my affair with him began – centuries ago – I thought: 'When all this is over I shall go away . . . start again . . . turn over a new leaf . . .' Now I realise how little I have left with which to start afresh. Markus has taken it all away. He has torn my soul to pieces. I have given him more than I have ever given to any man. We have been together nearly every day again this week. This afternoon we went for a long walk in the country and watched some horses in a field and stroked their noses when they came close to us. I felt happy with him.

After tea, in my flat, we began suddenly and for the first time, to discuss our relationship. He asked me whether his assumption was true that I have been thinking of breaking with him. (It's quite frightening, how he sees through me.) I lied of course. No, I said, no, no. We had a long, long conversation. He said he resented that, from the start, I did not really love him. I replied that, although I had a weakness for married men, I was not stupid enough to throw away my life for one.

But he was wonderful tonight, magnificent. For a few hours I worshipped him. He had made me sad and unhappy, I didn't enjoy lovemaking, but I saw Markus at his finest, just as I want to remember him. Earlier in the evening Mrs Pinhorn had invited us to her drawing room for a chat, and he behaved impeccably and I was proud of him. When he was about to leave me I felt very sad again and he saw that I was almost crying. "You mustn't cry, my darling," he said. "I don't mean anything nasty that I say to you, ever."

As soon as he had gone I decided to finish the affair. The idea would not go away, and I knew that it would keep me awake. I thought with dread of the weeks and months ahead unfolding themselves, empty without Markus. My whole attention has been on him all these months and there is no one to take his place, nor can I imagine anyone doing so. I know his many faults, but I know too that I have done him an injustice, that I don't understand him, that he is not a happy man but has never talked about that. I like to think that I was the sunshine of his life, if only for a short time, a lovely, sunny holiday which had to end, as all holidays must.

Now I am going to write that letter to him. And then? Just nothingness. Even dying won't matter.

15th January 1950

No. I can't. I can't. I can't write that letter to Markus. I am incapable of it. Let nature take its course. Nothing is as important now as the fact that Markus must remain in my life. I can't part with him. I can't do it. I have given him too much. I rely on him, I need him, he needs me. I am lost and alone without him. I want to die.

20th January 1950

The weather is freezing. To keep warm, Putz and I went to the pictures on Monday evening; we saw a film called *Murderers Amongst Us*. Afterwards I had coffee at her place. The Wrens' sitting room is always nice and warm. On Wednesday I was at the Howards' again, enjoying Gretel's baking. Mr Calé was there, too. I never ask after WB but Mr Calé sometimes talks of him, and of what has been happening at Parkers' foreign department. I'm so glad I'm not there any more.

I had a long conversation with Mr Rosenthal on Wednesday. His office is on the floor above mine, and next door to it is Miss Grierson's room. She's the accountant; she is an elderly, classy spinster and has worked here for many years. Mr R. showed me a copy of *Max and Moritz* in Latin! I have not seen many interesting books here but this was one of them. Another, though I didn't see it, is Hitler's Complete Shakespeare, with his ex-libris in it. "It looks as if it had never been opened," Mr R. commented. But most books have titles like *Academia nobilissimae Artis Pictoriae* and *Metoposcopia libris tredecim* and cost hundreds of pounds. I admired a painting of Paganini which hangs in Mr R's room and said that he – Paganini – looked liked Jean Louis Barrault. Mr R. agreed. His passion is music and Dr Ettinghausen's is Judaica. A woman called Mrs Koch also works here, part-time. She's expecting a baby and will shortly leave.

I've discovered that there's some kind of a feud going on between the packer, Peter Grainger, and our bosses, Mr R. and Dr E. When I told Peter how much I liked both of them, and the job, he replied that I would soon be disillusioned; that they are both mean and money-grabbing and he had never had a rise or been allowed any time off that he had ever asked for. I found all that very hard to believe, but as I make the coffee every morning in the packing-room no doubt things will become clearer in time.

One other person works here and that is a little old man who comes to clean the office at 6pm. Yesterday I was amazed to see him chuck the contents of the tea pot onto the carpet. He explained to me that there was no better way to clean carpets than with damp tea leaves. What a lot I've learnt since coming to work here.

I'm spending this weekend at Sara's in Wheatley.

I haven't seen Markus for a week.

*24th January 1950 (I still remember the **23rd** of January, 1941 . . .)*

On Saturday morning I took Sara to Chris and Ted's. I'm always apprehensive about introducing my friends to each other, for fear they won't jell; they're all so different from one another. 'Show me your friends and I'll tell you who you are,' the saying goes. I'd like to know who I am: there's no telling from my hotchpotch medley of friends. We went to Chris's kitchen in the basement where the children were playing and drawing. Valerie wore a woolly hat as she had ringworm and has had her hair shaved off. Chris is very embarrassed about this – and so was I, when Sara said pleasantly to Valerie, "Hello, why are you wearing a hat?"

Chris explained, blushing, but Valerie didn't mind; she's too young. Sara and I didn't stay long as we were taking Michael out to coffee at Ellistons'. He was very excited, in a quiet way, for he's a gentle, quiet little boy. He wore a tie and his best trousers and was extremely well-behaved in town.

After we had taken Michael home Sara and I went to Wheatley by bus. We chatted about this and that. She congratulated me on having left Parkers' and 'that Mr Brown'. Suddenly she said, "Who was that attractive man I saw you with the other day?"

"I didn't know you saw me with an attractive man the other day."

"I did. In town. Who was he?"

"Markus."

"Markus who?"

"You don't need to know that."

"Will you introduce me to him?"

I was appalled. "No, I won't," I said firmly.

"I'll get you an invitation to a dance at Claridges if you do," said Sara. "Is that a bargain?"

"No," I'd be as out of place at a dance at Claridges as a blind man at a cinema. "Why do you want to meet him, anyway?"

"He looks nice. And a lot older than you. Is he married?"

"Yes."

"I thought he might be. You'll have to bring him over one day."

We got off the bus and visited her grandmother before going to Bleak House. The grandmother was tall and distinguished-looking and dressed entirely in black. She reminded me of pictures I had seen of Edith Sitwell.

There were other visitors at Bleak House, Sara's home. They were called Peggy, Basil and Susan. The following day, Sara and I looked after her little brother, Trevor, while her mother went out. After lunch Sara came to the bus stop with me.

"You'll bring Markus over one day, won't you?" she said.

"I don't know," I replied, and waved her goodbye from the bus. "Thanks for a nice weekend," I called, as we moved off. The idea of taking Markus to the Mostyns seems preposterous.

I wish tomorrow would never come: I've allowed Victor to take me to the pictures to see *Paisa* and have supper with him at the Continental afterwards. Every minute spent in his company is agony.

Markus is at one of his disappearing tricks again. Since that memorable Saturday evening, when we didn't arrange anything as he said he might have to go to Bristol for a few days, I have neither seen nor heard from him. I know that one day it will happen like this, just exactly like this, the end of our affair, and he knows it, too. I can never get in touch with him because of Diana, and he has only to press the button, so to speak, when he thinks the time is ripe. Which lets me off. My attitude to Markus at the moment is like my attitude to smoking which I've recently given up; I know that I'm better off without it, and while I'm without it I'm so proud of my accomplishment it makes up for my abstinence; but when on rare occasions I give in to desire and have a cigarette, that cigarette tastes like ambrosia and satisfies me for a very long time.

29th January 1950

He was only busy. He called on Thursday and stayed for the evening. He came again unexpectedly on Friday, but I had to go babysitting at the Dauries'. Sometimes I don't want him at all, I reject him fiercely; at other times I imagine myself in his arms and I can't wait to be with him again, and experience all the wonderful things that will happen, but somehow never do quite. Why not? I've never even been completely in the nude with him. We have never spent a whole night together; we have never discussed the future.

This afternoon, Sunday, I was at Markus's house for some telepathy experiment he is conducting. Diana and the children were away. Also taking part in the experiment were Mr White and Professor Pryce. Markus is interested in Dr Rhine's experiments using Zener cards, which have different symbols on them, and we were subjected to this test. Markus seemed pleased with the results, and said they confirmed his belief in E.S.P. 'extra-sensory perception'. I remained unconvinced. It's not for nothing Jean-Claude used to call me 'disbelieving Thomas'!

Putz and I saw *Kermesse Hérorique* with Francoise Rosay yesterday afternoon about which I had heard so much. For this reason perhaps, I was a little disappointed in it. In the evening I was at her place, tonight she was at mine. We never run out of conversation.

Mr Rosenthal and 'the Doctor', as Dr Ettinghausen is known, were away for two days this week. On Wednesday I left work early to go to the Music Faculty and to Christ Church with some books. I have still not seen everywhere in this building: right on the top floor there's a flat and this is occupied by Peter the packer. Peter has a wife called May who is away at a teacher training college but is here most weekends. He has invited me to have supper with them.

Being friendly with Peter makes things a bit awkward for me, as he is constantly at war with Mr R. and the Doctor, with whom I get on so well. To me they are not like bosses at all: the Doctor treats me more as if I were his daughter, and when I tell you what Mr R. said to me today you will agree that this is not at all an average boss's comment to his secretary: I've mentioned that we often have long talks, which are always strictly intellectual. During one of these today he told me how much he adored Italy, with its marvellous Art and Architecture, its beautiful language, its glorious climate. He advised me to go there for a holiday some day. I said I didn't know enough about Art and Architecture and I didn't speak one word of Italian. "That doesn't matter," he said, "You can admire Art and Architecture without understanding it; and everyone speaks English there."

"Anyway," I said, "I've been told one should be fair-haired to go to Italy; one gets really well-treated if one is blonde." And then he said this thing, which so took me by surprise that it silenced me – and pleased me immensely.

"But you would be a sensation whatever colour your hair," he said. "You'd be admired wherever you went." He is such an attractive man that I was quite overcome with joy at hearing him say this. Compliments are my undoing. I remembered Markus saying to me on that train journey after Joan's wedding: "A fascinating young lady like you . . ." Is there perhaps some message in my eyes? But what or who put it there? The technique of married men should be crystal clear to me by now, but is a surprise every time. Afterwards, back at my typewriter, I thought how nice it is to be still a mystery to somebody, to have my weaknesses still unknown . . .

4th February 1950

I saw Mrs Zuccari at Exeter College Library on Wednesday; she invited me for tea on Sunday. I've also seen Enid Carter again. I met her in the street and she told me she was engaged. In complete contrast to my usual social activities, yesterday evening I was invited to a 'Jewish supper' at the Kochs'. Another practising member of the Jewish faith was present called Lucy Haiman. I felt like a fish out of water. I know nothing about Jewish customs, much to the Doctor's chagrin, and can honestly say I felt more at ease in the C of E working-class home of Enid Carter. Mr Rosenthal, incidentally, like me, is only Jewish by birth.

Which brings me to an episode that happened today when Markus was with me. The evening can be summed up: quarrel – hell – bed – heaven. I really hated him today. He was particularly unpleasant. I was fed up with the continual ups and downs of his moods, and with forever kidding myself. We said very angry things to each other, and we were dead serious. I meant every word I said. I wanted him to go away. "You're a Jewess, you're a Jewess," he suddenly taunted me. It was the worst thing he could have said to me, and he knew it. My loathing for him at that moment mingled with feelings of shame and inferiority. Markus is of course himself a Jew, and probably as little pleased with this particular card life has dealt him as I am. As if he knew he had gone too far, he suddenly pulled me in his arms. And I didn't struggle. That was the strange part. Now everything I had been feeling only moments earlier turned into excitement. A curious recipe for perfect lovemaking, but perfect lovemaking is what resulted. In as far as I was capable of thinking, the thought flashed through my mind: 'Sex is not overrated, after all.' And then it was like waking up after a long sleep. I remembered everything. I watched Markus put on his clothes, his vest first of all, then his shirt and tie. He said, "Don't look so unhappy, darling!"

I lied firmly that I wasn't unhappy. Then we were suddenly talking about his son's homework, Diana's cold, Diana's cooking. Anything is better than quarrelling, I told myself. I pretended to be interested. But I felt deeply sorry for myself. "Oh, you don't do so badly," another voice inside me made itself heard. I left it at that.

I feel today to have been a good criterion because, although I experienced both hell and heaven, I am perfectly able to discriminate. Markus likes everything in moderation, yet he can engender such extremes of emotion. However, today he was quite stripped of his veneer and I shall surely never be taken in by him again?

Last Thursday Putz and I saw *1066 and All That* at the Playhouse and laughed so much that we left the theatre feeling quite intoxicated.

14th February 1950

Last week a strange young woman was in the office when I arrived at 9.30. She was wearing a purple silk overall. The Doctor introduced us. She was Miss Fiammetta Olschki, an Italian cousin of Mr Rosenthal's whose father is also an Antiquarian bookseller, in Florence.

"She speaks four languages fluently," the Doctor explained. "And she sings."

While in Oxford for six months, she will come to the office regularly to do some work. I was duly impressed with this illustrious girl and her many talents but Peter Grainger, with whom I had supper at his flat upstairs on Friday, had not a good word to say about her, either.

"They are all decadent," he said. I should have been babysitting at the Dauries' that evening but it was pouring with rain, so cycling was out and it's financially not worthwhile going there by bus.

Markus didn't turn up last Saturday evening. Instead he came on Sunday morning, full of apology and excuses. Nothing he does surprises me any more. I was and wasn't pleased to see him. We were a bit awkward with each other. Perhaps that was why I blurted out what I hadn't meant to mention to him at all. "You have an invitation to visit my friend Sara with me," I said. Me and my big mouth.

He was instantly cock-a-hoop. "Who is Sara?" he asked. "Why didn't you tell me before?"

"Sara Mostyn. She used to work at Parkers' with me."

"Mostyn? I know that name."

I told him what I know of the family and he continued to insist that he knew them. I promised him to arrange a visit, without of course mentioning the dance at Claridges about which I hope Sara has forgotten and which was to be my payment.

Markus having enhanced my interest in psychology, I'm going to a lecture at the Institute of Psychology on Thursday evening. I expect it will be way above my head.

Why, when spring comes, am I always out of love? Why does everything beautiful always end up ugly? Is it because life must end in death?

If I wanted to marry Victor I could do so. He is now a Fellow of Magdalen College and lives in lavishly furnished rooms at the College. I was there this evening, after supper at the Continental with him. He told me that he was not as sick in mind as I probably believed him to be, and was not prepared to bang his head against a brick wall forever: in short, he had been seeing another girl. I said I was very pleased for him (I wasn't) and hoped he would be luckier this time. He didn't try to kiss me or touch me at all. I admired his rooms and looked at his books. I felt it couldn't last, and it didn't. At ten o'clock he removed his veil of pride and triumph. We were in the middle of a conversation, I forget what about, when he suddenly said:

"But it is, after all, you I am still in love with. The other girl's only a compensation. Let me make love to you! Please! Just once! Later on, not now, whenever you want . . . We might still marry, you and I, mightn't we? Mightn't we?" I was pleased that he still loved me, and might now continue to do so without bothering me since he had chosen a substitute for his immediate requirements. How disgusting human nature is. I am frequently disgusted with my thoughts and feelings.

17th February 1950

The Doctor had just finished dictating one of the numerous letters he writes to a book collector, Mrs Amzalak in Lisbon, when he said to me, "By the by, forget about being temporary. That's all over. You're so good . . ."

Needless to say, I was very pleased. I feel I fit into this establishment perfectly, I love it, and yet I realise more and more how little I belong anywhere. The more people I meet and form superficial friendships with, the more alone and an outsider do I feel. This is a strange thing, but it has a firm grip on me. I have made friends with all the people working at Rosenthals'; they are all interesting people with far more interesting backgrounds than mine, and I wonder what they see in me, and then I feel more alone than ever.

There is Mrs Koch, a little self-centred refugee woman from Germany, an orthodox Jewess in her late thirties or early forties who recently married and is pregnant; there is the Doctor himself, another orthodox Jew, a scholar, intellectual and lover of books, whose earliest memory is watching the funeral procession of Victor Hugo from a Paris window when he was about three years old, and who for some reason likes me; there is his partner Albi Rosenthal, highly attractive, in his mid-thirties, always perfectly dressed, cultured, with a charming voice and a passion for music, who telephones barons and dines with distinguished musicians and has numerous equally brilliant relatives scattered all over the world; there is Peter Grainger with a chip on his shoulder and no time for anyone who seems better off than himself, and a pretty half-Indian wife at college; there's Mrs Ettinghausen, the Doctor's second wife, a converted Jewess and very much inferior to him, but well-meaning and kindly; and lastly there is Mr Rosenthal's cousin *Fiammetta Olschki from Italy, who formed a friendship with me as rapidly as I expect her to break it but I like her. I was invited to her rooms in Woodstock Road for lunch today, and discovered that she has yet another talent – she's a super cook. The house where she lodges belongs to a friend of Rosenthal's – Mrs von Hoffmansthal to whom I was introduced; she is the widow of Hugo von Hoffmansthal who wrote the libretto for the *Rosenkavalier*. The only person whom I have not got to know is elderly Miss Grierson. She used to work for the Doctor in Paris, and it is said that she had hoped to become his second wife. I can well believe it; there is an air of disappointment about her.

All these people are vastly different from each other: how is it they all like me? Why are my friends so different from one another? I have no cosy circle of friends – they are a mixed bunch,

October 21st 1963: I hope I'm as wrong now about other unpleasant hunches as I was about this one: The 'Italian Cousin' is still one of my best friends, 13½ years later. She is married to Mario and has a boy of 10 and a mind that basically works like mine.

gathered here and there at various stages of my life, each appealing to a different part of me. I never knew that one can have a large number of 'friends' and still be lonely. Perhaps lonely is not the right word, for to be lonely one must be alone; have no one to do things with, no one to talk to in the evenings. Perhaps I should say they make me aware that I always seem to be a spectator, am never in the swim of things, always on the outside, don't belong anywhere, have no proper background. But perhaps working at Rosenthals' will change all that, perhaps in time I shall feel I really belong here among these people who are so nice to me. I once had a real friend – Willy Brown. But that is another story.

And so one lives, or drifts. And one watches other people do the same, only they appear to do it so much better, and with so much more success.

21st February 1950

Fiammetta, who is a few years older than I am, had introduced me to Mrs von Hoffmansthal as "the niece of Dr Bruno Furst, the art historian." This certainly gave me an identity I may have in theory, but is not acknowledged in practice. Anyway, he's only a cousin of my father's, not really an uncle, and he might be rather shocked if told he had a niece.

I've been puzzled for some time about something referred to as 'Biscuits' in many of the letters dictated to me. Now I've found out what these 'Biscuits' are: nothing less than Royal documents signed by Queen Isabella of Spain allowing Christopher Columbus to take provisions of biscuits on his voyage – and worth £10,000! Their whereabouts is a secret, but they belong to Rosenthals' and are being offered for sale.

Last Saturday after tea at Chris and Ted's, Chris and I fetched Micky from a birthday party on our bikes. On Sunday afternoon I was again at Markus's house for more telepathy experiments. Afterwards we went for a walk. Markus lives in a fictitious world, a world of illusions in which no one with whom he has any contact is real, least of all himself. I too am made unreal by him. He is continually changing and it's quite impossible to keep adapting oneself to these changes. I once told him, "Kaleidoscope should be your middle name," but he was not amused. I suppose you can't expect a psychologist to understand himself. He used to be so charming at the beginning of our affair, but now he just takes me for granted. I am his mistress, Diana is his wife, there is no need to be nice to us any more. The loveliest part of a love affair is the very beginning, just after the ice is broken, when each is still new to the other and a mystery and it is still necessary to be polite and to impress. One can still pretend and play-act. I have known men who have treated their wives with brutal indifference – notably Dr Beschorner – and I'm determined this shall never happen to me.

Yesterday I had to pay a visit to Dr Pick to have a filling replaced. He is still bad-tempered about the Health Service. In the evening I had supper with Peter and May Grainger in the flat upstairs. It was rather a slapdash supper. Some time afterwards I saw May crying, and Peter explained to me that she didn't want to go back to college and leave him. I thought this very odd – like a little girl who doesn't want to go to school. This evening Putz and I had dinner at Mrs King's; after the Graingers' meal of the evening before, I really appreciated the nicely cooked and served food.

25th February 1950

It was Election Day on Thursday. I voted Labour, of course – and a Labour Government has been elected. Mrs Ettinghausen said, "Now we're stuck with this rubbish for another 5 years." Earlier a customer who had come to the office had said, just after the election result was announced:

"What do you think of the bad news?"

I remained non-committal both times.

On Wednesday evening I had supper with Dr and Mrs Ettinghausen in their beautiful flat in Beaumont Street. Their food is vegetarian and kosher and even Bonny never gets meat. Afterwards they took me to the Playhouse, a few doors away, to see *The Mikado*. The Doctor, like me, is a great fan of Gilbert and Sullivan.

The following evening, the little girl who had been taken for a treat by her substitute parents turned into a woman again, a bad woman who has affairs with married men. Markus came, and there was a second perfect time. Each time I think it will be the last. How many more will there be? On Sunday we are having lunch at the Mostyns' in Wheatley. I'm very apprehensive. Does Mrs Mostyn know about us? Perhaps she's looking for material for a novel.

But my biggest news today is that *Peter Grainger has been sacked!* I don't know what to think about this or whose side to take. Has he done something I don't know anything about? If not, why should he be sacked? It is very strange.

This evening Putz and I were at Bruno and Erna's and, naturally, talked mostly about Labour's success in the election, even though they only got a narrow majority – very different from 1945. Human nature is never satisfied for long: enthusiasm for a political party wanes, as does love for a lover. How sad. Otto Paecht, another art historian, was there too, and later Egon Wellesz, the composer whom I remembered coming to Parkers'. But of course he didn't remember me.

27th February 1950

I have just returned from another Oxford Union Debate with Mrs Ettinghausen – Markus having provided me with the tickets. But I want to tell you about yesterday, when Markus and I had lunch at the Mostyns'. Not that there is much to tell. Sara met us at the bus stop, perhaps to get a preview of Markus. I think he made a good impression all round. Sitting around the table at lunch were Mrs Mostyn, Sara, her sister Jo-Jo, Trevor, and Markus and I. We talked a great deal about writing fiction, and Mrs Mostyn said that she made her living entirely by her pen. That is something, I thought, even if nobody has heard of you. Sara said she has also had a dab at writing stories. I said I had written three short novels but they weren't publishable. "Keep trying," advised Mrs Mostyn. After lunch we played various games.

On the bus journey home Markus said, "I could write a much better novel than any of you. I have a perfect novel in my head. But I can't be bothered to write it down."

"That's the difficult part," I said, marvelling at his conceit.

"Oh no," said Markus, "it isn't."

There was no point in arguing about it.

r

5th March 1950

I spent most of this weekend on a tatty old houseboat on Port Meadow which Peter Grainger has bought and on which he and May plan to make their home. He is renovating it and I just watch and keep him company and chat with the other boat people. I know nothing about boats but it is a pleasant way of spending a Saturday and Sunday morning, in the fresh air, on the river. Peter has already found another job, at Morris Motors in Cowley, which is well-paid but must be deadly. At the same time he will attend night school and get some qualifications as he intends to become a teacher, like May. He claims he was sacked because he voted Labour. Curiouser and curiouser.

I had a scene with Dr Pick on Tuesday as I was a few minutes late for my appointment. I shall now have to find another dentist. The Ettinghausens took me to a service at the Synagogue on Thursday evening! I hadn't been to a Synagogue since I lived in Vienna and then only on rare occasions. It was just entertainment to me, like going to a theatre or a cinema, but it pleased the Doctor.

I must say church services are far more impressive. I wonder what a Mosque would be like?

7th March 1950

I went to the pictures with Sara today and then we called at her friends, the Drummonds. She said Markus and I go well together and her mother liked him, too. Not a word about our illicit relationship.

Mr Calé wants to have lunch at the Tackley with me on my birthday, Thursday, and I agreed. He can pass on to WB all my news about Rosenthals' and how much nicer a place it is to work at than Parkers'. Putz and I are going to Cobham for the weekend, to celebrate my birthday there.

A woman came to be interviewed for Peter's job. She was tall, with bright blonde hair and a foreign accent and she was wearing a leopard skin coat. Not at all the sort of person to spend her days packing parcels. She got the job. I asked Mrs Ettinghausen who that was.

"That was Mrs Spender," she told me. "Some relation of

Stephen Spender's."

"Goodness," I said. "What sort of relation?"

"I forget. The Doctor will know."

She always calls him 'the Doctor', just like the rest of us do. Later I learnt that Mrs Spender is the sister-in-law of Stephen. I wonder what she will be like?

The Doctor said to me, "That Grainger is a bad egg. You don't need to feel sorry for him." This arose because a letter he had dictated to me about the upstairs flat contained the sentence: 'The present occupant has the delightful habit of hanging the frying-pan on the wall dripping with hot fat, which accounts for the stain all down the wallpaper.' I had modified this slightly, as it seemed so unkind, thinking the Doctor wouldn't notice. But he did. "You'd better write what I tell you, young lady," he said to me more in sorrow than in anger, and made me write the letter again. And that was how he came to say that Peter Grainger is a bad egg.

I do miss God when I'm unhappy or indeed very grateful for something. Praying used to be second nature to me, and it has left a gap. This wonderful, fine spring weather with its fresh new smells makes me feel so melancholy and depressed I feel like dying. Why? Everyone else seems happy about it. I wish I were in love. I wish I was getting married on a beautiful day like today with the world looking its best, washed clean by spring rain and blown dry by spring breezes. People talk of doing new things in the spring, of buying new clothes and cleaning their houses and acquiring new hobbies. But for whom should I do these things? I think spring is wasted on me.

15th March 1950

Mrs Ettinghausen gave me a jar of homemade marmalade for my birthday and the recipe for it; it's from the *Observer* and never fails, she promised.

When I was in Cobham for my birthday weekend, Anni, Putz and I went to the cinema in Esher and saw the *Forsyte Saga*. I have been thinking about this film ever since. It pushed my own life right out of sight.

How can I ever grow tired of Markus when, like Proteus, he assumes so many shapes? Diana cut me in the street the other day. She simply turned away and didn't speak to me. I don't blame

387

her, but I should like to tell her that I don't want to take Markus away from her, I don't want more of him than I know and have; he has to be taken in small doses, like oily sardines, otherwise he becomes too much, he makes you sick.

With my rise in taste, my fastidiousness, I'm altogether becoming much harder to please. I would rather be alone than in the company of unattractive men or silly boring women. I harbour a craving, hollow, burning longing for someone to love, someone to excite me, but my own company will have to do in their absence. I suppose it is my youth which, against all the odds, keeps me so remarkably hopeful that, sooner or later, I shall meet someone who possesses the wholesomeness of WB, the gaiety of Jean-Claude, the brilliance of Bill, the charm of Jonathan, the goodness of Ray, all rolled into one, and that this marvel of a person, against even stronger odds, will like me, and be free to like me. Could such a miracle ever happen?

Mrs Ettinghausen has invited me to see *Bless the Bride* with her, and on the 25th March I am going to my second cousin, Lisl Webern's wedding in Welwyn Garden City. Maybe I shall meet someone there?

19th March 1950

At last I have done it! What, you ask? Decided to travel the world? Told Markus I never want to see him again? Smoked twenty cigarettes and to hell with good intentions? No, none of these things.

I have been to Parkers' and seen WB again. It was my loneliness which drove me back to him, but perhaps I would have gone back sooner or later anyway. I have written him many letters that I never sent. For some time now I have felt that I needed him dreadfully badly. He was my only real friend. There was nothing I could not talk to him about. I know now that I was never in love with him, that he was more like a father, though that was not at all how he wanted our relationship to be. But he filled this gap. And so we kept clashing. And then I lost him, and it was terrible. I used to think: I'd like to tell WB that or WB would understand, if only he were still accessible . . . And so, for the first time since Christmas, I opened Parkers' shop door and went straight to the foreign department. It was Saturday morning and the shop was busy, but I saw at once that WB was not there. Mr Calé, however, was. So were most other people who used to work there with me. All were pleased to see me. I was just chatting to June when suddenly I heard my name – and the voice belonged to the only person who mattered there – WB. He said my name again. I wondered if he had altered, but no, he seemed just the same. "It's been a long time," he said. "What brings you here?" How could I tell him?

"I came to see you," I said, "and Mr Calé, and everyone."

I stood with him at his desk and we arranged to meet for lunch. If he had been angry with me for walking out as I did, without giving in my notice, he has long since forgiven me.

Cycling home, I thought: must I always return to WB like a murderer to the scene of his crime? Except for one other man, I have been good at forgetting the rest. Even Raymond, in spite of one photograph of him in my album to remind me – even he has become a ghost. I can smile about our 'affair' and think: Ah, Raymond! The perfect one, the god-like one. How peaceful it was to be with him. But it is over. And Jean-Claude, a bagatelle, a delightful operetta, enjoyable but quickly forgotten, too featherweight to make a lasting impression. And the one man I can never forget, from whom all I have are 3 letters and the memory of one night? Not even a photograph. Almost nothing, yet that almost nothing I have of Jonathan is unforgettable. I tried for a year to forget him, I thought when J-C came to England again last summer, he will make me forget. A night with a Frenchman after all . . .

But it didn't work. I thought all along: WB will talk me out of this dream, will laugh it off with me, but that was no good either. Then Markus came. And went. And came back again. I can't forget Jonathan but at least I have WB back, who has such funny ideas sometimes, about whom one can't be very romantic but who is my very best friend and now happily no longer my boss.

Markus called this morning and I told him about Peter Grainger and his houseboat and that I was going to join him on Port Meadow in the afternoon. At about three o'clock I was sitting on deck watching Peter work, hammering nails into wood, and rattling away about stemmed and dumb barges and the different design of their hulls, for my edification, when who should suddenly appear but Markus and his children.

"Can I come to see you tomorrow evening?" he whispered, as soon as an opportunity presented itself.

"Why not?" I said casually, not caring much whether Anthony and Mary heard or not.

This evening Peter came for tea. He looked rather grubby. I always feel bourgeois in his company, which I'm not. When he had done with running everything at Rosenthals' down, he talked of his wife May, who was illegitimate and never knew her father and, in order to shock me, I suppose, suddenly said, "Do you know, there are some men who have never kissed their wife's vagina?"

"Are there?" I said. But I suppose I was a bit shocked really, that he should have made this comment to me.

20th March 1950

"Do you know who that was?" Mr Rosenthal asked me. He was talking about a little man who had just been in the office, talking music to Mr R.

"No. Who was it?" I asked.

"That was Gerald Finzi. He's getting to be quite a well-known composer."

I had never heard of him, but decided to remember his name. Other well-known people often come to Rosenthals' – it's amazing how many of them are book collectors. Cecil Roth, the Jewish historian, comes at least once a week, and one day Peter and Iona Opie came and bought some books on children's games, on which they are an authority. I should start collecting autographs again.

I told Markus today, "You can't really afford me any more – emotionally." He smiled, as if he either knew, or didn't care, what I meant. He has been ill, he told me. As a matter of fact, I had been quite looking forward to this evening. I thought: At least there's still something to absorb and interest me, although I know it to be hopeless and often disagreeable. If Raymond was perfection personified, WB reliability and Jonathan sex, then Markus without any doubt is the personification of instability, of imposture, of . . . I don't know what the right word is. Nothing quite fits. There's something fictitious about him, as if he didn't properly exist. Even his children, when with him, look out of place and don't seem to belong to him. He's a character out of a bad writer's imagination.

Sometimes his unpredictable behaviour is quite amusing: this evening, at 9.30pm, he put his coat on and announced, "I must go home to do some work," and then suddenly opened his trousers and made love to me, with his coat still on – after having sat with me the whole evening. I didn't enjoy it at all and told him so. But it's futile to tell him things; you can't tell fictitious characters anything. They don't hear you because they aren't really there. The thing to do with Markus is to pretend to take him seriously, and sometimes to try and make him laugh. But often it is difficult to know what sort of things he feels in the mood in to laugh at.

26th March 1950

Peter Grainger left Rosenthals' on Tuesday and Mrs Spender arrived the following day. She is clearly a connoisseur of antiquarian books and will not only be packing parcels.

I went to Cobham on Friday – by coach – and on Saturday, Anni, Felix and I went to my second cousin Lisl Webern's wedding in Welwyn Garden City. We went there by car. There was nobody very interesting at the reception, the nicest man by far being Lisl's husband, Peter Cohn, a research chemist. Instead of the usual decoration on the wedding cake there was a chemical formula in icing but I've forgotten what it meant.

"Do you think Lisl is a virgin?" I asked Anni after we had returned home.

"Yes. I'm sure of it," she replied. "She's not a girl who would give something for nothing."

Is that what I've done wrong then, I wondered? Is there no hope for me any more, because I gave something for nothing?

Dr and Mrs Ettinghausen are going to London for a week on Friday. It is the feast of Seder(?) which I can't spell and have only the vaguest recollection of, but Mrs Koch has invited me to her home to join in the celebration on Saturday evening. So I shall either have to hide my ignorance or try and find out what exactly it is.

Britta, my old school friend from Vienna who has been to a concentration camp, is coming to Oxford for the day on Sunday. I wonder what she will be like, after her terrible experiences?

6th April 1950

Putz was in Stratford last weekend so she didn't meet Britta. I took her sightseeing and we had a long walk. She has changed very little, and is still the round-faced, good-natured, rather highly-strung girl I remember from our schooldays. Although I longed to do so, I did not ask her anything about the concentration camp, and she didn't mention it, but her ghastly experiences, at which I can only guess, walked with us like a ghost, silent and sinister, at our side.

Fiammetta spent the whole of Monday in the office, sorting and collating books; usually she only comes in for half a day, for she can please herself. What a nice life. We chatted a lot and I'm getting to know her quite well. In the Ettinghausens' absence there isn't so much for me to do – Mr Rosenthal now dictates most of his letters to Mrs Spender – so I've been going home early.

Gerda came for coffee on Tuesday evening. So long as I know her the memory of Jonathan won't fade. On Monday evening (I got my chronological order wrong again!) I went to the pub with Chris and Ted and then had supper with them. Tomorrow is Good Friday, and Putz and I are going to Bristol to visit our cousin Herta and her husband Ernest, who's also a doctor. They have a house and a car and a dog and are expecting a baby in July, and if I were in that situation I would have nothing left to wish for. But I have nothing and no one and nowhere, I'm free as a bird, I could go anywhere in the world. Where shall I go? To France, to Switzerland? To South America, to China, or back to Austria? Total freedom is terrible because it means no one cares enough to restrain you. It paralyses me. And so I go nowhere. Besides, what would happen to my cabin trunk? And my equally beloved bicycle? They would have no home.

By keeping a diary I live twice through all my experiences, like a cow regurgitating its food. And it is as necessary to me as it is to the cow.

11th April 1950

Herta and Ernest made us very welcome over the Easter weekend. They showed us the suspension bridge which we crossed by car, we went to Bath where we had tea and saw the Roman Bath and imagined people bathing in it 2000 years ago, and Sunday we drove to the Cheddar Caves where I slipped and fell down but didn't hurt myself, and returned via Weston-Super-Mare. It was lovely to see the sea again. When we got back to Herta's house I borrowed her scalpel to make ridges in the soles of my slippery shoes.

Myself with Herta's dog, Fling.

"Locking the stable door after the horse has bolted," Ernest said. He's a nice fellow and easy to get on with. My falling down in the Cheddar Caves has become a joke.

Next weekend the clocks go forward one hour. I have invited Fiammetta for tea on Sunday. As I can't compete with her superb cooking, nor her knowledge of books and music, nor her talent for languages, I'm not wholeheartedly looking forward to the occasion. I always see myself in black or white – I'm the best, the most attractive, brilliant person in the world whom no one can resist, or I'm the worst, the stupidest, the dullest whom no one wants. Years ago I read in my horoscope: 'You are very easily discouraged: don't be.' It sticks in my mind because it is so true. The slightest criticism or sign of failure hurls me into the depths of misery. I never cease to be amazed that so many people find their right partners. It seems such a thing could never happen to me. I don't fit into any group and yet surely there must be many other individuals like me? Perhaps I'm destined to remain a spectator for the rest of my life, with no husband, children or even a dog But enough of introspection for today.

393

18th April 1950

Peter and May seem determined to find me a boyfriend and asked if they could bring their Australian friend, Bill, tomorrow evening. I couldn't tell them that any friend of theirs is unlikely to appeal to me, especially if he's called Bill!

Putz and I are going to Cobham again at the weekend, by coach. I always feel so relaxed there, especially as all we mostly do is lounge in the garden and gossip and go to the village and for short drives in 'Geoffrey' and play games with Lixl. Anni is nice to talk to and makes me feel better about things.

A few days ago Mr Rosenthal came into the office as I sat typing. No one else was there, not even Bonny. He said, "Do you know what Jacqueline said to me?" Jacqueline is his 7 year old daughter, a lovely blonde and blue-eyed little girl who sometimes comes to the office with her father.

"What did she say?" I asked.

"She said, 'Isn't Miss Jacoby pretty!' " Luckily I was wearing my dark-brown polo-neck pullover that I still have from Vienna which I feel good in, and so I wasn't too embarrassed.

I said, "She's pretty, too."

Once the Doctor had said to Jacqueline, "What do you want to do when you grow up, Jacqueline?"

"Play the piano," she had replied.

"Which piano?" he'd teased her, to the amusement of the adults present, but not to Jacqueline, who was years away from a reply to such a joke, and looked very surprised.

Since the arrival of Mrs Spender I hardly ever see Mr Rosenthal alone but I did again a few days ago, in the early afternoon. The Ettinghausens had not returned yet from lunch and Mrs Spender was out. Miss Grierson, shut away in her office upstairs, does not usually emerge unless she knows the Doctor is here. I had been saving a question for Mr R. and I now asked it. "Mr Rosenthal," I said, "what exactly does 'the Cadenza is Beethoven's own' mean?" He explained, in his gentle, charming voice, that composers frequently did not write their own cadenzas and that often Joachim wrote Beethoven's. I wished I knew more about music and didn't have to ask such questions.

A few days ago I saw Victor in the street. He saw me too, and before I had a chance to escape, manoeuvred his way over to me and said cheerfully, "Come and see me some time. I'm still at Magdalen." It sounded harmless enough and I felt sure he had got over me by now. An evening in those lavish rooms might be quite pleasant if I was being invited merely as a casual acquaintance, which I believed I now was.

"All right," I said. The date was fixed for Monday evening, last night.

It was ghastly. Is there anything in the world quite so repulsive as being kissed or even only touched by a man one doesn't want? But I couldn't hurt him, he's such a nice boy and I am really sorry for him. He told me he still liked me better than any girl he had ever known (which probably isn't very many), he begged me to like him a little, he talked of marriage and children. He wants all the things I do, that is the irony. How can life be so cruel?

"Will you come to the Commem. ball with me in June?" he asked.

"I don't know yet, Victor," I said. But of course I did know, I felt bored and sick and wretchedly unhappy.

"Why won't you? Why won't you?" he asks me incessantly, and when I make evasive replies so as not to hurt his feelings with the truth, he calls me Sphinx-like and impenetrable and becomes almost aggressive. Beware of pity! It can only lead me to where I don't want to go. Some time during that dreadful evening we talked of things that people were afraid of – I don't recall how we arrived at this subject – and I said I was afraid of about everything it is possible to be afraid of. "Ah," said Victor "so that is why you won't let me make love to you! You are afraid!" I wanted to deny it hotly, but then thought better of it. Why not let him believe that, if it makes him feel better? The more unbearable his caresses became the more sorry I felt for him, the more lies I told him, and the more encouraged he became. I thought: if he finds me out I shall feel like a burglar who has been caught in flagrante, or at best like a bad actor whose acting is too amateurish for belief. It would then no longer be pity I would feel for him, but contempt.

Victor's inept fumbling reminded me of Harold's embarrassing kisses at a time when I knew no better, and presently of the incident, which at the time I was too inhibited to mention even here, when Jimmy Dickens kissed me and ejaculated after two minutes, and how he had grown scarlet and excused himself and run to the lavatory.

After I left Victor I thought I can't bear him ever to touch me again, the very recollection of his sexless kisses made me shudder. There's nothing sexy about Victor, and I am disgusted with myself for allowing my pity for him to let him do even the little he did.

Being with an unloved, unlovely man is my 'Huis Clos'.

27th April 1950

We had snow on Tuesday!

Putz and I saw a marvellous Italian film called *Bicycle Thieves*. I've also been to the Playhouse – with Mr Calé and Eileen Cox from Parkers' – to see *Crime Passionel*, which is based on a book by J. P. Sartre called *Les Mains Sales*. I love Sartre. His philosophy and lifestyle fascinate me. On Sunday the Film Society starts again, it being the beginning of term. An Italian girl is staying with Bruno and Erna and they have invited us to meet her on Sunday and arrange some English conversation lessons with her. The famous Mrs von Hoffmansthal will be there, too. This Italian girl apparently is very attractive and accustomed to being stared at in the street in Italy. When she found that Englishmen don't indulge in this pastime to the same extent, she was quite offended and wanted to return home, but of course she didn't.

WB rang me today; we arranged to have lunch at the Tackley next Tuesday.

The anniversary of my meeting with Jonathan has passed, and with it Jonathan must be erased from my memory. I met him when he was looking for the ideal woman and I for the ideal man, and for a brief spell, we thought we had found them. Maybe he has found her by now. Or maybe I dreamt the whole episode and it never really happened. If it did, it is the greatest tragedy of my love-life. I expect nothing worse.

3rd May 1950

Yesterday I had lunch with WB. I suppose the question will always remain unanswered – the question of my relationship with WB. He is the steady rock in my life, my criterion of reality. I like being with him, he puts the whole confusing and terrifying world into a harmless nutshell for me, he shelters me from my torments, he's a refuge for my tortured soul. With him I see everything in its proper perspective and my stupid worries become ridiculous. But the truth is, were we to work together again we would fight again.

The truth, however, has always stood very little chance. Everything else is stronger. WB says I am against myself, I want to see myself lose. Since WB could make me win, he's an obstacle. The result is conflict.

Of course, there wasn't any Sachertorte at the Tackley.

Sylvia Montini, the Italian girl, had her first English Conversation lesson with me today. During the course of it she discovered that I usually cut my own hair, and also my cousin Herta's in Bristol, and she asked me if I would do hers, too. I said I would. Tomorrow she, Putz, Fiammetta, Mrs Spender and I are going to the Opera Club to see the *Zauberflöte*.

Eva Deutsch, a girl of my age whom I used to know in Vienna and who now lives in Sao Paulo with her family, is coming to Europe all by herself, armed with addresses of old friends of her family. The Deutschs' were friends of my parents. My father asked me to find a room for Eva in Oxford for a few days.

10th May 1950

My present situation is like the present political one – hopeless from every aspect. I have suddenly become modest and small whereas not so long ago I felt wanton and robust. Furthermore I am bored. What is to become of me? Life seems too stupid sometimes, like a silly dream one tries to understand the meaning of, but it hasn't any meaning.

Last Friday Sara came to see me at Rosenthals'. She brought me a story she has had published in *Isis*. It's called 'The Toaster'. A woman wants to buy an electric toaster. The shop assistant lists all its virtues. This toaster, he says, is a brilliant invention. It cuts the bread, toasts it, butters it and spreads marmalade on it. She buys it. The toaster does all the things the shop assistant had promised. Then it ate the toast. I thought it an excellent story and wrote and told Sara so. I didn't tell her that, although I've never had anything published, I have this vague, conceited notion that when I do, it will by far exceed this. Miss Kitty used to say it is very important to believe in yourself, and if you don't blow your

397

own trumpet nobody else will. Now seems a good time to bear this in mind, because I'm feeling so low.

An undergraduate called Mario Witt who, like Fiammetta, lives in the house of Mrs von Hoffmansthal, was also at the Opera Club on Thursday. His real name was Wittkower and his parents are friends of Bruno and Erna's. We heard a superb performance of the *Zauberflöte*.

Peter Grainger's houseboat has been moved to Folly Bridge. I went to see him there on Sunday. He's lonely, and probably misses May, his half-Indian, schoolgirl wife; I quite like being on the boat if I have nothing better to do at weekends. I've never thought of Peter as anyone other than someone to pass a few hours with when there's no one better around, so imagine my surprise when he said on Sunday:

"If I weren't married already, I'd marry you."

For a moment I was lost for a reply. After all, it was a compliment.

"Story of my life," I replied, when I had recovered from this confession.

If he had tried to kiss me, I think I should have been sick. He tries hard to be continental and passionate, and I think was more influenced by the cultured and intellectual people and atmosphere at Rosenthals' than he would admit, but sadly will never make that world, and so pretends to despise it.

WB no longer attracts me physically either. I didn't want him to touch me at all the last time he came to see me. When it was time for him to go, he said I visibly perked up.

"You remind me of the baby of friends of ours," he said. "When they have visitors it cries most of the time, but as soon as they get up to go, it smiles happily and enthusiastically waves goodbye." This made me feel very guilty. Perhaps it was a mistake to go back to him? I'm seeing him again for lunch next week.

13th May 1950

Mrs Spender knows Jonathan Sofer!

They were at Cambridge together. "A fantastic man," she said. Did she have an affair with him? She laughed when I asked her. "What a lot you want to know," she said. So you see I am not allowed to forget him.

She's very worried, and I should be too, about a possible war because of the situation in Korea: North Korea has invaded the South and there is a war there which could involve the whole world, as the principle of communism versus democracy is at stake. Already armed forces from fifteen nations have been dispatched there to intervene. It all seems so far away.

Mrs Spender is very nice to me and we frequently have lengthy discussions, but everything about her is shrouded in mystery. I only know that she is divorced from Michael Spender, the poet Stephen's brother, and has a 14 year old son away at boarding school. She speaks perfect German but claims to be half Danish. Books, especially antiquarian ones, are her great love. One day she brought me a book to look at which she was about to post to a customer in America. "Look at this," she said to me. "Isn't it heavenly?" It was called *Notes sur l'Amour, avec dessins originaux de Pierre Bonnard*. She placed it before me. It cost £21 – cheap by Rosenthal standards. I wished I could feel as enthusiastic as she, and gave a poor imitation of enthusiasm. Before I worked here, I thought I liked books. Now I know that I don't like them nearly enough, and don't understand most of them. But I can't think of anything I like or understand better. I still want to be a writer one day.

WB told me that someone called Brian Aldiss now works at Parkers', in the second-hand department, who also wants to be a writer, and that I must meet him. I've actually seen him around, usually on his bicycle. Once I cycled behind him on St Giles. He and his wife or girlfriend were cycling side by side, holding hands!

Putz has been wanting to leave Wolsey Hall for some time and has been looking for another job. I always read the *Oxford Times* on Friday evenings at the Dauries', and yesterday I spotted an advertisement for a secretary at the Human Anatomy department at the university. I cut it out for her, and she is going to apply for the job. We had tea and spent the evening at Clem and Beryl Wood's today whom we had not seen for a long time. As the weather was fine we sat in the garden.

21st May 1950

Last Monday I fetched Fiammetta from the music club after work, we went to the pictures and saw a marvellous film called

Maskerade, and afterwards I had supper at her place. Mario was there. Fiammetta can make a simple dish like scrambled egg taste like ambrosia. Whether she is serving up her delicious food, or talking about books, or singing, she makes me feel very inadequate. I can't think why she likes me. When Mario is there, I am a bit more relaxed as his levels of intellect and ability are more like mine.

I have found a room for Eva Deutsch with a Mrs Goodbank; Eva is coming to Oxford on the 30th.

Victor has once again persuaded me to have supper with him, against my better judgement. Afterwards we went for a walk. It was awful again. Every minute in his company is agony. Such harmless things as having a meal and going for a walk with somebody can be wonderful or unbearable according to who that somebody is. I told Chris about Victor and she said, "Why do you go out with him if you don't like him?"

It seems so simple. But it isn't. I just said I felt sorry for him.

On Wednesday I missed Putz for lunch at Connors'. I had lunch by myself and afterwards went to her digs. She wasn't there but arrived after about five minutes. She had been for her interview.

"Guess what," she said, looking very happy. "I've got the job at the anatomy department."

I was very pleased. "Thanks to me," I reminded her.

"Yes, thanks to you."

She starts there on the 12th of June.

We are going to Cobham for the Whitsun weekend.

25th May 1950

I had lunch with Mr Calé today, and last night WB spent the evening with me. I gave in to him . . .

Monday and Tuesday were Jewish holidays and the Doctor strictly forbade me to go to the office, although I knew Mr Rosenthal and Mrs Spender would be there. It seemed strange to be free on a weekday. Monday morning I went to town. I visited Mrs Zuccari at Exeter College Library and called at Parkers' and chatted with the girls. Then I met Mr Brun in the street. He's the man from Radio Rentals who comes to see to my radio from time to time. He asked me if I knew of a couple who want to go to

Austria for a two week holiday in July and share expenses of the car journey with him and his wife. "I want to go to Austria," I said, half-jokingly.

"But we'll need two people."

"I'll mention it to my sister." I was so enthusiastic that he must have considered the matter clinched. What have I done? I thought immediately afterwards. I mentioned it to Putz yesterday, her birthday – and she agreed! We have until the 7th July to make arrangements and save some money.

Sylvia came for another English lesson on Monday afternoon, and I cut her hair. She was very satisfied with my effort. In the evening, on the boat with Peter, he tried to get intimate, which I had been dreading for some time. I told him to remember May away at college, and suggested we go for a ride on our bicycles. He sheepishly agreed. We bought some chips on the way.

On Tuesday, the second Jewish holiday, I had coffee at Ellistons with Fiammetta and afterwards a walk in the University Parks. WB came for lunch and in the evening I was at Chris and Ted's. They have a puppy! I'd like to have a dog.

29th May 1950

Cobham was, as always, wonderfully relaxing, an antidote to everything I don't like about my life. On Saturday Anni took Putz, me, Trudl and Elsa to Epsom for the DERBY, by car. We had a sandwich lunch there, a gypsy told us our fortunes, and I lost 5/- on a horse. We stood in the field rounding the bend at Tattenham corner, about half a mile from the finish, but saw very little of the race – just a flash past lasting a few seconds. A horse called Galcador won. I wish the gypsy had known that! It was all very exciting. I wonder if Mr Herbert is still placing bets on horses and as usual, losing money?

On Whit Sunday my father and Betty came out for the day and we all went to the nearby rhododendron woods and later had tea in the garden. Putz went back to Oxford in the evening but I stayed till the following day which, after Anni and Lixl had seen me off at the station, I spent in London with Britta. We went to the Whispering Gallery in St Paul's Cathedral, had lunch at her friends', the Loebls, and in the afternoon we visited Regents Park zoo. I like Britta better now than I ever did at school in Vienna.

Back to Oxford in the evening – and whom should I meet on Paddington Station but Mrs Spender! What a surprise. We returned to Oxford together. The antidotal weekend in Cobham will soon be only a memory. I think everything in the world is made of glass. It doesn't last long. Soon it breaks up into a thousand splinters that bear no resemblance to what they had once been.

2nd June 1950

Today I feel six years younger. I ought to have made this entry six years ago. I feel almost adolescent again. But let me start at the beginning:

Eva Deutsch arrived in Oxford on Tuesday. We had not seen each other since we were 10 or 11 years old, and from the pretty little girl with the baby face I remembered she had turned into a beautiful young girl, with short auburn hair, perfect features and a wonderful slim figure. She was friendly and easy to get on with. In my lunch hour we walked in St John's gardens and one of the first things I asked her was whether she remembered the incident at her flat in Vienna when she and Ruth conspired against me; we had all three been playing together when Eva took me aside, Ruth having mysteriously disappeared, and suggested we play a joke on her. I was to stand behind the door, and when Ruth approached, I was to jump out and spit a mouthful of flour at her. I had been suspicious before, now I was sure the joke was on me for even I knew that you can't spit flour out. I declined. Eva had no recollection of the episode and laughed about it. I laughed too, but without meaning it. Pain inflicted in childhood never leaves you and never becomes funny.

After I finished work, Eva came to my flat for tea. She liked my little attic bedroom and admired the imitation Chinese screen which conceals the washbasin, the little desk under the window, the general cosiness. She thought it very exciting to live as independently as I do. She remembers much more German than I because she lives with her parents. She taught me a Viennese song I had long forgotten. I remembered being told by my grandmother that Mrs Deutsch had a toad run down her naked back on her wedding-day for good luck, and it certainly paid off, for the family escaped together from Hitler, and Eva seems to be a happy girl with not a care in the world.

I wasn't entirely surprised when she rang me the following day and said she had met some undergraduates while sightseeing and arranged an outing for the evening, and would I come along? I didn't particularly want to go, and felt a bit like Faust who wasted his youth because he never learnt to enjoy it. However, I did go. We went to the Trout and the Perch and had drinks and danced a little in the garden. The two boys were called Frank and Blair and I knew at first sight that they would be boring. We met Gerda in the Perch and she joined us and walked home with us.

The following day, Blair, who was Eva's 'boyfriend', invited her, Putz and me for coffee at his College, Magdalen, where we were joined by two more students called Tim and Ronald. Afterwards we went punting. Blair's gramophone came too. Ronald, quite definitely, was the nicest of them. He had just come back from Vienna. I looked at him and I thought: 'What a pity that I could never take him seriously. He is so fresh and young and clean.' He reminded me a little of Bill Emerson when I first knew him. But I am a woman now and I know what I want. Somehow Ronald became my partner for the evening. We sat next to each other in the room at college, then in the punt. Pressed against him as we glided down the river at night, with the music and the moon and the summer air wrapped around us, I was even a little excited over this fair, young English boy. I felt 17 again. And I'm only 23! But how I have grown up in these six years. How short that adolescent period was with me when every shy, blue-eyed look meant happiness. With some girls it goes on until marriage.

Sometimes I wish I were unspoilt again, as unspoilt as I'm sure Eva is, and innocent and susceptible to those blue-eyed looks. Last night I pretended I was. I pretended I didn't know what it is like to be touched by a real man who knows how. And so I enjoyed myself a little last night. I almost forgot my owl-like wisdom of life and abandoned myself to the pleasures of the evening where the moon meant romance and holding hands would end at best in an innocent kiss.

But I did quite like that boy and was sorry he did not kiss me. I wondered if he would ask to see me again, but he didn't. We all walked home at one o'clock in the morning and for Eva it was goodbye; she was very sad. I saw her off at the station this morning. She's going to Austria next. Would I have been like Eva,

I wonder, if things had gone for me as they have for her? At any rate I had another glimpse of that innocent world – and it was like being confronted with one's dolls when one is grown up and has put them away years ago. Eva and those boys are still children as far as I am concerned. They don't know much about life. They don't know how to touch you. They must always laugh about everything. They can only enjoy themselves when they are laughing. No, I'm not envious. I laughed too, last night, and I enjoyed it, but it wouldn't do for long . . .

"Il faut chercher l'amour . . ." I'm cherching it.

7th June 1950

It is terrifically hot and Putz and I spent the weekend sunbathing alternately in her and my garden. When she used to live at the Blaschkos in Park Town, we always sunbathed in the communal Park Town garden which was for residents only; usually we had it all to ourselves.

On Monday night I had supper at Gerda's and was introduced to a girl called Maureen; later a boy called Gordon came. Gerda has a lot of friends. Last night I went to the pictures with Fiammetta; we saw *Mayerling*. Afterwards I had supper at her place. Mario was there too. We chatted until midnight.

'The Doctor' and Bonny.

WB came for lunch on Tuesday and is coming again on Thursday evening. Putz and I ate sandwiches for lunch in the University Parks as the weather is so fine, and we shall do so again tomorrow, if the fine weather continues.

We have chosen our destination in Austria: it is the Hotel Hohe Munde in Telfs. It costs £3 a night. We can hardly believe that in a month's time we shall see Austria again.

The Doctor said to me, "Who is this Mr Brun? Are you sure he's all right? Two young girls

404

trusting themselves to a relative stranger . . . Does your father know?"

I laughed. "He's quite all right, Doctor," I said. "Our father knows. And Mr Brun's wife is going too, anyway."

"So he says."

"She really is." I was touched by his concern. Mrs Spender is always teasing me about the Doctor's protective attitude towards me – which she doesn't think I need.

8th June 1950

I don't know whether I am surprised, pleased or just indifferent: Ronald has written to me, asking to see me again. I'm going out with him next weekend – and he has a car! I've never known a man with a car. Of course there's no point in my going out with him except for a little harmless amusement, and as a sort of farewell to my adolescent world.

This evening WB was here. What a contrast! He always reads this diary and knows everything about me. Last time he was here, we enjoyed quite pleasant intimacy but this time we only talked. I hope I shall not fail to recognise love, in my frantic search for it.

13th June 1950

Today is my mother's birthday. I am always sad on this day. I wake up in the morning with a pain in my heart that won't go away and that pervades whatever I'm doing for the rest of the day.

Last Sunday I was invited to a garden party at Sara's in Wheatley. There was a barbecue and people danced on the lawn, neither of which I liked, though dancing out of doors and in the dark is not quite so bad. The food tasted burnt on the outside and raw inside. I decided I preferred my sausages and potatoes cooked in the usual way. On Monday evening, Mr Calé and I went to see *A Midsummer Night's Dream* in New College grounds. I enjoyed it very much until the mosquitoes spoiled it for me.

Fiammetta returns to Italy at the end of the week and is coming for a 'last supper' on Friday. On Sunday she's singing at a concert to which we're all invited – Putz and I, Silvia, Fursts,

Mario, Mr Rosenthal and Mrs Spender.

And now about Ronald: I cannot understand it, is it really not possible for a man to be with me for more than half an hour without asking me to go to bed with him? Victor once said, "Every man who sees you must surely want to take you to bed at once. You're so attractive." How right he apparently was, and how disastrous for me! I never knew I looked like a prostitute. Such women come to a sticky end, and no doubt a similar fate awaits me – not because of what I do but because of how I look.

The evening began quite pleasantly. Ronald (Ferrier is his surname) called for me and we drove to the Trout in his car. It is my mother's birthday as I've said, and I didn't expect to enjoy myself wholeheartedly, but when after only a very short time, Ronald asked me to come away with him in his car, enjoyment of any kind was out of the question. I was so angry that I wanted to say: "I despise dilettantish, Anglo-Saxon slugs and I wouldn't sleep with you if you were the last man on earth." I didn't say that, of course. I simply said no. It seems he's not quite as inexperienced as I thought, and has been about quite a bit, as he was quick to let me know, and what with my bedroom eyes or whatever it is, he came to a wrong conclusion. The evening left me feeling disgusted, and reminded me of evenings spent with Bill Emerson. I don't want to go back, I want to *go on*. I'm glad God made me fastidious, otherwise where would I be now?

I don't know whether I ever told you that Markus left Oxford some time ago, without saying goodbye to me. Recently I had a letter from him to which I did not reply. In the letter he asked me whether I missed him and begged me to write to him and come to see him.

I did write a letter to Victor, however – telling him I would not come to the Commem. Ball with him. As you can see, I'm carrying on a kind of Bolshevik purge campaign at the moment.

14th June 1950

The more I think of it, the more it appals me: the cold, matter-of-fact, loveless way in which that boy said to me, "Will you come away with me for the weekend?" Who does he think I am, to ask me such a thing? Does he really imagine that I would in cold blood lie in bed with a man I don't know and don't love?

Ah yes, I know. There was Jonathan. I certainly didn't know him either. The more I think about how I could have done such a thing, the more incomprehensible it becomes. I can only explain it because I fell in love with him, almost immediately. Jonathan did not coldly say to me, without smiling, "Come to bed with me." Jonathan said it with his eyes. He was not an adolescent Englishman showing off his new confidence. And Jonathan loved me for three hours. Yes, for three hours, until I disappointed him. I shall believe that until I die. If I feel only shame about that night with him, it's because of its sentimentality; it was quite the most sentimental thing that ever happened to me, and that is why it can still make me cry.

I am beginning to know Jonathan well now. I am learning more and more about him. For instance, I know now that he's a good swimmer, that he used to be a Zionist and a Communist, that he has a new and beautiful girlfriend. How do I know these things? From Mrs Spender mostly, and also from Gerda, who frequently mentions him. So you see, if ever there was hope of obliterating him from my memory or imagining that he was only a dream, there is certainly none now. Almost imperceptibly, Jonathan is changing shape, the vision I've cherished becoming a man I can't recognise.

I still remember every moment with him so vividly. We had supper in a nameless restaurant I should never know again. During the meal, which I couldn't eat, our eyes suddenly met and we both stopped eating (picking at things on my plate, in my case) and stared at each other and then he took my hand, or stroked my face, or both, and when his eyes had told me everything already, he began to plead quietly, "Stay with me, stay with me . . ."

No one will ever revive that part of me that Jonathan killed.

And then I had missed my train and I was to be with him for a whole night and I loved him and I was so immensely happy that tears come to me eyes just remembering it. In my rush to write everything here at the time, I left many things out, and I remember now that after the meal I went to the lavatory and there was a woman being sick and I didn't feel sorry for her at all because I was blind and deaf to everything. When I returned Jonathan was waiting for me, smiling, and he put his arm around me. I told him about the woman who was sick but he only said,

407

scarcely audibly, "Let's go home."

That was a year and two months ago.

Why did I fail Jonathan sexually, when I was so excited myself? What stopped me from total abandonment, at that moment of exuberance?

Did Ronald Ferrier read this unforgettable experience in my eyes and think he could emulate it? Oh, Ronald, I pity you. When I see him on Saturday – for I agreed to go for a drive with him before he goes down at the end of term until October, as I so love riding in cars – I shall tell him that he can save his breath and make no more indecent suggestions to me as he means about as much to me as a stone in the road, and certainly not as much as his car.

17th June 1950

What happened this evening is so ridiculous that the most unskilled novelist would refrain from using it in a plot.

The day was Saturday. I spent a pleasant afternoon at Chris and Ted's; it was Micky's birthday and there was a special tea. Ted's mother was there and after tea we all went for a walk with the dog. With these wholesome and agreeable things still on my mind, Ronald arrived at my flat in his car at around seven o'clock. It is going to bore me to tell you what happened next, but I should like to remember it and tell it to friends and to the man who may one day love me, and perhaps even to my grandchildren if ever I have any. I asked Ronald where we were going and he replied, "To Thame." Good, I thought, that's a nice long drive.

He got into the car and opened the door for me. I was about to sit down on the passenger seat – when it collapsed. Ronald was very embarrassed and apologetic. I had to sit in the back, which made me feel silly, and like a passenger in a taxi. However, we chatted in a light-hearted way and the drive was over all too quickly.

We reached Thame. Ronald said, "Ah, there it is," and stopped the car.

There is what? I wondered. I saw a hotel named The Golden Eagle. Perhaps he meant to go there for drinks.

He said, "Well, I'd better get out first and make sure about the room."

I visualised a private room he had booked for dinner, such as I have often seen on films, and though the whole thing was not quite clear to me, I didn't query it. He had told me last time that he always voted Conservative because his parents did and he had been brought up that way, and I presumed this was the Conservative way of doing things.

"Oh, you booked a room," I said cheerfully, hoping he had booked a special meal to go with it.

"Yes," he said. "Just for the night."

I stared at him in utter amazement. I thought at first it was a joke, or else that he had gone completely crazy.

"Are you mad?" I said.

The poor boy turned scarlet. He explained that he thought I had agreed to his suggestion last time and had gone straight ahead with booking a room. He was desperately embarrassed but remained calm, serene and polite throughout, though he could see how angry I was. Only a Conservative could behave like that. I felt quite sorry for him, after my first anger had passed. There he sat, that drippy, callow puppy, frustrated in his attempt to spend a night of love (or sex, rather) – perhaps his first with a woman. I played the shocked, mortified, innocent girl. I said I was hurt and insulted. I accused him of cold-bloodedness and heartlessness. He continued to mumble apologies and then we drove back in silence. He dropped me at my house and we said goodbye – forever, I expect. I wondered whether the hotel would make him pay for the room. I hope so. Serve him right.

24th June 1950

I had an accident on my bike on Monday. A car passing me came too close and knocked me down in Banbury Road. I wasn't hurt, just shocked.

Putz has started her new job at the Human Anatomy Department. She is secretary to Dr Weiner, who is an anthropologist. The head of the department is Professor Le Gros Clark. The milieu is right up her street. Today we went to town and bought a few things for our Austrian holiday. I bought a bathing costume; it's pale blue with a small nondescript pattern and a white border.

Miss Feith from Mrs Wawerka's office and Professor Maas, who is a classics scholar, spent last Wednesday at Rosenthals', typing. Every morning I arrive at the office I tell myself how lucky I am to be working here. It really is an interesting establishment. The Doctor has issued further warnings about my Austrian holiday which is less than two weeks away: I must in no circumstances wander off on my own in the mountains, in view of what happened to Miss Munro recently.

On Monday WB had lunch with me again. I feel differently towards him, physically, every time I see him. We laughed about my experience with Ronald Ferrier. But later I thought: it wasn't really funny at all. It was sad. I'm a girl men only want to sleep with, not to marry. I'm a foreign girl, there for the taking, with no family to shield me, and no respect due. I could murder Ronald.

29th June 1950

It would be nice to be dead, I often think, but with that is linked the romantic notion of death, of being found dead, of the publicity, of suddenly becoming important albeit when one no longer requires it. The imminent war – and Mrs Spender is sure there will be war because of the situation in Korea – is not much consolation. Most of us would die, and there would be no trace left of our bodies after the atom bomb. It terrifies me. I don't often think of these things except when, as now, I'm in a morbid mood.

"Soon you will be happy, darling," my beloved WB always tells me. I hope he is right. Assuming there's no war, that is.

BRITISH WOMAN MURDERED IN AUSTRIA

FROM OUR OWN CORRESPONDENT

VIENNA, Monday.

Miss Helen Munro, 42, whose home is at Park Town, Oxford, was found murdered yesterday in an isolated valley on the Patscherkofel mountain, eight miles east of Innsbruck. She disappeared on Saturday.

Her body had severe head and shoulder injuries, and was said to be partly covered by slates. Earlier Innsbruck police said she seemed to have been strangled.

Her handbag was missing. It contained £35 in notes, some French francs and Austrian schillings, and between £30 and £40 in traveller's cheques.

Austrian police with bloodhounds are searching for a South Tyrolean, Guido Zingerle, 45, whom they want to question. He is described as having bushy eyebrows and wearing grey check trousers and wooden clogs. Italian police have been warned to watch for him in case he tries to cross the border.

Miss H. Munro.

Miss Munro had been Southern Regional Director of the Arts Council of Great Britain since 1946. She lived at Redington-road, Hampstead.

WALK ON SATURDAY

She arrived at the Patscherkofel Hotel, with her mother, on Saturday, and later in the day went for a walk. While she was away there was a violent thunderstorm. When she had not returned by yesterday morning hundreds of police combed the area.

Her brother, Mr. Alexander Munro, left for Innsbruck to-day. It is believed that Miss Munro will be buried there.

Miss Munro was a daughter of the late Dr. Munro, Rector of Lincoln College, Oxford, and studied at the Slade School of Art in London. After leaving Oxford, where she took a First, she worked for the B.B.C.

"Fine Type"

Mr. M. J. McRobert, deputy secretary of the Arts Council, said in London yesterday: "I knew Miss Munro well and she always struck me as a conscientious worker and a fine type of woman."

4th July 1950

Eva Deutsch sent some photographs from Austria. I compared them to the one I have of her taken in 1930 which Hedi Engl brought after the war. Unfortunately she has her back to the camera. She was 3 years old, and so was I. on this old photograph I am in my mother's arms. My paternal grandparents, Uncle Hans and Aunt Lea, Mr & Mrs Deutsch and their older daughter Agi and Putz standing next to our mother, are also in the photograph.

Putz and I had tea at Mr and Mrs Brun's on Cumnor Hill the other day. It was so hot that I walked barefoot up the hill leading to their house because my shoes hurt (as usual). The holiday in Austria is now arranged to the last detail and I can hardly contain my excitement. We are leaving at 5.30 on Friday morning and crossing from Dover to Dunkirk.

The weather has been very hot for some time. Mr Calé and I went canoeing on the river on Saturday, and on Sunday I went swimming on Port Meadow with Chris, Ted and the children – and some cows, who waded into the river with us. We also went to their allotment (the Hayes', not the cows).

After babysitting at the Dauries' on Friday, I had a long political discussion with them. Mr Dauries, who has always voted Labour, surprised me by saying that, next time, he would vote Conservative. This is because he thinks it is best not to go too far in one direction for too long. It is not a point of view I have ever heard or considered myself. Yesterday I saw Anthony, Markus's small son. It brought Markus back vividly, as if it had all only happened yesterday. I wanted to say to Anthony: "Your father was my lover." What would he have replied? In theory it was the fulfilment of my schoolgirl dreams. But, as I should know by now, dreams are better left as they are.

This time next week I shall be – in Austria! What awaits me there? An alien land, as unrecognisable as the child who grew up there? Hitler lurking behind every tree? A new love?